HISTORY OF THE SWEDES OF ILLINOIS ...

HISTORY OF THE SWEDES OF ILLINOIS ...

Vol. Pt1

Ernst Wilhelm Olson , Martin J. Engberg , Anders Schön

HISTORY OF THE SWEDES OF ILLINOIS ...

Vol. Pt1

Ernst Wilhelm Olson , Martin J. Engberg , Anders Schön

ISBN : 8888006791168

First Published 1908, reprint 2017 in India by

Facsimile Publisher
12 Pragati Market
Ashok Vihar, Ph-2
Delhi-110052, India
E-mail: books@facsimilepublisher.com

HISTORY

OF THE

SWEDES OF ILLINOIS

The Linné Monument, Lincoln Park, Chicago

HISTORY

OF THE

Swedes of Illinois

PART I

EDITED BY

ERNST W. OLSON

IN COLLABORATION WITH

ANDERS SCHÖN AND MARTIN J. ENGBERG

ILLUSTRATED

CHICAGO

The Engberg-Holmberg Publishing Company

1908

TABLE OF CONTENTS

PART I

PART II

PART III

INTRODUCTION

HEN in the forties of the last century the great influx of Swedish immigrants to the United States began, by far the largest number settled in Illinois. Even at that early period Swedes had begun to form sporadic settlements in the territory to the north and west, but these were of little consequence as compared to the populous Swedish communities that sprang up in the soil of the Prairie State.

The Swedes of Illinois, therefore, rank as the pioneers of this great migratory movement. In later years they have been outnumbered by the Swedes of Minnesota, and nearly all the western and many of the eastern states now have each a very considerable Swedish population, yet the Illinois Swedes retain pre-eminence from a historical point of view.

Illinois was the central point from which the Swedish population spread in various directions, chiefly to the west and the northwest. The Swedish settlements in the eastern states and on the Pacific slope are of more recent date and have no direct connection with the pioneer history of Illinois.

In intellectual culture as well as in material development the Swedes of this state led the way for their countrymen in other parts. In Illinois we meet with the first properly organized Swedish churches —the mother churches of no less than five distinct denominations. In Illinois was founded the first Swedish-American newspaper of permanence, and the great bulk of the Swedish publishing business in this country has always been done here. In Illinois was founded the first Swedish-American institution of learning, followed in later years by a score of others, but still remaining the foremost educational institution among the Swedish people of the United States. In Illinois were put forth their first endeavors in the literary field, which, although modest, yet formed the nucleus of a distinct literature. In the cultivation of the fine arts of music and painting as well as in manufacture, craftsmanship, invention and industrial art, the Swedes of Illinois also led, and in the succeeding pages will be found the names of Swedish pioneers in a variety of fields.

In public life Swedes have been active in this state principally after the close of the Civil War. In that conflict large numbers of them fought as volunteers, contributing skillful commanders and brilliant tacticians as well as gallant soldiers in the ranks. Their military history goes back not only to the Civil and Mexican Wars, for there were Swedes also among the Illinois troops in the War of 1812. In the politics of this state a Swede made his mark while Illinois was still a territory.

Chicago being one of the first points settled by the Swedes and having gradually grown to be their greatest center of population, also became the center of culture; and this city is, in a figurative sense, the Swedish-American capital.

Illinois having thus become, from the first, the seat of culture as well as the fountain-head of material development among the Swedish-Americans in general, it is fair to assume that the Swedes of this state in the past sixty years have exerted an appreciable influence not alone upon their fellow-countrymen elsewhere, but also upon the civic life of the state and the nation.

The story of the Swedes of Illinois, showing the part they have played in the making of this commonwealth, is here told for the first time in the English language and thus placed within ready access of the general public.

CHAPTER I

Summary of the History of Illinois

Early French Explorations in North America

OT long after the discovery of the West Indies by Christopher Columbus, in 1492, and the successive discoveries of Central and South America, those regions were explored and settled by Europeans, while the colonization of the North American continent was accomplished only by slow degrees. Although re-discovered in 1497 by John Cabot, after having been found originally by Leif Eriksson and his Norse followers about five hundred years earlier, and explored during the first half of the sixteenth century by parties landing here and there on the southern, eastern and western coasts and penetrating into the interior, it was not until the early part of the seventeenth century that the European nations obtained a firm foothold in this part of the New World. So slow was their westward progress that the discovery of the Pacific coast was practically without results up to the latter part of the eighteenth century, when finally the first successful colonies were founded.

The Spanish, the French, the English, and to a slight extent, the Dutch share the credit for the discovery and exploration of the various parts of the North American Continent. The Spaniards directed their energies principally to the South, the Southwest and the West, the French traversed and colonized the extreme eastern part, the region of the Great Lakes and the Mississippi, the English settled the eastern coast from Maine to South Carolina and the Dutch a limited area on the Hudson River.

Sweden also claims a chapter in the colonial history of this country. Through the colony of New Sweden, founded in 1638, extending over part of the present territory of Delaware, Pennsylvania and New Jersey, and conquered by the Dutch in 1655, Sweden contributed a noteworthy share toward the earliest development of North American civilization.

The discovery and primary colonization of the territory now forming the state of Illinois was the work of the French explorers and pioneers. Before narrating these events, let us view, in retrospect, their causes and the historical factors leading up to them.

As early as 1504 the French began to frequent the banks of New Foundland, attracted by the abundance of fish in these waters. These fishing expeditions have continued to this day, and but for them the French government might never have had its attention directed to this part of America. King Francis I., in 1524, sent an Italian traveler, John Verrazani, to explore these regions. He sailed along the coast from the present site of Wilmington, North Carolina, to Nova Scotia and, without founding any colonies, took possession, in the name of the French crown, of the entire territory termed New France.

Ten years later, in 1534, a Frenchman by the name of John Cartier, discovered the St. Lawrence River and on his second expedition sailed up the river as far as the present city of Montreal. On his third expedition, in 1541, he founded Quebec, a fort which formed the center of a penal colony, recruited from the French prisons. In 1541 a French nobleman by the name of Francois de la Roque had been appointed viceroy of New France. He arrived and took up his duties two years later, but finding his province a wilderness and his subjects deported criminals, he returned to France within a year.

During the next fifty years the public mind of France was entirely engrossed with the strife between the nobility and the royal house on the one hand and the equally bitter conflict between the Calvinists and the Catholics on the other; meanwhile the colonial interests in the New World were well-nigh forgotten. Not until the beginning of the seventeenth century the project was revived. Samuel Champlain, a noted naval officer, having explored anew the shores of the St. Lawrence (1603), Sieur de Monts, a Calvinist, received a large portion of this territory as a grant from the government. Two years later he founded Port Royal, which rapidly grew to be a large and flourishing settlement.

In the meantime the cause of converting the Indians of New France to the Christian faith was taken up in the mother country, and numerous missionaries, many of them Jesuits, were sent among the natives, gaining great prestige among them in a short time, owing to their judicious methods. Missionaries, fur traders, settlers and soldiers soon found a basis of operation in the settlement of Quebec (1608) and that of Montreal (1641), from which points they gradually pushed on along the St. Lawrence River, into the region of the Great Lakes, and through the Mississippi basin, planting the Catholic standard of the Cross and the flag of the fleur de lis in the Indian villages as far down as the Mississippi delta. In a short time France laid claim not only to all of Canada, but to Maine, Vermont, New York, the two Carolinas, as well as the entire territory between the Alleghanies and the Mississippi.

It was during this gradual conquest of the West and the South that Illinois was first seen and traversed by white men. As early as 1641 French missionaries had penetrated to the outlet of Lake Superior, and in 1658 traders had visited the western end of the lake. Among French missions founded in these distant regions after the year 1660 was one at Green Bay, Wis., established in 1669, and named after St. Francis Xavier.

The French learned through the Indians at this and other missions that a journey of several days would bring them to the banks of a great river, known among the natives, on account of its size, as the Mississippi, the Father of Waters. This fact was reported to the French governor at Quebec, who determined to take possession of the river and adjacent regions. In order to carry out this enterprise without molestation, it was necessary to obtain the friendship and co-operation of the tribes dwelling along its banks. For this purpose Nicholas Perrot was dispatched westward in 1671, with instructions to assemble the surrounding tribes in council at Green Bay. After this meeting Perrot set out with an escort of Pottawatomie Indians on his journey southward, traversing what is now Illinois and visiting, among other points, the present site of Chicago, then included in the territory of the Miami Indians. Perrot is said to have been the first European to have set foot on Illinois soil.

In the following year two Jesuit fathers, Claude Allouez and Claude Dablon, left the Green Bay mission on a journey to western and northern Illinois, visiting the Fox Indians along the Fox River and the Masquotin tribe that dwelt at the mouth of the Milwaukee River. These missionaries claimed to have extended their explorations as far as Lake Winnebago.

Explorations of Marquette and Joliet

Father Jacques Marquette and Louis Joliet, a fur trader, were subsequently commissioned to continue the exploration of the Mississippi and the territory through which it flows. In the spring of 1673 they entered upon their task, accompanied by five other Frenchmen and two Indian guides, and supplied with two canoes. Starting from the St. Ignace mission, opposite Mackinaw Island, they followed the north shore of Lake Michigan. They soon reached Green Bay and the St. Francis Xavier mission, the uttermost outpost of French civilization

The Departure of Marquette and Joliet on Their First Voyage to Illinois

westward and southward. Here the party rested until June, and then pressed on into the wilderness. They traveled up the Fox River as far as the ridge forming the Wisconsin watershed, and, carrying their canoes across, proceeded down the Wisconsin River to their sought-for goal, arriving the 17th of June on the banks of the majestic Mississippi. Enraptured by its grandeur, and mindful of the divine protection of

Jacques Marquette

Louis Joliet

the Virgin throughout his perilous journey, Father Marquette in her honor named it Conception River.

The exploring party took a short rest on the banks of the great river, but soon embarked, more eager than ever. Floating down with the current, they had on either hand vast stretches of prairie, where the bison roamed in countless herds, but not a human being did they see. It was like traveling through a mysterious land whose inhabitants

"We are Illini"

some strange power had spirited away. The mouth of the Des Moines River was reached June 25th. On these shores human footprints were discovered at last. Following up the tracks for about two leagues, the party came upon three Indian villages, beautifully located on the banks of the Des Moines, belonging to the Peoria tribe.

As soon as the natives noticed the strangers, four chiefs set out to meet them. "Who are you?" demanded Father Marquette, in the Algonquin dialect. "We are Illini," one of the chiefs replied. The Peorias belonged to a coalition of tribes, including also the Moingwenas, the Kaskaskias, the Tamaroas and the Cahokias. The name Illini meant simply men, and had been adopted by these tribes to distinguish them from their hereditary foes to the eastward, the Iroquois, whom they abhorred on account of their cruel and bloodthirsty disposition, deeming them no better than brutes. In course of time the name Illini was altered by means of the French suffix -ois, and finally this name was applied not only to the Indian tribes but to all the newly discovered region. When in recent years this tract was made a territory of the United States, this name was made official, and later on naturally passed to one of the states parcelled out of the territory.

The fearless little band still pressed on, arriving in July at the junction of the Missouri and Mississippi. They shortly passed the mouth of the Ohio River, reaching the confluence of the Arkansas River and the Mississippi a few days later, and found there several Indian villages. From that point the mouth of the great river was to be reached in a short time, yet Marquette and his party hesitated to proceed farther, fearing a conflict with the Spaniards, who laid claim to all the surrounding territory by right of discovery by Ferdinand de Soto in 1541. Geographically, further progress was unnecessary, Marquette being already convinced that the Mississippi emptied neither into the Atlantic, nor the Pacific, but into the Gulf of Mexico. On July 19th, therefore, he turned back, retracing his course as far as the mouth of the Illinois River, which he entered and continued up this waterway.

The Death of Marquette

At one of the villages of the Kaskaskia Indians, near the present site Utica, La Salle county, the party halted. The French named the village La Vantum, and before departing, Marquette baptized the village chief Cassagoac, together with several leading tribesmen. Continuing up the entire length of the Illinois, the party entered its tributary, the Des Plaines River, carried their canoes across the watershed between this and the Chicago River, and finally by way of the south branch of the latter reached Lake Michigan. Here they rested for several days, then pursued their way along the west shore northward to Green Bay, returning thither before the end of September the same year. Thus was the Illinois River traversed for the first time by whites, and the surrounding territory brought within the sphere of civilizing influences.

Joliet immediately returned to Quebec in order to report to Frontenac, then governor of New France, the results of the expedition, while Marquette was compelled by illness to remain at the Green Bay mission.

In spite of ill health Marquette a year later, on the 25th of October, 1674, revisited the Kaskaskia village, accompanied by two young Frenchmen, Pierre and Jacques, together with a number of Indians. Retracing the course of the journey northward, they reached the mouth of the Chicago River December 4th. Here Marquette's condition suddenly grew worse, forcing the party to tarry. Near the head of the south branch of the river his companions erected a block-house, which sheltered them until early spring, when Marquette was so far restored that they could continue their journey, arriving at their destination on the 8th of April.

In this wilderness, with no sanctuary but the primeval forest, no choristers but the winged songsters, Father Marquette, with all the solemnity that the occasion afforded, performed the Catholic mass and subsequently proclaimed the sovereignty of France over the explored territory in the name of the Savior, the Holy Virgin and all the saints. In the same year he made another tour along the Illinois, exploring thoroughly its banks and adjacent regions.

Divining that his end was near, Marquette with his companions started on his way back to Canada, following the east shore of Lake Michigan, but was overtaken by death in the vicinity of present Sleeping Bear Point, in the state of Michigan, and was buried on the shore by his companions. The next year, however, Indians exhumed his remains, which were brought thence to the St. Ignace mission and solemnly interred in the mission chapel. After death, Marquette was long revered almost as a saint, to whom the sailors on Lake Michigan would pray for deliverance in the hour of danger.

Journeys of La Salle—French Forts Erected in Illinois

At this time there lived at Fort Frontenac (now Kingston), located at the point where the St. Lawrence River forms the outlet of Lake Ontario, a former Jesuit named Robert de La Salle, who had emigrated to New France in 1667. Devoting himself to fur trading, his vessels visited almost all the bays of Lakes Ontario and Erie. In 1675 he was knighted and received Frontenac as a grant from the crown on condition that he erect a fort there. He was rapidly accumulating wealth through agriculture, cattle raising and a lucrative Indian trade, when Joliet on his visit to Quebec brought him the first report of the discovery of the Mississippi. This enterprising man immediately conceived the idea of founding French settlements in the Southwest and opening up mercantile communications between France and the Mississippi region.

In pursuance of this purpose he returned to France without delay, submitted his plan to the government, and was authorized to continue the exploration begun by Marquette and Joliet, obtaining also the exclusive right to the trade in buffalo hides. He returned to New France in 1678, together with an Italian veteran by the name of Tonti, a Franciscan monk, Louis Hennepin, and carried with him a number of artisans and sailors and a large cargo of chandlers' supplies and merchandise for the Indian trade. In the fall of the year a small vessel with a capacity of ten tons was built near Fort Frontenac. In this ship La Salle and his followers soon sailed across the Ontario to the mouth of the Niagara River where a small fort was erected as a protection for a trading post. Above the falls, on the shores of the Erie, he built a sailing vessel with a tonnage of 120,000 pounds, named it the Griffin and freighted it with chandlery and ironware, designed for the fitting out of another vessel to be built on the Illinois River. The Griffin was launched August 7, 1679, with the firing of cannon and the singing of songs. This was the first sailing vessel to plow the waves of Lake Erie. With it La Salle and his crew crossed the lake, passed the straits into Lake St. Claire, sailed thence across Lake Huron and through the straits of Mackinaw, where another trading post was established, and

finally down Lake Michigan to Green Bay. Here the cargo was transferred to smaller boats for further transportation down the Illinois

Renè Robert Cavelier de La Salle

River, while the Griffin took a cargo of furs and returned to the starting
point.

La Salle and his crew navigated Lake Michigan as far as St.
Joseph, Mich., where a trading post was established, protected by

Starved Rock

palisades and known as Fort Miami. They waited until December for
the return of the Griffin, but were disappointed, the vessel having gone
ashore on its way back to Niagara. Then they prepared to continue
their voyage. There were two routes between Lake Michigan and the
Illinois River, used by the Indians from time out of mind, the one being
that taken by Marquette and Joliet on their return, the other leading
up the St. Joseph River to the turning-point near South Bend, Ind., and
thence across the watershed to the Kankakee and down that river to
the Illinois. La Salle chose the latter. His company consisted of Tonti,
Hennepin, two Franciscan monks, besides thirty sailors and colonists.
Reaching the aforesaid Kaskaskia Indian village, and finding it abandoned, they continued the journey down the Illinois, not stopping until
they reached, on January 1, 1680, that expansion of the river called
Lake Peoria. Here they found Illini Indians, with whom La Salle entered into a treaty of friendship, obtaining also permission to build a
fort, which was located on the east shore of the river, near the south
end of Lake Peoria.

The situation of La Salle was, however, far from enviable. Fifteen
hundred miles from the nearest French outpost, his followers despair-
ing of a successful issue of the enterprise and anxious to return, he was
doubtless himself in deep distress, as evidenced by the name given to
this stronghold, viz., Fort Crevecœur, meaning Broken Heart.

In spite of untoward circumstances, La Salle did not lose heart, but
set about building the intended vessel. The work had not advanced
far when several of his men deserted him, forcing a temporary delay
and necessitating his return to Fort Frontenac to secure other workmen. With three companions he started March 1st, reaching the
objective point May 6th, after many hardships and perils.

Meanwhile Hennepin and two other Frenchmen, Du Guy and
Michael d'Accault, journeyed down the Illinois to the point where it
empties into the Mississippi, and then started on a new exploring tour
up that river. They pressed on as far as the present site of Minneapolis
and discovered the great falls, named from St. Anthony of Padua,
their patron saint, the St. Anthony Falls. A cross having been erected
here, a mass was held and possession claimed in the name of France.
All that summer they tarried in this delightful region, returning in the
fall, not to Illinois, but to Green Bay.

Tonti, who had been requested to build a stronghold on a high cliff
on the south shore of the Illinois, which is now known as Starved Rock,
had left Fort Crevecœur simultaneously and started for that point.
The fort was completed and received the appropriate name of Rockfort.
While Tonti was engaged in this work nearly all the remaining Frenchmen fled, after having razed Fort Crevecœur and thrown all its supplies

into the river. Only six men of the garrison, including two priests, remained faithfully at their post. To complete the disaster, a band of Iroquois Indians arrived Sept. 10th, threatening the fortress with anni-

HENRI TONTI

hilation. The remaining Frenchmen fled. At Rockfort Tonti was taken prisoner and upon his release returned to Mackinaw.

Upon his return the following year with the advance guard of his newly recruited force of men, La Salle, to his dismay, found both fortresses deserted. He returned with his men to Fort Miami, where he met the main body of the new expedition, and quartered it there for the winter.

In furtherance of his plans, La Salle promoted a defensive alliance between the Miami and the Illinois Indians against their old enemies the Iroquois. In December he called a council of tribesmen at Fort Miami, choosing eighteen out of their number who, together with his twenty-three Frenchmen, were to accompany him to the mouth of the Mississippi. In the meantime Tonti's whereabouts had been revealed, he was sent for and put at the head of the expedition, which started southward Dec. 21st. The supplies were carried on sleds to the Illinois and there stowed into canoes, in which the expedition embarked for the desolated Fort Crevecœur.

The half finished vessel was found almost intact. It was quickly completed, whereupon the expedition set sail for its destination. The mouth of the Mississippi was reached April 6, 1682. At length, La Salle had thus reached the goal for which he had strived untiringly for several years. The French possessions in America, which had been bounded by the Great Lakes, were now extended to the Gulf of Mexico. Nor was La Salle slow in taking possession of this vast territory with the customary ceremonies, consisting of the erection of a cross, the holding of a mass, and the planting of a standard, bearing the royal arms of France. All of this new territory was named Louisiana, in honor of Louis XIV.

The expedition returned, doubling on its former course, and at the mouth of the Illinois, Tonti, with a few men, remained to establish the claims of France by actual possession. His first work was to erect a fort as a protection against the Iroquois tribes and a nucleus for the contemplated settlements in these parts. In December, 1682, Starved Rock was for the second time selected as the site of a fort, and the new stronghold was named Fort St. Louis. The necessity for protection against the Iroquois was all the more urgent, as these savage tribes were furnished with arms and ammunition by the English colonial governor at Albany, on the Hudson River, and sent westward to harass the French and destroy their lucrative Indian trade in the region of the Great Lakes.

La Salle now returned to Quebec in order to obtain authority to colonize the newly explored territory. Unfortunately, he found that Governor Frontenac had been recalled and replaced by La Barre, who was his personal enemy and antagonistic to his plans. In vain he pleaded with La Barre to co-operate with him in realizing the colonization plans. Where he had expected to find sympathy, he was met with derision. La Salle then resolved to return to France in order to obtain the privileges denied him by the governor, and embarked in the autumn of 1683. In the meantime, La Barre sent a man named De Baugis to Illinois to assume the command at Fort St. Louis, which was cheerfully relinquished by Tonti. Although deprived of the command, Tonti soon afterwards bravely beat back a savage attack by the Iroquois.

A better location than Starved Rock the experienced frontiersman could scarcely have found for the building of a fort. It consists of an isolated and almost inaccessible rock 130 to 140 feet in height. The side facing north toward the Illinois River is almost perpendicular, the opposite side forming a steep slope. The rounded top has an area of three-fourths of an acre. About a mile to the southward was the main village of the friendly Illinois Indians, called La Vantum and numbering at that time 6,000 or 7,000 inhabitants. With these he expected to carry on a profitable trade, while depending upon them to assist in repelling the attacks of their mutual enemies, the Iroquois. Furthermore, a fort at this point would form the strategic key to this part of the lower Illinois valley as well as the Mississippi valley.

Fort St. Louis consisted of earthworks and palisades, surrounding a storehouse and also a blockhouse, serving the double purpose of trading station and barracks for the garrison. By means of a windlass water was hoisted from the river. Two small brass cannon, mounted on the breastworks in such a position as easily to dominate both the river on the north and the plain on the south, completed the armament. The fort was solemnly dedicated by one Father Membre and soon became the favorite rendezvous of the natives of La Vantum and the surrounding country.

Although anticipating subsequent events, the history of Starved Rock may as well at this point be told to the end. Fort St. Louis was garrisoned until 1702, when the garrison was withdrawn. As a trading post the fort was still maintained until 1718, when it was captured and burned, supposedly by the common enemy, the Iroquois Indians. The Illinois were thenceforth left in peace until 1722, when the Foxes made an unsuccessful attack. In order to avoid further molestation the

The La Salle Monument in Lincoln Park

remainder of the dwellers about the fort removed to their tribesmen that dwelled along the Mississippi. The few that stayed behind fell an easy prey to their enemies. In the year 1769 they were attacked by tribes from the north, and, being severely pressed, sought refuge on the high rock formerly covered by Fort St. Louis. Here they were besieged by the enemy for twelve days, and then, exhausted from lack of food and water, made a desperate night attack with the hope of breaking through the lines. The attempt failed totally, all but one, an Indian half-breed, being slaughtered and scalped. Long afterwards, when the whites again began to settle here, human bones lay thickly scattered on and about the rock, as grewsome evidences of that savage battle, and to this day bones are said to be found here and there in the accumulated soil. It was this siege and the starving out of the captives that gave the name to the historic landmark, known ever afterwards as Starved Rock.

Having thus briefly sketched the history of Fort St. Louis and its famous site, we return to the story of La Salle and his colonization of Illinois.

La Salle had better success with the king of France than with his obstinate representative at Quebec. The government set aside a suitable sum to defray the expenses of colonizing the western territory, and in July, 1684, La Salle was able to return to America with a flotilla of four ships, laden with all the necessaries of the prospective settlements and carrying 280 colonists. Of this number one hundred were soldiers, the remainder farmers and their families, sailors, and members of monastic orders. The bulk of these emigrants, however, had been picked up haphazard in the cities and proved to be poor material for colony building.

After a long stay on the island of San Domingo, the expedition at length entered the Gulf and arrived in the first part of January, 1685, off the Mississippi delta, where Tonti with twenty Frenchmen and thirty Indians awaited his arrival. The expedition, however, by some miscalculation, sailed past the mouth of the river, and when La Salle discovered the mistake, he was unable to persuade Beaujeu, the commanding officer of the fleet, to turn back. He obstinately held to westward until they reached the Matagorda Bay, where they landed in boats. When the vessels subsequently entered the bay, the supply ship struck a shoal. Part of the cargo was landed during the day, but the following night a severe gale wrecked the vessel and scattered the great bulk of its cargo over the waves. To add to the disaster, the Indians of the surrounding region flocked to the shore, intent on plundering the stores saved from the wreck. A fight ensued in which several natives were killed. Two of the remaining ships immediately set sail for France, leaving La Salle and 230 Frenchmen behind, "to shift for themselves as best they might," according to the obstinate Beaujeu.

After having searched the region in all directions without finding any of the channels of the Mississippi delta, La Salle determined to found a colony with fortifications on an eminence west of Matagorda Bay. The purpose was accomplished and the settlement named St. Louis. The stores landed would have sufficed for several years, had the colonists been industrious, provident and peaceful among themselves. Being quite the reverse, the colonizing scheme thus forced upon La Salle by circumstances proved a complete failure.

In December, 1685, La Salle undertook another expedition in search of the Mississippi, but failed again. In April of the following year, accompanied by twenty men, he made an expedition to New Mexico in search of gold, but again Fortune frowned upon his undertaking. On his return the discouraging news awaited him that the colonists had been reduced to the number of forty, the remaining ship lost, and the last of the provisions consumed.

Still undaunted, La Salle determined to bring recruits and provisions from Canada. On January 12, 1687, with a company of sixteen, he started on a march northeast through the boundless wilderness. In this party he had a stanch friend in a relative of his, a young man by the name of Moranget, but also two secret enemies, Duhaut and L'Archeveque, who held La Salle responsible for the loss of all their property, which they had risked in his enterprise. At one of the tributaries of the Trinity River these men killed Moranget in a quarrel, and then lay in ambush for La Salle himself, who on his arrival at the spot was shot down by Duhaut. The slayer and his accomplice then plundered the corpse and left it on the prairie, a prey to the wild beasts. Thus ended the strenuous career of a brave and illustrious explorer.

Shortly after the foul deed the murderers and the rest of the party became involved in a fight among themselves, in which Duhaut fell, whereupon his sympathizers joined an Indian tribe. The remnant of the expedition, a small group, numbering seven men, reached Canada after an arduous journey, replete with privation and peril.

The colony thus founded by La Salle in Texas, though originally intended for Illinois, was destroyed soon afterward by Spaniards from Mexico, who invaded this region and established their claim on Texas territory.

French Missions and Colonies in Illinois

Marquette's visit to the Kaskaskia Indian village, near the present site of Utica, and the baptism of Chief Cassagoac was the first step towards christianizing Illinois. During his second visit in 1675, this zealous missionary of the church established the mission of the Immaculate Conception and built a chapel of logs and bark, the first house of worship in Illinois. This missionary work was resumed April 27, 1677, by the aforesaid Jesuit priest, Father Claude Allouez, who in 1686 took up permanent residence at the mission. He died in 1690 and was succeeded by Father James Gravier who in 1693 succeeded in establishing the mission post on a more permanent basis. A small French settlement grew up gradually on the outskirts of the Indian village.

When the French in 1699 founded a settlement at Biloxi in the present state of Mississippi, several Indian tribes of Illinois prepared to move there and locate in the neighborhood of the colony. Among those that actually broke camp were the Kaskaskias who, however, traveled southward only as far as the river that bears their name. Here they settled down, about six miles above its confluence with the Mississippi, and built a village, to which the old Kaskaskia mission also was removed, both retaining the old name. At the head of the mission at this time was a priest named Francis Pinet. A French colony was gradually formed, which as early as 1721 had attained such development and importance that the Jesuits deemed it expedient to found a convent and a school at that point. Four years later the village was incorporated as a town by permission of King Louis XV. of France.

The reason why the French colonies were attracted to southwestern Illinois is supposed to be a desire to locate near the thoroughfare between the French settlements in Canada and those at the mouth of the Mississippi. Travelers and traders alike had now practically abandoned the route via Lake Michigan and the Chicago River for the one along the Fox and Wisconsin rivers to the Mississippi. Kaskaskia, in its most prosperous days, about the middle of the eighteenth century, numbered 2,000 to 3,000 inhabitants. Toward the end of the century this number gradually lessened, amounting in 1765, when the town was taken by the English, to only 450. Of the fate of this town we will have occasion to speak in subsequent pages.

A few months prior to the founding of the new Kaskaskia, certain French Jesuits established nearby, at or near the present location of Cahokia, St. Clair county, a mission, around which there sprang up a settlement which has the distinction of being the earliest permanent French colony in Illinois. In 1701 the mission work here was left in the hands of priests educated at the French seminary in Quebec. These eventually limited their endeavors to the French settlers, leaving the spiritual care of the natives to the Jesuits. They continued their work at Cahokia until that point was surrendered to the English. After that event this old town also began to decrease in population and importance. Farther on in the course of the narrative it will again claim our attention.

After the destruction of Fort Crevecœur, friars of the Recollect Order began a mission on the same site, but the work was soon abandoned. In 1711 we find, however, a French missionary station located on the western bank of the river and surrounded by French settlers. These were the first inhabitants of the present city of Peoria. It is positively know that there was a colony at this point in 1725.

Other French colonies grew up around the original three heretofore mentioned, such as St. Philip, forty-five miles south of Cahokia, Prairie du Rocher, northwest from Kaskaskia, and west of the Mississippi, in

Ruins of Fort Chartres. The Powder Magazine. (Photograph taken in 1903.)

the present state of Missouri, St. Louis and St. Genevieve. As early as the second decade of the eighteenth century France thus possessed a considerable colony in the Mississippi valley, midway between its Canadian settlements and those founded, also in the early part of the same century, near the Gulf of Mexico. About the year 1730 these Mississippi settlers numbered 140 French families and about 600 converted Indians, together with quite a number of traders. For the protection of their midland possessions the French in 1718-20 erected Fort Chartres, sixteen miles northwest from Kaskaskia. The fort was built of limestone from an adjacent hill on a very low site, near the river bank. The ground plan was an irregular rectangle formed on three sides by stone walls of a thickness of 2 feet and 2 inches and on the fourth by a ravine which the spring freshets filled with water. This was the seat of government in Illinois during the French colonial period. At the outbreak of the French and Indian War in 1756, the fort was rebuilt at a cost of a million French crowns and was then considered the strongest fortress on the North American continent. Its story will be continued in succeeding pages.

The Fox tribe of Indians vacillated between the English and the French in disposing of their peltries. They had control of the portages of the St. Joseph and Des Plaines rivers to Lake Michigan and exacted toll from the French traders. To remove this barrier to commerce, the French determined their destruction, and one branch of the Foxes was exterminated in 1712 by the French and their Indian allies. Massacres followed in 1716 on the Wisconsin River, and the Foxes were driven away in 1728. In 1730 they were on their way east to seek protection from the Wea Miamis in northern Indiana. They were overtaken by the French under the command of St. Ange, the commandant at Fort Chartres, and by the Kickapoo, Mascoutin and Illinois tribes. The Foxes took refuge at the Big Creek of the Rock River, in Kendall county, and built a fort. But they and their enemies were both starved, and a part of the besieging force deserted. On September 8, 1730, a violent storm arose, during which the Foxes made their escape. The next day they were overtaken and 300 warriors were killed or taken prisoners, their women and children, numbering one thousand, also falling into the hands of their enemies. The facts about this massacre were until recently buried in the archives of France

To the history of the French in Illinois may be added that slavery was introduced by them at this time. The first slave trader was Pierre F. Renault, who about 1722 sold a number of slaves to settlers at Kaskaskia. Henceforth, slavery continued in Illinois for 120 years. The constitution of 1818, when Illinois was granted statehood, forbade the bringing of slaves into the state, yet such were found up to the year 1840, when they disappeared, at least from the census records.

Illinois Under English Rule

With envious eye England watched the extension of the French possessions toward the west and the south, while its own were limited to a comparatively narrow tract along the Atlantic coast. Before long, disputes arose over the boundary lines between the English and the French possessions, resulting in a war which materially reduced the French dominion in America. The territory thus ceded to England included the present state of Illinois.

The first cause of dispute was the chartering of a colonizing syndicate, entitled The Ohio Company, consisting of eight members, among whom George Washington, the man who was to play such a decisive part in the shaping of the civic destinies of the North American continent. The charter gave this company the right to colonize a large tract of land in the present state of Ohio. In order to obtain possession, the company began erecting a fort on the present site of Pittsburg, but the men engaged in building it were driven away by a large force of Frenchmen and Indians. This was the beginning of the French and Indian War, one of the bloodiest conflicts in the history of our country.

The war lasted from 1754 to 1759, simultaneously and in connection with the Seven Year's War in Europe. In the colonial war the Indian tribes of Canada, the region of the Great Lakes and the Ohio basin fought on the side of the French, while the Iroquois, the Delawares, the Shawnees, the Miamis, the Wyandottes and various other Indian tribes took up the cause of the English. The French colonists who fell into the hands of the English or their savage allies were treated with the utmost cruelty. The war was carried on with ever changing fortunes, until the English finally gained the upper hand. The last decisive battle was fought on the Plains of Abraham, south of Quebec, Sept. 12, 1759, where the English commander, General Wolfe, with a well trained army corps of 5,000 men utterly defeated the French army under General Montcalm, which, though numerically equal, consisted chiefly of militiamen. Of these 500 fell and 1,000 were taken prisoners. The English loss was, however, almost as great, 600 men being killed or wounded. Both generals fell. Five days after the battle Quebec, the main stronghold of New France, capitulated, whereby the key to the French possessions in America fell into the hands of Great Britain.

The preliminary peace protocol was signed at Montreal, Sept. 8, 1760, by General Amherst, the British commander-in-chief, and Governor de Vaudreuil of New France. Thereupon the English immediately began to take possession of the conquered domains. This, however, proved no easy task. From generation to generation the Indians had become warmly attached to the French and had fought side by side with them in the war just ended. No Englishman had heretofore settled northwest of the Ohio River; the Indians still held possession without the slightest fear of being dispossessed by the English. They were willing, as before, to carry on commerce with English traders, but this was the extent of their courtesies.

On Nov. 29, 1760, the British under Major Robert Rogers captured Detroit. The following summer they took possession of Michilimackinac, at the outlet of Lake Superior, also Green Bay, St. Joseph and Sandusky, which with their fortifications had remained intact during the war. This was true also of Forts Vincennes and Ouatanon on the Wabash River, as well as of the French villages and forts in Illinois. Far distant as these were from the arena of war, they had not been threatened with attack. But before any steps had been taken to subjugate these points, the western tribes determined to drive out the English from the strongholds already captured. The brave Chief Pontiac, their leader, headed a secret conspiracy to attack and recapture at a preconcerted moment all the strongholds lost to the English. The plan was carried out and all the forts recaptured, with the exception of Detroit and Fort Pitt (Pittsburg). The Indians were again undisputed masters of the entire Northwest. They kept up the siege of Detroit until August 26, 1763, when General Bradstreet with a large force of Englishmen came to the relief of the garrison and dispersed the Indians, who for one whole year kept the place so completely blockaded that no provisions could be smuggled in. Fort Pitt was similarly besieged until General Bouquet, about the time of the relief of Detroit by Bradstreet, came to the rescue. Nothing more remained for the English to do to fulfill the terms of the protocol but to capture Forts Vincennes and Ouatanon and subdue Illinois.

Four years had elapsed since the signing of the protocol, and still the English made no show of penetrating into the wilderness, hesitating, no doubt, on account of the vast areas of forest and plain which stretched between the English colonies in the East and the French settlements in Illinois. Their first attempt was the sending of a numerous expedition by boat up the Mississippi in order to preclude attacks by Indians with French sympathies. The expedition, numbering 300 men, was led by Major Loftus. In flat-bottomed boats they left the English fort, Bayou Manchae, on the Gulf, and proceeded up the river. They were, nevertheless, soon attacked by natives of the Tonica tribe, encamped on both sides of the river, and Major Loftus had no recourse but to return.

Meanwhile, peace had been declared between France and England, also other participants in the Seven Year's War, and the treaty of Paris, signed in 1763, advanced the frontier of the English dominion in America from the Ohio to the Mississippi, thereby subjecting Illinois, nominally at least, to British rule.

While waiting for the final treaty of peace, French traders in Illinois, as heretofore, carried on their commerce in hides and furs with the Indians, disposing of their stock in St. Louis and New Orleans at high prices. This put new obstacles in the way of the final ratification of the peace treaty, for as soon as this was done the English traders would supersede the French and the commerce would seek a channel over the Great Lakes instead of the Mississippi, and England deemed the Indian trade of Illinois of so great importance that Sir William Johnson, superintendent of the British Indian Bureau, was authorized to secure control of it at once. To gain this end, Sir William Johnson appointed George Crogan, an accomplished officer and a man of experience in similar matters, as his special commissioner. Crogan set out from Fort Pitt for Illinois in May, 1765. After various Indian skirmishes, a delegation of natives under the leadership of the haughty Chief Pontiac met him in council in the month of July, this being the first time the Indians would meet the British in peaceful negotiations. After Pontiac had agreed to cease hostilities, to use his influence for peace with kindred tribes, and in their behalf to guarantee the British undisputed possession of Illinois, Crogan had no further purpose in proceeding westward, but turned back and visited Detroit, where another council with the Indians was held. Thence he returned to Sir William Johnson, whose headquarters were on the Mohawk River, and reported the successful outcome of his mission.

In accordance with the original plan, the British military forces started from Fort Pitt in the fall of the same year to take formal possession of Illinois. It consisted of 120 men of the Forty-second Highlanders under Captain Stirling. The company arrived at Fort Chartres near the junction of the Ohio and Mississippi rivers on October 10th. The same day the French flag was hauled down and the British colors hoisted in its stead. Henceforth Illinois was British territory in fact as well as in name.

The first official act after the occupation of Fort Chartres was the issuance of a proclamation guaranteeing to the inhabitants civil and religious liberty. The latter was all that these Frenchmen coveted, holding, as they did, that hardly anything could be done to extend their political freedom. But the idea of reorganizing their communities along British lines, with various office holders, did not enter their mind. They continued their patriarchal form of village government, with the priest as chief advisor in worldly as well as spiritual affairs.

Three months after his arrival at Fort Chartres, Captain Stirling died and Major Frazier succeeded him as governor of Illinois. Though under British rule, the French pioneers continued so peaceful and law-abiding that the British troops in the spring of 1766 were sent away as superfluous. The soldiers departed by way of the Mississippi, destined for Pensacola, Florida, whence they sailed for Philadelphia, arriving June 15th.

One Colonel Reed succeeded Frazier as governor, but his despotic manner brought him into such disfavor with the people, that he was soon in turn succeeded by Colonel Wilkins, who arrived at Kaskaskia Sept. 5, 1768. The 21st of that month the new governor was ordered by General Gage, his superior, to establish a court at Fort Chartres. Seven judges were consequently appointed and on Dec. 9th of that year the first English court of law in Illinois opened its sessions. After existing for a century without a court of law, the French had established such a court in 1722.

The principles of British territorial government were clearly set forth in the proclamation of Oct. 24, 1765, by King George the Third, and in the successive proclamation of 1772. In these acts private ownership of realty was forbidden, which fact leads one to believe that the government purposed to divide the land in large estates to be granted to favorites by the crown. Fortunately, British supremacy in Illinois did not last long enough to bring about a system so dangerous to the future development of the territory.

June 2, 1774, the British parliament adopted an act, known as the Quebec Bill, by which the boundaries of Canada were extended so as to embrace all of the territory north of the Ohio River. This was the first action of parliament that aroused actual dissatisfaction among the colonists, principally those of Virginia. It encroached upon the territory of that colony, whose original grant stretched across the Ohio, and was particularly odious to the private colonizing companies which at that time planned to direct emigration into the valley of the Ohio. Certain acts of Lord Dunmore, the last colonial governor of Virginia, angered the people on the frontier, and they made their displeasure known in a way that unmistakably presaged a coming uprising, long before any revolutionary tendencies could be discerned in Boston and Philadelphia.

Captain Hugh Lord seems to have been the last of the English governors of Illinois, and no more troops were sent there. The population, now made up of half-breeds as well as French and Indians, was left to govern itself under the direction of Philippe Francois de Rastel, Chevalier de Rocheblave, in the capacity of military commander, territorial governor and judge of the provincial council. Rocheblave was the last commander in Illinois under British sovereignty, continuing in that capacity until the Americans claimed possession.

Fort Chartres remained the seat of government until 1772, when one side of the fort was destroyed by a Mississippi flood. On a hill near the Kaskaskia River, opposite the town of the same name, the English erected Fort Gage the same year, making this the administrative headquarters. Fort Gage was built entirely of wood, being inferior to the former stronghold now left to fall into ruin. The river floods have long since completed the work of demolition, leaving no vestige of this whilom proud and forbidding citadel.

The American Occupation

The Continental Congress, made up of representatives of the thirteen colonies, assembled in Philadelphia Sept. 5, 1774. This congress soon set about forming an American home government to take the place of the British, which had became oppressive and odious. On June 13th of the following year three Indian departments were instituted, viz., the Southern, the Northern and the Central, the last named embracing Illinois.   As its officers were chosen Benjamin Frank-

Brigadier General George Rogers Clark

lin and James Wilson of Pennsylvania, and Patrick Henry of Virginia. Owing to the remoteness of the territory under their supervision no practical benefits accrued to it, the plan simply denoting the first official act in the acquirement of the western territory.

On April 10, 1776, Col. George Morgan, a former trader at Kaskaskia, was appointed Indian Agent for this department to succeed

Franklin and Wilson. He resided at Fort Pitt, but his office required him to visit the Indian tribes of the West for the purpose of befriending them. The British agents, however, had already obtained their friendship, and Morgan's efforts proved needless.

In the meantime the revolutionary movement made great strides. Among its most enthusiastic promoters, and those who made the greatest sacrifices in its support, were the people on the Virginia frontier. Prominent among them was Col. George Rogers Clark, himself a Virginian. He was one of a number of men who had founded settlements in Kentucky, but had returned Oct. 1, 1777, to submit to Governor Patrick Henry of Virginia a plan for the occupation of Illinois. After repeated representations the governor finally approved the plan, and Col. Clark prepared to carry it out.

The utmost precaution was needed, for had the British learned of the enterprise, they would have immediately sent troops from Detroit to interrupt the Clark expedition and prevent further progress, and in all likelihood would have reinforced Fort Gage with a strong garrison. The expedition embarked at Pittsburg, following the Ohio River down to a point near its junction with the Mississippi, whence it proceeded overland to Kaskaskia, then a town of about 1,000 inhabitants.

In the evening of July 4, 1778, Clark and his men arrived at Fort Gage. No English were found there, only a handful of French doing garrison duty under the command of Rocheblave. The inhabitants of Kaskaskia were completely taken by surprise by the Americans, and no resistance was offered. A Pennsylvanian who chanced to be among the occupants of the fort secretly admitted the Americans at night. So complete was the surprise that the commandant himself was found by the entering enemy soundly asleep by his wife's side, and was rudely awakened only to be put in irons, as were also a number of his men, while the remainder of the population were forbidden to leave their houses, on penalty of being shot without mercy. To add to the alarm of the peaceful citizens, the Americans patrolling the streets marched back and forth, making night hideous by noise and shouting.

Rumor had portrayed the American soldiers as a band of rowdies. Clark, knowing this, determined to take advantage of the fact. His purpose was at first to strike terror into the inhabitants by stern, relentless severity, and afterwards gain their friendship and confidence by merciful and considerate treatment. He succeeded admirably. Before they had any inkling of his purpose, the inhabitants sent a delegation headed by their priest, Father Gibault, with a humble request that they be permitted to assemble once more at church to bid each other a last farewell before being scattered in various directions, as they feared. Their request was granted on the specific condition

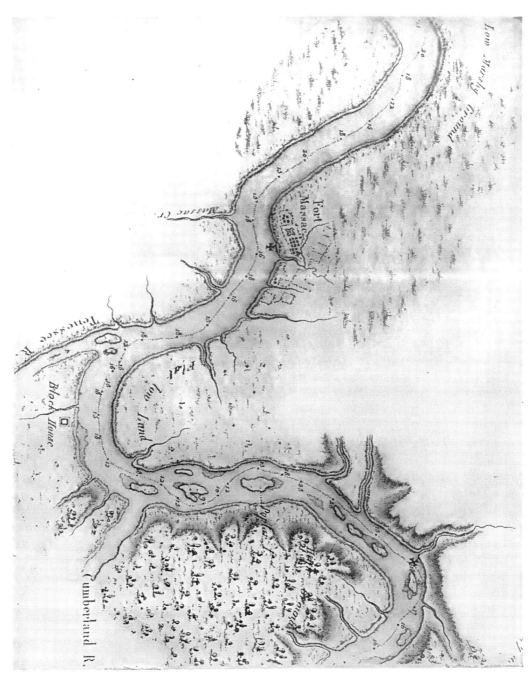

Map Showing Fort Massac and Vicinity (1826)

that no one leave the town. After the meeting in the church Father Gibault and a committee again called on Clark, praying that, as they were about to be exiled from their homes, they might be permitted to take with them provisions and other necessities, and that mothers might not be separated from their children. Clark listened to their supplications with visible surprise and then exclaimed: "What! Do you take us for savages?"

It were needless to say that the reverend father and his companions were equally surprised and elated at this good-natured retort. Then this fierce colonel and his band of Americans had not come to drive them from their abodes and deprive them of their property and religious freedom! On the contrary, they had come merely to institute the new government and place Illinois under its protection, the settlers learning now for the first time and to their satisfaction that this government had been officially recognized by France. Cahokia and the other French villages in Illinois willingly recognized the authority of Clark, and Illinois had thereby all but nominally ceased to be a British dependency.

Clark's position was, however, rather precarious. Fort Pitt, the only point from which he could obtain reinforcements in an emergency, was situated five hundred miles away, with the French village of Vincennes and Fort Sackville, still held by the British, intervening between him and his military base of supplies. It was, therefore, of the utmost importance that this point be taken and that the British be prevented from sending reinforcements from Detroit. Father Gibault and one Captain Helm, together with a small number of men, offered to go to Vincennes and persuade the French to take up the American cause. Their mission succeeded, and Captain Helm was made commandant at Fort Sackville, but all too soon the fears of Col. Clark were realized. On Dec. 15th, Henry Hamilton, the English governor at Detroit, appeared outside of Vincennes with a force of thirty British soldiers, fifty French volunteers and four hundred Indian warriors. At the fort Captain Helm stood ready to fire what appears to have been the only cannon of the fort. When Hamilton and his soldiers had arrived within hearing distance, Helm shouted a thundering "Halt!" To this Hamilton replied with a demand on Helm to capitulate. This Helm agreed to do, on condition that he might depart without the customary military honors. Hamilton consented, and out marched the commandant and the entire garrison—one lone soldier.

This made Clark's position more perilous than ever, but he proved himself master of the situation. Having been informed in January, 1779, that Hamilton had somewhat reduced the garrison at Fort Sackville by sending a small force to blockade the Ohio River in order to cut off the retreat of the Americans, the fearless Col. Clark deter-

Site of Old Fort Massac, Showing Earthworks

mined to take the fort by surprise.   Forming a company of French volunteers, which raised his fighting strength to 170 men, he marched on Fort Sackville, while a vessel under John Rogers' command, with a crew of 46 and a cargo of supplies, was dispatched down the Mississippi and up the Ohio and Wabash rivers to co-operate with the land forces.   It was only with the greatest difficulty that Clark and his men succeeded in crossing the swollen Wabash.   The vessel failing to arrive on time, he temporarily provisioned his forces at an Indian village and advanced bravely on Fort Sackville.   They arrived Feb. 24th, and after a hard-fought battle of twenty-four hours, the fort surrendered. This was practically the only battle incident to the conquest of Illinois by the Americans.

Previous to this battle, the Americans had made preparations for a system of government for the territory.   The legislative assembly of Virginia in October, 1778, resolved to institute a temporary government, and on this act Col. John Todd, second in command under Clark, based a proclamation, issued June 15, 1779, declaring the entire territory a county of Virginia, to be known as the county of Illinois. The same year a fort was erected on the east bank of the Mississippi, a short distance below the mouth of the Ohio, designed to protect the territory against the Spanish, who, besides other extensive possessions in the New World, since 1762 claimed the entire territory west of the Mississippi.   Col. Todd fell in the battle of Blue Licks, Kentucky, August 18, 1782, and was succeeded by Timothy Montbrun, a Frenchman, as commandant of Illinois.

An old trading post named Fort Massac was established about 1700 by the French in southern Illinois, on the Ohio River.   In 1758 they rebuilt it as a bulwark against the English during the French and Indian War.   After having been ceded to the British in 1765, the fort was left unoccupied.   This made it possible for Gen. Clark to float down the Ohio River unmolested.   The fort was rebuilt in 1794 and was occupied by an American garrison until after the War of 1812, when it was abandoned.   As late as 1843 it was decided to build an arsenal here, but this was instead established at Rock Island.   Earthworks still mark the site of the fort, which is now a state park.

In 1782 the first American settlement in Illinois was founded in present Monroe county and significantly named New Design.   The settlers were James Moore, Shadrach Bond, James Garrison, Robert Kidd and Larken Rutherford, the last two having served in Clark's little band of soldiers.   In the summer of 1781 these men came with their families across the Alleghany Mountains, boarded a river vessel in Pittsburg, and were carried down the Ohio to the Mississippi, and up this river to the point selected for the settlement.

By the treaty of Paris, Sept. 3, 1783, England recognized the independence of the United States. The territory thereby ceded to the new republic included Illinois, and after the ratification of the treaty of peace by the congress at Philadelphia, on Jan. 14, 1784, Illinois became an integral part of the United States and passed into a new and important epoch of development.

Illinois as a Territory and a State in the Union

On July 13, 1787, congress passed the Northwest Ordinance, by which all the region north of the Ohio River was organized as the Northwest Territory. October 5th of the same year Arthur St. Clair,

The Old Cahokia Court House (1795)

an officer of prominence in the Revolutionary War, was appointed governor. July 9th of the following year he arrived at Marietta, a newly founded settlement on the Muskingum River, designated as the seat of government. The first county in Ohio was organized under the name of Washington. In June, 1790, Hamilton county was organized, and a few weeks later the governor together with Winthrop Sargeant, the territorial secretary, made a journey to Kaskaskia and organized the settled portions of Illinois as a county, named St. Clair in honor of the governor. A court was established at Cahokia, and a justice of the peace appointed in each village. Five years later the increase in population necessitated the organization of another county, which was named Randolph.

By an act of congress May 7, 1800, the Northwest Territory was divided in two, the one comprising Ohio, the other Indiana, Illinois, Wisconsin and portions of Michigan and Minnesota. Simultaneously, William Henry Harrison was appointed governor and John Gibson secretary of the latter, called Indiana Territory. Vincennes was chosen

Ninian Edwards, Territorial Governor 1809-18. United States Senator 1818-24. Third Governor 1827-30.

capital and the new governor arrived Jan. 10, 1801. By order of the governor a territorial legislature was elected Jan. 3, 1805, and assembled at Vincennes. Shadrach Bond and William Biggs were elected representatives of St. Clair county and George Fisher representative of Randolph county. These three men, the first members of a legislative body in Illinois, met for their first session July 29th of the same year.

Previously, however, Indiana Territory had already been divided by an act of congress, passed Jan. 11, 1805, the lower Michigan peninsula forming a separate territory. Four years later, in February, 1809, a second division took place, making a new territory, named Illinois, out of the present states of Illinois and Wisconsin and the upper peninsula of Michigan. Kaskaskia was made its capital and Edwards, the first governor, entered upon his administration the following 11th of June. The census of 1810 showed a population of 12,282 in the

Old Kaskaskia house, in which the first Territorial Legislature
is said to have met in 1812

territory. Three new counties, Madison, Gallatin and Johnson, were organized, and the territorial privileges were gradually enhanced. Thus it was given a seat in congress in 1812, Shadrach Bond being the first territorial delegate.

In January, 1818, Nathaniel Pope being the delegate, the territorial assembly petitioned congress for statehood. The petition was granted, and out of the aggregation of small and widely scattered settlements was formed a state of the Union with all the rights and privileges thereunto appertaining. The boundaries then fixed have remained intact. The following summer a constitutional convention was held at Kaskaskia, with attending delegates from all the counties then existing, viz., St. Clair, Randolph, Madison, Gallatin, Johnson, Edwards, White, Monroe, Pope, Jackson, Crawford, Bond, Union, Washington and Franklin. The constitution was adopted in August and the first state election took place in September, resulting in the unanimous election of Shadrach Bond, the only candidate, as governor, Pierre Menard as lieutenant governor, and Elias Kent Kane as secre-

Shadrach Bond, First Governor of Illinois

tary of state. These entered upon their duties the 6th of October following.

In 1820 Vandalia became the capital of the new state, and Kaskaskia from that time began to fall off in population and importance. Today only a small group of dilapidated buildings bear evidence of its former dignity.

A similar fate befell the still older community of Cahokia. Both places having for a time shared the functions of county seat in St. Clair county, Cahokia, after the organization of Randolph county, held that distinction alone until 1814, when Belleville became the administrative center. This meant the passing of Cahokia. In 1890 the place had but 100 inhabitants, a considerable number of whom were descendants of the early French settlers at that point.

Vandalia became, as stated, the capital of the new commonwealth. The first capitol building was a plain two-story frame structure. The first story contained a single room, used as the assembly hall of the House of Representatives. The upper story was divided into two rooms, the one occupied by the Senate, the other by the Council of Revision. For the use of the secretary of state, the treasurer and the state auditor individual offices were rented in the vicinity of the capitol. The state archives at the time of removal from Kaskaskia to Vandalia comprised a single wagonload of documents. The legislature at its first session in Vandalia resolved that this city be the seat of government for twenty years, beginning Dec. 1, 1820.

This modest capitol building was destroyed by fire Dec. 9, 1823, whereupon a larger and more commodious brick edifice was erected at a cost of $15,000, the citizens of Vandalia contributing $3,000 towards this amount. Regardless of the resolution pertaining to the location of the capitol, agitation was begun the very same year in favor of selecting another capital city, owing to the fact that the northern part of the state had become so densely populated that Vandalia was no longer the central point. At the legislative election in August, 1834, the question was submitted to a popular vote, the city of Alton receiving the largest number of votes, with Springfield second. One of the reasons urged in favor of a removal was that the capitol building, though little over ten years old, did not meet the growing requirements. The enterprising mayor of the capital was opposed to the plan, and to stop all talk of removal on account of the inadequacy of the structure, in the summer of 1836 set about tearing down the old building without reference to the will of the legislature, and subsequently put up a new building, utilizing the old and adding new material at a cost of $16,000. This coup proved of no avail, however, for on Feb. 28, 1837, the legislature, disregarding the popular vote of 1834, resolved to make Springfield the capital city. The legislature assembled in the state house at Vandalia in December, 1838, for the last time, thereupon turning the rebuilt structure over to Fayette county for a courthouse and school building. Remodeled in 1858-9, this same structure today serves as the county courthouse.

For the capitol building in Springfield the legislature appropriated the sum of $50,000 and the city contributed an equivalent amount, whereupon the cornerstone was laid with appropriate ceremonies July 4, 1837. On the same day two years later the administration moved into the new statehouse, which, however, was not completed until

1853, when it had cost the state $260,000 or more than double the original estimate of $120,000. The building was considered a masterpiece of architecture as well as a structure of extravagant magnitude, yet fifteen years after its completion the enormous growth of the state had shrunk it into inadequacy. The legislature, therefore, on Feb. 25, 1867, resolved to sell it to the city of Springfield and the county of Sangamon at a price of $200,000 and to erect a new capitol, the

The State Capitol at Springfield

fifth in the history of the young state. The cost was fixed at a maximum of three million dollars. The cornerstone was laid Oct. 5, 1868, and twenty years were required to complete the building. It then represented an expenditure of about $4,500,000. During this long period the tax payers had repeatedly found fault with the extreme laxity in building operations as well as the unwarranted waste of the funds of the state. At all events, a capitol worthy of the state was erected. It is a worthy monument to the enterprise of a commonwealth that had so suddenly sprung from an isolated territory to become one of the most flourishing and influential states of the Union.

Among the early problems that pressed for a solution was the question of improved transportation facilities. The state had a number of navigable waterways, such as the Mississippi, the Ohio, the Wabash, the Illinois and the Rock rivers, yet the vast stretches of prairie that intervened were traversed only with great difficulty. The old commercial route, leading from Lake Michigan along the Desplaines and Illinois rivers to the Mississippi, again came into extensive use as the white population increased, but carrying merchandise in canoes and on horseback was now considered too slow a mode of transportation. The idea of connecting the Mississippi with Lake Michigan by means of a canal suggested itself, and the first step in the realization of the plan was the organization of the Illinois and Michigan Canal Association in 1825. The following year a memorial was sent to congress by the legislature, requesting a grant of land by the government toward defraying the expense to be incurred by the project. In 1827 congress appropriated 224,322 acres of land for this purpose. In 1836, nine years later, the work of digging was begun, and twelve years later the canal was completed. This waterway remained for many years one of the principal transportation routes in the state.

During the construction of the canal, an epidemic of speculation raged throughout the state. Villages, towns and cities sprang up—on paper, and lots sold rapidly at exhorbitant prices. It proved the golden age of the real estate agents and promoters. Finally, in 1836, the fever spread to the legislature itself. The lawmakers devised a plan for the improvement of transportation facilities which, in point of extensiveness, challenges comparison. Bills were passed looking to the building of no less than 1,300 miles of railways crossing one another in every direction. Large amounts were set aside for the improvement of rivers and the building of canals. Counties not affected by these public enterprises were set at rest by means of an appropriation of $200,000 to be parcelled out among them. The legislature was in such a state of excitement that it gave orders for beginning work at both ends of the projected railroads simultaneously. The appropriations for the enormous enterprises amounted to a grand total of $12,000,000 and commissioners were sent out to negotiate loans to that amount. Considering that the railway was still in its infancy and was looked upon as the greatest of luxuries, that there were entire counties that could scarcely boast a single settler's cabin, and that the entire population of the state numbered less than 400,000, the legislature of the young state certainly expended a tremendous amount of energy in its efforts to develop the resources of the commonwealth. Meanwhile the legislature established new state banks, the earnings of which were to be used to defray part of the expense for the new lines of transportation.

This forced and abnormal development was soon followed by the inevitable crash. This came in the form of the great financial panic of 1837 which, while it affected the entire country, yet caused the most serious disturbance in this state. Business was practically stagnant and all public enterprises had to be abandoned for the time being. The state banks discontinued cash payments, and the credit of the state was still further impaired during the next few years by a vigorous propaganda in favor of repudiating the public debt. So great was the financial embarrassment that state bonds offered at 14 cents on the dollar went begging in the money markets. Taxes and state revenues narrowly sufficed to defray current expenditures. After August, 1841, no further efforts were made to pay the interest on the state debt, and in the early part of the following year the state banks went out of business entirely. The state debt at this time amounted to $14,000,000, an enormous sum for a young state with a small population and with its natural resources still undeveloped.

In 1842 Illinois thus stood on the verge of bankruptcy. From such a catastrophe it was saved by Governor Thomas Ford, an energetic man, through whose endeavors a plan for the payment of the state indebtedness was formed and successfully carried out. This marked the beginning of a gradual improvement in the finances of the state.

Long before the Illinois and Michigan Canal was opened for traffic, the first steamboat had appeared on the Illinois River. This was in 1826, but several years elapsed before steamboats came into general use for river traffic. In the late thirties railway building was begun in Illinois as well as in the eastern states. The first railway in the state was the Northern Cross, with Jacksonville and Meredosia as its terminal points. This stretch of road, which proved the beginning of the great Wabash Railway system, was completed in 1839, the first locomotive having been imported the foregoing year. This railway was built at state expense.

In 1847 work was begun on the first railway out of Chicago, namely, the Galena and Chicago Union, which had been chartered eleven years before. This was the beginning of the great North-Western Railway system, which has contributed so largely to the material development of the state. The Chicago and Rock Island Railway was built in the early fifties, opening an important thoroughfare from Chicago to the Mississippi and the West.

In the financial crisis of 1837, Illinois was one of the states which suffered the greatest loss. Business was at a standstill and all public enterprises were indefinitely postponed. Business operations were resumed by slow degrees, however, and Illinois swung again into the path of progress. A new period of prosperity was inaugurated in 1850 by an act of Congress appropriating extensive land grants for the completion of the Illinois Central Railway. Immigrants came in great numbers, and towns and villages sprang up quickly along this railroad as it neared its completion in 1856. The public debt of the state had increased enormously during the panic of 1837 and grew continually, reaching its highest point, $16,724,177, in 1853.

Another great stride in the development of the state was taken in 1848, when the telegraph system, established a few years prior, was extended into Illinois.

At this point we may fitly mention an event in the early history of Illinois which at the time was considered very noteworthy. In the spring of 1825, at the initiative of Governor Coles, the renowned

General Lafayette

General Lafayette of revolutionary fame paid a visit to Illinois. The governor had formed the general's acquaintance in Paris, and when the latter was about to visit the young republic which he had so materially helped to establish, the governor insisted that the journey ought to be extended to what was at that time known as the far West. Lafayette's visit to Illinois was hailed with the utmost enthusiasm by the Americans and not least by the descendants of the old French settlers. The expenses of the trip were paid out of the state treasury, amounting to $6,743, or one third of the tax revenue for the year.

While long and bloody conflicts were raging between the whites and the Indians in Ohio and Indiana, Illinois was spared the ravages of Indian warfare, owing largely to the French element, which had early gained the confidence of the redskins and long exercised a dominating and wholesome influence over the Indians and the population in general. During the war of 1812 between England and the United States, the Indians as allies of the British committed certain outrages, which were, however, of small significance as against the cruelties perpetrated before and after in other western territories.

The most serious conflict of this kind in Illinois was the Black Hawk War of 1832. Black Hawk, who in 1788 had succeeded his father as chief of the Sac Indians, sedulously guarded the interests of his tribe against the inroads of the whites. Bitter rage filled the chieftain's heart, when certain other chiefs of the Sacs and Foxes in 1804 disposed of their lands, comprising a stretch of 700 miles along the Mississippi, to the whites for an indefinite amount payable in annual instalments of $1,000. He held that his fellow chiefs must have been drunk when signing such an agreement. Nevertheless, Black Hawk himself renewed the agreement in 1816. Having thus become homeless on their former domains east of the Mississippi, the tribesmen were compelled to withdraw in great numbers to the government reservation opened

BLACK HAWK

to them in 1823 in Iowa, near the present site of Des Moines. Black Hawk and a number of others, however, remained on their native soil. In 1831 the last tract occupied by the Indians was sold to white settlers. When these began to plow up the little patches already planted by the Indians, the anger of the savage chief and his followers knew no bounds and they swore bloody vengeance. To prevent an outbreak, the state militia was called out, and Black Hawk and his warriors were forced to retreat beyond the Mississippi under promise not to return to Illinois without permission. He soon broke his promise and invaded the state in the spring of 1832, at the head of a band of fifty warriors, but was met and repulsed by the militia. The band was broken up into small groups that attacked the white settlers wherever found, killing, scalping and devastating. General Scott was sent with a small force to put a stop to the savagery, but his operations were hampered by an outbreak of cholera among the soldiers. The Indians were at last driven up to the Wisconsin River where General Dodge dealt them a telling blow on July 21st and General Atkinson, on August 2nd, totally defeated them. Chief Black Hawk was taken prisoner, and a treaty was made by which the remainder of the lands claimed by his tribe were sold and the remaining tribesmen, about 3,000 in number, were transferred to the aforesaid reservation in Iowa. The chief himself, two of his sons and seven warriors who were held as hostages by the government for some time, were taken through a number of the larger cities in the East and finally imprisoned at Fort Monroe. They were liberated June 5, 1833, and permitted to rejoin their tribe. This famous chief of a dwindling tribe died at the reservation on the Des Moines River on Oct. 3, 1838, at the ripe age of seventy.

The Mormons at Nauvoo

Peace had scarcely been restored, when a new disturbance aroused the inhabitants. This time the Mormons were the disturbing element. In the state of New York Joseph Smith had proclaimed the alleged revelation of the hidden tablets of gold, by the aid of which he had written a book embodying a new religion. In April, 1830, he had organized a small band of followers who were called Mormons after that weird fabric of truth and falsehood, the Book of Mormons. Joseph Smith and his faithful settled in Kirtland, Ohio, where the sect grew so rapidly that Smith and his assistant, Sidney Rigdon, soon were obliged to select a larger tract farther west for the accommodation of the colony. A suitable location was found at Independence, Jackson county, Missouri, and here they determined to found a New Jerusalem and build their temple. Smith and Rigdon returned to Kirtland and set about raising the funds needed for the removal. They decided to establish a bank as the easiest means to that end, but omitted, as useless, the formality of obtaining banking privileges from the government. While issuing bank notes of highly questionable value, they provided for the numerical growth of the sect by sending out missionaries to various parts of the country. In January, 1838, the bank was forced to close, while Smith and Rigdon escaped being imprisoned as swindlers by leaving the city by night and making their way toward Missouri with numerous creditors on their tracks.

In the meantime, large numbers of Mormons assembled there, the influx being marked by sharp friction with the inhabitants, who, with or without cause, charged the strangers with robbery, incendiarism and murder. After numerous conflicts with enraged mobs, they were driven from one county to another and settled at last in the town of Far West, in Caldwell county, where Smith and Rigdon rejoined them. The conflicts with the Missourians continued, while an internal feud threatened disintegration among the Mormons themselves. This strife was quickly settled, whereupon the colony again presented a united front to their neighbors. Toward the close of 1838 the conflict had assumed the proportions of a rebellion. The Mormons armed themselves and assembled in large numbers in fortified villages, openly challenging the authorities. Finally the governor was forced to call out the militia, and Smith and Rigdon were arrested, charged with fomenting a revolt.

Realizing the fruitlessness of armed opposition to the people of the entire state, the Mormons now submitted to the authorities and agreed to leave the state. To a number of 15,000 they crossed over into Illinois in 1839, receiving a friendly welcome in spite of reports of the trouble they had caused in the neighboring state. Smith meanwhile fled from prison and here reunited with his flock and his comrade Rigdon, who had been released through habeas corpus proceedings. On a tract of land in Hancock county, placed at their disposal on speculation by one Doctor Isaac Galland, the Mormons began to build the town of Nauvoo. By sharp transactions in real estate Smith amassed a fortune in a few years.

On the strength of an alleged new revelation, Joseph Smith issued a decree to his followers in various parts of the world, commanding them to assemble in Nauvoo, whereby the population of the town increased by thousands in a short time. A charter was issued by the legislature, entitling the city to certain exceptional privileges, which placed Smith and Rigdon, together with other leaders, in a position to assume almost unlimited power over the community. Among other privileges was that of organizing a military force. This resulted in the forming of the Nauvoo Legion, comprising nearly all ablebodied men in the town. Smith assumed the chief command with the title of Lieutenant General. Besides this, he was mayor of the city and president of the Mormon denomination. Having thus united in his own person the civil, the military, and the ecclesiastical power, he was not slow to exercise the prerogatives voted him by his own followers and a short-sighted state legislature. He had purposely so worded the Nauvoo city charter as to deprive the state authorities of almost every vestige of jurisdiction within its limits. It was a proud moment for Joseph Smith, when on April 6, 1841, at the head of the Nauvoo Legion and surrounded by a glittering military staff, he performed the pompous ceremony of laying the cornerstone of the temple, designed to be the civil and religious shrine of the dreamed-of Mormon empire.

Up to this time the Mormons had sustained fairly peaceful relations with the people of the state, but when Smith in 1843 announced a new revelation instituting polygamy, the situation was at once changed. The leaders publicly disclaimed and denounced the doctrine but to no avail, for it was generally known that Smith himself had lived in plural marriage since 1838. Certain men, whose wives Smith had approached seeking to induce them to enter into illegal relations with him, established a newspaper, the "Expositor," which mercilessly exposed the immoral life of the prophet. The result was that on May 6, 1844, a number of Smith's faithful attempted to destroy the office and property of the paper. The perpetrators were ordered arrested but refused to follow the officer of the law who read the warrant, fortifying themselves by the charter of special privileges, and the officer was driven

The Mormon Temple at Nauvoo

out of town by force. The county authorities called for military aid in preserving law and order; the Mormons also took up arms and bloodshed seemed imminent. This was prevented by the governor, who persuaded Smith and his brother Hyrum to submit to a trial. They were taken to the prison in Carthage where guards were posted for their protection. In the evening of June 27th the prison was attacked by a mob; the guards were overpowered, shots were fired at the prisoners through doors and windows, and Hyrum Smith fell dead on the spot. The prophet returned the fire, defending his own life with a revolver until his ammunition was spent, then made a dash for safety through a window, but was hit by a bullet and fell dead in his tracks. This ended the career of Joseph Smith, the religious adventurer.

Profiting by past experience, the legislature annulled the charter of the city of Nauvoo the following year, and the Mormons were forced to seek new quarters. A considerable number broke camp in February, 1846, and gathered in Council Bluffs, whence they travelled afoot across the plains and mountains to Utah. The remaining Mormons had a second conflict with their neighbors. In September, 1846, the city was fired into for three consecutive days and the inhabitants were finally driven out at the point of the bayonet. In the year following there was another exodus to Utah, but not until May, 1848, did the main body of the Mormons break up from Nauvoo and follow in the path of the advance guards. In the fall of the same year their destination was reached. In Utah the Mormons soon founded the city of Salt Lake and various other important communities. Judging from the continued history of the Mormons, particularly that of the fifties, the state of Illinois is to be felicitated upon its fortunate riddance, after but a few years, of this lawless and obstinate element.

The Icarian Community

When the Mormons evacuated Nauvoo in 1846, the place was immediately occupied by a party of French settlers, known as Icarians, who formed a community, the story of which has a peculiar interest.

Etienne Cabet, born at Dijon, France, the son of a cooper, became in the time of Louis Philippe one of the leading French jurists and ultimately attorney-general during the Second Republic. He was a novelist of some note, his best known works being entitled, respectively, "Voyage to Icaria" and "The True Christianity." Having lived through the horrors of the revolution, Cabet founded the Icarian Community, based on ideas advanced by Victor Hugo in a novel called "Icaria." A number of his adherents preceded him to America, landed at New Orleans and planted a colony in Texas, on the Red River, opposite Shreveport, La. Finding the climate unfavorable, they returned to New Orleans, where they were joined by Cabet, who appointed a committee of three to sail up the Mississippi to select a site for final settlement. This committee visited Nauvoo and agreed to purchase about twelve acres of the Mormons' property, on which the party subsequently located.

On leaving, the Mormons tried to burn their temple, a handsome structure built largely of massive stone, with the upper portion and steeple of frame. The fire destroyed only the upper parts, which the Icarians set about reconstructing. A terrific storm undid their work and also tore down part of the masonry, whereupon they used what was left of the temple in erecting other buildings. The principal ones were a large structure, the lower part of which contained one vast hall, which served the double purpose of dining room and auditorium, the upper story containing living rooms. The hall accommodated 1,200 diners, who were all served almost at the same time. The next largest building in Icaria was a schoolhouse.

The administration consisted of president, secretary, treasurer and seven directors, styled ministers, all elected yearly by the members of the community, females of eighteen and males of twenty-one being entitled to vote. They also elected a General Assembly, a legislative body which held session every Saturday evening. Père Cabet, the founder of the community, was its president for many successive terms. Admission into the community was conditioned by the payment of 300 francs. The applicant was put on probation for three months, then voted on and, failing of election, his money was returned. If elected, the applicant was required to turn over all his property to the community. The colony was strictly communistic in every detail.

There was a general director of work, with special foremen appointed monthly for each line of employment, and each man or woman could select the work desired, with the privilege of changing occupation at times to relieve the monotony. The children were put in school at seven and kept there until adjudged competent. In the highest classes the sciences, astronomy, geometry, etc., were taught to both sexes. The instruction was liberal in the extreme. So good was the school considered that outsiders went there to receive their education. In religion they were also liberal, most of them being free thinkers; but church affiliation was no bar to membership. Sundays were generally set aside for recreation. After dinner the great hall was cleared and given over to discussion or to music, an excellent orchestra of fifty pieces being maintained. On Sunday evenings in winter the colonists were usually regaled with some play, there being several actors of talent and a stage at one end of the hall. After the show, adults and children indulged in dancing. There were hospitals for the sick, an athletic field for public sports and playgrounds for the children. Civil cases and cases of misdemeanor were tried by the assembly. Criminal cases, if any, were turned over to the municipal authorities, for the colonists were loyal subjects of the United States. They had a periodical, the "Icarian," issued more for proselyting purposes than for the news it contained. Copies circulated in France from time to time won new members, particularly from the communistic party. When Napoleon III. ordered the arrest of the communists, many fled to America and a number joined the Icarians at Nauvoo.

The Icarians were largely skilled workmen, such as mechanics, tailors and shoemakers. To dispose of the overproduction by the latter two crafts, a store was opened in St. Louis for the sale of clothing and shoes. Other surplus products were sold in Keokuk, Ia. The colony had flour mills, sawmills, a cooper shop, a wagon factory and a distillery. Much of their textile goods was manufactured at home.

All told, there were about 1,800 Icarians during their sojourn in Nauvoo, but never more than 1,200 at one time. Most of the members were French, with a sprinkling of other nationalities. Early in the fifties, forty-eight of the colonists were sent to pre-empt government lands near Council Bluffs, Ia., and acquired some 8,000 acres, the community apparently foreseeing the day when its present quarters might become too cramped. In the course of time the serpent of disruption entered the Icarian Eden. Though most economically managed, the maintenance being but 7½ cents daily, per capita, the colony was going slowly but surely to the wall. To reduce the constantly growing indebtedness, the more practical members urged that the plan of keeping skilled workmen on a plane with common laborers should be abolished and the former set to work in manufacturing goods on a larger scale for the general market, enabling the colony to liquidate the debt. This clashed with the theory of "Father Cabet," who held that commerce and intercourse with the outside world would spoil community life. He also claimed the position of supreme dictator for life. When at the next election he was defeated for president, he withdrew in disappointment, going to Cheltenham, near St. Louis, with his minority of about 200 colonists. He did not long survive the defeat; his adherents disbanded or joined the settlement in Iowa; the community property was sold to pay the debts. Today the only trace left of the Icarian community is a group of some forty members, engaged in fruit farming in California.

Having in the foregoing pages followed the material development of Illinois through its successive stages, we turn now to a brief review of its constitutional history. The successive territorial governments were similarly organized, consisting of governor, secretary and judge, appointed by the president. This same organization was retained when in 1809 Illinois was separated from Indiana and became a distinct territory. The governor was clothed with almost unlimited power in the matter of appointments, the only official not appointed by him being the secretary. The legislative power lay in the hands of the governor and three judges appointed by the president. This tribunal met June 16, 1809, and framed a code, embodying the principal laws in force up to that time. ,

This administrative system obtained until 1812, when congress entitled the territory of Illinois to local self-government, implying the right of the people to elect their own county and town officials, members of the legislature, and the territorial representative in congress. The franchise was granted every citizen who paid taxes to the territory. The legislature comprised two houses, called the Legislative Council and the House of Representatives, and made up of five and seven members respectively. The governor had absolute veto power, enabling him to set at naught every act of the legislature at his own discretion. The first members elected to the assembly met in Kaskaskia Nov. 25, 1812, and ratified, during their first session, all the laws passed to date by the Indiana legislature and the governor and judges of Illinois.

In the year 1818, as we have seen, Illinois was raised to the dignity of statehood. The state constitution then adopted was a brief document, patterned after the constitutions of Kentucky, Ohio, New York and Indiana. A proper distinction was drawn between the legislative, the executive and the judicial authorities, the maximum of power being lodged in the first-named branch of government, while to the second was allotted a comparatively small share. The governor, the lieutenant governor, the sheriffs, the coroners, the county commissioners and, as a matter of course, the members of the legislature and the state representatives in congress, were elected by the people. The secretary of state was appointed by the governor with the advice and consent of the legislature. Almost all other officials were directly or indirectly chosen by the legislature, which designated them either for appointment by the governor or election by the citizens of the various counties. The governor's veto was replaced by a Council of Revision, consisting of the governor and the members of the state supreme court. This tribunal was empowered to examine all acts of the legislature and resubmit all disapproved legislation for further action. An absolute majority was required for the passage of any bill or act over the veto of the Council of Revision.

The ever growing demand for local self-government soon forced the legislature to surrender part of its appointive power to the people. Thus the offices of justice of the peace and of constable were filled by election after Dec. 12, 1826, and that of probate justice of the peace in a similar manner after March 4, 1847.

The right to vote was the prerogative of every white male citizen having attained to the age of twenty-one years and resided six months in the state. General elections were held every four years. All voting was done viva voce. It is a remarkable fact that this, the first constitution of the state, was never submitted to the people for ratification.

As the commonwealth grew and developed apace, and new exigencies arose, the need of a new constitution became imperative. This was spoken of as early as 1824 and again in 1842, but not until April, 1847, were delegates to a constitutional convention chosen. The convention met in June of that year and completed its work in August. The new constitution was submitted to a vote at the next election, March 6, 1848, was then ratified, and went into effect on the first day of April the same year. The idea of local self-government which had steadily gained ground throughout the country since 1818, was asserted in the new constitution through a curtailment of the extensive appointive power of the legislature. This power was transferred to the people, who were given the right to fill the great majority of offices at the general elections, while the right of local self-government was made almost absolute. The ballot was given to all white males who had attained their majority and had resided one year in the state. To the governor was given the right of veto, formerly exercised by the Council of Revision. Even in other respects the prerogatives of the legislature were curtailed. The financial experiences of the last decade which had cost the state dearly, caused the insertion of a clause strictly forbidding the legislature to use the credit of the state to further building operations or for other purposes. Henceforth, such public works devolved upon the various communities singly or in common. Every county was granted the right to subdivide itself into townships, this in deference to the wishes of the people of the northern part of the state, who had come largely from New York and the New England states.

During the rapid industrial development from 1850 to 1860 new problems arose, which could not be solved under the constitution of 1848. The increasing number and power of the corporations was generally considered a serious public menace, in the absence of restrictive legislation on that point. It was feared that these would abuse their power in an effort to procure special legislation in their behalf, hence the desire to place them under state control. A proposed constitution, formulated by the constitutional convention of 1862, was deemed inadequate and failed of ratification at the subsequent election; but the need of a new constitution remained and caused the calling of a fourth constitutional convention in 1869. This convention labored with better success than its predecessor, and on May 13, 1870, submitted the draft of a new constitution, which was accepted at an election held on the second day of July following, and went into effect August 8th of that year. It augmented the veto power of the governor, prohibited special legislation in favor of corporations, limited the bonded debt of state, county and municipality to amounts not to over-burden the taxpayers, enlarged the influence of the people on legislation, while limiting in a measure the authority of the legislature, added to the responsibility of the judicial executives, and placed restrictions upon the operations of railroads and other business corporations.

The Slavery Question

A remarkable chapter in the history of Illinois is that dealing with slavery and the attitude of its people toward that question from time to time.

To the French the credit is due for the discovery and exploration of Illinois and the founding of its earliest colonies; theirs is the blame for the introduction of slavery into its territory. Shortly after the establishment of the first French settlements, certain Frenchmen, acting on the supposition that all kinds of valuable ores were to be found here, organized two companies with a view to exploiting the ore fields. The second established headquarters in the St. Phillips settlement, with a Frenchman by the name of Philip Francis Renault as its representative.

In 1720 Renault purchased 500 negroes in San Domingo and brought them here to work in the prospective mines. No ore beds could be found, however, and part of the slaves were put to work in the lead mines discovered near the present city of Galena, as early as the year 1700, also near the site of Dubuque, Iowa, and in similar mines in present Missouri, while the remainder were sold to French settlers in Illinois. This event marked the beginning of the slave trade in the state. In the latter part of the eighteenth century, when the English and the Americans in turn invaded Illinois, protection of life, liberty and property was guaranteed to the French settlers and their rights and privileges were safeguarded. The slaves were naturally classed as property. In the Northwest Ordinance of 1787, by which all the tract northwest of the Ohio River was made one territory, slavery was expressly forbidden within its borders, yet the inhabitants, particularly the French and Canadian settlers, by exemption were permitted to follow their established customs. This stipulation was commonly interpreted to mean that, while the statutes prohibited traffic in slaves and the extension of slavery in the territory, they implied that the slaves already in the territory, and their descendants, were to remain in bondage forever. However, protests were raised, questioning the validity of this stipulation in the ordinance on the ground that congress, in passing it, had exceeded its authority. Others maintained that all children born to slaves after 1787 were free. Still another group insisted that no material prosperity would be possible without slavery. In the course of time a considerable number of inhabitants inclined to this view. After the division of the Northwest Territory in 1800, the slave question grew more serious than ever, the adherents of slavery obtaining strong support in William Henry Harrison, governor of Indiana Territory. A convention to discuss the question was called by him at Vincennes in 1804. Then and there a petition to congress was drawn up, demanding that the section in the ordinance of 1787 prohibiting slavery in the Northwest Territory be rescinded or modified. The congressional committee to which this petition was first referred, reported adversely, but a second committee recommended that the slavery clause be suspended for a period of ten years. Congress, however, took no action in the matter. In 1807 a counterpetition with a great number of signatures was sent to congress, where it met the same fate. In the meantime the advocates of slavery kept up a vigorous agitation and succeeded in having a territorial law passed which, under certain limitations, authorized the bringing in and enslavement of negroes and mulattoes over fifteen years of age. According to the same law, slaves under fifteen years of age could be procured and held in bondage, males to the age of 35 and females to the age of 30 years. Descendants of registered slaves were to serve the owner of the mother up to the age of 30 and 28 years, respectively, according to sex. As a result of this law, which was ratified in 1812, the number of slaves increased rapidly in the territory.

The first state constitution of Illinois, adopted in 1818, prohibited all form of slave traffic in the future, causing great dissatisfaction among the slaveholders. An agitation was set on foot in 1822 to force a change in the statutes, making Illinois a slave state. Their first effort was directed toward securing a new constitutional convention. For a year and a half a bitter fight was waged between the so-called Conventionists and their opponents. At a general election August 2, 1824, the Conventionists were defeated by a heavy majority, this being the final settlement of the slavery question in Illinois.

The negroes and mulattoes already in servitude remained slaves during the term stipulated. The census of 1820 thus showed 917 slaves in the state. Ten years later their number had been reduced to 747 and in 1840, when they last figured in the census report, their number was 331. Before 1850 the last trace of slavery had been wiped out in the state.

Edward Coles, who had just become the second governor of Illinois, had been private secretary to President Madison and was an intimate friend of Thomas Jefferson and Patrick Henry. He had inherited a plantation and a number of slaves in Virginia. Disliking the institution of slavery, he had removed in 1820 with his slaves to Illinois and set them free, giving to each head of a family 160 acres of land. In his inaugural address in 1822 he recommended that the legislature revise the laws so as to prevent the kidnaping of free negroes, a crime then

Edward Coles

Edward Coles, Second Governor of Illinois

committed with impunity. He devoted his four years' salary, amounting to $4,000, to the anti-slavery cause. Coles was a forerunner of Lincoln and his influence was paramount at a critical period in the preservation of Illinois as a free-soil state.

The champions of slavery continued their efforts, in spite of their defeat in 1824, fighting the abolitionists at every point and with all the means at their command. Two eminent leaders in the anti-slavery movement were Elijah Parish Lovejoy, a Presbyterian minister, and his brother Owen Lovejoy, a clergyman of the Congregational Church. In the early '30s Elijah Lovejoy published from St. Louis a religious weekly, the "Observer," condemning the slave traffic in unsparing

The Elijah P. Lovejoy Monument at Alton

terms. His life being threatened by enraged slaveholders, he removed to Alton, Ill., in July, 1836, continuing the publication from that point. He waged a fearless campaign for the noble cause which he had espoused, and a year later he and a number of sympathizers organized a secret league for the abolition of slavery. But not even on Illinois soil was he permitted to carry on his work unmolested. In the course

Owen Lovejoy

of one year his printing shop was attacked three different times by violent mobs, which destroyed his presses and other property. After he had purchased his fourth press, a number of his friends offered to protect it from the assaults of the rabble. In the evening of Nov. 7, 1837, a mob surrounded the building where it was kept and, to make short shrift with it, one of their number climbed to the roof for the purpose of setting the building on fire. Stepping outside, together with two of his friends, to see what was going on, Lovejoy was shot from ambush and died in a few moments. His fellow abolitionists considered him a martyr to the cause, and his death formed the theme of many a bitter invective against the slave power. His example became an inspiration to every friend of the downtrodden serfs and his violent death aided materially in strengthening the anti-slavery sentiment at the North.

Owen Lovejoy lived to take a distinguished part in the great final struggle for abolition and the preservation of the Union. He was elected to congress in 1856, and Lincoln had no more faithful and loyal supporter of his policy in congress than was Owen Lovejoy. It was the consciousness of this fact, which, after the anti-slavery champion's death in 1864, called forth from Lincoln the warmest tribute to his memory.

Abraham Lincoln, the Greatest Illinoisan

At this juncture, there passed from a humble pioneer home out in public life a man foreordained by Providence to become in due time the deliverer of the slaves, the great emancipator, Abraham Lincoln. A review of the history of Illinois would be incomplete and lacking in value without the name and achievements of him, the noblest of its citizens.

Abraham Lincoln was born in Kentucky and came as a young man of 21 to this state, to the progress of which he gave the best efforts of his mature manhood. Scarcely two years had passed from the day he began splitting rails for the enclosure of the homestead the family selected in Menard county, when, after serving both as a private and an officer in the Black Hawk War, he appeared as a candidate for the state legislature. He was defeated, but two years later he reached the goal of his first political ambitions, having in the meantime successfully completed a course in law and also worked as a surveyor, showing skill and aptness for the vocation. In the legislature he was made a member of the committee on appropriations and accounts. After re-election in 1836 he was appointed on the committee on finances; and, being re-elected again in 1838 and 1840, he was twice the Whig candidate for the speakership. Recognizing the wants of the state, he advocated a uniform system of public improvements. In March, 1837, the Democratic majority in the legislature passed several resolutions favorable to the slave power; against these Lincoln went on record by registering a forcible protest. According to the best information at hand, this was Lincoln's first public pronouncement on the slavery question.

The same year Lincoln was admitted to the bar, and henceforth we often find him in court, defending those charged with assisting runaway slaves from the South. Owing to the steady growth of his law practice, he was obliged to decline renomination for the legislature in 1842. As a candidate for presidential elector in 1840 and 1844, he electioneered with great energy for the Whig candidate for president. His debates with Stephen A. Douglas on the burning question of the times, held before great audiences in a later campaign, are a matter of history. Lincoln was a warm admirer of Henry Clay, whose defeat caused him deep regret.

Having up to that time devoted himself to Illinois politics, Lincoln in 1846 was elected to congress and became a national figure. His Dem-

Abraham Lincoln

ocratic opponent in this campaign was Peter Cartwright, the famous Methodist clergyman. In congress Lincoln strenuously opposed the policy of President Polk, and pronounced the war with Mexico a national infamy. He voted for the anti-slavery petitions laid before congress, urged an investigation as to the constitutionality of slavery in the District of Columbia, and in 1849 moved its abolition. He might have had the renomination, but declined. In the Whig national convention in 1848 he furthered Taylor's nomination to the presidency and made a campaigning tour in New England during the subsequent campaign. In 1849 he stood for election to the senate, but was defeated by General Shields. President Fillmore offered him the governorship of Oregon Territory, which was declined.

The repudiation of the Missouri Compromise caused Lincoln again to enter the political arena, and in a short time he became the recognized leader of the Republican party, then in process of formation. At the national convention of that party in 1856 he was by the delegation from his state put in nomination for the vice presidency, but failed to get the requisite number of votes to confirm the nomination. In June, 1858, the Republican convention held at Springfield nominated Lincoln for United States Senator to succeed his old antagonist, Stephen A. Douglas, who sought reelection. During the campaign the two held seven public debates, principally on the leading issue whether Kansas should be admitted to the Union free or slave. It was generally admitted that Lincoln was the superior of his astute political opponent in argument. He received a majority of 4,000 votes over him in the following election, but the legislative districts were so gerrymandered, that the Democrats succeeded in getting a majority of eight on a joint vote in the legislature, and Douglas was seated.

Lincoln, however, continued his crusade against the slave power in forceful speeches, delivered in various parts of the country, including Kansas and the New England states. Not only his own opinion, but the prevailing sentiment of the Republican party was thus voiced.

The strain between the North and the South, owing to the slave question, was ever on the increase. Slavery was, or was claimed to be, an essential factor in the economy of the South, and the slave owners looked upon the anti-slavery movement as a danger to be warded off at all hazards. Fear of economic collapse was the ultimate cause of the desperate tenacity with which they held fast to the slave system and fought the abolitionists. The theory of state sovereignty was urged in behalf of the slave states, and the secessionist movement began in earnest, aiming toward the establishment of a new confederacy of states—all for the purpose of preserving to the South this institution on the plea that it was indispensable.

The slavery question was brought to an issue when the Republican party at its national convention in Chicago in May, 1860, adopted a platform emphatically declaring that neither congress, nor the state legislatures, nor any individuals were empowered to legalize slavery in any part of the United States, and at the same time nominated Lincoln for the presidency. When he was elected in November of that year,

Wigwam in which Lincoln was nominated May 18, 1860

thereby defeating his intrepid opponent Douglas, who was one of the three presidential candidates of the disintegrated Democratic party, the slaveholders took this as a sure sign of the impending destruction of their cherished system of economy, although it was well known that Lincoln was by no means disposed to precipitate the change.

In order to prevent the abolition of slavery, the slave states determined to withdraw from the Union and set up a government of their own. South Carolina, whence originated the principle of state sovereignty, led the way by calling a convention, which on the 20th of

December, the same year, voted in favor of secession. Within six weeks the states of Mississippi, Florida, Alabama, Georgia, Louisiana and Texas took similar action. These states subsequently united under the name of the Confederate States of America, and, on the 8th day of February, 1861, elected Jefferson Davis president. Lincoln thus entered upon his duties as president in March, 1861, under the most trying circumstances. He realized from the first that a peaceful settlement af the contest was impossible; that the Union could be saved only by an appeal to arms. On March 13th two commissioners of the Confederacy appeared at Washington offering to treat with the government regarding the questions arising out of the secession. The govern-

The Lincoln Family

ment, however, refused to recognize them on the ground that the secession was illegal and without the consent of the people of the United States. This reply was made public April 8th, and on the 12th the rebels fired on Fort Sumter. This was the opening gun of the Civil War.

The account of that great conflict does not enter into the plan of this work. Attention may, however, be called to the enormous task that was thereby thrown upon the shoulders of President Lincoln, as well as to the tireless perseverance, the lofty statesmanship and the glowing patriotism he evinced throughout; how he, with the great goal of human freedom ever before him, issued, on Sept. 22, 1862, his Emancipation Proclamation, by which slavery was abolished in the United States; how he was again elected, with an overwhelming majority, in 1864; how he, with the faithful aid and support of the people, brought the war to a close, with honor to the North, benevolence to the entire country, and the restoration of the Union, one and inseparable; and, finally, how he, after his life had often been placed in jeopardy by persons seeking revenge for the alleged losses sustained by his great work of emancipation, died by the hand of an assassin.

The people of Illinois will ever point with pride to the fact that this man, the peer of Washington in our history, was one of their

Richard Yates, War Governor of Illinois

number. And as long as the human heart cherishes the deeds of the great, they will visit, with a reverence akin to worship, the mausoleum at Springfield, where Abraham Lincoln lies entombed.

Among the earnest supporters of the national administration in its measures for the suppression of the rebellion was Richard Yates, governor of Illinois, 1861-4, who was later styled "the Illinois War

Governor.'' He served as United States senator 1865-71, and died in 1873.

One of the military heroes produced by Illinois was John A. Logan, a member of congress at the outbreak of hostilities. ,Leaving his seat, he fought in the ranks at Bull Run. Commissioned colonel of the 31st

John A. Logan

Regiment Illinois Infantry by Governor Yates, he went to the front and was rapidly promoted to major-general. He was in 1884 an unsuccessful candidate for the vice-presidency with James G. Blaine. Logan died in 1886 as a United States senator.

The greatest military figure brought out by the Civil War was furnished by Illinois in the person of Ulysses S. Grant, who was in

1861 a tanner in Galena. After serving as clerk and drill-master he was commissioned colonel of the 21st Illinois Volunteers. As brigadier, general he captured Forts Donelson and Henry in 1862. He soon had charge of all western operations and his capture of Vicksburg after a siege was the chief Union victory of 1863. He became major-general

Ulysses S. Grant

and then lieutenant-general in 1864, taking command of all the Northern armies. Grant personally directed the campaign against Richmond which resulted in the surrender of Lee at Appomattox on April 8, 1865, and the downfall of the Confederacy. The rank of general was created for him in 1866, after which the nation chose him president in 1868 and again in 1872. During the years 1877-9 he made a tour of the world and was received everywhere with the highest honors. General Grant died July 23, 1885.

Illinois during the Civil War contributed to the Union army 214,133 men, 34,834 of whom fell in battle or died of disease during service in the field or as war prisoners in the South.

In spite of the Civil War of 1861-1865 the economic development of the state progressed almost unimpeded. In 1860 Illinois already took first rank among agricultural states, and its industrial progress was rapid. During twenty years, 1850-1870, Illinois advanced from fifteenth to fifth place as a manufacturing state. At the present time it stands third in rank with reference to manufactures and varied industries. This phenomenal growth was principally due to the rapid extension of the railroad system, that work going forward at such a pace that Illinois in 1870 had more miles of railway than any other state in the Union, a distinction which it still enjoys.

Up to 1870 agriculture was the chief occupation of its people, the farmers outnumbering those of all other occupations combined. Since then, however, this condition has changed, and in 1900 those engaged in manufactures and varied industries outnumbered the agricultural population. The number engaged in commerce and transportation was almost as large as the industrial class, there being, however, no material difference in the numerical strength of the three groups.

With respect to the value of the crops, Illinois in 1900 ranked first among the states, and in coal production it had second place. Its banking business gives it a place among the leading commercial states.

No better exponent of the development is found than the census records, which give the increase in population by decades as follows:

Year	No. of Inhabitants	Year	No. of Inhabitants
1820	55,162	1870	2,539,891
1830	157,445	1880	3,077,871
1840	476,183	1890	3,826,351
1850	851,470	1900	4,821,550
1860	1,711,951		

The Educational System

The first step in establishing free public schools in the part of the country now comprising the state of Illinois was taken by congress May 20th, 1785, in adopting "An Ordinance for Ascertaining the Mode of Disposing Lands in the Western Territory." By this act the system of survey still in force was introduced into the United States. The system was the work of Captain Thomas Hutchins, who at the same time was appointed surveyor-general. The act stipulated that section

16 of every township was to be reserved for the maintenance of public schools within the township. The same provision was made in all subsequent ordinances pertaining to the disposal of public lands. In

University of Illinois—Library Building

the Northwest Ordinance, adopted in 1787, this declaration was made: "Whereas religion, morals and education are necessary to human happiness, the establishment of schools and other means of education should be constantly encouraged." The stipulations regarding land grants for the support of schools were renewed in an act of congress April 18, 1818, giving to the people of the Illinois Territory the right of self-government, and they were formally adopted by the first constitutional convention. This act also included a provision that, besides the lands set aside for school purposes in the act of 1804, an entire township was to be reserved for the maintenance of a seminary of learning and that three per cent. of the proceeds of the sale of public lands in the state should be devoted to the promotion of education as directed by the legislature. One-sixth of this fund was to be used for establishing and endowing a college or university. These acts and resolutions form the foundation of the educational system of the 'state.

Prior to their adoption, however, primary schools had been established. One John Seeley is said to have begun teaching school in a blockhouse in present Monroe county as early as 1783, thus being the first known public school teacher in Illinois. Seeley was followed by Francis Clark and a man named Halfpenny. Among the early educators during a later period we note John Boyle, a soldier in the little army commanded by Col. George Rogers Clark, who taught in Randolph county some time during 1790-1800; John Atwater, who taught near Edwardsville in 1807, and John Messinger, a surveyor, who was a member of the constitutional convention of 1818 and speaker of the first general assembly. The last named taught in the vicinity of Shiloh, St. Clair county, at the point where Rev. John M. Peck's Rock Spring Seminary was subsequently erected. These schools, all of a primitive nature, were supported privately by the parents of the pupils.

The first effort to establish a general school system for the entire state was made in January, 1825, when Joseph Duncan, who was afterwards elected congressman and governor, submitted to the legislature a bill to appropriate two dollars out of every $100 of state revenue for distribution among those paying taxes or otherwise contributing to the support of schools. The revenues of the state at this time were, however, so insignificant (a trifle over $60,000 per annum), that the sum thus realized for school purposes would have amounted to about $1,200 annually, if the act had been enforced. It remained a dead letter until 1829, when it was nullified, and the state authorities began to dispose of the seminary lands and use the proceeds of the sale for defraying current expenditures. In this manner 43,200 acres were sold, leaving only four and one-half sections, and the sum realized was less than

$60,000. The first sale of township school land took place in Greene county in 1831, and two years later the greater part of the school lands

University of Illinois—College of Agriculture

in the heart of present Chicago were sold for about $39,000. These sales continued until 1882 and brought an average of $3.78 per acre. Certain lands were sold as low as 70 cents per acre. These meager results were not chargeable to the system, but to the administration of it. Had the authorities exercised foresight, the school fund doubtless would have grown vastly greater. The first free public school in the state was opened at Chicago in 1834, the second at Alton in 1837, the third at Springfield in 1840, and the fourth at Jacksonville the same year.

The present school system dates from 1855, when a law was passed creating a permanent school fund by general taxation. Since then the school law has been frequently amended, yet the fundamental principle that every child is entitled to the advantage of an elementary education has always been carefully guarded. It may be said without exaggeration, that the Illinois school system in the last forty years has been developed into one of the best in the country. The following figures will convey a fair idea of this remarkable development:

In 1902 the state had 12,855 free public schools with 27,186 teachers, 6,800 male and 20,386 female, and 971,841 pupils. The cost of maintenance was $19,899,624.54, including teachers' salaries to the amount of $12,075,000.14. In the same year the private schools in the state numbered 3,961 teachers and 144,471 pupils.

There are, furthermore, 350 high or continuation schools, supplementing the public schools. These are the natural results of the development of the educational system, not the creation of any legislative statute. Eighty-eight of the 350 high schools own buildings valued at $4,000,000, and one has a permanent endowment fund, while the others are maintained by local taxation. They were attended in 1902 by 41,951 pupils, 5,230 of whom were graduated.

Higher education in Illinois dates from the time when it was still a part of the Indiana Territory. In November, 1806, the territorial legislature, assembled at Vincennes, resolved to establish at that point an institution to be known as the University of Indiana Territory. The necessary funds, estimated at $20,000, were to be raised by means of a lottery. A board of regents was at once selected, with General William Henry Harrison as chairman. This enterprise advanced as far as the erection of a building and then collapsed.

Twenty-one years later, in 1827, the first successful effort at establishing a higher institution of learning in Illinois was made. The credit belongs to Rev. John M. Peck, a minister of the Baptist denomination. Peck was born in Litchfield, Conn., in 1789, settled in Greene county, N. Y., in 1811; took charge of a congregation in Amenia, N. Y., in 1814, and was sent in 1817 as a missionary to St. Louis, Mo. During the following nine years he made extensive journeys in Missouri and Illinois, and finally settled in Rock Spring, St. Clair county, where he founded in 1826 the Rock Spring Seminary and High School for the education of clergymen and school teachers. This was the predecessor of Shurtleff College, established by the Baptists in 1835 at Upper Alton,

University of Illinois—Engineering Hall

being subsequently merged with that institution. In promoting his enterprise Peck traveled thousands of miles, collecting meanwhile the sum of $20,000, a considerable amount in that day. For many years he continued a member of the board of directors of the school. This educational pioneer of Illinois was awarded the honorary degree of

Doctor of Divinity by Harvard University in 1852. He died at Rock Spring March 15, 1858.

In 1828 a Methodist seminary was established at Lebanon under the name of Lebanon Seminary. After two years it was made a college and named after Bishop McKendree. Illinois College was founded in

University of Illinois—Campus Scene

December, 1829, at Jacksonville with the support of the Presbyterians, and from this institution the first graduates in the history of Illinois schools were sent out in 1835. These schools of learning were legally recognized by the state the same year. Next in order came Knox College, founded by Presbyterians in 1838, at Galesburg, and the Episcopalian Jubilee College, established in 1847, at Peoria.

For the promotion of general education there were held, during the thirties and forties, a series of educational conventions, attended not only by teachers but also by legislators and others devoted to the cause. The first convention was held in the then capital city of Vandalia, in 1833. In 1854 these conventions resulted in the organization of the State Teachers' Institute, its name being changed three years later to the State Teachers' Association. The question of electing a state superintendent of public instruction had been raised as early as 1837 and debated at the educational conventions, in the educational journals, and in the state legislature, but not until 1854 did the proposition materialize in the establishment of that office.

It was during this progressive period that the idea of founding a state university was conceived. At a farmers' convention, held Nov. 18, 1854, at Granville, Putnam county, one Prof. Jonathan B. Turner from Jacksonville, Ill., proposed the plan for a uniform system of polytechnic schools throughout the United States, with one scientific school in each state and territory, and a national institute of science in the federal capital. The same plan was received with favor elsewhere, especially in New York and New England, and not without interest in Illinois. The meeting at Granville was followed by others, and at one of these conventions, held at Springfield in January, 1852, was organized the Industrial League of the State of Illinois to further the project and arouse popular interest by means of lectures throughout the state. It was decided at this meeting to petition congress for land grants out of the proceeds of which to support these institutes. In 1853 Illinois, through its legislature, unanimously recommended the plan and

University of Illinois—College of Law

requested its senators and representatives in congress to promote its adoption. The matter was taken up in congress and a bill authorizing such institutions was passed, but annulled in February, 1859, by the veto of President Buchanan. The matter was again taken up and a bill passed, which received the approval of President Lincoln July 2, 1862.

Thus a great movement in the Prairie State, advocated by an Illinois man, supported by Illinois people, was confirmed by an Illinois president.

By this act the national government donated to each state in the Union public land scrip in quantity equal to 30,000 acres for each senator and representative in congress "for the endowment, support,

University of Illinois—Auditorium

and maintenance of at least one college, whose leading object shall be, without excluding other scientific and classical studies, and including military tactics, to teach such branches of learning as are related to agriculture and the mechanical arts * * * in order to promote the liberal and practical education of the industrial classes in the several pursuits and professions of life."

On account of this grant, amounting to 480,000 acres in Illinois, the state pays the university, semi-annually, interest at the rate of five per cent. on about $610,000; and deferred payments on land contracts amount, approximately, to $35,000.

To secure the location of the university several counties entered into competition by proposing to donate to its use specified sums of money, or their equivalent. Champaign county offered a large brick building in the suburbs of Urbana, erected for a seminary and nearly completed, about 1,000 acres of land, and $100,000 in county bonds. To this the Illinois Central railroad added $50,000 in freight.

The state has from time to time appropriated various sums for permanent improvements, as well as for maintenance. For 1907—1908 it appropriated $305,000 for the College of Agriculture, $900,000 for ordinary operating expenses, and $502,790 for various extensions, besides which $100,000 was set aside for the Graduate School, $250,000 for a physics laboratory, and $150,000 for an addition to the Natural History Hall. The present value of the entire property and assets is estimated at $3,250,000.

The institution was incorporated February 28, 1867, under the name of the Illinois Industrial University, and placed under the control of a board of trustees, constituted of the governor, the superintendent of public instruction and the president of the state board of agriculture, as ex-officio members, and twenty-eight citizens appointed by the governor. The chief executive officer was called Regent, and was made an ex-officio member, of the board and presiding officer both of the board of trustees and of the faculty.

In 1873 the board of trustees was reorganized, the number of appointed members being reduced to nine and of ex-officio members to

University of Illinois—Woman's Building

two—the governor and the president of the state board of agriculture. In 1887 a law was passed making membership elective at a general state election and restoring the superintendent of public instruction as an ex-officio member. There are, therefore, now three ex-officio members and nine by public suffrage. Since 1873 the president of the board has been chosen by the members from among their own number for a term of one year.

The university was opened to students March 2, 1868, when there were present, beside the Regent, three professors and about fifty students—all young men.

During the first term instruction was given in algebra, geometry, physics, history, rhetoric and Latin. Work on the farm and gardens or about the buildings was at first compulsory for all students, but in March of the next year compulsory labor was discontinued, save when it was made to serve as a part of class instruction. A chemical laboratory was fitted up during the autumn of 1868. Botanical laboratory work began the following year. In January, 1870, a mechanical shop was fitted up with tools and machinery, and here was begun the first shop instruction given in any American university. During the summer of 1871 the present engineering laboratory was erected and equipped for students' shop work in both wood and iron.

By vote, March 9, 1870, the trustees admitted women as students. During the year 1870-1871 twenty-four availed themselves of the privilege. Since that time they have constituted from one-sixth to one-fifth of the total number of students.

In 1890 the congress of the United States made further appropriations for the endowment of the institutions founded under the act of 1862. Under this enactment each such college or university received the first year $15,000, and thereafter $1,000 per annum additional to the amount of the preceding year, until the amount reached $25,000, which sum was to be paid yearly thereafter.

On May 1, 1896, the Chicago College of Pharmacy founded in 1859, became the School of Pharmacy of the University of Illinois. Its building is located at Michigan ave. and 12th st. in Chicago.

Pursuant to action of the board of trustees, taken Dec. 8, 1896, the School of Law was organized, and opened Sept. 13, 1897. The course of study covered two years, in conformity with the existing requirements for admission to the bar of Illinois. In the following November, however, the supreme court of the state announced rules relating to examinations for admission to the bar which made three years of study necessary, and the course of study in the law school was immediately rearranged on that basis. On Feb. 9, 1900, the name of the School of Law was changed to College of Law.

Negotiations looking to the affiliation of the College of Physicians and Surgeons, of Chicago, with the university, which had been going on for several years, were concluded by the board of trustees in March, 1897. According to the agreement made, the College of Physicians and Surgeons became in April, 1897, the College of Medicine of the University of Illinois. The college is located at Congress and Honore streets, Chicago.

In 1897, the matter of the reorganization of the University Library was considered by the board of trustees, with the result that the School of Library Economy, which had been established in 1893 at the Armour Institute of Technology, in Chicago, was transferred to the university, and the director of that school was appointed librarian of the University Library. In accordance with these plans the State Library School was opened at the university in September, 1897.

Pursuant to action taken by the board of trustees in March, 1901, a School of Dentistry was organized as a department of the College of Medicine. The school was opened October 3, 1901. The name was changed to College of Dentistry in 1905.

The land occupied by the university and its several departments embraces 220 acres, exclusive of the stock farm, experimental farm, and forest plantation, which embrace some 400 acres additional. The principal buildings are: the university hall, agricultural building, armory, library building, astronomical observatory, chemical laboratory, engineering hall, laboratory of applied mechanics, mechanical engineering laboratory, metal shops, wood shop and foundry, natural history hall, men's gymnasium, woman's building and auditorium. The general university library contains 90,400 volumes and pamphlets, and has a subscription list of 1,100 periodicals. To this is added the library of the state laboratory of natural history, 6,000 volumes and 16,500 pamphlets, and those of the college of medicine and dentistry, and the school of pharmacy, in Chicago, and the college of law. The department of education has a special collection of 1,500 books and 3,000 pamphlets. An art gallery was established in 1874, the gift of citizens of Champaign and Urbana.

The appropriations made by the congressional act of March 2, 1887, were for the purpose of establishing and maintaining, in connection with the colleges founded upon the congressional act of 1862, agricultural experiment stations, "to aid in acquiring and diffusing among the people of the United States useful and practical information on subjects connected with agriculture, and to promote scientific investigation and experiment respecting the principles and applications of agricultural science." Under this provision the Agricultural Experiment Station for Illinois was founded in 1888 and placed under the direction of the trustees of the university, and a part of the university farm, with buildings, was assigned for its use.

The federal grants to the station have been liberally supplemented with state appropriations, until its revenues have become the largest of those of similar institutions throughout the world.

Investigations are conducted in the growing and marketing of orchard fruits, the methods of production of meats and of dairy goods, the principles of animal breeding and nutrition, and in the improvement and the economic production of crops. All the principal types of soil of the state are being studied in the laboratory under glass and in the field. A soil survey is in progress which when finished will map and describe the soil of every farm of the state down to an area of ten acres. Twenty to thirty fields and orchards are rented in different portions of the state for the study of local problems, and assistants are constantly on the road for the conduct of experiments or to give instruction to producer or consumer. The results of investigation are published in bulletins, which are issued in editions of 40,000, and distributed free of charge.

The Engineering Experiment Station was established by action of the board of trustees, in December, 1903. It is the first and, so far as

University of Illinois—College of Medicine (Chicago)

known, the only experiment station connected with any college of engineering in this country. Its purposes are the stimulation and elevation of engineering education, and the study of problems of special importance to professional engineers, and to the manufacturing, railway, mining, industrial and other interests of importance to the public welfare of the state and the country.

Up to the present time, eleven bulletins, of value to engineering science, have been published. The experiments have related chiefly to tests of concrete, reinforced concrete beams, tests of high speed tool steels, the resistance of tubes to collapse, fuel tests, and the holding power of railroad spikes.

In 1885 the legislature passed a bill transferring the State Laboratory of Natural History to the University of Illinois from the Illinois State Normal University, where it was founded in 1877 by the present director, Dr. Stephen Alfred Forbes, a noted scientist, who is also state entomologist. This laboratory was created for the purpose of making a natural history survey of the state, the results of which should be published in a series of bulletins and reports, and for the allied purpose of furnishing specimens illustrative of the flora and fauna of the state to the public schools and to the state museum.

The herbarium contains about 50,000 mounted specimens of plants. The flora of North America is fairly well represented, the collection of species of flowering plants indigenous to Illinois is particularly complete, and a considerable collection of foreign species has been made. The collections of fungi amount to 32,000 named specimens and include a full set of those most injurious to other plants, causing rusts, smuts, moulds, etc. There are specimens of wood from 200 species of native trees and shrubs, which well illustrate the varieties of native wood.

The work of the state entomologist's office has been done at the University of Illinois since January, 1885; and by legislative enactment in 1899 it was permanently established at the university. It is the function of the entomologist to investigate the entomology of Illinois, and particularly to study the insects injurious to the horticulture and agriculture of the state, and to prepare reports of his researches and discoveries in entomology for publication by the state. Over 700 pages of reports have been issued from this office. He also inspects and certifies annually all Illinois nurseries, and maintains a general supervision of the horticultural property of the state as respects its infestation by dangerous insects and its infection with contagious plant diseases.

The chemical survey of the waters of the state was begun in September, 1895, by Dr. Arthur W. Palmer. In 1897 the legislature authorized the continuance of the work, and directed the board of trustees to establish a chemical and biological survey of the waters of the state. Its purpose is to collect facts and data concerning the water supplies of the state; to demonstrate their sanitary condition by examination and analysis; to determine standard of purity of drinking waters in the various sections, and publish the results of these investigations. Analyses of water for citizens of the state are made on request.

An act of the general assembly on July 1, 1905, provided for the establishment of a bureau to be known as the state geological survey.

University of Illinois—Electrical and Mechanical Laboratory
and Laboratory of Applied Mechanics

Its purpose is primarily the study and exploitation of the mineral resources of Illinois. Field parties are organized for the investigation of clay, coal, stone, artesian water, cement materials, road materials and general scientific investigations. The bureau is charged also with the duty of making a complete topographical and geological survey of the state. The topographical work will lead to the publication of a series of bulletins and of maps, eventually covering the entire state.

The attendance at the state university increased very slowly year by year, until the nineties, when an exceptional increase set in. In 1889-90 there were but 469 students. In 1891-2 the number of students was 583, but six years later it reached 1,582, and in the school year of 1901-2 the 3,000 mark was passed. Four years later the number exceeded 4,000, and the summer of 1906-7 showed 4,316 students in attendance. In 1907-8 the attendance was over 4,700 students.

John Milton Gregory, the first president, came to the university in 1867 and laid the plans for the new type of college whose appropriate motto was chosen as, "Learning and Labor." His life-work was fostering the idea of laboratory education. His faith and earnestness of purpose made the present university possible. He resigned in 1880, died in 1898, and is buried on the university grounds.

Selim Hobart Peabody, the second president, had been professor of mechanical engineering and consequently was well acquainted with Gregory's plans. It was in 1885, the sixth year of his presidency, that the legislature was persuaded to change the name of the institution to University of Illinois. It was perhaps this as much as any other fact that awoke the people of Illinois to the splendid opportunities of their own institution. Dr. Peabody resigned in 1891.

From 1891 to 1894 Vice President Thomas Jonathan Burrill administered the affairs of the university. He declined the presidency, preferring to devote his entire time to botany. During this period the natural history hall and the engineering building were erected.

Andrew Sloan Draper became the third president in September, 1894. The university grew phenomenally, not only in numbers, but in material equipment. Eighteen buildings were erected on the campus during his term of office. He resigned in 1904 to resume the position of commissioner of education in New York state, which he had held before.

Edmund Janes James, the fourth president of the university, was born May 21, 1855, at Jacksonville, Ill. He prepared at Illinois State Normal School and continued his studies at Northwestern University in 1873, at Harvard in 1874, and at University of Halle 1875-7, receiving the degrees of M. A. and Ph. D. Returning to this country, he was principal of the Evanston, Ill., high school 1878-9, then transferring his activities to the Illinois State Normal School, at Normal, where he was professor of Latin and Greek, and principal of the high school department until 1883. After a year of research in Europe Dr. James was called to the professorship in public administration at the University of Pennsylvania. He organized the graduate school and was director of the Wharton School of Finance and Economy at that university. Owing largely to his efforts similar departments have been established in the Universities of California, Chicago, Michigan and Columbia University. His report on commercial education to business men in Europe, made in 1892, has become a standard authority on this subject. Dr. James is the author of more than one hundred papers and monographs on various economic, legal, educational and historical topics. He is president of the Illinois State Historical Society, and is a member of various patriotic, historical, scientific and educational societies. Dr. James is a man of broad attainments and the University of Illinois is, under his guidance, rapidly advancing by leaps and bounds toward its probable position as the greatest of the American state universities.

University of Illinois—Men's Gymnasium

The development of the school system necessitated provision for the education of competent teachers. The initiative was taken by the legislature Feb. 18, 1857, in authorizing the establishment of the Illinois State Normal University, at Normal, which was opened October 5th of the same year. This was the first teachers' seminary in the Mississippi valley, and it has furnished teachers to the majority of the normal schools since established in various states. At the same time the legislature established the State Board of Education, comprising a state superintendent of public instruction and fourteen other members.

The normal school soon proved inadequate to meet the demand for teachers, and on March 9, 1869, the legislature resolved to found a second institution of the same order, which was located at Carbondale, being completed June 30, 1874, and known as the Southern Illinois Normal University. During the nineties three other normal schools were established, namely, the Eastern Illinois Normal School at Charleston, and the Northern Illinois Normal School at DeKalb, by act of the legislature May 22, 1895, both being opened in September, 1899, and last the Western Illinois Normal School at Macomb, authorized by the legislature April 24, 1899, and opened before completion in September, 1902.

In addition to the aforesaid institutions, the state maintains four special schools, viz., the Institution for the Education of the Deaf and Dumb, and the Institution for the Blind, both at Jacksonville, the

Asylum for the Feebleminded, at Lincoln, and the Soldiers' Orphans Home at Normal.

The religious denominations maintain a great number of educational institutions, the mere enumeration of which would require pages. The most prominent ones are the Chicago and the Northwestern Universities, which will be dealt with in a subsequent chapter on the City of Chicago.

With this synopsis of the educational system this outline of the history of the state of Illinois may fitly end.

CHAPTER II

The City of Chicago

Early History

HICAGO, as a city, date from the year 1837, but its early history stretches back into the latter part of the sixteenth century. The name Chicago or Chikagou first occurs on a map of Illinois drawn by the Frenchman Franquelin in 1684. It was applied both to a river emptying into the Desplaines just above the mouth of the Kankakee and to a point on the shore of Lake Michigan identical with the present site of Chicago. Some years later the French explorers used the name Chekagou to denote the present Desplaines River.

The next recurrence of the name was in the memoirs left by the aforementioned Tonti. This explorer, who in 1685 made a journey from Canada to Illinois, writes: "October 30, 1685. I embarked for Illinois, but on account of the ice I left my canoe and proceeded by land. Having traveled 120 leagues, I arrived at Fort Chicagou where M. de la Durantaye was commandant." There is no doubt that Fort Chicagou was one of the strongholds erected by the French to secure their possession of the newly discovered territory, nor is it questioned that the fort was situated on ground now a part of the great metropolis. The time and circumstances of its founding are unknown. From the memoirs of Tonti we learn that in 1699 there was a mission, where the gospel was preached to the neighboring Miami Indians. It appears from contemporary reports that adjacent to the mission and the fort was a French village of modest size, but we find no information as to how long this settlement was maintained.

The name Chicago is an Indian word, concerning whose original meaning philologists are not agreed. Some hold that it meant onion or garlic, others skunk, still others derive it from two Indian words meaning "wood gone." The first interpretation is based on the prolific growth of garlic along the Chicago River in early days; the second on the supposition that skunks were plentiful in the neighborhood; while the third presupposes that the place at one time had been covered with woods which were afterwards cut down. In the absence of definite knowledge on this point one explanation may be as acceptable as another.

About 1730 the name was also borne by a chief of the Indian tribes of Illinois. When these tribes in 1736, through a treaty with the French, had reached the acme of their power, D'Artaguette, a French-Canadian, asked their aid against the Chickasaw Indians of Mississippi, who were making war upon the French at New Orleans. At the

CHIEF CHICAGOU

head of a force of 500 braves Chief Chicagou accompanied him to the land of the Chickasaws, where they were to join a French force under Bienville. The latter did not arrive at the time and place appointed, and the Illinois warriors together with the fifty French soldiers proceeded, under the command of D'Artaguette, to capture and occupy two of the Chickasaw strongholds. In a third attack D'Artaguette was wounded and made prisoner. Chief Chicagou then returned with his men to Illinois, while the Chickasaws, with the enemies' scalps at their belts, marched in triumph to Georgia on a visit to Governor Oglethorpe, with whom they had made a friendly treaty.

Certain historians claim that the name Chicagou was applied to a long line of subsequent chiefs of the Illinois tribes. Whether or not these chieftains had any connection with the place bearing that name is not established.

Not until a hundred years after Tonti's visit at Chicago, do we find the place again mentioned in the early accounts. In 1796, we are told, a mulatto named Jean Baptiste Pointe du Sable, who was born in San Domingo, settled on the north bank of the Chicago River, near its mouth, built a hut and began trading with the Indians. A short time afterwards, he sought to become their chief, which would indicate very friendly relations. His effort failed, however, and in his chagrin he sold the hut with the surrounding patch of cultivated soil to a French fur trader, named Le Mai, and moved to Peoria.

Fort Dearborn

After the purchase of the Louisiana tract from Napoleon Bonaparte in 1803, it became necessary for the United States to establish a fort for its protection. A commission was sent from the war department at Washington to select a suitable site, and on its recommendation it was decided to build a fort at the mouth of the St. Joseph River, on the east shore of Lake Michigan. Preparations for building had al-

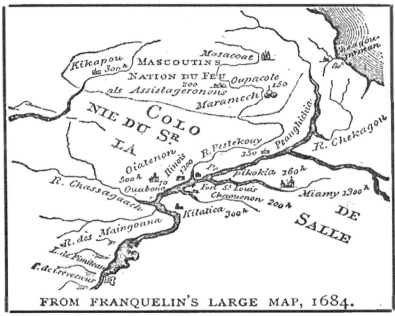

FROM FRANQUELIN'S LARGE MAP, 1684.

Early Map of Illinois River Basin

ready been made when the Michigan Indians refused to grant the necessary site. To force their consent was deemed unwise and hazardous, therefore the government chose the alternative of erecting the fort at the mouth of the Chicago River, where it owned a tract comprising six square miles of ground ceded by the Indians as early as 1795.

To build a fort so far out in the wilderness was a risky undertaking, but no other site being available, the building orders were issued in the early summer of 1803. At that time Detroit and Michilimackinac were the farthest western outposts of the United States on the Great Lakes. A military company was in garrison at Detroit under command of Captain John Whistler, and to him was given the duty of supervising the erection of the fort as well as the command at the new outpost. The other officers at Detroit were two lieutenants, his oldest son, William Whistler, and James S. Swearingen from Chilli-cothe, Ohio. The latter was ordered to head the soldiers afoot through the forests to Chicago, while Captain Whistler himself, together with his wife and their son, the lieutenant, with his young bride, embarked in the government schooner Tracy for the same destination.

Chicago at this time consisted of three little huts occupied by as many French fur traders with their Indian wives and half-breed children. One of these traders was the aforesaid Le Mai, the others Ouilmette (after whom the town of Wilmette has been named) and Pettell. The schooner arrived off the mouth of the Chicago River July 4th and anchored at a sand bank just opposite. Here its cargo of arms, ammunition and provisions was loaded into small boats and brought ashore at the point on the river bank selected as the site of the fort to be erected.

Two thousand Indians were assembled on the shore to witness the landing. The schooner itself was the object of their especial interest and admiration, and was styled "the great winged canoe." After debarking, Captain Whistler ordered the crew to return with the vessel to Detroit, and soon its sails disappeared at the eastern horizon. The total force left at Chicago, aside from the three commissioned officers, consisted of four sergeants, three corporals, four musicians, a surgeon and fifty-four privates, numbering altogether 69 men.

Their first duty was to build a blockhouse for shelter. This would have been an easy task, except for the fact that the logs had to be brought from a considerable distance. For lack of horses or oxen the soldiers themselves were obliged to drag the required timbers from the nearest woods to the point selected for the blockhouse. This point was on the south side of the river, on rising ground near present Rush street. The river did not, as at present, flow directly east, but curved southward and emptied into the lake at the foot of Madison street. On the ground within this bend the fort was subsequently erected. The whole summer and part of the fall had passed before the building was so far advanced that it afforded shelter for the men, and the fort was not completed until the following year. The fort then consisted of two blockhouses, one in the southeastern, the other in the northwestern corner of a palisaded area sufficiently large to serve as military drill grounds. From the palisades a subterranean passage led to the river's edge. The armament consisted of three small cannon. West of the palisades was built a loghouse two stories high, with shingled roof and walls. This was to serve as the warehouse of the Indian agency which was established simultaneously and served as a distributing center for large quantities of goods sent by the government as gifts to the Indians by way of winning their confidence and good will. The Indian agent also served as the quartermaster of the

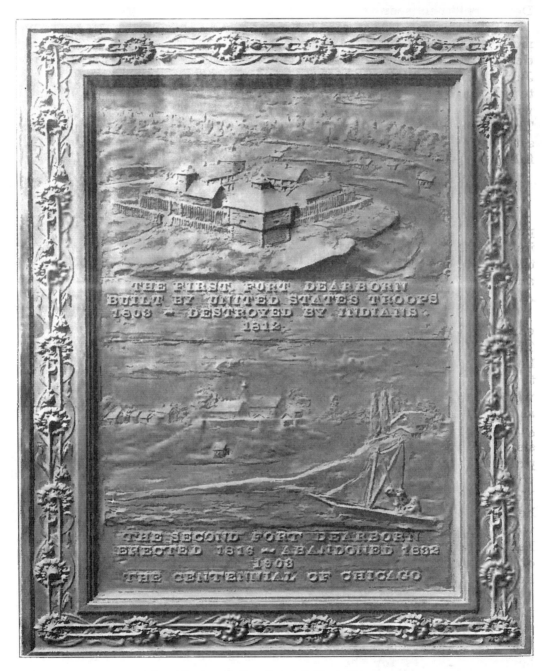

The First and the Second Fort Dearborn

garrison. The post was named Fort Dearborn after General Henry Dearborn, then secretary of war under President Thomas Jefferson.

Life at Fort Dearborn during that first winter was a dreary monotony, which must have seemed like exile or imprisonment, particularly to Lieutenant Whistler's girl wife of sixteen, formerly Miss Julia Fenson of Salem, Mass. There was practically no opportunity to associate with people outside the stockade, there being no whites, with the exception of the three French fur traders with Indian wives. The monotony was somewhat relieved by a number of Americans settling in the vicinity of the fort in the next few years. In the following pages we will introduce a few of these Chicago pioneers.

John Kinzie and His Contemporaries

In 1804 John Kinzie, a fur trader, arrived at Fort Dearborn and purchased from Le Mai the house built by Du Sable and changed by its second proprietor into a general store. This house was situated on the north bank of the river, directly opposite the fort. Kinzie enlarged and improved the building, which may thus be considered the first American private residence in Chicago.

John Kinzie was born in Quebec in 1763, of Scotch parents, and came with his mother and stepfather to New York at an early age. There he was sent to a school on Long Island at the age of twelve, but he soon ran away from home and returned to Quebec where he went to work as a jeweler's apprentice. Later Kinzie rejoined his parents who, meanwhile, had removed to Detroit. Here he established himself as a jeweler and began trading with the Indians. He wedded a young girl, Margaret McKenzie, from Virginia, who together with her younger sister, Elizabeth, had been carried off by an Indian Chief and held prisoner for years. After McKenzie's return to Virginia together with his two daughters, Kinzie removed in 1800 to the St. Joseph River. No sooner had he heard of the establishment of Fort Dearborn than he decided to move there with his second wife, Mrs. Eleanor McKillip, widow of an English officer. He arrived in 1804, as stated, and established himself as an Indian trader, gaining and retaining the confidence of the natives. On account of his craft, they called him Shaw-nee-aw-kee, the silver man.

Already in 1805 Kinzie had established auxiliary trading posts in Milwaukee, on the Rock, the Illinois and the Kankakee rivers, and in the region now named Sangamon county. Every post had its representative, its French servants, called voyageurs or engagés, and horses, boats and canoes for the transportation of merchandise. From the majority of posts furs were carried on horseback to Chicago and goods for trading purposes brought back in the same manner. Ordinarily, two sailing vessels arrived at Chicago annually, in the spring and fall.

In these the furs were shipped to Mackinaw where the depots of the great fur companies were located. In other seasons of the year, the furs were sent in open boats to the same destination. With the exception of the garrison at Fort Dearborn, everybody at the fort was directly or indirectly interested in fur trading, and the percentage of servants in proportion to the total population was exceptionally high. But the masters themselves were mostly subordinates of the large fur companies.

There were two of these companies that early established commercial relations with Chicago. These were the Hudson Bay Company and the Northwest Fur Company, and a third competitor was the Mackinaw Company, until John Jacob Astor formed the American Fur Company, and in conjunction with the Northwest Company purchased the stock of the Mackinaw Company, forming the Southwest Company, its stockholders being largely English capitalists. In 1815, however, Congress prohibited foreigners from engaging in the American fur trade, whereupon Astor purchased the stock held by Englishmen and two years later formed a new concern named the American Fur Company.

John Kinzie was doubtless one of the shrewdest fur traders of his time. Though a frontiersman, he had killed but one man and that an Indian interpreter, Lalime, whom he killed in self-defense, in 1812. Kinzie had several children with each of his two wives, one of his daughters, Ellen Marion, being the first white child born in Chicago, and some of these settled at Fort Dearborn, whither other members of the Kinzie family were gradually attracted, so that in a decade or two the place had a considerable white population. They dwelt principally on the north side of the river, near the fort, but in the course of time huts began to dot the plan at some distance from it.

The first Indian agent at the fort was a Virginian, named Charles Jouett. He retained the position until 1811 when he was succeeded by one Captain Nathanael Heald. Jouett was also the superintendent of a so-called factory established there by the government. The circumstances were as follows: When the government learned of the enormous sums earned by the great fur companies in the fur trade with the Indians, it was deemed expedient, by way of improving the financial condition of the young republic, to establish factories or trading stations at the frontier forts with a view to sharing the prosperity of the private enterprises. The government purposed to make honest payment for all furs bought of the Indians in the form of necessaries of life. The presumption was that the natives would rather deal with the government representative than with traders who usually made them drunk and then cheated them shamefully. But the government agents proved vastly inferior to the private traders in shrewdness and ex-

MAP—ILLINOIS IN 1912-1814.

perience, this resulting in the total failure of the factory system. The American Fur Company, after its reorganization in 1817, swept away the government factories as well as all the individual traders and for a time enjoyed a practical monopoly of the fur trade in the Northwest. The government withdrew from the field none the richer but much the wiser from its experiment in trafficking with the Indians.

The second, and presumably the last, Indian agent at Fort Dearborn was one Matthew Irwin of Philadelphia, who occupied that position from the year 1811 until the destruction of the fort in the following year.

The Fort Dearborn Massacre

Although the relations between the savages and the Americans were less cordial than the friendship that had existed between them and the French, yet the Fort Dearborn garrison had nothing to fear from them during the first few years, and could go about their peaceful pursuits in and about the fort in comparative safety. Soon, however, lowering clouds threatened the settlement, its fort and garrison with the storm and stress of warfare.

During the winter of 1804-5, Tecumseh, the brave, sagacious and eloquent Shawnee chief, and his brother Elskwatawa, called the Prophet, started on a tour from tribe to tribe in the Northwest, persuading the tribesmen to form a federation for the purpose of driving out the Americans. In spite of Tecumseh's glowing eloquence and his brother's auguries, based on revelations from the Great Spirit, that the campaign would be successful, the Illinois redskins remained peaceful. In 1810, a council of the Pottawatomies, Ottawas, and Chippewas was held at St. Joseph, Mich., resulting in a compact not to join the Tecumseh federation. General Harrison's victory over the Shawnees and other tribes in the battle of Tippecanoe, Ind., Nov. 7, 1811, highly enraged even the Illinois Indians against the encroachers, and in April, 1812, unfriendly hordes of Winnebagoes appeared in the neighborhood of the fort, terrorizing the settlers, many of whom sought refuge within the palisades.

After the United States declared war against England in 1812, numerous Indian tribes allied themselves with the English, hoping with their aid to drive the hated Americans from their territory. The fortunes of war at first favored the British. On the 9th of August the friendly Pottawatomie chief, Winnemeg, came to Fort Dearborn as a courier from General Hull at Detroit, bearing the message that on July 16th the formidable Fort Michilimackinac, the headquarters of the fur traders, had fallen into the hands of Indians. He also brought orders for Captain Nathanael Heald, who a year before had succeeded Captain Whistler in command at Fort Dearborn, to abandon the fort and retreat with the garrison to Detroit. Almost simultaneously the Indian swarmed around the fort, demanding the distribution among them of supplies stipulated, as they claimed, in previous treaties.

The Fort Dearborn garrison consisted of only 54 regulars, 12 militiament and besides the commander, 2 officers, namely Lieutenant L. T. Helm and Ensign R. Ronan. Of the men a number were ill, reducing the available fighting strength to about forty. Besides, there were about a dozen women and twenty children under their protection. Captain Heald knew only too well that under such unfavorable circumstances it would be difficult, if not impossible, to defend the fort, and equally precarious to hazard a retreat. Contrary to the advice of John Kinzie, Winnemeg and other friends, to evacuate the fort before

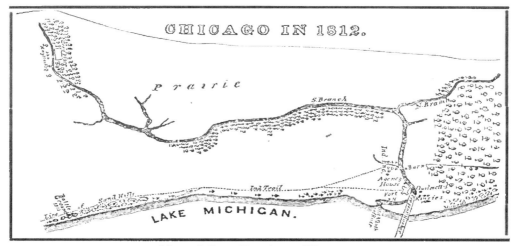

CHICAGO IN 1812.

Site of Fort Dearborn Massacre

the Indians had time to complete a plan of attack, he delayed action for six days, faintly hoping that the formerly friendly Pottawatomies, through whose territory he planned to march away, would permit him to depart without annoyance. Meanwhile, 500 or 600 Indian warriors gathered near the fort. With these Captain Heald held a parley on August 12th, promising them all the supplies and other property found at the fort and the agency in return for safe escort to Fort Wayne, Ind. The Pottawatomies agreed, knowing that the fort held large quantities of ammunition and whisky. At this juncture (August 13th) Captain Wells, the Indian agent at Fort Wayne, arrived with an escort of 30 friendly Miamis. Captain Wells, who was an uncle of Mrs. Heald, decried as senseless the idea of abandoning these supplies to the savages, Kinzie and the officers and men of the garrison joining in support of his view. Heeding the advice, the commander had all the arms and ammunition he was unable to take with him destroyed and the casks of whisky emptied into the river.

The news reached the ears of the Indian chiefs, who charged Captain Heald with gross deception and treachery and disclaimed ability to keep their warriors from attacking the Americans. A council of war was held, resulting in a decision to massacre the garrison and settlers in the vicinity of the fort just after their departure. At 9 o'clock in the morning of August 15th the gates swung open and the garrison marched out. At the head rode Captain Wells, followed by 15 of the Miami escort, the remaining 15 bringing up the rear. A number

The Fort Dearborn Massacre Monument, Chicago—Black Partridge
Saving Mrs. Helm

of Pottawatomies also joined the party, explaining that they desired to reinforce the escort. Kinzie, however, having heard that the Pottawatomies intended to ambuscade the retreating garrison, joined the soldiers, thinking his influence with the Indians might dissuade them from carrying out their savage plan. Before starting he left in the care of two trusty Indians a boat containing Mrs. Kinzie, her younger children, Grutte, the nurse, a bookkeeper, two servants, two other

Indians and two oarsmen. The soldiers marched slowly southward along the Michigan shore. Their wives and children followed in wagons and on horseback. The Pottawatomies soon separated from the escort and hurried away beyond the sand dunes to lie in wait for the company.

Captain Wells at once suspected their purpose and rode back to the main body apprising the soldiers of the treachery and telling them to prepare for a fight. They did not wait long for the expected attack. Officers and men resisted the onslaught with great bravery, but what did a handful of men, however courageous, avail against hundreds of savages? The provisions soon fell into the enemy's hands; many women and children were butchered. The Miamis fled in consternation at the first attack. Of the whites, Captain Wells, Ensign Ronan, and Surgeon Isaac Van Voorhis fell dead; Captain Heald and his wife, Lieutenant Helm and his wife, a stepdaughter of John Kinzie, and many others were wounded. The killed were scalped, and the heart of Captain Wells was cut out and distributed in small pieces among the tribes. In a few moments the Fort Dearborn garrison and population had been reduced to 25 men and 11 women, who were spared through the magnanimity of Black Partridge, a friendly chief, on condition that they lay down their arms. The prisoners were subsequently sent to the British commander at Detroit. The battle here described is known in the annals of Illinois and Chicago as the Fort Dearborn Massacre.

On the day after the massacre the Indians, having looted the fort and the agency during the night, set fire to the buildings, which soon burned to the ground. The same day General Hull surrendered not only the fort with its garrison and supplies at Detroit but all Michigan into the hands of the British and their Indian allies.

While the Fort Dearborn garrison fought the Indians among the sand dunes, John Kinzie's craft with its passengers still lay moored at the mouth of the Chicago River. The purpose had been to depart at once for St. Joseph across the lake, but the trip was interrupted by the battle. After the massacre the boat was brought back to the fort, and the members of the Kinzie family, Mrs. Heald and the rest returned to the Kinzie home under the protection of friendly and faithful Indians. Here they were threatened with destruction by a horde of Wabash Indians that had arrived for the purpose of participating with the Pottawatomies in the plunder, but found to their exasperation that they were too late. The Pottawatomie warriors and their sons were already disporting themselves in the articles of feminine apparel left behind at the evacuation.

Through the intervention of several chiefs, and particularly through the efforts of one Billy Caldwell, a brave and sagacious half-breed, the little company was saved from annihilation, whereupon the Kinzie family, under the guidance and protection of an Indian escort, was brought to St. Joseph, thence in November to Detroit, where they were delivered up as prisoners of war to Col. McKee, the British commander. During the winter John Kinzie himself also was brought as a prisoner to Detroit. He was at once set at liberty on parole, but was again arrested some time afterwards under suspicion of corresponding with General Harrison of the American army, and was then separated from his family and sent to Canada. Four years later he returned, together with his family, to the desolated homestead on the

Wolf's Point, Chicago, in 1832. A Trading Post Conducted by Wolf at the Fork of the North and the South Branch of the Chicago River

Chicago River. One by one the scattered settlers returned and settled once more on Chicago's banks.

The second war with England was ended by a treaty signed Dec. 24, 1814. This also put an end to the Indian wars, it being stipulated in the articles of peace that thenceforth neither power should arouse the Indians against the other. The American government was now left to arrange matters peaceably with the western tribes. In 1816, by a treaty signed at St. Louis, Mo., it purchased from the Ottawas and Chippewas a tract along Lake Michigan, extending ten miles north and ten miles south from the Chicago River and back as far as the Kankakee, Illinois and Fox rivers. In order to keep up communications with the vast territory purchased thirteen years before from France and to protect the fur trade and other mercantile interests, a fort on Lake Michigan was deemed necessary. The following year, therefore, the government issued orders for the erection of a new Fort Dearborn on the ruins of the old. The commission was given to Captain Heze-kiah Bradley, who arrived on the site July 4th of that year, just thirteen years after Captain Whistler, the builder and first commander of the first Fort Dearborn, landed with his men.

The new fort was built on a larger scale than the old. To the administration building and barracks were added magazines and a supply storehouse, and the buildings were protected by a square of palisades and two bastions in opposite corners. This fort was evacu-ated in 1823, reoccupied in 1828, and again abandoned in 1831, only to be taken possession of by a new garrison the following year, at the out-break of the Black Hawk War. The final evacuation occurred in 1836, after the Indians had withdrawn west of the Mississippi. The fort shared the fate of many other historic structures, being left to gradual decay and final annihilation at the hands of vandals. Thus one Judge Fuller, some time in the forties or fifties, had part of the administration building and one other structure torn down and rebuilt on sites owned by him on the south side. In 1857, one A. J. Cross, a city employee, had the remaining buildings torn down, except one, and the sandhill on which the fort had been located, graded to a level with the sur-rounding grounds. The remaining structure was moved to another part of the Fort Dearborn site. The great Chicago fire of 1871 re-moved this last trace of Fort Dearborn.

The development of Chicago in its early stages was very slow. In 1823 Major Long wrote: "This village offers no promise for the future, in view of the fact that, although quite old, the place numbers only a few huts, inhabited by a lot of miserable creatures, little better than the Indians whose descendants they are. Their loghouses are low, dirty and uninviting, lacking every requirement of home comfort. In a business sense, it holds out no inducement to strangers, the busi-ness of the village being limited to the disposal of the cargoes brought here by five or six schooners annually." As late as 1825 the village numbered only 75 or 100 inhabitants, 14 of whom owned taxable prop-erty. Real estate being non-assessable, the total value of taxable property amounted to $9,047. The most well-to-do settlers were, John Crofts, agent of the American Fur Company, with property worth $5,000, John B. Beaubien, worth $1,000, Archibald Clybourn, worth $625, Alexander Wolcott, worth $572, John Kinzie, worth $500. From the last item it appears that Kinzie, who is improperly called "the father of Chicago," at this time was a man in very moderate circum-stances. Kinzie died Jan. 6, 1828, at the age of 65 years.

The village site was first surveyed in 1829 and divided into lots, a plat of which was made the following year. This survey embraced three-eights of a square mile. A post office was established in 1831.

It was a primitive affair, according to the report that Jonathan Bailey, the postmaster, nailed up old bootlegs on the wall as receptacles for incoming and outgoing mails.

Chicago as a Town and City

In the year 1833 the former Indian village and trading station entered upon a new stage of development. On August 10th of that year it was incorporated as a town, and a town council of five members was elected, with John V. Owen as its president. The town comprised an area of 560 acres, 175 buildings and 550 inhabitants, 29 of whom were entitled to vote. The property value was $60,000, with an assessed value of $19,560, and the taxes for the first year amounted to $48.90.

Nov. 6th of that year the first newspaper was issued, being the first issue of "The Chicago Democrat;" and the following year the first public school was established in Chicago, being also the first in the state. Several brick buildings were erected, and a bridge was built across the river, which since 1831 had been crossed by means of a ferry. In 1835 were added a courthouse and a school.

In four years the town of Chicago grew to be a point of no small importance commercially, as the following figures will show: In 1833 four vessels with a total tonnage of 700 arrived at Chicago; in 1834 one hundred and seventy-six vessels with a tonnage of 5,000, entered this port; in 1835 two hundred and fifty, with a tonnage of 22,500, and in 1836 four hundred and fifty, with a tonnage of 60,000. A shipyard was established, and on May 18th of the last named year, Chicago's first vessel, the sloop Clarissa, went down the ways. On July 4th the entire population witnessed the turning of the first sod in the work of digging the Illinois and Michigan canal, a waterway which, completed, became an important line of transportation for Chicago's commerce and for general traffic.

The great financial panic of 1837 naturally affected Chicago, but it could not stop the development so recently begun. Even at this early date Chicago seemed to possess a goodly amount of that spirit of enterprise for which it has since become famous. In the midst of the general crisis, the town sought and obtained a city charter, dated March 4, 1837. On the 1st of May following the first city election was held, at which W. B. Ogden, a wealthy and influential citizen, was elected Chicago's first mayor. The first census was taken July 1st, when the city was found to number 4,179 inhabitants.

To give a detail account of the city's further development would require volumes, but a brief outline will answer our present purpose.

In its second year as a city, the foundation was laid for that enormous line of commerce, the wheat trade, for which Chicago becam known in the markets of the world. The first cargo of wheat, 100 bushels, was now shipped east from Chicago. Before that time, grain and flour had been shipped to Chicago from the East. When the farmers in the vicinity of Chicago learned that there was a market for their grain, they hauled their wheat to the city by the wagonloads, and the buyers and sellers made their deals in the street. The unpracticability of this method led to the establishment of the Chicago

Chicago in 1858. Northeast View, Taken from the Old Court House

Board of Trade, which in a short time did an enormous business. As early as 1854 Chicago exported more grain than New York.

Other steps in the making of Chicago followed in quick succession. Its first railroad, The Chicago and Galena Union, was begun in 1847. The following year telegraphic connection was established, first with Milwaukee, then with the Atlantic coast cities. The same year (1848) the Illinois and Michigan Canal was opened for traffic, giving Chicago through the Illinois and Mississippi rivers a waterway to St. Louis and the Gulf cities. In another two years a gas lighting plant was established. Steamer routes between Chicago and other points on Lake Michigan were established in 1852. During the fifties several railroad lines radiated from Chicago, viz., the Michigan Southern and the Michigan Central in 1852, the Chicago and Rock Island in 1854, the Chicago and Alton in 1855, and the Illinois Central in 1856. A waterworks system was established in 1854, and in 1859 the first fire engine was purchased, marking the initial step in introducing a modern fire-fighting system. The same year the first street railway was built in Chicago.

The growth of the system of transportation was followed by a phenomenal business development. The volume of business in 1852 was $20,000,000, in 1856, $85,000,000, and in 1860 $97,000,000.

The manufacturing industry increased correspondingly. In 1850 the value of Chicago manufactures was $2,562,583; ten years later it had increased to $13,555,671. The banking business naturally kept pace with the increase in other lines of business.

A powerful factor in the speedy development of Chicago was the influx of immigrants to the West. This began in the early forties and increased steadily for each succeeding decade. Labor and capital met in Chicago, making that city, in the course of a few decades, a center of business enterprise and human activity without a parallel.

Intellectual and spiritual development went hand in hand with the material growth. Congregations of various denominations were early established, increasing rapidly in numbers. Imposing church edifices were erected at short intervals. The public school system was carefully nurtured and improved; many higher institutions of learning were founded, among which several medical schools. Various kinds of charitable institutions sprang into existence. The Chicago Historical Society was organized in 1856 and the Academy of Sciences the next year.

The press has been not the least essential factor in the upbuilding of Chicago. "The Chicago Daily American," its first daily newspaper, was established in 1839. During the following two decades several large newspaper enterprises were launched, such as "The Evening Chicago Tribune" in 1847, and "The Chicago Times" in 1854.

This progress along all lines continued throughout the sixties. Figures to show this progress would prove a bewildering array, suffice, therefore, the bare mention of the principal enterprises of that decade. First in importance beyond compare was the establishment of the Union Stock Yards. The packing industry of Chicago dates back to the forties, but not until the founding of the Stock Yards did it assume the proportions of a giant industry. The Stock Yards proved a powerful stimulus to the stockraising industry of the West and Southwest, and in a few years Chicago was the leading live stock market in the United States. The exports of the packing plants increased year by year, making Chicago a household word abroad as well as at home. The shipments of cattle to Chicago shows the following increase: in 1857, 48,524 heads, in 1866, 384,251, in 1870, 532,964; the corresponding exports were, 25,502, 268,723 and 391,709 heads. The hog shipments to Chicago were, in 1857, 244,345, in 1866, 1,286,326, and in 1870, 1,953,372 heads; the corresponding exports were, 123,568, 576,099 and 1,095,671 heads.

In the iron industry Chicago also made a name for itself. At the Illinois Steel Works North Chicago plant was rolled in 1865 the first

THE SAUGANASH HOTEL.
Built by Mark Beaubien on the S.-E. Corner of Lake and Market
Streets, Previous to the Black Hawk War

iron rail manufactured in America. This marked the new birth of the railway system in the United States.

The constant increase in population made new demands on the sanitary drainage system. The sewerage, emptied into the Chicago River and carried by its current out into the lake, made the city's water supply a source of danger to the health of the inhabitants. To circumvent this peril, the city in 1864 began the construction of a two-mile water tunnel, terminating in a crib or intake. This tunnel was completed in 1866 and opened for use in March the following year.

The bridges spanning the river soon became inadequate for the lively traffic between the various portions of the city. This led to the construction of tunnels under the river for the transportation of passengers. The Washington street tunnel, the first of its kind in the United States, was built in 1868, and the La Salle street tunnel two years later. A third street railway tunnel was constructed at Van Buren street.

During the same decade the laying out of Chicago's extensive park system was begun. Three park boards, authorized in 1869 by the state legislature, were appointed and charged with this work on the north side, the west side and the south side respectively.

In 1866-70 a considerable stretch of the Illinois and Michigan Canal was deepened and improved at a total expense to the city of $3,251,621.

The Great Chicago Fire

As described in the preceding outline, such was Chicago in the beginning of the seventies. In some thirty odd years it had grown from an insignificant village with three or four thousand inhabitants to a great metropolis with a population of 300,000. In point of rapid growth it had outstripped almost every other city in the world. There yet seemed to be no limit to its development.

Then came that great catastrophe which with one fell swoop reduced to charred ruins the structure of three fruitful decades. Chicago, the young, the undaunted, was vanquished by the fiery fiend. In a few hours the conflagration completed its work of destruction, swept over an area of 2,100 acres, or nearly 3¾ square miles, reduced 17,500 buildings to ashes, made 98,500 people homeless, and destroyed property to the value of $190,000,000.

Great in its prosperity, Chicago proved itself grander still in adversity. What seemed like a crushing blow only served to spur it on to greater exertions towards a new and greater development. Ere the ashes had cooled, preparations were made for rebuilding the city, and out of the ruins there rose, in less than a year after the fire, a new Chicago, great in wealth and power, compelling the admiration of the world.

The Chicago fire was the worst disaster of its kind in history up to that time, being more destructive than the great London fire in 1666, those of New York, 1835, Hamburg, 1842, Constantinople, 1852, and is only surpassed by one similar calamity—the burning of San Francisco in April, 1906.

This terrible disaster occurred on the 8th and 9th of October, 1871. The main conflagration was preceded by a smaller fire which broke out in the evening of Saturday the 7th, on Clinton street, near Van Buren, on the west side, and, fanned by a strong wind, destroyed buildings on an area of twenty acres, causing a property loss of about $700,000 on dwellings, lumber yards and coal supplies, and leaving several hundred families without shelter.

The following Sunday was a bright autumn day. Tens of thousands visited the churches while other tens of thousands preferred to pace the streets, viewing the splendid decorations in honor of the expected visitor, Grand Duke Alexis of Russia. Many a devout churchgoer doubtless breathed silent thanksgivings to the Almighty for having averted the visitation that had threatened the city the night before. The great mass, on the contrary, seemed to have no thought of the disaster, oblivious as ever of the misfortunes of others, and intent only on their pleasures.

In the evening the city presented, if possible, a still more animated aspect. The devout again thronged toward the houses of worship, while the frivolous in still greater numbers surged to the theaters and other places of entertainment, how to find the greatest possible enjoyment being the question uppermost in every mind. The inhabitants of Pompeii and Herculaneum were probably no more light of heart the evening before they were buried in a rain of ashes and a stream of glowing lava than were the people of Chicago in the evening of the fated 8th of October.

At half past nine o'clock in the evening, just as the people were leaving the churches at the conclusion of the evening services, while the theatrical performances were nearing the acme of interest and dancing was in full swing in the halls of social pleasure, the fire alarm was given anew. The fire fighters, exhausted by the exertions of the previous day, again hurried with engines, hose carts and ladders to the field of battle on the west side. This time a fire had broken out at the corner of Jefferson and DeKoven streets, a point far to the south of the area devastated the night before. Following is the generally accepted story of how the fire started. An old Irishwoman, Mrs. O'Leary by name, who during the day had entertained a crowd of merrymakers, went out to the stable in the back yard at this late hour to milk her cow. A lamp which she placed beside her was kicked over by the animal, the litter of the stall was saturated with the oil and set on fire; the flames soon reached the fodder supply, and in a few seconds the stable was ablaze. The flames spread rapidly to neighboring frame buildings.

During the entire fall no rain had fallen; the frame structures with their shingled roofs were very dry and burned like tinder. To add to the disaster, the strong wind of the previous day had increased almost to a hurricane, adding to the fury of the rapidly spreading flames. In vain the firemen tried to stop the spread of the fire northward; step by step they were driven back. The fire soon divided its forces into two mighty columns which raced northward with incredible speed. The storm flung masses of sparks toward the northeast, and these advance scouts made independent attacks, setting buildings on fire far in advance of the main column of the fire-fiend. In this manner the firemen were repeatedly surrounded and forced to beat a hasty retreat or perish.

The public as well as the firemen hoped that the fire would die out from lack of sustenance upon reaching the burnt area from the night before. This hope, however, proved a delusion. That point was

Fleeing Across the River from the Flames

reached at half past eleven in the evening, but the flames leaped quickly over the charred district, at once attacking the planing mills and factories on the west bank of the south branch of the river, which furnished ample nourishment. A sudden shift of the wind now hurled firebrands across the river to the main business district.

While the fire was limited to the west side, the inhabitants of the south and north sides felt comparatively safe, trusting to the skill and perseverance of the fire brigade. Besides, the river was depended upon to stop the onrushing element. But this last hope fled when they saw the firemen rushing their engines at top speed across the bridges to the business district, and flames began to shoot up from the roofs of buildings in the heart of the city. It was now apparent that this district also was doomed, and the work of saving portable property here was at once begun amid the stampede of the panic-stricken thousands.

Meanwhile the fire grew in extent and fury, being now absolutely beyond control. As it raged through the business district it afforded a spectacle well-nigh indescribable in its terrible grandeur. Great six and seven story buildings of brick and stone melted down like tapers before the fire. So intense was the heat that an ordinary building would be leveled with the ground in the brief space of five minutes. The moment the flames penetrated into a structure the windows would glow as though reflecting a sunset; in an instant the flames would leap skyward, forming a colossal pillar of fire which, erect but for a second or two, would waver in the wind and then be hurled down to ignite adjoining structures. This process was repeated again and again. A sea of fire rolled its gigantic waves over the city with nothing to impede their course. Now and then, when the flames reached a shop or storehouse containing explosives or highly inflammable liquids a series of explosions would hurl firebrands and redhot rocks high in the air, as from the crater of a volcano in action. The flames would take different colors according to the materials consumed, thus producing a play of color, remarkable for its varied splendor. Like varicolored snakes flames crept along cornices of copper or zinc, until they mingled in the fiery blast as the walls fell in. The spectacle was reflected in the heavens, which for miles around were glowing red, while the darkness beyond hung as a dark pall about the awful picture.

The noises produced by the fire were infinite in variety and made a weird concert that no hearer can ever forget. Writhing flames hissed, firebrands crackled. When the limestone walls of the buildings were exposed to the extreme heat, the masonry would scale off, particles flying in all directions with a sound as of a discharge of musketry. The roar of the storm and the incessant thunder of falling walls constituted the bass in this infernal orchestra. Through the terrific din came now and then the mournful sound of a bell. It was the bell in the courthouse tower, which up to 2 o'clock in the morning kept sounding the death-knell of the passing city.

The people of the doomed city became frenzied. Judging alone from their appearance and actions, one would have been led to the conclusion that the entire population had gone mad. The jam and panic in the streets beggared description. Crowds of men, women and children rushed along, howling and gesticulating like maniacs, stumbling over one another and colliding in great numbers at the street corners. Not all, however, lost their senses. Some cool heads there were who took the matter philosophically, some even who looked on the ludicrous side of it all. Such stoical characters shrugged their shoulders and drew their faces to a grim smile while witnessing the process of annihilation that plunged them in a moment from opulence to poverty. Others gnashed their teeth in helpless rage to see the results of years of toil shattered thus beyond repair. Still others, apparently hale and strong men, wept like children.

Sidewalks and yards to the south of the burning district were heaped with furniture and household articles of every description. The gilded trappings from the mansions of the rich were thrown helter skelter among the modest belongings of the pauper. Among these scattered fragments, rescued from a thousand homes, the owners, men or women, had generally stationed themselves so as to keep a watchful eye on their chattels. Proud ladies, who ordinarily would not stoop to the menial duty of lifting a chair, were seen staggering under the weight of trunks or heavy loads of books, pictures, and other articles of value. Some decked themselves out in all their jewels and finery, only to be relieved of their valuables by the first robber they

Ruins after the Great Fire. Clark St., North from Washington

encountered. Young girls strained their tender frames in carrying away pieces of furniture or heavy burdens of clothing and household goods, while aged women tottered along with armfuls of personal effects. Here and there groups of children stood guard over the property of their parents; other groups were bitterly bewailing the loss of parents or guardians in the crush of humanity. At one point a bareheaded woman would be kneeling on the ground before her crucifix, telling her beads with nervous fingers and mumbling silent prayers; at another a man, crazed by misfortune, would shake his clinched fists in the face of heaven as if challenging the Almighty. Again a rather peaceful and bucolic scene might be witnessed in the midst of the havoc, for instance, a family, having saved little or nothing besides the coffee pot and the necessary ingredients, settling down in the open to enjoy the popular beverage cooked over a heap of glowing embers in the street.

Numbers, however, sought comfort in far more stimulating beverages than coffee during that grewsome night. The lower elements were afforded the most ample opportunities to indulge their taste for liquor. Saloons were recklessly plundered, casks of whisky and wine were rolled out in the street, the heads were knocked out, and men and boys crowded about, draining the contents till they staggered and fell, many

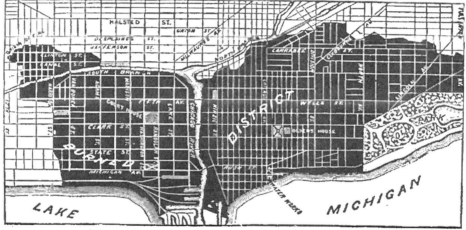

The Great Fire. Map of the Burned District

perishing where they lay when the flames reached them. Others succeeded in crawling out of harm's way, and dropped into sobering sleep in yards and alleys.

When the fire threatened the jail, the prisoners were set free. These immediately joined the criminals at large in a riot of loot and plunder. Without the slightest hesitation they would enter the merchant's shops, hurl articles of value to their accomplices at the door, and depart with their plunder, with the air of having saved their own property, not a hand being raised to prevent their escape through the crowds. However great the losses by theft that night, they were probably insignificant as compared with the amount of goods and chattels destroyed in the streets or consumed by the flames. Many purposely destroyed their own property rather than have it stolen or burned.

With the aid of draymen many succeeded in having their goods hauled to places of safety far from the burning area, but these men, who were often unscrupulous, charged a rate of cartage amounting to a high percentage of the actual value of the goods saved. Thus, a hundred dollars might be demanded for hauling a load of goods only a few blocks. Early in the evening the bridges leading to the north side became so crowded with people and vehicles that many were severely injured in the crush. Many businessmen on the south side had goods worth millions brought to the river bank, where loads upon loads of valuable merchandise was destroyed by fire before morning.

At 3 o'clock in the morning, the fire had practically finished its triumphal march through the business district, leaving nothing but smoking ruins behind, and prepared to cross the river to the north side, having previously sent scouts ahead in the form of sparks and fire-brands hurled across by the wind. It was also feared that the flames would again be directed toward the west side, the main portion of which was still intact, but the danger was averted by a systematic protection of the buildings nearest the river. The people of the north side, many of whom had retired for the night, were in turn, like the inhabitants of the west and south-sides, routed out of bed and forced too flee for their lives. It was high time they did, for the flames were already hovering over their roofs. The gas plant soon caught fire and was shattered by a tremendous explosion, instantly followed by the ex-tinction of the street lamps, leaving the district in darkness but for the reflection from the blazing buildings to the south. In a short time the flames reached the water works at the foot of Chicago avenue, nearly a mile north of the river. With that, the fire department was com-pletely disarmed, all hope of resistance was gone, and the phalanxes of the fiery conqueror marched on undeterred.

Here was repetition of the scenes already enacted on the south side, while the terrorstricken inhabitants were engaged in precipitous flight for safety. Thousands took refuge westward across the north branch of the river, while other thousands fled to the lake front. The latter soon discovered their mistake. As the fire approached, they were enveloped in dense clouds of smoke and exposed to a shower of sparks and flying embers that ignited the personal property deposited there. The heat grew more suffocating for every passing minute and finally became unendurable, forcing those who had not fled north along the lake front to wade into the water for protection and remain there until they could be taken away in boats. The flames spared not even the city of the dead. The Catholic cemetery near Lincoln Park was ravaged, charred wooden crosses and cracked marble shafts bearing evidence of the destruction wrought.

Not until 4 o'clock on Monday afternoon had the fire run its course. Its spread southward had been checked by volunteer fire fighters, assisted by a military troop in command of General Philip Sheridan. On the north side, however, the fire raged as long as any houses remained. At Fullerton avenue, where lay a stretch of open prairie, the flames died out at last. ·

A host of people were left homeless, penniless, without clothes or shelter against the cold autumn night. Many camped on the prairies outside the city or among the mounds of the dead in the cemeteries, not a few doubtless heartbroken, and wishing that they too were asleep under the sod. Their future seemed as black and cheerless as the area strewn with the ruins of the Chicago of yesterday.

The one bright spot in the desolate picture was the energetic assistance and succor furnished by city authorities and the people of the intact portion of the city. Churches, schoolhouses, stationhouses and other public buildings were thrown open and turned into asylums for the distressed, while tents were furnished to thousands of other sufferers. The railways offered free transportation to all who desired to seek shelter with

Ruins after the Great Fire. Honore Block, N.-W. Corner of Adams and Dearborn Streets

relatives and friends elsewhere or simply wanted to leave the stricken city for anywhere. It is claimed that about 15,000 people availed themselves of the opportunity and left on outgoing trains the same day.

While the fire still raged on the north side, the mayor, jointly with the department chiefs of the city administration, issued a proclamation to the effect that the City of Chicago assumed the liability for all expenses incurred in rendering aid to the fire sufferers, and promised protection for all exposed personal property. As soon as the disaster had been telegraphed abroad, money and supplies began to pour in from all parts of the country, and later from almost every part of the civilized world. The first outside aid was in the form of provisions, sent from Indianapolis, reaching Chicago by express at 3 o'clock Tuesday afternoon. This was followed in a few hours by another train from St. Louis, bringing clothing and provisions, and a delegation of citizens bearing this greeting: "Brethren, be of good cheer! All that we have is at your disposal until you get on your feet again. We have come to stay and help you." Similar messages were received from other points. Troops were called in from Fort Leavenworth, Kansas, to assist a volunteer corps in patrolling the burned district, and the better to preserve order General Sheridan placed the city under military rule. The Chicago Relief and Aid Society was organized and took charge of the distribution of incoming supplies. On Nov. 7th, one month after the fire, there had been subscribed for the relief fund $3,500,000, $2,050,000 of which had been paid in. Sixty thousand people were then receiving assistance.

Shortly after the fire, the state legislature was called in extra session and appropriated a generous sum to the relief work. The relief funds in cash already amounted to $4,820,148.16, out of which $973,897.80 had been contributed from foreign countries. The total value of all funds and supplies aggregated almost seven millions of dollars.

To the figures given in the foregoing, the following are subjoined to show the full extent of the disaster. Among the buildings destroyed were 69 church edifices and convents, 32 hotels, 29 bank buildings, 15 academies and seminaries, 11 public schools, 10 theaters and other places of amusement, 9 offices of daily newspapers, 7 orphan asylums, 5 hospitals, 5 telegraph offices, 5 grain elevators, 3 railway stations, besides the courthouse, the customhouse, the postoffice, the board of trade building, the gas plant and the water works.

The fire loss was estimated at $190,000,000, including $50,000,000 on buildings and $140,000,000 on other property. If the loss by shrinkage in realty values and reduced incomes be included, the sum total would pass $200,000,000. All city property, real and personal, was valued at $620,000,000 just before the fire. Thus about one-third of this had been wiped out. The loss was partly covered by insurance totaling $96,533,721, of which $6,000,000 had been written by foreign companies. The insurance paid amounted to only $44,000,000, owing principally to the fact that not less than 57 fire insurance companies were bankrupted by the enormous losses sustained.

The exact loss of life was never determined, the approximate number of people who perished being set at three hundred.

The setback given to the commercial development of the city was of short duration. Before winter set in, many businessmen were established in temporary quarters in various parts of the city. The homeless, who could not be otherwise provided for, were sheltered in temporary wooden barracks. Free coal, free provisions and free lumber was distributed to the most unfortunate victims. Within a year a large portion of the burned district had been rebuilt at a total cost of $40,500,000, while the increase in the volume of business and manufactures had surpassed all previous records. With remarkable energy, equalled nowhere, the work was pursued night and day. Wages were high and laborers were plentiful. In two years the population was increased by 68,419.

Three years after the fire, almost every trace of the catastrophe had been erased. A remarkable chapter in the annals of Chicago closed with the great fire of 1871, and another, equally wonderful, opened with the rebuilding of the city.

Later Development of Chicago

During the thirty-six years that have elapsed since the great fire, Chicago has developed into one of the great cities of the world, with the evil as well as the good features of a metropolis. Following are a few of the important facts in its latter history.

Lincoln Monument—Lincoln Park

Less than three years after the fire the city was again threatened with destruction. July 14, 1874, another extensive conflagration destroyed property valued at four million dollars before the flames could be subdued.

As has been shown, Chicago early attained importance as a business center and shipping port. Its industrial phase next added new activity, giving the city high rank as an industrial community. Besides the great stock yards and slaughter houses, immense steel mills, farm implement factories and other similar establishments were founded. The year 1880 marks a new epoch in the industrial history of Chicago. Then the Pullman Palace Car Company, organized in 1867, founded the town of Pullman, twelve miles south of the heart of Chicago. The new community, comprising the extensive car factories and cottages for its thousands of workmen and their families, grew rapidly and soon became, in many respects, a model town.

Workmen from all parts of the civilized world flocked into Chicago, making it pre-eminently a city of labor and of laborers. Here, as elsewhere in industrial communities, the war between capital and labor was soon raging. The fight waxed all the more fierce on the labor side, owing to the fact that the labor movement had been taken in charge by German socialists in the early seventies, a few years after the fire, they having emigrated from their native land on account of the iron rule of Bismarck. Thus Chicago soon became famous for her labor organizations and their incessant struggle for what they held to be their rights. Shorter hours, increased wages and legislation favoring the working classes were the demands made by the socialists and supported by them on the rostrum and in the press. The ballot, they declared, was their most powerful ally.

Unfortunately, this agitation soon sunk to the level of anarchistic propaganda. In the late seventies and the early eighties there arrived from Europe a number persons intimate with the leaders and the principles of anarchy and nihilism, and these succeeded in acquiring a controlling influence over the labor organizations. These held the ballot to be altogether too ineffectual a weapon with which to fight the capitalists and their hirelings, the civic authorities as well as the unorganized workingmen being classed with the latter. Guns, revolvers, bombs, these were the great emancipators of the workers, the means of overturning the effete social order of the present.

The first great strike in Chicago occurred in 1877, when the railway employees struck work here as in Baltimore, Pittsburg and other eastern centers. The dragon's teeth sown by anarchy gave its harvest on July 25th, in the form of a skirmish between the strikers and the police, the former being worsted in the fight. This had a cooling effect on the hotheaded leaders, causing all violence to subside and gradually bringing the strike to a close.

The anarchistic propaganda, however, being carried on unchecked, brought about conspiracies among labor organizations, designed to make short shrift with the capitalistic class and every other form of opposition in the next conflict. The German anarchist papers in particular openly urged force and bloodshed. In February, 1886, an event occurred which caused renewed activity in the anarchistic camp. At the great McCormick Harvester Works a strike of the workmen was promptly met by a lockout. When the strikers found that their former employers had arranged to supplant them with non-union workers, their rage knew no bounds. Two organizations, the Metal Workers Union and the Carpenters Union No. 1, agreed to arm themselves with guns, revolvers, and bombs in order to prevent the strike breakers from

The Ottawa Indian Monument—Lincoln Park

taking their places. For reasons unknown, the fight never took place, and on March 1st the new men, protected by a squad of police, went to work unmolested. Before and after noon of the same day, however, fighting occurred between the strikers and the police guarding the factories, resulting in the arrest of several strikers and the discovery of bombs and other weapons in their possession.

It was believed that the anarchists, after having made such a lame showing, would take a new tack, but this hope proved illusive. They operated in secret and were biding their time. The crisis came on May 1st, when from 40,000 to 50,000 workmen in various trades struck for an eight hour day. The McCormick works were now running almost full force, thanks to the strike breakers or so-called scabs. In the vicinity of the factory was held a mass meeting attended by about 8,000 strikers, 3,000 of whom were Germans and an equal number Bohemians belonging to the Lumber Shovers Union. August Spies, the editor of the radical "Arbeiter Zeitung," and one of the foremost leaders of the anarchists, climbed into a dray and made a speech to the crowd, characterizing capitalists and employers as oppressors and vampires, and the laborers as their slaves. His words struck fire in the minds of the assemblage, and the speaker had scarcely finished when a mass of strikers stormed in the direction of the factory, breaking the windows of the gatekeeper's house and maltreating the workmen first encountered. The crowd soon forced its way into the factory yards, with the evident purpose of wreaking bloody vengeance on the "scabs" and destroying the works. This plan was defeated by the police who hurried to the scene and, after a brief but sharp encounter, cleared the grounds and put the strikers to flight. Although firearms and missiles were freely used, no one was killed. The leaders of the raid were arrested the same day.

At this sorry outcome of the onslaught on the powers that be, the anarchists were still more enraged, and swore terrible vengeance. Spies hurried to his editorial room and wrote a circular in English and German, urging the strikers to arm themselves and take remorseless revenge upon the police. Immediately thereupon, he published in his paper an incendiary article, relating to the disturbance his words had caused. In this he charged that four strikers had been shot to death by the police, despite the fact that not a man had been seriously wounded.

In the afternoon of May 3rd, representatives of all the anarchist organizations in the city held a secret meeting, at which it was resolved that at the next encounter with the authorities the anarchists at a given signal would simultaneously blow up the police stations with dynamite and shoot all surviving policemen. Then they would march to the heart of the city, where the principal struggle was to take place. The main buildings were to be burned, the jails stormed and the prisoners set free, to make common cause with the revolutionists. In order to arouse the populace to a high spirit of vengeance against the police a mass meeting was called at Haymarket Square, at Desplaines and Randolph streets, the following evening. The anarchist delegates separated after agreeing that the word "Ruhe" (peace) inserted in the "Letter Box" in the columns of the "Arbeiter-Zeitung" was to be the signal for a general uprising.

During Tuesday, May 4th, a number of anarchists were busily at work manufacturing bombs of every description, while others distributed circulars announcing the great mass meeting. In the evening "Zeitung" the ominous word appeared, advising every anarchist in the city that the hour of vengeance had come. The fact that the city had a powerful militia at its disposal and that well disciplined United States troops were at hand, ready to step in at once, should the Chicago police be unable to cope with their antagonists, evidently had not entered the minds of the revolutionists.

The Haymarket Tragedy

It was the evening of May 4th, a memorable date in the history of Chicago. At 8 o'clock about 3,000 people had gathered at the appointed place. Editor Spies and the other anarchist agitators were promptly on hand. A few moments later, Spies mounted the speaker's stand and entered upon a severe criticism of the McCormick Company's treatment of the strikers. This, the speaker maintained, ought to teach the workingmen to arm for their own protection against the capitalists and their hirelings. The next speaker was Albert R. Parsons, editor of the American anarchist paper, "The Alarm." His speech was also of an inflammable character. Next in order came Samuel Fielden, a teamster, whose untutored eloquence seemed to impress the crowd more strongly than the polished harangues of his predecessors. "The advance guard skirmish with the capitalists forces has taken place; the main battle is yet to be fought," said he.

Fearing an outbreak, the authorities had detailed a force of 176 policemen to the Desplaines street police station, under command of Inspector John Bonfield. When he learned through detectives at the meeting that the speakers were growing extremely bold in their expressions, and the masses showed signs of threatening disorder, he marched his forces to the square. From his elevated position in a dray wagon, Fielden saw the police approaching and shouted:

"The bloodhounds are upon us! Do you duty! I will do mine."

A minute later, the front line of police halted a few feet from the wagon, and Police Captain Ward stepped up, saying:

"In the name of the people of the state, I order you to disperse peaceably at once."

Fielden, who had meanwhile jumped from the wagon, shouted aloud: "We are peaceable!" This seemed the secret signal of attack (compare the watchword, "Ruhe"), for the next instant an object resembling a lighted cigar was hurled through the air and fell between the lines of the second platoon of police. One second more, and the impact of an explosion shook the air far around. Numbers of policemen were hurled in all directions, some dangerously, others slightly injured.

The exploding bomb, thrown by some anarchist, was taken as a signal for general fighting with revolvers and pistols between the revolutionists and the police. In a moment the latter force had regained its presence of mind and made a concerted sortie upon the masses, which, though armed, were unable to withstand the attack, and were soon dispersed.

The three agitators were among the first to seek safety in flight. The projected slaughter at Haymarket Square, the destruction of the police stations, and the incendiary raid of the business district had been set at naught. The anarchists, comparatively few and undoubtedly cowardly as they were, had lost their first and, one may well hope, last battle in Chicago.

The bloodshed at this encounter was considerable. One policeman fell dead and seven others were fatally wounded. Besides these, sixty-seven of the police were injured more or less seriously in the affray. A number of the rioters were shot and seriously wounded by the police. The number who died from their injuries never became known, for their relatives, prompted by fear or shame, refused to make known their exact loss. It leaked out, nevertheless, that several anarchists were secretly buried at night shortly after the riot. Of the wounded policemen two died May 6th, one May 8th, one May 14th, one May 16th, and the seventh and last on June 13, 1888.

A great number of suspects were at once taken into custody, among others almost the entire working force of the "Arbeiter-Zeitung." Other arrests were made later at short intervals. The police investigations soon revealed the fact that the principal conspirators, besides Spies, Parsons and Fielden, were Adolph Fischer, foreman of the printing office, Michael Schwab, assistant editor, Balthasar Rau, an agent of the paper, Louis Lingg, a carpenter, George Engel, a painter, Oscar W. Neebe, a yeast dealer, and others. Lingg was found to be the most energetic manufacturer of bombs, and the one causing the destruction on Haymarket Square was doubtless his handiwork. The man who hurled it at the police platoon was Rudolph Schnaubelt, who was also arrested but again set free on the strength of an impression made on the police authorities that he was innocent. Schnaubelt lost no time in leaving Chicago for parts unknown. Thus it happened that the actual perpetrator of the crime escaped trial and punishment, while most of the conspirators who had planned the foul deed paid the penalty with their lives.

Thanks to the thorough work of the police, a mass of evidence against the prisoners was gathered, and on May 17th they were indicted by the grand jury. The trial was begun June 21st, and the selection of a trial jury consumed four weeks, the actual trial of the prisoners opening July 15th, and lasting until the 19th, when the case went to the jury. The following day they brought in a verdict of guilty and fixed the penalty at death on the gallows for Spies, Schwab, Fielden. Parsons, Fischer, Engel and Lingg as the instigators of the Haymarket bloodshed, and fifteen years' imprisonment for Neebe for complicity in the crime. The counsel for the defense immediately asked for a new trial, but on Oct. 7th the motion was denied. The only recourse was an appeal to the state supreme court. The appeal was taken in March, 1887, and on Sept. 14th this tribunal struck dismay to the hearts of the anarchists and their sympathizers by sustaining the verdict of the lower court. But even then the culprits clung to a faint hope, and took an appeal to the court of last resort, the Supreme Court at Washington.

The Schiller Monument—Lincoln Park

The appeal was taken up for consideration Oct. 27th, resulting on the second of November in a decree sustaining the former verdict. Parsons, Engel, Fischer and Lingg, still headstrong, then petitioned Richard J. Oglesby, governor of Illinois, for unconditional pardon, while Spies, Fielden and Schwab made the more humble request that the death penalty be commuted to life imprisonment. The governor's answer, given Nov. 10th, granted the petition of Fielden and Schwab but denied the request of the other four.

Before the governor's reply came, Lingg seemed to have a premonition that all hope was gone. To go to the gallows and submit to the authority of law and social order was revolting to this sworn enemy of the law, and he found another way. In some mysterious way he had a bomb, consisting of a piece of loaded gaspipe, smuggled into his cell by a friend, and on the morning of Nov. 10th, he placed this in his mouth, lay down on his bed and lit the fuse with a candle. The explosion tore away half of the face. At 2.45 o'clock in the afternoon of the same day death relieved him from his sufferings.

The remaining four were executed the following day, Nov. 11th,

Newberry Library

at the county jail. They were unrepentant to the last, giving vent to anarchistic sentiments on the very scaffold. On the same day, Fielden and Schwab were committed to the penitentiary at Joliet.

The general insurrection threatened by the culprits as a sequel to the execution failed to materialize. Not a sign of a revolutionary movement could be discerned. The energy and promptness with which the authorities had acted deprived the lawless league of all inclination toward a renewal of violence, and in a short time the anarchist propaganda had been silenced in Chicago. The labor movement was again directed into its normal course.

After six years, Fielden, Schwab and Neebe were pardoned out of prison on June 26th, 1893. Since that time they have not been known to plan any new social order to be brought about by means of bombs and bloodshed.

In the same year that witnessed the anarchist uprising, a strike was declared on November 7th among the packinghouse workers in Chicago. Two regiments of the national guards were ordered out to preserve order. No disturbances occurred and the troops were withdrawn on the 15th of the same month. The next great strike was enacted April 7th, 1890, when seven thousand carpenters threw down their tools to enforce their demand for an eight hour day. Four years later there came a new conflict between capital and labor, when, on the 12th of April, 1894, a general lockout of workmen in all the building trades was declared, throwing 10,000 workmen out of employment. The 11th of May following, 2,000 employees of the Pullman Car Company went on strike, and to make this more effective all other labor organizations were called upon, June 28th, to boycott all railway lines using Pullman cars.

This move resulted in violence, for the quelling of which President Cleveland ordered out government troops. This was done July 3rd. Two days later, Governor Altgeld demanded the withdrawal of the troops on the ground that their presence was not needed. The President replied to this on July 8th by declaring Chicago under martial law. This action, together with that of the federal grand jury, indicting Eugene V. Debs, President of the American Railway Union, for declaring a boycott interfering with the United States mail service, hastened the settlement of the difficulties. On July 19th both the strike and the boycott were declared off, and quiet was restored. Since that time a number of strikes have occurred in Chicago, resulting favorably to one side or the other, but none has been attended by disorder necessitating military interference.

Facts and Figures of the Chicago of To-day

In the course of time, the city has grown rapidly to the north, south and west, while new suburbs have sprung up on every hand, in turn merging with the metropolis according as their interests dictated. Not less than sixteen annexations have thus been effected. The largest addition of territory was acquired in 1889, when the towns of Lake View, Hyde Park, Lake, Jefferson and part of Cicero were absorbed. Since then considerable areas have been added from time to time, bringing the total area of the city of Chicago up to 190.6 square miles.

The Chicago River divides the city into three sections known as the south side, the west side and the north side. These sections are connected by means of 60 bridges, mostly of the swinging type, which are gradually being replaced by the more modern bascule bridges.

The total street mileage is 3,946. The longest street is Western avenue, extending 22 miles, and Halsted street extends nearly the same distance north and south. The city has fifteen parks, the largest being Lincoln, Humboldt, Garfield, Douglas, Washington and Jackson parks. These are connected by wide and attractive boulevards and thus form as extensive and fine a park system as any city can boast of. The entire system, including boulevards, has an area of about 3,300 acres, the latter having a total length of 48 miles. Under the streets extends a system of sewers measuring about 1,600 miles in length. The city's water mains have a combined length of approximately 2,000 miles. By means of enormous pumps the water is forced into the city from a series of cribs located far out in the lake, through water tunnels running under the lake and underground a total distance of 38 miles, and emptying into an extensive network of watermains and smaller pipes. The pumping stations have a combined capacity of 529,500,000 gallons daily. The lighting system is equally extensive. Numberless gas mains and electric conduits form an underground mesh extending

Franklin Monument—Lincoln Park

far out to the most distant suburbs. There were in 1905 37,000 gas and electric street lamps.

The preservation of law and order is entrusted to a police force of 3,300 men, distributed among 45 police stations. · The fire department comprises 1,200 men, divided into 92 larger and 27 smaller companies. About 15,000 people are variously employed in the service of the city.

From Chicago radiate 20 lines of railroad, several of which extend to the Atlantic and Pacific coasts, Lake Superior, and the Gulf of Mexico. There are six great railway terminals having a system of common track connections. The incoming and outgoing trains, through and suburban, number 1,600 per day and carry, on a rough estimate, several hundred thousand passengers.

The street railway system is one of the most extensive in the world, comprising about 120 separate lines with a total of 1,000 miles of track. Including the suburban and elevated system, the trackage is 1,360 miles.

The principal motive power is electricity. The daily average number of street car passengers exceeds half a million, but the full capacity of the system is claimed to be one million and a half. Equally important as a system of passenger transportation are the four elevated railway lines, with their branches. One of these, the Northwestern Elevated, has four tracks, runs express as well as local trains, and is claimed to have the only complete traction system of the kind. The elevated railroads have a combined trackage of about 150 miles. In 1905 the daily average number of passengers on surface and elevated lines was 1,354,450.

Chicago has 235 large and a great number of small hotels, capable of accommodating 200,000 guests. There are over 1,000 restaurants and cafés, with a daily capacity of several hundred thousand guests. Many of the hotels are palatial, famous at home and abroad for the comfort and luxury they afford. From twenty to thirty thousand people daily visit the city's theaters, which are 40 in number. Besides these public entertainment is furnished at a number of other places of amusement. In the history of Chicago theaters there must be recorded that appalling catastrophe, the fire in the newly built Iroquois Theater, at Randolph st., on the 30th day of December, 1903, the flames starting in the scenery and sweeping out over the auditorium, throwing the audience into a panic, and causing the death of 588 persons by burning, crushing and suffocation.

There are fifty clubs of different kinds, many of which having their own club houses. The sick are being cared for in not less than 68 hospitals. To these must be added fifty other charitable institutions, such as asylums and homes for the feeble-minded, the crippled and the aged. For the care of the poor and indigent there are eighteen large and a number of smaller benevolent associations. Sick benefit societies and others for mutual assistance in emergencies are too numerous to be counted, as are also the organizations for social pleasure.

The educational system of Chicago is world-renowned, and rightly so. The number of public schools in 1906 was 250, with 5,900 teachers and 287,000 pupils. Higher courses of study are pursued in fifteen high schools. For the education of teachers there is a normal school, besides two training schools. The schools founded by religious denominations and public spirited individuals number twenty-two. Principal among these are the Armour Institute and the Lewis Institute, both technological schools of a high order. The well-known Chicago Musical College leads a number of excellent musical schools conducted here. Higher education is represented by two great universities, the Northwestern University of Evanston and the University of Chicago.

Libraries and museums are not lacking. Of the former there are thirteen, the largest being the Chicago Public Library, which on June

1, 1906, contained 323,610 volumes, the Newberry Library, with 218,525 books and pamphlets on Oct. 1, 1906, and the John Crerar Library, with 194,000 volumes and 50,000 pamphlets on Oct. 1, 1906. The museums

Chicago Historical Society Museum and Library

are, the Academy of Sciences, containing natural history collections, the museum of the Chicago Historical Society, with a large historical collection pertaining to the early history of the city, the Field Columbian Museum, with extensive ethnological collections, and the Chicago Art Institute, comprising a considerable collection of paintings, sculptures and art objects from the remotest to the most recent times. The Art Institute includes a school of art with a large annual attendance.

The Chicago Historical Society was founded in 1856 for the purpose of collecting and preserving the materials of history and to spread historical information concerning the Mississippi valley. The great fire of 1871 destroyed the priceless collection of 100,000 volumes and manuscripts, among them being the original draft of the emancipation proclamation by Abraham Lincoln. The nucleus of a new collection was consumed in 1874. A third collection was started which now numbers more than 140,000 volumes, manuscripts and pamphlets. Among the manuscripts are the James Madison papers, James Wilkinson papers, Ninian Edwards papers and Pierre Menard papers. There are letters in the handwriting of Joliet, Allouez, Tonti, Frontenac and La Salle. The collections comprise also many oil paintings, bronzes and antiquities. A fire-proof granite building was erected 1892-6 at Dearborn ave. and Ontario st., at a cost of $190,000. Historical lectures are maintained each winter. Some forty papers on subjects presented at its meetings have been published, besides which four large volumes of historical collections have been issued. The library and museum are open daily to visitors.

Almost every church denomination in the United States is represented in Chicago. The number of church edifices is about 800. In this connection may be added that there are forty cemeteries, a number of which are maintained by church organizations.

About 600 newspapers and periodicals are published in Chicago, a large number being in foreign languages. The leading daily newspapers are, "The Chicago Daily Tribune," "The Chicago Record-Herald," "The Inter Ocean," "The Chicago Daily News," and "The Chicago American." Several of these are issued in enormous editions.

The book publishing business has likewise attained gigantic proportions. A great number of houses are annually putting out immense editions of original and reprinted works of every description. One result of this is a high development of the publisher's art and all its auxiliary branches.

The mail service of the city is excellent. At the central post office and the 47 district stations, 2,600 persons are employed in handling the enormous mass of incoming and outgoing mail. The collection of mail from letter and parcel boxes and the distribution of incoming mail matter requires the service of 1,650 collectors and carriers. The free delivery system prevails. In addition to the district post offices there are 246 sub-stations distributed throughout the city for the accommodation of the public in the matter of stamps, postals cards, money orders and the registry of letters. The volume of the Chicago postal business is shown by these figures: during the year ending June 30, 1906, 1,139,084,480 pieces of mail were handled, the total weight being 126,542,509 pounds. The total income for the department for the same year was $12,885,149.

The building and real estate interests are extremely active. During 1905, not less than 8,442 buildings were erected at a total cost of $63,970,950. The dealings in realty are equally brisk. The year 1902

The Grant Monument—Lincoln Park

showed 18,063 real estate transfers aggregating $111,441,112 in value, those figures having since been materially increased.

The taxable value of realty in Chicago in 1905 was estimated at $295,514,443 and that of personal property at $112,477,182, making a total valuation of $407,991,625. The tax levy was $27,959,908.

Enormous progress in manufactures and varied industries has been made since the great fire. In 1900 Chicago had within its limits 19,203 manufacturing establishments with a combined capitalization of $534,-000,689. These employed 262,621 persons, who were paid $131,065,337. The cost of materials used amounted to $538,401,562 and that of the finished product to $888,945,311. For comparison, the value of manufactured products in the entire state in 1905 was $955,036,277, and in Chicago alone about $500,000,000, or more than half of the total.

The greatest of Chicago industries is the slaughtering and packing industry. During the year named, it embraced thirty-eight packing plants, with a capital of $67,137,569, 25,345 workers, with wages aggregating $12,875,676, a consumption of live stock and other materials amounting to $218,241,331 and an output valued at $256,527,949, this latter sum representing 35.6 per cent. of the product of the entire packing industry of the country.

Second in order of importance is the foundry and machine manufacturing industry, represented by 441 separate establishments, capitalized at $36,356,168, employing 20,641 workers, paying $11,264,544 in wages, consuming $20,070,516 worth of raw material and showing an annual production valued at $44,561,071.

The manufacturing of agricultural implements stands third, with six plants, a capitalization of $36,025,355, 10,245 workers, and an annual expenditure of $5,180,958 for labor. The materials used cost $10,842,299 and the finished products sold at $24,848,649.

The tailoring industry ranked fourth with 874 shops, $12,991,669 of capital involved, 13,855 workers employed, $5,551,561 in wages, and a production of $36,094,310, at a cost of $17,547,665.

In the fifth place comes the iron and steel industry, with nine plants, a total capital of $24,271,764, 6,112 workers, $4,329,342 paid in wages, $22,448,511 as the cost of production and an output estimated at $31,461,174.

Other large industries are, the building of railway coaches and street cars, with an annual output of $19,108,085, printing and binding, with $18,536,364, and brewing and distilling, with $14,956,865 as the value of their respective output.

Chicago is the headquarters for the grain market of the great West. There are in the city twenty-six immense grain elevators with a total capacity of 32,550,000 bushels. The grain market shows no steady increase but fluctuates according to the crops and other trade conditions dependent thereon. For instance, in 1886, 192,778,757 bushels of grain was inspected here, in 1890, 290,251,109 bushels, in 1895, 265,737,585 bushels, in 1900, 462,758,523 bushels, in 1902, 287.337,599 bushels, in 1903, 237,532,024 bushels, and in 1905, 260,675,693 bushels.

Although not a seaport, Chicago is the greatest shipping point in the United States, a fact not generally known. Its shipping will doubtless acquire still greater proportions when the new waterways in process of construction shall be completed, giving access to the Mississippi and the Gulf. During 1897, 9,156 vessels, with a combined tonnage of 7,209,444, entered, and 9,201 vessels, with a tonnage of 7,185,-324, left this port. In 1903, 7,456 vessels, with a combined capacity of 7,603,278 tons cleared out of the Chicago port, and in 1905 the arrivals and clearances were, respectively, 6,949 vessels, of 7,218,641 tons, and 7,014 vessels, of 7,281,259 tons. The decrease in shipping in later years is mainly chargeable to the obstructed condition of the river.

These figures regarding Chicago's grain trade and shipping show the city to be one of the foremost commercial centers of the country. Some additional figures will serve to substantiate the statement. The value of goods sold by Chicago's wholesale and jobbing houses during 1903 was more than $1,058,000,000. This includes dry goods and carpets, $162,500,000, groceries, $115,500,000, iron and steel wares, $70,-500,000, lumber, $70,500,000, men's ready-made clothing, $66,000,000, goods sold through mail order houses, $55,000,000, boots and shoes, $48,000,000, coal, $47,000,000, diamonds and jewelry, $40,000,000, metal wares, $34,000,000, furniture, $34,000,000, books and music, $20,500,000, paper, $20,000,000, leather, $17,500,000, tobacco and cigars, $16,500,000, medicines and chemicals, $16,000,000, musical instruments, $15,500,000, hats and caps, $15,000,000, furs, $15,000,000, women's clothing, $12,-500,000, baskets and wickerwork, $12,000,000, millinery, $11,000,000, china and glassware, $11,000,000, wool, $10,000,000, etc.

During the last-named year the following packing house products were shipped from Chicago: cured meats, 580,282,643 pounds; preserved meats, 1,835,035 pounds; dressed meats, 1,252,233,792 pounds, tallow, 373,000,959 pounds; beef, 82,010 barrels; pork, 175,795 barrels.

Farm products were received and shipped as follows: cheese, received, 82,129,852 pounds, shipped, 57,277,361 pounds; butter, received, 232,031,484 pounds, shipped 197,620,859 pounds; eggs, received, 3,279,-248 cases, shipped, 1,699,302 cases.

During 1902 imports from foreign countries to Chicago reached $18,329,390, duties on same amounting to $9,565,452.96.

In that year Chicago paid internal revenue on spirituous liquors, tobacco, oleomargarine, playing cards, etc., amounting to $8,839,042.06.

It is but natural that a city with so extensive manufacturing and commercial interests should develop a banking business of great magnitude. In June, 1904, the number of banks was 44, with a total capital of $50,875,000 and deposits amounting to $550,068,287. The bank clearings of the year 1902 were $8,395,872,351.59.

The Population of Chicago

In previous pages we have endeavored to show how Chicago grew from an insignificant Indian village to a trading station, from trading station to town, from town to city, and from city to metropolis. The rapidity of this development is best exemplified by figures giving the population by decades, as follows:

Year	Total Pop'n	Year	Total Pop'n
1837	4,179	1870	298,977
18o.	4,470	1880	503,185
1850	28,269	1890	1,099,850
1860	112,162	1900	1,698,575

Chicago is a cosmopolitan city, nearly every nation in the world being here represented. More than three-fourths of the inhabitants are foreign born or descendants of foreigners.

According to the school census of 1902, the city had 2,007,695 inhabitants, as follows:

Nationalities	Population.	Nationalities	Population.
German	534,083	Dutch	18,555
Irish	254,914	French Canadian	13,533
Polish	167,383	Hungarian.	11,658
Swedish	144,719	Swiss.	7,922
Bohemian	109,224	French	7,493
English	72,876	Welsh	4,863
Russian	61,976	Greek	1,493
Norwegian.	59,898	Chinese	1,179
British Canadian	48,304	Belgian	1,160
Italian	42,054	Finnish.	416
Austrian	29,760	Miscellaneous	3,132
Scotch	28,529		
Danish	25,355	Total	1,651,079

Subtracting this from the grand total of population, 2,007,695, the remainder, 356,580, indicates the number of native born Chicagoans. This, however, includes all descendants of foreign born parents after the first generation, all persons of mixed foreign and native parentage and some 35,000 colored. Should their number in turn be substracted, there would be a very small remainder, denoting the number of Americans in the limited sense of the word.

It may be added that the most recent estimates of Chicago's population vary from 2,049,185, the figures given by the health department, to 2,300,500, the more sanguine estimate based on the city directory.

Northwestern University

May 31, 1850, three clergymen, three lawyers, two businessmen and one physician, all members of the Methodist Church, met in the little office of Attorney Grant Goodrich, on Lake st., near La Salle st., in Chicago, to lay plans for the establishment in that city of a university, under the patronage of that church. At that time there was not one higher institution of learning in Chicago, and in the entire state of Illinois only a few, including McKendree, Illinois, Knox and Shurtleff colleges. At this meeting three committees were appointed, one to procure a charter for the projected institution, a second to enlist the interest and moral support of the various Methodist conferences, and a third to canvass the field for possible pecuniary support.

After three weeks the first named committee had the proposed charter drafted. Northwestern University was the name suggested, and the charter, being granted by the legislature, was signed by Governor French on Jan. 28, 1851. The first trustees were a number of Chicago residents, besides representatives of the Rock River, Wisconsin, Northern Indiana, Iowa, and Michigan conferences of the Methodist Episcopal Church.

These held their first meeting June 14th the same year and organized for the great task before them. A college was first determined upon, its president to serve as professor of philosophy. Other professors were suggested for the chairs of mathematics, natural sciences, and ancient and modern languages. Another resolution was passed to establish a preparatory department in the city and to purchase ground for the necessary buildings. A lot was purchased at the corner of La Salle and Jackson sts., at a cost of $9,000. September 22, 1852, the

Northwestern University Building, Chicago

board of trustees decided to erect a building accommodating three hundred students, and also appointed a committee to select a site for the proposed college building. Simultaneously, a request was issued to the members of all the aforesaid conferences that no other higher institutions of learning be established, but that all energies be concentrated upon this one, to the end that the university plan might be realized. At this time, also, the board decided to petition the legislature for authority to establish branch preparatory schools in various parts of the Northwest and to merge already existing schools with the proposed university.

The decision to erect a building in Chicago for the preparatory school was never carried out. The ground purchased for that purpose is now occupied by the Illinois Trust and Savings Bank which pays a large rental to the Northwestern University. At a meeting of the trustees June 23, 1853, Dr. Clark T. Hinman was unanimously elected its first president. Being a man of unusual energy, he at once took up the work with great vigor. A plan to raise funds through the sale of scholarships was inaugurated. These scholarships were of different kinds. One kind was a permanent scholarship of one hundred dollars, entitling the holder, his son, or grandson, to free tuition at the institution for a fixed term. Another form was the transferable scholarship, which could be bought and sold, always entitling its holder to the privileges therein set down. The one hundred dollar scholarship entitled the holder to $500 in tuition, while one quoted at fifty dollars guaranteed $200 in tuition. One-half of the income from scholarships was to be used for paying teachers' salaries, the other half to go to a fund for the purchase of a tract of land, not exceeding 1,200 acres, partly to be used as a site for the university buildings, partly to be sold in lots for the benefit of the building fund. Dr. Hinman filled his gripsack with scholarship certificates and started out to peddle them among the people. So great was his power of persuasion and such the enthu-

Northwestern University Medical School, Chicago

siasm for the prospective university that he succeeded in disposing of $64,600 worth of scholarships in Chicago and elsewhere in a very short time. In the meantime, other persons raised $37,000 in the same manner.

The committee appointed to select a site recommended the purchase from John H. Foster of a tract of 280 acres situated on the lake shore eleven miles north of the city hall. The price asked was $25,000, one thousand to be paid in cash and the balance in partial payments during the next ten years. The offer was accepted and the deal closed in August, 1853. The following October the trustees offered for sale thirteen acres of this tract at a price of $200 per acre. February 3, 1854, the site of the projected university was named Evanston, in honor of John Evans, M. D., then president of the university corporation. Soon after, other portions of the tract were platted and put on the real estate market.

One Eliza Garrett had founded a Methodist theological seminary called the Garrett Biblical Institute. Upon invitation extended in February, 1854, by the university trustees, this institution was removed to Evanston, where it occupies ground leased from the university. It has always been in close co-operation and has served as the theological department of the university, but is an independent institution financially and in other respects.

In June of the same year, the resources of the university, including real estate, notes and subscriptions, amounted to $281,915, while the liabilities stopped at $32,255.04.

When the board of trustees met in March, 1855, Dr. Hinman, the president of the university, was no more. His successful career in the service of the institution had been ended by death. His last effort had been to increase the fund accumulated by disposing of scholarships to $25,000 and the building fund to $100,000, and if death had not claimed him, he doubtless would have attained the goal. Meanwhile, one build-

Northwestern University—University Hall,
Evanston

ing had been erected, being a wooden structure, with suites of rooms for six professors, a chapel, a small museum, meeting halls for several literary societies, and a few student's rooms in the attic.

In this building, the college department of the university began work November 5th of that year. It was a modest beginning: only two teachers and a small group of students. A year later, in 1856, R. S. Foster, D. D., was elected president at a salary of $2,000 per year. At his suggestion, the board proceeded to plan permanent university halls and a library building.

The same year (1856) steps were taken to incorporate the Garrett Biblical Institute and the Rush Medical College in Chicago with the university in order that they might issue diplomas. A girl's school, the Northwestern Female College, had also been founded in Evanston, but the similarity between its name and that of the university caused the latter so much annoyance that the board requested the girl's seminary to change its corporate name. The request was not granted, the institute continuing under that name and later under the name of Evanston College for Ladies until 1873, when it was absorbed by the university. The proposed absorption of Rush Medical College did not materialize.

In 1857 the board made arrangements to establish a department of law, a preparatory department and a chair of science. At this time

Northwestern University—Orrington Lunt Library, Evanston

the library contained 2,000 volumes, and a museum of natural history had been established. In April, 1859, the proposed law school began its sessions, not, however, as a part of the Northwestern University, but of the old University of Chicago. In June of the same year the college department held its first graduation.

The following year Dr. Foster resigned the presidency. Dr. Erastus O. Haven, who was chosen his successor, declined the position.

During the Civil War, the activity of the new university was greatly impeded, several of its professors and many of its students enrolling in the Union army.

Through wise administration, the university, during this same period, freed itself of debt, whereupon the board devoted all its energies to the erection of necessary buildings. The first of these was a dormitory. In 1865, the sum of $25,000 was set aside for the erection of a main building to cost, when completed, $100,000. This building, called University Hall, was begun in 1866 and completed in three years.

Charles H. Fowler was called to the presidency in 1866, but resigned the following year before entering upon his duties.

The university now comprised a divinity school, a college and an academic department, and next was added a medical school in the following manner. Since 1859 there had existed in Chicago a medical institution, connected with the Lind (now Lake Forest) University. In 1864, this connection was severed, and the school became independent,

Northwestern University—Fayerweather Hall of Science, Evanston

under the name of the Chicago Medical College. This same school in 1869 was merged with the Northwestern University, but retained its name until 1891, when it was changed to the Northwestern University Medical School. This branch of the university occupies buildings specially erected for that purpose at Dearborn street, between 24th and 25th streets, in Chicago, in close proximity to the Wesley, the Mercy and the St. Luke's hospitals, where its students obtain their clinical training.

The same year that the medical school was incorporated with the university, the library received a valuable addition in the form of a collection of 20,000 volumes, purchased for the institution by one Luther Greenleaf. That year also, Erastus O. Haven was a second time called to the president's chair, which he occupied till 1872, when he was succeeded by the aforesaid Charles H. Fowler, who served with great credit for four years.

The aforesaid school of law also became a department of the Northwestern University in 1873 and then assumed the name of Union College of Law. It continued in connection with both universities until 1886, when it became an independent institution. In 1891, it was reorganized and again became a part of the Northwestern University, being named Northwestern University Law School.

In 1881 Joseph Cummings, senior of the Methodist Episcopal university professors and for many years president of the Wesleyan University, was made the head of the Northwestern. During a period

Northwestern University—Dearborn Observatory, Evanston

of ten years, he filled this responsible position, gaining, meanwhile, the highest respect of teachers and students alike. During his presidency, in 1886, the Illinois College of Pharmacy, just established, was made a part of the university. In 1891 its name was changed to the Northwestern University School of Pharmacy. The Dental School, established in 1887, three years later was added to the university. This department in 1896 absorbed a similar school, the American Dental College.

A donation of $25,000 by James B. Hobbs in 1888 enabled the university to erect the Dearborn Observatory, where the valuable instruments of the old observatory of the same name, located in Chicago, were moved and set up.

After the demise of Dr. Cummings, Dr. Henry Wade Rogers was elected his successor in 1890. He also served for ten years, and like his predecessor, accomplished much useful work for the institution. During his term of office, in 1891, the Woman's Medical College, connected with the Chicago Hospital for Women and Children, was added; this department, however, was discontinued in 1902 on account of the great expense to the university.

In 1893, the Orrington Lunt Library, an imposing structure, was erected, with funds raised by the platting and sale of 157 acres of land near Wilmette, donated to the university in 1865 by Orrington Lunt, one of its founders. A musical school was established in 1895, and two years later a building was erected for its special use.

In the summer of 1899, Dr. Rogers resigned the presidency. He was succeeded in 1902 by Dr. Edmund James, formerly a member of the faculties of the Universities of Pennsylvania and Chicago. This election was satisfactory to all the friends of the university, who knew Dr. James as a man of erudition and power, of whom much energetic work might be expected. Dr. James, in 1904, accepted the presidency of the University of Illinois, the next choice for president being Dr. Abram W. Harris, who entered upon his duties in July, 1906. Dr. Harris was born and educated in Philadelphia, studied at the Wesleyan University at Middletown, Conn., and in the Universities of Munich and Berlin. President Harris organized for the Department of Agriculture the Bureau of Experiment Stations. He spent some years in teaching and in 1892 was called to the presidency of the Maine State College. Under his direction it expanded and became the University of Maine. In 1901 he resigned to become the Director of the Jacob Tome Institute at Port Dupont, Md., which in five years assumed a high place among secondary schools.

One of the greatest acquisitions of property of the Northwestern University was the purchase in 1901 of the old Tremont hotel building, located at the corner of Dearborn and Lake sts., in Chicago. For this property the institution paid half a million dollars and expended an additional $275,000 for changes and repairs. This structure, known as the Northwestern University Building, now contains the Law school, the Dental school and the school of Pharmacy. In 1907 the university property was valued at $9,034,212, and the current expenditures for educational purposes alone in 1906 amounted to $606,189.

From its college department about 2,000 students have been graduated, from the medical 2,200, from the woman's medical school 559, from the law school 1,800, from the school of pharmacy 1,500, from the dental school 1,600, and from the school of music 300, making a total of 10,000 graduates.

During the year 1905-6 the total number of students attending the university was 3,863.

The University of Chicago

This institution, planned, as it is, on a large scale, has a history dating back to the fifties. Stephen A. Douglas, the renowned statesman, whose home was in Chicago, in 1854 offered to donate ten acres of ground at the southern limits of the city as a site for an institution of learning, on condition that a building costing $100,000 would be erected for this purpose within a specified time. The cornerstone of the future university building was laid July 4, 1857, but the general business depression then prevailing caused a long delay in completing the building. The liberal donor, therefore, granted additional time, but even this did not hurry the work, and finally he concluded to donate the site without any conditions.

Under the name of the Douglas University and with Rev. John C. Burroughs as president, the university was opened in 1858. According to the plan, it was to comprise a preparatory, a college, a law and a theological department. The university was started under the auspices of the Baptist denomination. The law department was added the following year.

The theological department was not added until the following decade. Its early history reads as follows:

At a meeting of Baptists in Chicago in 1860 a society, called the Theological Society of the Northwest, was formed. This was followed by the organization of another society, termed the Baptist Theological Union, which was incorporated Aug. 27th of that year. February 16, 1865, it was granted a charter to found and maintain a theological seminary. A beginning was made the same year, when Rev. N. Colver, D. D., began giving theological instruction to a limited number of students. The following year this instruction was given at the university, where Prof. J. C. C. Clarke was made assistant instructor in theology. These arrangements were merely temporary. The theological department, however, soon was permanently organized, for in 1866 two professors of theology were called, followed, one year later, by a third, whereupon the regular theological department was opened in the fall of 1867. Two years later it was provided with its own building, located at the corner of Rhodes ave. and 34th st. This building, costing $60,000, had accommodations for sixty students, besides the lecture halls. The department, having no permanent funds to draw on, was maintained by private contributions. During the first five years the Baptist Union Theological Seminary, as it was called, was attended by 97 students, of whom 37 were graduated.

During the seventies, the school was on the verge of collapse. The great fire of 1871 made it impossible for its friends to contribute as generously as before, and the second fire in 1874 still further demoralized it financially. The trustees were forced to look about for another location. One was found in Morgan Park, where the Blue Island Land and Building Company in 1876 donated to the seminary fifty acres of ground and a large brick building, into which the seminary moved in the fall of 1877.

During this decade a Scandinavian department was added to the seminary, designed to equip pastors for the Scandinavian Baptist congregations in America. The history of this department will be told in

The University of Chicago—Across the Campus

a succeeding chapter on educational institutions of the Swedes of Illinois.

Now the seminary owned its own site and its own building, had a faculty and students, but still funds were lacking. Up to this time all efforts at establishing endowments had failed. The trustees were driven to extremes in their efforts to provide the requisite means for its support from year to year. They had to draw continually upon the liberality of the congregations. Evidently, this could not go on indefinitely. The seminary must have permanent funds or cease to exist. A wealthy Chicagoan, E. Nelson Blake, at this juncture came to the assistance of the trustees by donating to the institution the sum of $30,000. With great exertions, they succeeded in raising $70,000 from other sources, thus creating an endowment of $100,000. But this proved inadequate, and an equal amount had to be raised in order to continue the work of the institution with any degree of success. Toward this amount John D. Rockefeller, the oil magnate, contributed $40,000 and other persons $11,000, whereupon the subscription work was at a standstill for a long period, threatening failure. Finally, after nearly ten years' effort, the second one hundred thousand dollar fund was completed.

Still the requirements of the institution were not fully met. New buildings were needed. The building donated by the land company had up to this time housed every department of the institution, containing, as it did, library, chapel, lecture hall, students' rooms and dining hall. Owing to the cramped quarters, the library, which then contained 25,000 volumes, was partly arranged on shelves along the walls of the lecture hall, partly packed down in boxes and thus inaccessible for use. For the same reason only about half of the students could be housed at the seminary. In 1886 a call was issued with a request for $50,000 to be used partly for the erection of a building containing lecture halls and chapel, partly for a library building. Mr. Rockefeller at once donated $10,000, and promised $10,000 more, provided the remaining $30,000 were raised before May 1, 1887. The condition was successfully met, and the same year the first named building was erected at a cost of $30,000. It was named Blake Hall, in honor of the aforesaid E. Nelson Blake, who had given one-third of the required sum. Later the library building was also erected.

During all these years the inner development of the institution kept pace with its outward progress. The faculty was reinforced time and again and the number of students increased until in 1891-92 it reached nearly 200. During the twenty-five years of its existence, the seminary had graduated several hundred Baptist ministers, of whom a large number had gone to distant lands, while the remainder were scattered throughout the Union. In the new library building the books were systematically arranged and catalogued, available for use by students and teachers.

The Baptist Union Seminary was, as stated, a part of the Douglas University, or, as it was soon called, the University of Chicago. Each had its own administration, and if the finances of the seminary were in a bad way, those of the university were still worse. While the former gradually improved, the latter deteriorated year by year, until the university found itself in a precarious position. In 1885 its mortgages amounted to $320,000, and the board could no longer pay the interest accruing and make payments as they fell due. In these straits the board turned to the Baptist clergymen of Chicago for advice, and the matter was taken up at one of the weekly meetings, held Feb. 8, 1886. President George W. Northrop of the theological seminary then expressed as his opinion that any attempt to maintain the university would prove futile. Better, then, rent a few rooms, retain the faculty, and look about for a suitable president. Further, the sum of $10,000 ought to be raised annually for three years to defray current expenses, while efforts were made to raise a fund of $250,000. The financial difficulties experienced by the board would, in his opinion, urge well-to-do Baptists to come to the rescue of the institution with liberal donations, so that within ten years an excellent institution might be firmly established. Dr. Thomas W. Goodspeed spoke to the same purport. He recommended that ground be purchased ten miles south of the southern limits of the city, a new charter procured and a new board of regents elected. Now, said he, is the time to act.

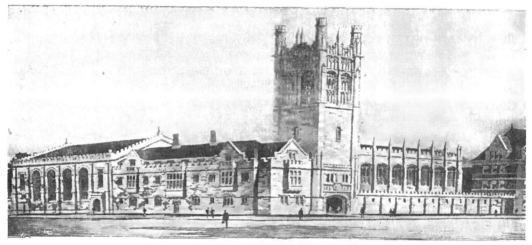

The University of Chicago—The Tower Group

After a lengthy discussion those present gave formal expression to the prevailing opinion to the effect that it was practically impossible to raise the funds wherewith to lift the mortgages on the university property, and recommended that a committee of fifteen, appointed the previous year at the educational convention held in Farwell Hall, Chicago, be empowered to plan a new university. The result of these resolutions was the conveyance of the university property to the mortgagees, the Mutual Union Life Insurance Company, the same year and the closing of the university.

Thus the old University of Chicago disappeared after an existence of 29 years of pecuniary embarrassment. Its patrons, however, desired that it be supplanted by a new institution, and this view was shared by prominent Baptists in other parts of the country. During the next two years the project was discussed extensively at meetings and through correspondence. The first move towards realizing the plan was made in May, 1888, when a society, called the American Baptist Education Society, was organized in Washington, D. C., for the purpose of establishing a college in Chicago—a university they dared not think of—and to raise funds for the support of Baptist institutions of learning in other parts of the country.

These initiative steps were followed with great interest by Mr. Rockefeller, who, as already shown, had contributed to the maintenance of the theological school. He conferred with Professor Willam R. Harper, of Yale University, a man who then already had attained a reputation as a scholar and a man of exceptional executive ability. These two men soon agreed that the Baptist Church should again take up its educational work in Chicago and on an enlarged scale. Mr. Rockefeller declared his willingness to contribute several hundred thousand dollars to such an institution.

In December, 1888, the preliminary work had advanced to a stage, where the plan could be laid before the directors of the American Baptist Education Society. The plans were approved, and they pledged their hearty support in carrying the enterprise forward, instructing their secretary, Rev. Fred T. Gates, to do everything in his power to insure its success. Early the following year Rev. Gates opened negotiations with Mr. Rockefeller, and, after numerous conferences between them, a committee of nine was appointed to draft a plan for the new institution, propose a site, estimate the amount of money required for safeguarding the enterprise financially, and to learn to what extent the support of the Education Society might be counted upon. Prof. Harper was the first man appointed on that committee.

After thorough inquiries this committee submitted a full report on the basis of which the Education Society, at its annual meeting in Boston, in May, 1889, passed a formal resolution to establish the proposed college in Chicago. Immediately, a letter from Mr. Rockefeller was read, wherein he pledged himself to give $600,000 as a fund for the institution, on condition that others contributed $400,000, before June 1, 1890, to be used for the purchase of a site and the erection of buildings. Shortly after this meeting, another one was held in Chicago, attended by fifteen Baptist clergymen, and fifty-five businessmen. At this meeting a college committee of thirty-six members was chosen to issue a call for subscriptions toward the $400,000 fund. Before this meeting was adjourned, one quarter of the amount required had been subscribed by those in attendance.

In January, 1890, Mr. Marshall Field, the Chicago millionaire merchant, announced his willingness to donate a tract of land, situated between Washington and Jackson parks, to the proposed college, provided the conditions set up by Mr. Rockefeller were met. At the meeting of the board of the Education Society in the spring of that year it was announced that the aggregate sum of $402,000 had been subscribed, books and scientific apparatus valued at $15,000 promised, and that subscriptions were still coming in at the rate of $1,000 a day.

These numerous and generous responses to the call for funds made it clear to the committee that the previous plan to establish a college, which was to be gradually enlarged to a university, had to be abandoned and the institution laid out on university lines from the start. This line of action was subsequently followed. To begin with, ground was purchased adjoining the tract comprising one and one-half blocks, donated by Mr. Field. The Education Society board for the sum of $132,000 bought of Mr. Field an equal tract, making a total of 20 acres,

The University of Chicago—The Walker Museum

bounded on the north and south by 56th and 59th streets and on the east and west by Greenwood and Ellis avenues. Shortly afterwards, the block located farthest north was traded for one bounded by 57th and 58th streets, and Greenwood and Lexington avenues, whereupon still another block was purchased, completing a quadrangle two blocks square in a beautiful and rapidly developing part of the city. A better location for a university would be difficult to find.

In order to prevent possible complications, arising from the fact that an institution named the University of Chicago had existed before, the directors of that institution met June 14, 1890, and formally authorized the use of that name for the new university. At another meeting September 8th the same board decided to call their institution The Old University of Chicago and to turn over all its books and records to the new university corporation. This was done partly to distinguish the graduates of the old institution, partly to enable them, if they so desired, to be recognized as graduates of the new university.

These and other preliminaries having been disposed of, the new university was chartered September 10, 1890, under the name of the University of Chicago, the incorporators being John D. Rockefeller, E. Nelson Blake, Marshall Field, Francis E. Hinckley, Fred T. Gates, and Thomas W. Goodspeed. The charter stipulated that the university regents should be twenty-one in number, two-thirds, as also the president, to be members of the Baptist Church. On the contrary, church affiliations were to play no part in the selection of professors and instructors.

Scarcely had the institution been incorporated when Mr. Rockefeller, on the 16th of September, made an additional donation of one million dollars, one of the conditions being that the Baptist Union Theological Seminary should be moved from Morgan Park to the university grounds, be made its theological department, and furnished with a special building. These terms were gratefully accepted by the Baptist Theological Union.

At their second meeting, held September 18th, the trustees elected as president of the university Dr. W. R. Harper, who after six months accepted the call and shaped the destinies of this great university with superior energy and ability.

The working plan of the university had already been prepared and submitted to the boards of more than fifty different universities and colleges for approval. Having been thus criticised, the plan was made public Jan. 1, 1891. According to this plan, the work of the institution was to be arranged under the following three heads, the university proper, the university extension work and the university publication work.

The first-named department was to comprise the following subdivisions: (a) Academies, or preparatory departments, the first to be established at Morgan Park and other branch institutions to be either formed from existing schools or erected anew, as opportunity offered; (b) Colleges, as follows, (1) the College of Liberal Arts, with a course leading to the degree of Bachelor of Arts, (2) the College of Science, leading to the degree of Bachelor of Science, (3) the College of Literature, giving also the degree of Bachelor of Science, (4) the College of Practical Arts, with comprehensive courses in practical subjects, leading to the degree of Bachelor of Science; (c) affiliated colleges, the nature of whose relations to the university was to be determined by the conditions in each individual case; (d) schools, as follows: (1) The Graduate School, to comprise all non-professional post-graduate work, (2) the Divinity School, with the customary theological courses, (3) the Law School, (4) the Medical School, (5) the School of Engineering, (6) the School of Pedagogy, (7) the School of Fine Arts, (8) the School of Music. The two first-named were to be established at once, the remaining six in due order, as financial conditions would permit.

The university extension work was to comprise, (a) regular courses of lectures, to be given in Chicago and elsewhere, according to the best plans for university extension; (b) evening courses in college and university subjects in and outside of Chicago; (c) correspondence courses in college and university subjects for students all over the country; (d) special courses in biblical subjects, studied from the original texts and translations; (e) library extension.

The university publication work was to embrace, (a) university bulletins, catalogues and other official documents; (b) special newspapers, journals and reviews of a scientific nature, written and edited by instructors in the various departments: (c) books written and edited by instructors of the university; (d) collection by exchange of newspapers, journals and reviews, similar to those published; (e) purchase of books and disposal of same to students, professors and to the university library.

In connection herewith the inner organization of the institution in the matter of faculties, officers, the division of the school year, etc., was mapped out. In these respects the University of Chicago was to differ materially from other universities and colleges in the United States. For instance, while most of these divide the scholastic year into three terms, viz., the fall, the winter and the spring term, with a long vacation following the latter, its year was to be divided into quarters, beginning with the first day of July, October, January and April, respectively, each quarter to comprise twelve weeks, with intervals of one week's vacation. In order to accommodate those desiring to spend a still shorter period at the university each quarter was subdivided into two terms of six weeks.

The advantages of this new arrangement were apparent. In the first place the waste of time under the old system was precluded; in the second, it enabled students to attend one or two quarters and spend the remainder of the year in some profitable occupation, earning the means to continue their studies; in the third, it was made possible to prepare for examinations in shorter time; in the fourth, the courses of instruction could be arranged more conveniently for the professors and instructors. While their term of service was nine months out of the year, they might be granted permission, at any time suiting their purpose, to pursue special studies or take a vacation for their health. By serving longer than the prescribed periods, they might earn either longer vacations or an extra income.

Another result of this division of the university calendar was the abolition of classes and their names, such as Freshman, Sophomore, Junior and Senior, and with that the class spirit. The result of the quarter system was that a student might begin his studies any time of

The University of Chicago—The Women's Dormitories

the year and take his examinations at the end of any of the four quarters.

The University of Chicago held its first convocation October 1, 1892. An imposing corps of professors and instructors had already been selected, comprising men who had served at American and European universities, and no less than five hundred students had then been enrolled. Adding to this the fact that the financial position of the institution had been further strengthened by new donations by Mr. Rockefeller and others, it will appear that the future of the new university was exceptionally bright. The rich promises given at the start have been most handsomely realized.

The development of the University of Chicago has been phenomenal in every respect, and at its present pace the university inspires the confidence that it will in a short time become one of the best organized and most largely attended universities in the world. A few figures may be quoted as showing most clearly the rapid progress already made during the first decade of its existence. The enrollment increased during the decade of 1892-02 from 698 to 4,450 and the endowment funds during the same period from $1,539,561 to $9,165,126, the value of the real estate, building, etc., from $1,618,778 to $6,000,000 and the total value of all the property of the university to $15,128,375; the number of professors and instructors grew from 135 to 323, and the current annual expenditures from $109,496 to $944,348.

This magnificent material growth was made possible by continued donations, aggregating over $18,000,000 for the same period. The principal donor is Mr. Rockefeller, whose gifts during this same decade amounted to more than $10,000,000. Since then he has donated millions more. Other wealthy men and women, especially Chicagoans, have contributed munificently to the university, such as, Miss Helen Culver, who gave one million to the department of biology; Mrs. Emmons Blaine, who donated over a million to the School of Education for the training of expert teachers; Martin A. Ryerson, who founded the Ryerson Physical Laboratory in memory of his father and gave large sums towards its equipment; Sydney A. Kent, who founded the Kent Chemical Laboratory; Charles T. Yerkes, who gave to the university the world's largest telescope and besides contributed liberally toward the equipment of the university observatory at Lake Geneva, Wis., which bears the donor's name; Marshall Field, who made large donations to the general funds; Silas B. Cobb, founder of Cobb Hall; George C. Walker, who donated the Walker Museum and has shown his generosity in other ways; Mrs. Charles Hitchcock, who erected the dormitory for boys as a memorial to her husband, Mr. Charles N. Hitchcock; Mrs. Caroline E. Haskell, who donated a building and established a lectureship in memory of her husband, Mr. Frederick Haskell, Mrs. Elizabeth G. Kelly, who founded Kelly and Green halls for female students; Mrs. Mary Beecher, Mrs. Henrietta Snell and Mrs. Nancy S. Foster, who have each had university halls erected, bearing their names; Adolphus C. Bartlett, who equipped the Bartlett Gymnasium in memory of his son, Frank Dickinson Bartlett; Leon Mandel, who founded the Assembly Hall; the William B. Ogden estate, which has donated property, the income from which was used in founding the Ogden Graduate School of Science; John J. Mitchell and Charles L. Hutchinson, who have also remembered the university with substantial donations.

The university buildings in 1902 numbered 20 and the grounds comprised 75 acres in Chicago and 65 acres at Williams Bay, Wisconsin.

By an agreement between the directors of the Rush Medical College, established in Chicago in 1837, and the regents of the University of Chicago, that renowned medical institution in April, 1901, became identified with the university to the extent that the medical students during the first two years of the course pursued their studies at the university proper. A year later the directors of the medical school proposed a complete merger which, however, has not yet been effected, owing chiefly to economic obstacles.

On March 11, 1902, the university regents appropriated $50,000 towards the purchase of a law library and the establishment of the law school already decided upon. Other professional and technical schools are to be established as the exigencies will permit.

The splendid progress made by this university is proof positive of the wisdom and care with which the broad and practical plans were mapped out.

The total attendance for the year ending July 1, 1907, compiled on the basis of three quarters or nine months to the school year, was 5,070. Of these 2,629 were men and 2,441 women. Since 1893 the number of grauates has been 4,131.

On Jan. 10, 1906, the university suffered an incalculable loss in the death of President William Rainey Harper, who had served through fourteen and one-half years. On the death of Harper, Harry Pratt Judson was appointed acting president of the university, and on Feb. 20, 1907, he was elected to the presidency. Judson prepared at Williams College, from which he graduated in 1870 and received the degree of A. M. in 1883; was principal of the high school in Troy, N. Y.; professor at the University of Minnesota 1885-92; received the degree of LL. D. from his alma mater 1893, and has the same title from the Queen's University, Ontario, the State University of Iowa and the Washington University, St. Louis; was co-editor of the "American Historical Review" 1895-1902; became professor of political science and head dean of the colleges of the University of Chicago 1892; after two years he was made head of the department of political science and dean of the faculties of arts, literature and science, a position held until 1907, when elected president of the university.

The World's Fair at Chicago

As the four hundreth anniversary of the discovery of America by Columbus drew near, suggestions were made from various directions that the event be celebrated by means of a world's exposition, just as in 1876 the one hundreth anniversary of the independence of the United States was celebrated. The first step toward the 400th anniversary celebration was taken in November, 1885, when the directors of the Chicago Inter-States Exposition Company passed a resolution declaring in favor of such a plan. The second step was taken July 6th of the following year, when the Iroquois Club of Chicago invited six other clubs of the city to co-operate with it in arranging for "an international celebration, in Chicago, of the four hundreth anniversary of the discovery of America by Columbus." With that the matter rested for some time.

The newspapers of the country, however, began to discuss the project and cast about for the most suitable location for a new world's exposition, Washington, New York, Chicago, and St. Louis being strenuously advocated by their respective papers. Then the citizens of Chicago no longer confined themselves to a discussion in the abstract, but took action long before the other three proposed cities had closed

World's Fair—Administration Building

the debate. Thus Chicago again went on record as a most energetic and progressive community.

After having advised with men of prominence, such as J. W. Scott, the editor of the "Chicago Herald," Thomas B. Bryan, the lawyer and politician, and others, Mayor Dewitt C. Cregier on July 22, 1889, laid the matter before the city council, which at once requested the mayor to appoint a committee of one hundred (later increased to 250) citizens to further the exposition project among the people and hold forth the advantages of Chicago for that purpose. Pursuant to this resolution, a large meeting was held August 1st, at which a set of resolutions, framed by Thomas B. Bryan, were adopted and subsequently published throughout the United States. An executive committee also was appointed, consisting of 51 persons, to take active charge of the preliminary preparations for the exposition. Its first act was to form an exposition company with a capital stock of $5,000,000 in shares of $10 each. So rapid was the progress made that the company, whose corporate name was The World's Exposition of 1892, was legally incorporated on the 14th of the same month, and at once proceeded to sell stock.

The competition among the four cities bidding for the exposition now grew extremely brisk. From New York and Washington it was urged that Chicago was situated entirely too far inland to attract foreign participation. These and other objections were successfully combated by the Chicago committee, which was ably assisted by the influential men of Illinois and neighboring states.

On Jan. 12, 1890, the committees of the four cities had a hearing in Washington before a special committee appointed by the senate. New York was represented by more than one hundred of its foremost citizens, whose combined wealth aggregated several hundred millions, and who lost no opportunity to press the claims of their city. But the Chicago representatives proved conclusively that their city had a greater volume of trade in portion to its population than New York and had a far more suitable site to offer.

While congress had the matter under consideration its decision was awaited with the greatest interest. Along towards spring the question was passed on, and Chicago was the choice.

On April 25, 1890, President Harrison signed the congressional act by which the quadri-centennial exposition was located at Chicago. According to the terms of said act, the president named eight commissioners-at-large together with two commissioners and two alternates from each state and territory in the Union and the District of Columbia. This commission chose as Director-General of the exposition Col. George R. Davis of Chicago, as President ex-senator Thomas W. Palmer of Michigan, and as Secretary John T. Dickinson of Texas. The commission delegated part of its authority to a Board of Reference and Control, half of its members being appointed by the exposition company.

Pending the act of congress, stock had been liberally subscribed, so that at the time congress took action the number of stockholders had reached about 30,000. These were called to meet in Battery D, on April 10th, when the organization was completed by the election of forty-five directors, picked from among the wealthiest citizens. Two days later the board of directors met at the Sherman House and chose a committee on finance and a committee to draft by-laws. At the next meeting April 30th, Lyman J. Gage was elected president of the board, Thomas B. Bryan first and Potter Palmer second vice-president. On May 6th the board elected William J. Ackerman auditor and Anthony·

F. Seeberger treasurer, and finally on July 11th Benjamin Butterworth secretary. The president of the board appointed a number of auxiliary committees to have charge of various departments of work.

June 12th the stockholders at an extra meeting changed the name to The World's Columbian Exposition Company, in accordance with the congressional act, and also decided to increase the capital stock from $5,000,000 to $10,000,000, to comply with another condition named by congress, that the time and place of the exposition should be fixed, the grounds and buildings assured and ten million dollars subscribed

World's Fair—Government Building

for the enterprise before the President of the United States would issue to foreign nations the official invitation to take part.

Besides these two boards there was still another, the Board of Lady Managers, consisting of two lady representatives and alternates from each state and territory and nine for the city of Chicago. Mrs. Potter Palmer of Chicago, a woman of prominence no less for her high intellectual attainments than for her great wealth and social position, was chosen as its president. To this board was entrusted the management of everything pertaining to the participation of women in the exposition and to the woman's department of exhibits.

In the matter of choosing a site a diversity of opinions arose. Some of the directors suggested Jackson Park, in the southern part of the city, while others favored a more central location. The former opinion prevailed, and building operations were begun as soon as a construction department had been formed, with Daniel H. Burnham as chief, John W. Root as architect, Abram Gottlieb as engineer, and the firm of Olmstead & Co. as landscape architects. In order to have the buildings constructed with a view to artistic beauty as well as practical uses, a board of consulting architects was picked from among the most skillful men of the craft in Chicago. Besides, architects from New York, Boston, and other cities were called in to assist in making the drawings. The expenditures for the grading of the site and the erection of the buildings were estimated at $16,075,453.

World's Fair—Illinois Building

Ground was broken for the exposition on Feb. 11, 1891. Swamps were drained, depressions filled, old lagoons and ponds dredged and new ones scooped out, walks and drives constructed and extensive improvements in the landscape planned. Piles were driven, foundations were laid, and soon the "White City" began to rise in splendor. In spite of changes that had to be made in the plans from time to time, the work progressed without interruption, thanks to efficient management both of the finances and the actual operations.

It was not an easy matter to raise the necessary ten millions, but the leaders of the enterprise were equal to the task. Through their influence, the state legislature was prevailed upon to grant Chicago the privilege of issuing bonds to the amount of five millions in order to invest said amount in exposition stock. But besides this amount and the aggregate amount subscribed by individuals, six or seven millions were still needed. Numerous plans to raise money were devised, but none was found altogether satisfactory. Finally, it was proposed to issue souvenir coins to be sold at an advanced price as a means of raising the additional amount required. The plan was laid before congress, which with some reluctance resolved that souvenir half dollars should be struck to the amount of $2,500,000 and sold at one dollar each, thus netting the exposition $5,000,000. Furthermore, the

World's Fair—Agricultural Building

exposition company issued bonds to the amount of $5,000,000 more, payable Jan. 1, 1894.

Neither plan brought the desired results, and new exertions were made. To the railway companies were sold $850,000 worth of bonds and several Chicago banks made loans to the exposition company taking unsold souvenir coins as security.

At the annual meeting in April, 1891, Lyman J. Gage resigned the presidency and was succeeded by William J. Baker.

Despite all preparations, there prevailed in the East and especially throughout Europe a lack of confidence in Chicago's ability to manage a universal exposition. The notion was general that Chicago was located on the outskirts of civilization and therefore incapable of producing a world's fair such as had been seen in London, Paris and Vienna. The exposition management resolved to overcome this prejudice and to that end appointed a special commission to visit the nations

World's Fair—Art Palace, Now Field's Museum

of northern Europe and their governments. This commission, consisting of five members, started for Europe in July, 1891, and performed its arduous work systematically and with marked success. As a result of its efforts, coupled with those of the government in the same direction, favorable responses to the invitation extended to the nations were received from a great number of governments and private corporations. To represent the exposition in a similar manner in southern Europe, Thomas B. Bryan and Harlow N. Higinbotham were appointed. The first gained an audience with the Pope himself and succeeded in gaining his co-operation and good will. The Holy Father with his own hand wrote a cordial endorsement of the enterprise, which

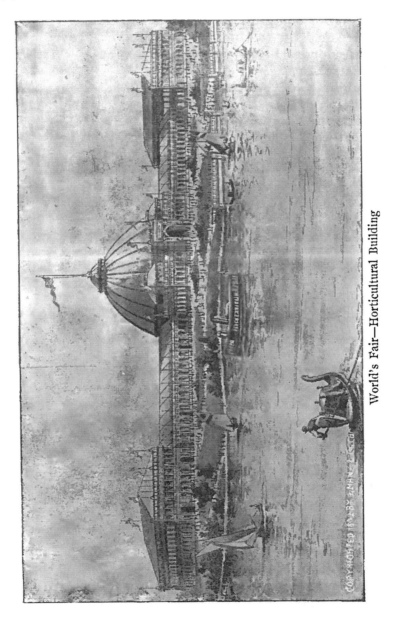

World's Fair—Horticultural Building

was subsequently translated into a number of languages and published far and wide. Its reassuming effect on the Catholic nations was unquestionable. The efforts of the two commissioners were crowned with success throughout. In recognition of his services, Mr. Higinbotham, upon his return to Chicago in February, 1892, was chosen vice-president of the exposition.

While this work was in progress abroad the exposition buildings were rapidly nearing completion and the time for the opening of the fair was not far off. Up to this time the board of directors and the board of commissioners had borne the entire responsibility for the financial administration. The number of members being equal in the two boards, a tie might easily result in important decisions. In order to preclude deadlocks and resultant delays a council of administration was created, consisting of members from both boards. As representatives of the directors were chosen Harlow N. Higinbotham and Charles H. Schwab and for the commissioners George G. Massey of Delaware and J. W. St. Clair of West Virginia. These elected Mr. Higinbotham their chairman, and he was about the same time chosen president of the exposition. This council had absolute authority to determine 'all questions of administrative policy, but were not empowered to pass appropriations beyond those made by the directors. One of the first acts of the council was to postpone the date of the dedication of the exposition from October 12th, the day fixed by congress, to October 21st. This was done partly because the city of New York had fixed on the former date for the holding of a grand naval review in commemoration of the 400th anniversary, partly from a desire to bring the celebration as near as possible to the date of the landing of Columbus on American soil.

The dedicatory exercises six months prior to the opening were held in order to publish to the world the extent of the preparation and the magnitude of the undertaking. The exercises opened with a salute of cannon at sunrise. In the forenoon the directors, commissioners, lady . managers and specially invited guests assembled in Michigan avenue, in front of the Auditorium hotel, where they formed in line, the parade passing, with flags flying and music playing, down the avenue and on to the World's Fair grounds. Here they were joined by Vice-President Levi P. Morton, representing the President of the United States, and President Thomas W. Palmer of the board of commissioners. In Washington Park 15,000 national troops from various points passed in review before the guests of honor, the procession then passing along Midway Plaisance to the entrance to the grounds. The place of assemblage was the gigantic Manufacturers' Building, where luncheon was served to 70,000 people. At the time set for the dedicatory ceremonies an immense mass of people crowded about the gateways to the exposition grounds, and at the command of President Higinbotham the gates were thrown open and the public given free admittance for that day.

The order of ceremonies was as follows: Columbian March, composed for the occasion by Prof. J. H. Paine of Cambridge, was rendered by the Columbian Orchestra and chorus. Following a prayer, offered by Bishop Fowler, an introductory address was made by

World's Fair—Fish and Fisheries Building

Director-General George R. Davis. Mayor Hempstead Washburne next welcomed Vice-President Morton and the foreign representatives, offering them the freedom of the city. Mrs. Sarah Le Moyne then read the World's Fair Ode, written by Miss Harriet Monroe, portions of the poem, set to music by George W. Chadwick, being subsequently rendered by the Columbian Chorus. Director of Works Daniel H. Burnham now presented the buildings to President Higinbotham and introduced to him the engineers, architects and artists who had constructed and decorated them. President Higinbotham responded, presenting to each of these a special medal in recognition of their work in behalf of the exposition. During this presentation the chorus rendered Mendelssohn's "To the Sons of Art."

Mrs. Potter Palmer, president of the Board of Lady Managers, then followed with an address on the work accomplished by that body, whereupon President Higinbotham presented the exposition buildings to President Palmer of the World's Columbian Exposition Commissioners, he in turn presenting them to Vice-President Morton, who dedicated them to their various uses. The Columbian Chorus sang the "Alleluiah Chorus" from Handel's Messiah; Col. Henry Watterson of Kentucky made an address, followed by another song, "The Star-Spangled Banner," by the chorus; another address was made by Mr. Chauncey M. Depew of New York, and the ceremonies were concluded with a prayer by Cardinal Gibbons of Baltimore, the singing of Beethoven's "In Praise of God" by the chorus and the benediction, pronounced by Rev. Henry C. McCook of Philadelphia. Immediately following the conclusion of the dedicatory ceremonies, the artillery post stationed in the park fired the national salute.

The opening of the World's Fair was set for May 1, 1893, and an enormous amount of work still remained to be accomplished during the intervening six months. Thanks to the energy and push of the directors almost all exterior work was finished in the time fixed. The arrangement of exhibits, however, required additional time, and the exposition, therefore, was not in proper order until the first of June.

The festivities in connection with the formal opening were held in that part of the grounds called the Court of Honor. Here gathered, in the forenoon of May 1st, the following guests of honor and officiating personages, namely, the Duke of Veragua, specially invited as the direct descendant of Columbus, together with his family; Grover Cleveland, President of the United States; Adlai Stevenson, Vice President of the United States; members of the cabinet, of the diplomatic corps and of congress; the three departments of the exposition management, namely, the Board of Directors, the Board of Commissioners and the Board of Lady Managers; foreign commissioners, members of the different state commissions and chiefs and other officials of the various exposition departments.

The opening of the exposition took place according to the following order of ceremonies: Music, Columbian March (John H. Paine), by the orchestra; prayer by Rev. W. H. Milburn of Washington, D. C.; poem, "the Prophecy," by W. A. Croffut of Washington; music, "Overture to Rienzi" (Wagner), by the orchestra; address by the Director-General of the exposition; address by the President of the United

World's Fair—Electricity Building

States; starting of the machinery in Machinery Hall, while Handel's "Alleluiah Chorus" was sung; official reception in the Manufacturers' Building, by President Cleveland and the World's Fair directors, of the foreign commissioners.

Immediately after the close of the President's address, the chief magistrate pressed the button of an electric line connecting with a great steam engine of 2,000 horse powers, starting the engine and this in turn bringing the fountains and cascades of the Court of Honor into play. At the same instant the flags of all the Fair buildings were unfurled to the breeze, and amid the roar of steam whistles throughout the city and harbor, the firing of cannon and the thundering huzzas of the sea of humanity assembled in the grounds, the Columbian Exposition was opened the the world. Chicago, Queen of the West, had reached the goal of her ambition: the World's Fair was an accomplished fact.

Before describing the further progress of the exposition and the manner in which the directors managed to carry the enormous financial burdens laid upon their shoulders, a comparison may properly be drawn between this and previous world's expositions with reference to area, number of exhibitors, and visitors, appropriations, etc. This is given in the following table:

Year.	Place.	No. of exhibitors.	No. of visitors.	Acres.	No. of days open.
1851	London	15,500	6,039,195	13.	144
1855	Paris	23,954	6,162,330	22.1	200
1862	London	28,653	6,225,000	25.6	171
1867	Paris	52,200	9,238,967	31.	217
1873	Vienna	42,584	7,254,687	56.5	186
1876	Philadelphia	60,000	9,910,966	236.	159
1878	Paris	40,366	16,032,725	100.	191
1889	Paris	55,000	28,149,353	173.	183
1893	Chicago		27,539,521	645.	183

The capacity of the various buildings of the Chicago exposition is shown in the following table:

Buildings.	Square feet.	Acres.
Administration	51,456	1.18
Agriculture	589,416	13.53
Art	261,073	5.99
Electricity	265,500	6.09
Fisheries	104,504	2.39
Government	155,896	3.57
Horticulture	237,956	5.46
Machinery	796,686	18.28
Manufactures	1,345,462	30.88
Mines	246,181	5.65
Transportation	704,066	16.16
Woman's	82,698	1.89
Minor	1,630,514	37.43
State	450,886	10.35
Foreign	135,663	3.11
Concessions (Midway Plaisance buildings, booths, etc.)	801,238	18.39
Miscellaneous	317,699	7.29
Total	8,176,894	187.69

Midway Plaisance was the name of the narrow stretch of open space extending from Jackson to Washington parks. This was at the disposal of the commissioners and was utilized for the extra attractions or side shows to the exposition. Here various semi- and uncivilized nations were assigned space for their exhibits and performances, showing the life and customs of various races. Great panoramas of natural sceneries from foreign lands were exhibited. Products and curios from every clime were sold, and in numerous variety theaters the plays and pastimes of the nations were more or less correctly presented. Also a great number of restaurants and cafés of various kinds were located there. One of the most original attractions of the Midway was the so-called Ferris Wheel, constructed by Engineer Ferris and named after him. It was the Chicago counterpart of the Eiffel Tower at the Paris Exposition of 1889. From the hanging cars of this gigantic wheel was afforded a charming birds-eye view of the White City and its environments.

Thirty-seven states of the Union had their own buildings at the Fair. The majority of these were a combination of exposition building for products of a state and meeting place for its citizens. Forty-seven foreign nations had made appropriations to the exposition and of these eighteen had their own buildings, besides being represented in one or more of the seventeen main departments. Exhibitors from no less than eighty-six countries were present.

Among exhibiting nations was the United Kingdom of Sweden and Norway, the Swedish riksdag having made an appropriation of 350,000 crowns for the purpose. A national pavilion of a distinct type, capped by an antiquated steeple, was built in Sweden, the material shipped over and the building reconstructed on its site at the exposition grounds. Portions of the Swedish exhibits were arranged in this pavilion, while the remainder were apportioned among the proper departments. The royal commissioner of the Swedish exhibit was Arthur Leffler, the secretary, Axel Welin. Tom Bergendal represented the Swedish Iron Institute, embracing fourteen industrial establishments, and a large number of manufacturers and institutions and organizations in Sweden had sent personal representatives to the exposition.

Besides the $2,500,000 appropriated by the United States in the form of souvenir coins, the national government set aside the amount needed for the erection of a splendid government building and $500,000 for a suitable exhibit therein. The total amount appropriated by the individual states was $6,120,000, Illinois alone expending $800,000. The total foreign appropriations were approximately $6,500,000. Private citizens of Chicago signed for shares $5,608,206, and the city of Chicago purchased shares for the sum of $5,000,000, raised by an issue of bonds.

In order to heighten the interest in the exposition a series of international congresses was arranged by a special board, established Oct. 30, 1890, as the World's Congress Auxiliary of the World's Columbian Exposition, headed by Charles Carroll Bonney, the originator of the idea. This work was divided into twenty departments, each of which was subdivided into various divisions, numbering altogether 224. The congresses held 1,283 sessions, making a total of 753 days. According to the printed announcements, there were 5,978 addresses and papers by 5,822 speakers and authors. The most noteworthy one was doubtless the Parliament of Religions, in which many prominent representatives of the principal religions of the world in addresses, treatises and discussions endeavored to show their relative positions.

Swedish Day at the World's Fair

A great number of festivals, special days set aside for various nationalities or occupations, memorial days, etc., furnished the additional events of the Fair. Among the national festivals, Swedish Day, July 20th, may be mentioned as one of the most successful and picturesque celebrations during the entire exposition.

Swedish Day at the World's Fair was a gala day for the Swedish nationality in Chicago. The celebration began early in the day with a street parade in the down-town district, participated in by 10,000 people, according to estimate. On the exposition grounds there was a second parade, followed by an afternoon concert at Festival Hall, exercises at the Swedish pavilion at sunset and a pyrotechnic display in the evening.

Early in the morning Swedish organizations of the north and west sides began to assemble on Chicago avenue. Marshalled by Dr. Sven Windrow and Mr. L. F. Hussander, they marched to Lake Front Park, to join the south side organizations and other participants. Forming in Michigan avenue, the parade wound its way through the city, on the following line of march: Michigan ave., Monroe st., State st., Lake st., Fifth ave., Madison st., Market st., Monroe st., Fifth ave., Jackson st., Wabash ave., Congress st., Michigan ave.

The parade, headed by Robert Lindblom as chief marshal, with N. N. Cronholm as adjutant, was made up of three divisions, in the following order: First division—platoon of police; band; American Union of Swedish Singers; distinguished guests and ladies in carriages. Second division—marshals; band; John Ericsson Legion, Select Knights of America; Belmont Legion of the same; First Swedish Uniformed Ranks, Knights of Pythias; Svea Society in carriages; Swedish Glee Club members in carriages; First Swedish Lodge of Odd Fellows; North Star Lodge, Knights of Honor; band; Svithiod Club members in carriages; Linnaeus Club members on horseback and in carriages; publishers and personnel of Swedish-American newspapers, "Svenska Ameri-kanaren," "Svenska Tribunen" and "Humoristen," in carriages; band; Gustaf Adolf Society; Court Vega Pleasure Club; Monitor Council, Royal Arcanum, in carriages; Nordenskjöld Lodge, Knights and Ladies of Honor; Götha Lodge of the same; Thor Society; Led-stjernan Lodge, Sons of Temperance; Court Stockholm, Independent Order of Foresters; band; Independent Order of Vikings. Third division—marshals; band; Svenska Gardet, preceded by their band; Uniformed Ranks, Knights of Pythias, South Chicago; Swedish Gym-

World's Fair—Swedish Building

nastic and Fencing Club; ladies in Swedish provincial costumes; Nord-stjernan Society, preceded by their band; United Brotherhood of Car-penters and Joiners; Iduna Society; Verdandi Lodge, K. of P., Burn-side; Balder Society; Linnea Society; Svenska Understödsföreningen; Pullman Band; Harmony Lodge, K. of P., Pullman; Lyran Singing Club, Pullman; Phoenix Lodge, No. 7, W. S. A., Englewood; citizens in carriages. Scattered through the parade were a number of picturesque and characteristic floats and groups, as follows: John Ericsson's "Mon-itor," furnished by John Ericsson Lodge; "A Feast in Valhall," by the Svithiod Club; "Svea, Columbia and Fama," by the Svea Society; "The Bellman Room," by Mr. Colliander; group of Laplanders, exhibit-ing at Midway Plaisance; groups of ladies in provincial costumes;

"Old Time Swedish Iron Smelter"; "Swedes of Delaware in 1638"; "Swedes and Indians", by Iduna Society.

From the piers on the lake front the paraders boarded the boats waiting to carry them to the exposition grounds. Upon arrival they were met by a procession from the Swedish pavilion, headed by the Swedish commissioner, Arthur Leffler, and his suite, escorted by a detail of Columbian Guards. At the Casino the paraders again formed in line and marched through the Court of Honor, past the principal buildings to the Swedish pavilion where they disbanded and scattered through the grounds.

Thousands repaired to Festival Hall, which was crowded long before four o'clock, the hour set for the grand concert, given under the auspices of the American Union of Swedish Singers. For this occasion no less than three celebrated artists from the Royal Opera at Stockholm had been engaged, namely, Caroline Östberg, soprano; C. F. Lundquist, tenor, and Conrad Behrens, basso. Adding to this the Theodore Thomas Orchestra and the United Singers, led by John R. Örtengren, a grand chorus of four hundred male voices, and the array of talent was such as to make this a notable Swedish musical event in Chicago, rivaled only by the appearance of Christina Nilsson twenty years prior.

Following the concert and after a medley of Swedish melodies had been played on the chimes in Machinery Hall by A. E. Bredberg of St. James' Cathedral, the people gathered for a folkfest at the Swedish pavilion. Addresses were made by Arthur Leffler, Swedish commissioner, T. B. Bryan, of the exposition directors, and Dr. J. A. Enander; songs were rendered by Mr. Lundquist and the A. U. S. S. chorus, and "greetings from fifty thousand Swedish-Americans" were telegraphed to his majesty, King Oscar II.

All day the flag of yellow and blue was everywhere in evidence, floating over the parading hosts, draping the interior of Festival Hall and waving beside the stars and stripes on many a pinnacle in the White City. The days' celebration added about 50,000 to the average daily attendance at the fair, raising the total to more than 126,000. It was a day of national inspiration to all Swedish-Americans participating and in every way a splendid success, fully comparable to the celebrations of other nationalities.

The principal historical celebrations were Patriotic Day, Independence Day and Chicago Day, the last-named in commemoration of the great Chicago fire in 1871. This celebration occurred October 9th and was marked by an enormous attendance from the city and the state at large. The number of visitors to the Fair that day was 716,880, this being undoubtedly the greatest concourse of people in the United States at any one time and place. During the summer the exposition management gave several banquets, the most brilliant affair being the reception given to the foreign commissioners October 11th. This was held at the Music Hall and was very largely attended.

During the month of May the total receipts amounted to $583,031, and during June to $1,256,180. The promise implied in these figures was made good. Thus the month of August showed the remarkable total of $2,337,856.25. The receipts of the exposition from all sources, including city, state and national appropriations, were $28,151,168.75. The gate receipts amounted to $10,626,330.76 and the special concessions realized $3,699,581.43.

The expenditures of the Exposition Company, including cost of organization, construction, and administration, were summed up March 31, 1894, at $27,151,800. If the expenses of the various states and the foreign nations are added, the total outlay for the Columbian Exposition will be found to reach almost forty-five million dollars.

Extensive preparations were made to close the Fair October 30th in a manner befitting its grandeur, but a lamentable event threw a pall over the city and made it expedient to simplify the closing celebration to a degree. On October 28th, Carter H. Harrison, the mayor of the city, fell by the hand of an assassin, an Irish fanatic, named Patrick Prendergast. In consequence the events of the closing day were marked by gloom rather than gayety. Festival Hall was packed with humanity. President Palmer of the Board of Commissioners stepped forward with the announcement that owing to the sad circumstances most of the numbers of the proposed program had been eliminated, whereupon he pronounced the exposition officially closed. After a few brief remarks, Dr. Barrows pronounced the benediction over the assembled hosts, which then regretfully departed from the hall to the strains of Beethoven's "Funeral March." The flags on the pinnacles of the exposition halls were lowered, the doors were closed, and the echo of the final artillery salute died as daylight waned on the domes of the exposition city. A strong sense of the vanity of all things created by the hand of man pressed home to every thoughtful spectator as he bade the fabulous beauty and splendor of the White City a last farewell. Thus the World's Columbian Exposition, the pride of Chicago and of the nation, passed into history.

The Chicago Drainage Canal

The growth of Chicago made it apparent to the municipal authorities that something had to be done to lead the flow from the extensive sewer system of the city into some other channel than the Chicago River, which empties into the lake, or the water supply from this last named source would eventually become entirely unfit for use. At first they tried to remedy the matter by deepening the Illinois and Michigan Canal so as to cause the river to run west instead of east, i. e., from the lake instead of into it. This work was carried out in 1865-1871. Although a pumping station was established at the juncture of the river and the canal at Bridgeport, calculated to assist in the reversal of the current of the river and force it into the canal, yet this experiment proved unsuccessful.

The intakes of the water works were then located several miles out in the lake, but even that arrangement was inadequate. Spring floods, storms and heavy rainfalls would at frequent intervals carry great volumes of impure water out as far as the cribs, where it would be absorbed at the intakes and carried back through the mains and be dis-

The Drainage Canal—Gates at Controlling Works, Lockport

tributed throughout the city, imperiling the health of its inhabitants. This condition was not to be tolerated, and other remedies were suggested from time to time, yet no plan, however plausible, pointed out a way of surmounting the chief obstacle, a lack of funds.

Toward the close of the year 1885, H. B. Hurd, who had served on the Board of Drainage Commissioners in 1855, was urged by a number of leading men to make a careful study of the problem. After he had convinced himself and others that the question offered no legal difficulties, provided the legislature would pass the necessary measures, the city council on Jan. 27, 1886, passed a resolution authorizing the mayor to name a commission, consisting of one engineer with a knowledge of sanitary affairs, and two assistant engineers, to investigate the water and sewer systems and submit a report on the result. The elder Mayor Harrison appointed as expert engineer Rudolph Hering of Philadelphia and as his assistants two Chicago engineers, Benezette Williams and S. G. Artingstall. At the next session of the legislature, in 1887, two bills on this subject were submitted. The one, the so-called Hurd bill, proposed that the necessary funds for sanitary improvements be raised by general taxation and by an issue of bonds; the other, known as the Winston bill, proposed special taxation, or assessment, for the same purpose. When it became evident that neither bill had any chance of passage, a new and simpler one, called the Roche-Winston bill, was submitted and passed toward the end of the session. This provided for a commission, consisting of two senators, two representatives and Mayor Roche of Chicago, to investigate the drainage question still further, and also proposed a canal running from the Desplaines River north of the city to Lake Michigan, to carry off the waters of that river

The Drainage Canal—The Bear Trap Dam, from Downstream

and the north branch of the Chicago River. Nothing, however, was accomplished to this end.

In the next legislature (1889) the commission made a favorable report, and a new drainage bill was submitted, essentially providing for the organization of a so-called Sanitary District, the digging of a drainage canal of suitable width and depth through the watershed between the basin of Lake Michigan and the Desplaines river valley, the appointment of a drainage board of nine members and the raising of the requisite funds by general assessment on all taxable property in the district created. The bill met with strong opposition, principally from the people dwelling along the Illinois River, who feared, partly that Chicago's sewage would permanently impair the wholesomeness of the river water, partly that the volumes of water from the canal would flood the bottomlands along the river. The friends of the bill urged to the contrary that if the canal were built and the Desplaines and Illinois rivers were dredged between Joliet and LaSalle, an excellent waterway between Lake Michigan and the Mississippi would be opened. During the eighteen months that this bill hung in the balance, largely attended conventions were held in Peoria, Memphis and other cities, at which the bill was warmly endorsed. The fear that the canal would lower the watermark in the lake was dispelled by experts, who explained that even with a flow of 600,000 cubic feet per minute, this being the maximum estimate, the surface of the lake would be lowered at most three inches.

This bill, so highly important to the city of Chicago, was passed by the legislature May 29, 1889. At the general election in Chicago Nov. 5th following, the proposition to organize the aforesaid sanitary district was carried by a large majority. This district comprises all that part of

The Drainage Canal—Seventeen Miles of the Canal are Sawed Out of the Solid Rock

Chicago north of 87th street, together with an area of about 47 square miles in Cook county, outside of the city limits. It measures 18 miles north and south, has a maximum width of 15 miles, its area being 185 square miles, with a population of 1,800,000. At a special election Dec. 12th the same year the members of the drainage board were chosen. Their first important duty was to make the authorized assessment, amounting to one-half per cent. of the tax value of all property found in the district. When later it became apparent that the amount thus realized was inadequate, the board was authorized to raise the assessment to one and one-half per cent. for a period of five years from 1895, at the expiration of which the former rate was to prevail. In addition, the board was empowered to raise funds by issuing bonds.

The financing of the entire enterprise was thus assured. But owing to differences arising among the trustees, actual work on the canal was delayed almost two years. Four trustees having resigned and other men elected to fill their places, the work was begun. The first sod was turned near Lemont Sept. 3, 1892, by Frank Wenter, president of the board. Necessary gradings, surveys, condemnations and letting of contracts had previously been made. The work was now pushed with vigor towards completion, despite obstacles of one kind or another. The route was divided into sections, each being let to one or more contractors according to the nature of the work to be done. For long stretches the bedrock was being blasted by means of dynamite, fired night and day by electric contacts, in other localities laborers, busy as ants, were digging through soil and clay, while still others were working like beavers constructing costly dams. The work progressed

The Drainage Canal—Walls of Solid Stone Artificially Laid

steadily, and seven years after ground was broken the canal was completed.

The drainage canal starts in the southwestern part of the city, at the point were Robey street crosses the south branch of the river, and runs parallel with the Illinois and Michigan Canal in a straight line southwest to Summit, a distance of eight miles. This stretch of canal has a width of 110 feet at the bottom and 198 feet at the waterline, and a minimum depth of 22 feet. At Summit the canal turns southward and a little farther down takes a westward course to Willow Springs, five miles from Summit. This section is 202 feet wide at the bottom and 290 at the water's edge, the depth being uniform throughout. From Willow Springs it runs west past Sag and Lemont to Romeo where it makes a sharp curve southward towards Lockport, the western terminus, located about fifteen miles from Willow Springs. This stretch is cut through solid rock and the corresponding measurements are 160 and 162 feet. The entire length of the canal is 28 miles.

The total excavations comprised 41,410,000 cubic yards, 28,500,000 being earth, clay and gravel and 12,910,000, rock. But other work was also necessary. The Desplaines River, which was cut or touched by the canal route at a number of points, had to be led into other channels, and for this purpose an extra canal, 13 miles in length, was dug and a levee built for a distance of 19 miles. The new river-bed is 200 feet wide at the bottom and represents an excavation of 2,068,659 cubic yards, bringing the total excavations up to 43,478,659 cubic yards. If all this material had been dumped into the lake it would have formed an island one square mile in area and 12 feet high above water level. The total cost of digging the canal was $33,525,691.20.

The Drainage Canal—Two Mile Curve at Romeo, Ill.

For the regulation of the current costly locks were constructed at the western terminal of the canal at Lockport. There are seven smaller locks 20 by 30 feet and one large one, the so-called Bear Trap Dam with a width of 160 feet and a vertical play of 17 feet. The latter consists of two huge sheet iron plates joined by means of hinges, the lower one being firmly fastened to a substantial substructure, while the upper one is so placed as to obstruct the current. This mechanism is operated by the power of the current itself, the water being let into special conduits and regulated by a set of valves placed directly under the iron dam. This is claimed to be the most ingenious piece of mechanism of its kind in the world. Near the locks there is a basin large enough to permit vessels of maximum draft to turn.

This gigantic piece of engineering work was completed in seven years. On Jan. 2, 1900, the current was turned into the canal, and on Jan. 17th, when this had been filled, the great locks were opened, causing the interesting spectacle of the Chicago River reversing its current. Its waters, thick with filth and sewage, foul-smelling and almost stagnant, yet sluggishly moving in the direction of Lake Michigan, now suddenly changed their course and began to move with a speed of a mile and a half per hour in the opposite direction, away from the river's mouth toward its source. Its color quickly changed from its traditional mud color to a light greenish tint, lent by the pure waters drawn from the lake. Thus the constant danger to the purity of Chicago's water supply was practically averted by reversing the current of a navigable stream. At the same time, a portion of waterway between Lake Michigan and the Mississippi, planned years before, had been completed.

The Hennepin Canal

For the sake of completeness, a brief sketch of this latter project is here subjoined. The old Illinois and Michigan Canal soon was found too narrow and too shallow for large deep draft vessels, and in the early seventies the question of building a new canal across the state was raised. A canal bill was presented in congress and in 1871 government engineers made a preliminary survey. In 1890 an appropriation bill, based on said survey, was submitted, and Sept. 19th the needed appropriation was granted. Work was begun at the western canal terminus in July, 1892, and at the eastern end in 1894, and has been in progress ever since.

The Illinois and Mississippi Canal, also termed the Hennepin Canal, starts at the Illinois River one and three-quarters of a mile above the city of Hennepin, at the point where the river changes its course from west to south. Passing the Bureau Creek valley it cuts the watershed between the Illinois and Mississippi rivers and empties into the Rock River at the point where the Green River empties into that stream, thence following the Rock its entire navigable length and reaching the Mississippi after flanking the rapids at the village of Milan. This the main line of the canal is 75 miles in length. A branch, or feeder, constructed at its highest altitude, extends from a point near Sheffield, located 28 miles from its eastern terminus, in a northerly direction to Sterling, where it taps the Rock Falls. A dam built at that point to force the current into the canal makes the Rock River navigable to Dixon, several miles northeast of Sterling. This feeder has a length of 29 miles, which, added to the main channel, makes a total of 104 miles of waterway, or seven miles more than the Illinois and Michigan Canal. From the Illinois River to the highest point there is a rise of 196 feet, and this section has 21 locks, varying in height from six to fourteen feet. From that point to the Mississippi the incline is 93 feet which is overcome by means of ten similar locks. The canal is 80 feet wide and 7 feet deep throughout. Along its entire length the banks are reinforced with solid masonry. The sluices are 170 feet in length and 35 feet in width, admitting vessels 140 feet long, 32 feet wide and with a tonnage of 600. The locks, bridges and aqueducts are all built of cement and steel, the smaller culverts of steel mains.

This canal shortens the route by water from Chicago to the Mississippi by no less than 400 miles by cutting across from the great bend of the Illinois River almost directly westward to the Mississippi. The extension of the old canal was the Illinois River which, after meandering through the state, empties into the Mississippi not far from the confluence of the Missouri. But in order to open a deep waterway all the way from the lakes to the Mississippi it will be necessary to deepen the old Illinois and Michigan Canal between the terminus of the drainage canal at Lockport and the city of La Salle, where the Illinois becomes navigable. The first steamer passed through the Hennepin Canal in November, 1907.

The cost of the Hennepin Canal was estimated at $6,926,000, including $1,858,000 for the feeder, but through certain changes in the course and reduced cost of material, a substantial saving was made.

CHAPTER III

The First Swedes in Illinois

Raphael Widen, the First Swedish Pioneer in the State

HE first Swede in Illinois was, so far as known to a certainty, one Raphael Widen. The year and place of his birth are unknown, but it is a matter of record that at the age of eight he was brought from Sweden to France where he was educated for the Catholic priesthood. It is not known when he emigrated to the United States. It is noted in the Territorial Records of Illinois that Raphael Widen was appointed justice of the peace of St. Clair county on Jan. 12, 1814, by the territorial governor, Ninian Edwards. He lived at Cahokia, the county seat, where he married, in 1818, into a French family of that place. Removing to Kaskaskia, Randolph county, he was one of the fourteen territorial justices who conducted the affairs of Randolph county during the interregnum from December, 1818, to May, 1819, the last meeting being held April, 19, 1819. Widen continued to act as justice of the peace as late as 1831 and presumably still longer.

Eleven manuscripts in Widen's hand are preserved in the Menard collection of manuscripts at the Chicago Historical Society. The earliest is a contract for the rent of a piece of land. It is written in French, is dated May 24, 1819, and covers two pages. The signatures of the contracting parties are made in Widen's hand, they each marking a cross.

A photograph of a promissory note written in French is reproduced on the opposite page. There are four notes in English, two executions and two summons papers. The latest date on the papers is Oct. 24, 1831. There is also a trust deed for $409.97 to secure a loan from Pierre Menard, first lieutenant governor of Illinois, to Maurice D. Smith and wife, Raphael Widen and Felix St. Vrains being named as trustees.

Widen became a man of more than local prominence. He was the representative of Randolph county in the second and third General

Assemblies of the young state (1820-24), and a member of the senate in the fourth and fifth General Assemblies (1824-28). During the second

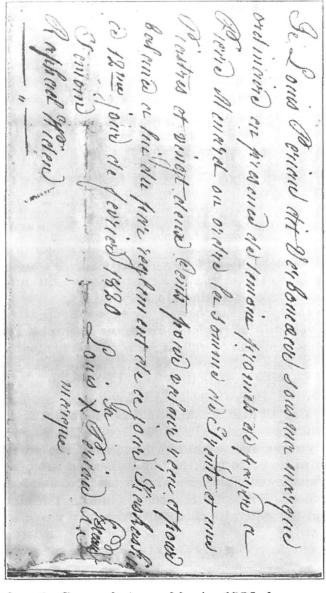

Specimen of Handwriting of Raphael Widen

session of the fourth General Assembly in 1826, he was president of the senate.

His career as legislator of the new frontier state was coincident with the period of heated debate over the question whether the state was to be slave or free. Widen took a stand by which he deserves lasting honor and respect. He was the sworn enemy of slavery and expressed his views freely and fearlessly in the legislature. When on the 11th day of February, 1823, while he was serving his second term as representative, a motion was made in the house to submit to a popular vote the question of calling a convention for the revision of the constitution in the interest of slavery, Widen was among those who voted resolutely against it. This is all the more notable when it is considered that he was one of the only two anti-convention representatives from the middle or southern portion of the state to oppose the bill. The motion carried with a majority of one vote in the house, after having passed the senate by a majority of two-thirds, and as told in foregoing pages, the question was submitted to the people at the election of August 2, 1824. The pro-slavery convention proposition was lost by a vote of 6,640 against it to 4,972 in its favor, settling the slavery question for all time in the state.

Widen lived in Kaskaskia when Lafayette made his visit at that place April 30, 1825. A reference has been found to "Edward Widen, the polished gentleman and enterprising merchant," as having been one of those present at the reception to the French hero. This undoubtedly refers to Raphael Widen in spite of the inaccuracy. Widen died in Kaskaskia from cholera in 1833.

That there were a number of Swedes among those who settled in Illinois in its territorial period admits of no doubt. Though Widen is the first of whom we have definite information, most likely there were others of whom we will never know. In the annals of early Illinois names characteristically Swedish are not infrequent. One Paul Haralson (also written Harrolson and Harelston), is said to have settled on the west side of the Kaskaskia River, near the mouth of Camp's Creek, in Randolph county, in 1802. He became a man of prominence in those early days and is said to have held the office of sheriff for a short time. In the period of 1803-09 he served as county commissioner, and also as county clerk of Randolph county, being the third man to hold that office. The public records make no mention of him as sheriff, but in the official list of surveyors the name of Paul Harrolson is third in order. His appointment by Gov. Edwards to the latter office was dated April 7, 1814. In the absence of proofs of his Swedish origin, we can merely suppose that he was a Swedish descendant, whose name was originally written Haraldson.

In looking over the lists of members of the Illinois militia in the War of 1812, several names instantly impress one as being Swedish. One is that of Bankson—an Americanized form of Bengtson, common among the Delaware colonists. One of the eminent personages among the Delaware Swedes was Andrew Bankson. And here we find the same name, borne by a man who was a lieutenant in the Second Regiment, from St. Clair county, before the war and during the war a private in a company of mounted riflemen. He was subsequently promoted second lieutenant under the name of Bankston, manifestly a misspelling.

On April 5, 1817, Andrew Bankson was appointed major of the second militia regiment by Ninian Edwards, the territorial governor, and on March 3, 1818, promoted colonel of the tenth militia. He resigned his colonelcy Sept. 9th following but the name of Col. Andrew Bankson reappears in the old records ten years later, in the list of thirty-three men chosen managers of McKendree College in 1828.

In the military lists are mentioned two other men of the same surname—James Bankson, sergeant of Capt. Nathan Chambers' company of infantry, and Patton Bankson, private in the same company. One Elijah Bankson was a brother of Andrew and Patton Bankson. Not unnaturally the inference may be drawn that these were descendants of Delaware families of the same name, but the probability, admittedly slight, is not strengthened by the known fact that the Banksons here encountered came to Illinois from Tennessee.

Among the comrades of Andrew Bankson was one David Eckman. That he was a Swede or of Swedish descent cannot be doubted. Of him we know nothing more than this, that he voluntarily shouldered the musket and risked his life to protect the community against its foes. Again, in the list of privates in the Fourth Regiment we find two names with a decidedly Swedish ring—John and Andrew Hallin. These men, presumably brothers, were members of Capt. Dudley Williams' company of the Fourth Illinois Militia.

Jacob Falström, Frontiersman and Missionary

In the Northwest Territory there lived among the Indians for about forty years, dating from the early part of the nineteenth century, a Swede by the name of Jacob Falström. He seems to have come to the West contemporaneously with Raphael Widen and is said to have arrived in Minnesota prior to the year 1819. Falström was born in Stockholm, July 25th in the year 1793 or 1795. He left home at twelve or fourteen years of age and went to sea with his uncle. Stories differ as to how he came to emigrate. One version has it that he lost his way in London and, unable to find his way back to his uncle's ship, took passage to America; another that he ran away from his uncle, who was cruel to him, both agreeing that he landed in Canada. Col. Hans Mattson, who met Falström at St. Paul in 1854, says that the boy deserted a Swedish ship in the port of Quebec and, picking his way through the wilderness, sought refuge among the Indians. He was content to stay among the redskins and ultimately became more closely allied with the natives by marrying into one of their tribes. He was a man well-known to the Hudson Bay Company, and to the early settlers in the upper Mississippi valley.

Falström, who spoke French and several Indian languages, was employed by the American Fur Company to trade with the natives around Lake Superior. With his Indian wife he had several children. Some of his descendants are still living in Washington county, Minn., where Falström staked a claim in 1837. In relating his experience to Col. Mattson, he stated that for about thirty-five years, or until he met the first Swedish settlers in the St. Croix valley, he had not heard a word of Swedish spoken and as a consequence had almost completely lost command of his native tongue. During his later years Falström was very religious and for a long time acted as a missionary among the Indians, apparently affiliating with Methodism. As a missionary he probably antedated all other Swedish pioneer preachers in the West. Falström passed away in the year 1859. He exerted but little of a civilizing influence, and his descendants are said to live in semi-savagery to this day.

Christian Benson, the First Swedish Farmer in Illinois

In the year 1835 a Swedish pioneer of Illinois arrived in the person of Christian Benson, who, however, made no mark in public life, but lived quietly as a farmer.

He was born in Göteborg in 1805, went to sea at the age of seven and followed that occupation until his thirtieth year. He first came to America in 1819. In 1827 he married Maria Bantherson at Providence, R. I. Later he returned to his seafaring life, coming to America for the third time in 1835. That year he settled in Portland township, Whiteside county, Illinois, not far from the present city of Rock Island, and went to farming. In his old age he was cared for by his two children. Benson was the first known Swedish farmer in the state. He was still living in 1880 and was spoken of as a stanch adherent of the Republican party.

Jonas Hedström, the First Swedish Clergyman in Illinois

Among the first Swedes to set foot on Illinois soil was Jonas Hedström. As Widen had acquired prominence in the field of politics, so Hedström became renowned as a pioneer in church work. He was the first man to preach the gospel in the Swedish language here and became the founder and pioneer of Swedish Methodism in the West.

An elder brother, Olof Gustaf Hedström, persuaded Jonas to emigrate to America. The elder Hedström was born in Tvinnesheda, Notteback parish, Småland, May 11, 1803. The parents were Corporal Hedström and his wife Karin, who had four sons besides Olof Gustaf, and two daughters. The eldest son was put to work as a tailor's apprentice at an early age, but in 1825, at the age of twenty-two, he left the old country and came to the United States the following year. His trip across the Atlantic was made under remarkable circumstances. He became secretary to the commander of a frigate named "af Chapman," one of the Swedish war vessels sold to the republic of Colombia, to be used by that and other South American colonies in their war for independence against Spain. This transaction, as every one familiar with Swedish history knows, caused international complications and came

Olof Gustaf Hedström

near involving Sweden in war. This, however, was averted when a later sale of three other warships was annulled. The frigate "af Chapman," which departed from Karlskrona in the summer of 1825 arrived safely at Cartagena, Colombia, but orders awaited Commodore C. R. Nordenskiöld, its commander, not to transfer the ship to the Colombian government. In March, 1826, the frigate was ordered from Cartagena to New York, where the expedition disbanded after numerous difficulties and complications, and the vessel was sold. Having been fully paid, the crew were granted passage back to Sweden, but young Hedström and several others chose to remain in New York.

Hedström had no intention of remaining permanently, but a misfortune forced him to do so. The same day that the crew was paid and mustered out of service, Hedström and a number of comrades went

ashore to see the city, and at night they took lodging at a hotel for
seamen. When he woke up in the morning he found to his chagrin
that he had been robbed of everything, even to his clothes. He told
his hostess, an Irishwoman, of his misfortune and she kindly procured

Jonas Hedström

a suit of clothes for him. Destitute as he was, a journey to Sweden was
out of the question, so he submitted to fate and remained where he was.

The trade he had learned in Sweden now proved very useful to
him. He was employed by an American tailor, Townsend by name,

and after a year or two he secured employment as cutter, earning good wages. In the same shop was employed a young woman, Caroline Pinckney, a cousin of Townsend, to whom Hedström was married June 11, 1829. She was of the Methodist faith, and through her influence Hedström a few weeks later joined that denomination, becoming at once an ardent worker in the church. Later he removed to Pittsville, Pa., where he opened a tailor shop of his own. The venture proved rather unsuccessful, causing him to sell out his stock. He returned to Sweden in 1833 apparently with a view to awakening his parents to their spiritual wants, a mission in which he seemed to have been successful.

On the return voyage the same year Hedström brought with him his younger brother Jonas, born Aug. 13, 1813, and at that time a youth of twenty. The trip was a perilous one. One awful night, when death seemed to lurk on every side, the younger Hedström underwent a total change spiritually, to the great joy of the elder brother. On their arrival in America, Olof Gustaf Hedström began to preach; in 1835 he was received, on probation, into the New York Conference of the Methodist-Episcopal Church; for ten years he labored as itinerant preacher among the American Methodists in the Catskill region. By dint of his fiery and convincing eloquence, equalled by few, he met with great success. It was, however, not among the American population, but among his own countrymen and other Scandinavians, that he was to perform his life-work. In 1844 he entered into earnest correspondence with friends in New York with reference to the opening of a new Methodist mission among the large numbers of Scandinavian seamen who annually visit that port and among the immigrants and the few Swedes that had already settled in New York City. The ship ''Henry Leeds'' was purchased with money subscribed for that purpose, the vessel remodeled as a mission ship with chapel and Sunday school rooms, re-named the ''John Wesley'' and anchored at suitable points in the North River. In this mission ship, better known as the Bethel ship, Hedström conducted the first services on Whitsunday, May 25, 1845. He was ably assisted by several others, among whom Peter Bergner, a former sailor and ship's carpenter. In 1857 a new Bethel ship took the place of the old one, but Hedström remained at his post. He made occasional trips to other ports, and founded the Swedish Methodist-Episcopal churches at Jamestown, N. Y., and Chandler's Valley, Pa., in 1851, and at Chicago the following year. In the summer of 1863 he re-visited Sweden, preaching in many places to large concourses of interested listeners. He labored without interruption until 1875 when he was forced to retire owing to failing health, but still retained much of his former fire and vigor even in old age. Hedström died in New York City May 5, 1877, at the age of 74. A handsome monument in Greenwood Cemetery, Brooklyn, marks his last resting place. By his side reposes his beloved wife, who died in 1890 at the ripe age of eighty-six years. They had three children, one being Dr. Wilbur Hedström, who is still living.

We have traced the life of the elder Hedström thus minutely by reason of its intimate connection with that of the younger brother, to whose career we now turn.

Jonas Hedström remained for a short time in New York, then spent some years in Pennsylvania, where he earned his living in the blacksmith's trade, and a very good blacksmith was he. At this time he formed the acquaintance of a family by the name of Sornberger which soon afterward removed to Knox county, Ill. The young Swedish artisan had formed an attachment for Diantha Sornberger, a daughter in the family, and in 1837 or 1838 Hedström followed. After marrying his affianced, he removed to the little village of Farmington, in Fulton county, where he opened a blacksmith shop. Shortly afterwards he began preaching, having been duly licensed by the local authorities of the Methodist Church. His license was renewed the next year. Later he removed to Knox county and became one of the founders of the town of Victoria, where he lived at the time of the first Swedish immigration to Illinois, and continued to reside until his death. By diligent and skillful application to his trade, he there acquired a sufficient income to build a rather comfortable home, where many a poor immigrant and weary wayfarer enjoyed hospitable entertainment. And he preached as energetically as he sledged. During the years following, he preached in the English language to the Americans in the various school-houses round about Victoria as well as in the neighboring towns of Lafayette, Knoxville and others. There being no Swedish settlers in that region or in any other part of the state at this time, he had no occasion to preach the Gospel in his mother tongue. By constant disuse, the Swedish language was gradually forgotten by him; but when in the early summer of 1845 he received a letter from his brother saying that he had been appointed missionary to the Scandinavian seamen and had already begun preaching in the Swedish language, it occurred to the younger brother that he also ought to revive his mother tongue, in order that he might expound the Gospel to the Swedish immigrants which his brother predicted soon would begin to arrive and settle in those parts. He, therefore, procured first a copy of the New Testament in Swedish and English, then a Swedish Bible complete, and fell to study his forgotten native tongue with great assiduity. His brother's predictions were soon fulfilled. Group after group of Swedish immigrants arrived at New York, where they were first met by the elder Hedström, who took a keen interest in their temporal as well as their spiritual welfare. With his knowledge of conditions in

Illinois, acquired through his brother, he was in a position to recommend that region as a desirable place of settlement. Many were they who followed his advice, journeying westward to Victoria where the younger Hedström stood ever ready to assist. By renewed use, in the next few years he again acquired the ability to speak the Swedish tongue fluently.

Although great tracts of good agricultural land were to be had much nearer, large numbers of Swedish immigrants came all the way to Illinois, owing to the activity of the brothers Hedström. To them is due also no small share of credit for the continued influx of Swedes into this state. But there is a third Swedish pioneer who, as we will presently see, played an important part in directing Swedish immigrants to Illinois.

Hedström preached his first sermon in the Swedish language Dec. 15, 1846, in a little blockhouse in the woods, about three miles southeast of the present town of Victoria, the occasion being the organization of the first Swedish Methodist Church. This congregation, started with five members, was also the first church organization of Swedish nationality in this country since the time of the Delaware settlements. The Erik Janssonists of Bishop Hill, who will be dealt with in the following chapter, had begun to arrive in July of the same year and constituted a sort of religious band, but could not as yet be said to exist as a church in the strict sense of the word. The Methodist propaganda among the Swedish settlers grew apace under the direction of Hedström, several new churches being founded in the course of the next few years. This growth will be more fully shown in the chapter dealing especially with Swedish Methodism in Illinois.

Owing to his restless endeavors and the great privations attending his constant travels in the service of his cause, Hedström's health broke down, compelling his retirement in the fall of 1857. His powers continued to wane, and on May 11, 1859, he ended his useful career, dying at the age of nearly 46 years. His body was buried in the Victoria cemetery, where a monument was placed upon his grave. His wife died in 1874 and was buried at his side. The pair had five children, two of whom are thought to be still living, viz., Luther Hedström and Mrs. Becker.

Hedström has been very differently judged according to the sectarian viewpoints of those making the estimate. By his adversaries he has been made out a lying, cheating, deceitful, fanatical and selfish person, while his close friends and brethren in the faith, on the other hand, ascribe to him every virtue and set him up as a model of perfection. Both sides, however, appear to have exaggerated his personal traits. During this early and formative period in our history, the lines were sharply drawn between the different religious groups.

To respect the opinions of others these early settlers had not yet learned, and intolerance reigned supreme. Hedström was fanatically devoted to Methodism and did everything in his power to disseminate its teachings among his countrymen. Possessing a greater proportion of zeal and enthusiasm than of erudition and good judgment, he frequently, by a lack of deference and tact, gave rise to serious controversies with representatives of other denominations, themselves devoid of spiritual moderation. That he acted from pure motives and with a sincere purpose of benefiting his fellowmen, no one, however bigoted, can deny.

As his elder brother, O. G. Hedström, may be styled the father of Swedish Methodism, and the Bethel ship in New York harbor its cradle, so Jonas Hedström may with equal justice be called the founder and pioneer of Methodism among the Swedes of the West, and the rude blockhouse near Victoria the starting-point of his endeavors. Jonas Hedström was not only the first Swedish preacher in Illinois, but the first Swedish exponent of material progress in these regions. For these reasons his name will always have a prominent place in the history of the Swedes in the state and in the entire country.

O. G. Lange, the First Swede in Chicago

O. G. Lange was another early Swedish pioneer of Illinois, and he also had the distinction of being the first known Swede in Chicago and Cook county.

Olof Gottfrid Lange was born July 4, 1811, in the city of Göteborg. July 27, 1824, he hired as cabin watch on an American brig, bound for Boston, where he landed Sept. 30th. He remained a sailor for more than ten years, serving in the American and the British navies.

In 1838 he abandoned the sea for the great West and arrived on Sept 18th at Chicago, which had received its city charter one year ago. If there had been any of his countrymen ahead of him, he would have had no difficulty in finding them, for at that time the city had a population of only 4,179. Several Norwegians, however, had settled here, and these he gave lessons in the English language, meeting his pupils at Fort Dearborn.

Later he opened a drug store near Chicago, at a point on the Illinois and Michigan Canal, which was then being dug. A severe attack of the ague soon caused him to give up the business, whereupon he went to Milwaukee and became, as in Chicago, the first Swedish settler in the community. It was his privilege to receive Gustaf Unonius and his companions, when they arrived in Wisconsin in the fall of 1841. In Milwaukee Lange became the manager of a hardware store, owned by a man who later became governor of Wisconsin. After a short time, Lange went into business for himself in co-partnership with one Hulbert Reed. It was at this time Fredrika Bremer, the Swedish authoress, visited the United States. When she left Chicago for Milwaukee in September, 1850, Lange received her into his home, entertained her for several days, and then accompanied her on a visit to the Pine Lake settlement founded by Gustaf Unonius.

Afterwards Lange became traveling representative of the Rathbone & Corning stove manufacturing company of Albany, N. Y. Having lived a short time in Charleston, S. C., he settled in Watertown,

Olof Gottfrid Lange

Wis., and became passenger agent for a section of the Chicago and Northwestern Railway. Not content with this occupation, Lange, who had cultivated a taste for change and variety, moved to Kenosha, Wis., in 1856 and there started a foundry which four years later was removed to the corner of Kingsbury and Michigan streets, Chicago. Thus Lange became a Chicagoan for the second time.

In 1866 he made a trip to Sweden for his health. On his return he brought a library of 500 volumes together with a number of art portfolios, for the Svea Society, a Swedish association already existing in Chicago. A large part of the collection was donated by

King Charles XV. of Sweden and his family. For this service to the society Lange was made an honorary member and presented with a valuable badge. The library of this society was totally destroyed in the great fire of 1871.

Lange is said to have tried his fortune at one time on the board of trade. The fact that he did not continue to trade on the board would seem to indicate that his venture was not successful. The last twenty-five years of his life he devoted to soliciting life insurance for various companies. With reference to the 250th anniversary of the landing of the Swedes on the Delaware, commemorated in the fall of 1888, Lange, in the issue of "The Swedish-American" for April 18, 1889, proposed that his countrymen in America annually celebrate "Forefathers' Day," and in many localities the suggestion was carried out during the next few years.

In July, 1893, the venerable pioneer had an attack of pneumonia and was prostrated at his home, 292 Irving ave., Chicago. During his illness he was visited by Rt. Rev. K. H. G. von Schéele, Bishop of Gotland, who, on his first tour of the United States, took the opportunity to bring cordial greetings from Lange's old schoolmates in the old country. July 13th, two days after this visit, Lange breathed his last. He reached the ripe age of 82 years. Having taken a deep interest in the Swedish fraternities, Nordstjernan, Balder and many others had, like Svea, conferred upon him honorary membership, and now showed their appreciation by sending large delegations to attend the obsequies. A bronze bust in memory of him may be seen in the lodge hall of the Svea Society.

Lange, commonly called "Captain" Lange, presumably on account of his early career as a sailor, was one of those Swedes who are not ashamed of their nationality. Although having spent the greater part of his life away from his native country, he never forgot or concealed his Swedish nativity, but took every occasion to glory in the fact and extol all that is best in Swedish character and culture. The best proof of the genuineness of his Swedish patriotism is found in his proposal of a Swedish "Forefathers' Day" celebration. Being kind-hearted and generous, he gave freely, but without ostentation, to his less fortunate fellows. He was twice married, his first wife dying early. With his second wife, Catharine O'Brien from Ireland, he was united April 23, 1843, the golden anniversary of that occasion occurring a few months before his demise. Mrs. Lange was a lady of refinement. Fredrika Bremer describes her as "a kindly little Irishwoman." They had five children, one son and four daughters. The eldest daughter was the wife of B. A. E. Landergren, deceased, who was for many years chief deputy in the Internal Revenue office at Chicago.

Sven Nelson, the Recluse of Andover

The next Swede to arrive in Illinois, following Lange, was doubtless Sven Nelson, like two of his predecessors a sailor. He came to the state in 1840 and settled in Andover, Henry county, a settlement founded five years before by Americans from the East. There he dwelt in peace and almost perfect seclusion for almost forty years, dying in the late seventies.

Nelson in the latter forties married a woman known by the name of Stigs Lena, who in 1849 came over from Hassela, Helsingland, with a party of Erik Janssonists.

Gustaf Flack, the First Swedish Merchant in Chicago

Following Sven Nelson, the next Swedish immigrant to Illinois was Gustaf Flack from Ålfta parish, Helsingland. The year of his arrival is unknown, as also his early life here. In the early forties we find him in Victoria, Ill., and in 1843 in Chicago, where he owned a small store near the ferry landing at Clark st. His stay in Chicago and America was cut short by his return in 1846, to Sweden, where he suddenly died on the way from the city of Gefle to his native home. During his sojourn in Illinois, Flack wrote letters to his friends at home freely lauding this state and predicting for it great future prosperity. His glowing descriptions primarily caused the Erik Janssonists to emigrate and settle here. Flack thus shares with the Hedström brothers the credit for directing the main current of early Swedish immigration to the Prairie State.

The Pine Lake Settlement in Relation to Swedish Immigration to Illinois

While only individual Swedes kept moving into Illinois, Gustaf Unonius and others in the early forties founded at Pine Lake, in the neighboring state of Wisconsin, the first Swedish settlement in America since the time of the Delaware Swedes. The history of this settlement and of its founder sustain so intimate a relation to that of the Illinois settlements as to merit a brief sketch in this connection.

Gustaf Elias Marius Unonius was born Aug. 25, 1810, in Helsingfors, the son of Israel Unonius, a barrister, and Maria Gårdberg, his wife. The father came of an old Swedish family in Finland, and removed to Sweden when Finland was ceded to Russia. He became postmaster and revenue collector at Grisslehamn. A military career was mapped out for the son, who at thirteen became a cadet at the Karlberg military school. Among his comrades were C. F. Ridderstad, Georg Adlersparre, and Wilhelm von Braun, whom he joined in literary pursuits, the results of which appeared in the literary periodicals of that time.

Young Unonius soon left the military academy for Upsala, where he finished his college course in 1830 and the course in law three years later. He subsequently entered upon a course fitting him for practice before the highest courts of the realm, but when in 1834 a cholera epidemic caused the closing of the sessions at the university, he took a position as assistant physician at one of the pest houses of Stockholm and became interested in that profession. When the epidemic subsided, he returned to Upsala to take up medical studies, but shortly after-

Gustaf Unonius

wards he again left the university to take a position in the provincial government offices at Upsala.

In 1841 he was married to Charlotta Margareta Öhrströmer, and soon afterwards, for reasons known only to himself, he decided to emigrate. On May 11th of that year the couple left Upsala for Gefle to embark for America together with a small company of friends and acquaintances. In the party were, an old maid-servant from the home of Mrs. Unonius, Christine by name, Ivar Hagberg, a young student of twenty-one, and a relative of Unonius by the name of Carl Groth. According to the statement of Unonius himself, he and his company were the first to take advantage of a recent decree granting the right to leave the country without obtaining a special permit from the crown.

For some reason the vessel did not get ready to weigh anchor until June 3rd. The vessel was named "Minnet," and its captain was C. J. Bohlin, with whom Unonius had contracted for passage for the entire party to the port of New York for a total sum of five hundred Swedish crowns, the passengers to supply their own provisions. Before they got ready to sail, still another person joined them, viz., one Vilhelm Polman, a former university student. The ship carried a cargo of iron. Having made the ports of Elsinore (Helsingör) and Portsmouth, the vessel finally reached its destination Sept. 10th, three months and seven days after weighing anchor. The emigrants stopped for a week

Unonius' Cabin at Pine Lake

in New York, where a Swedish merchant, named Brodell, together with the captain, who spoke English, rendered them every assistance. Inquiries were made as to the most suitable location for a Swedish settlement, and upon learning that large tracts of cheap land were to be had in Illinois, it was decided to settle there, whereupon arrangements were made for transportation to Chicago at $12 a person.

They started on their journey inland Sept. 17th, going by steamboat up the Hudson to Albany, thence via the Erie canal to Buffalo. Here they encountered fresh difficulties, the captains of the lake steamers refusing to recognize the validity of their tickets. Finally, through the good offices of one Morell, a Swedish jeweler who had spent many years in America, they were able to continue on their way, and went by boat to Detroit. Here Hagberg separated from the company and went to Cleveland, while the others proceeded across lakes St. Clair, Huron and Michigan, past Fort Mackinaw, to Milwaukee. Being now weary of travel, and having been told that Wisconsin was preferable.

to Illinois for agricultural purposes, they determined to stop here, after having spent two weeks on the way from New York. They took lodging at the principal hotel, where they found, first a Norwegian servant girl with whom they were able to communicate, and later met their countryman, Captain O. G. Lange, who had emigrated several years before.

After several days of rest, Unonius left the women in charge of a German family and, accompanied by Lange, set out to inspect the country. The date was Oct. 7, 1841. At that time Wisconsin was still a territory, with a population estimated at 45,000. The prospectors traveled afoot westward through forests and over prairies a distance of thirty miles, eventually reaching the dwellingplace of a man named Pearmain, for whom they had letters from the land office at Milwaukee. He lived in a log cabin, the first of its kind seen by the prospective settlers. With Pearmain as guide they traversed the surrounding country and, after a long and wearisome journey on foot, reached the shores of a picturesque little lake, called Pine Lake, from the fact that its shores were fringed with pine.

The lake was about two miles in length, with sloping, well-drained shores. Finding the region fertile and picturesque, the travelers determined to search no farther. The soil was found to be a deep black loam, mixed with clay; near the shores of the lake, the surface was rolling, gradually changing to a level and easily cultivated prairie.

Here the settlers determined to found their long wished for home. They selected a tract of land owned by a canal company which, having discontinued work on the canal, was likely to forfeit its title to the property, and on the advice of Pearmain and Lange they staked as their claim the west half of Section 33, Township 8, Range 18, expecting to get full possession under the pre-emption law, when after two or three years the title should revert to the government.

They now returned to Milwaukee and, having procured provisions, the pioneers, accompanied by Mrs. Unonius and the maid-servant, traveled back to the chosen site in a wagon, drawn by a yoke of oxen. The women got temporary lodging in the simple home of Pearmain, located on the present site of the city of Delafield, and the men began to open a road to the new homestead and to erect a loghouse. For temporary shelter they built a hut of logs, piled on one another in a square, and with a covering of dried grass. After Unonius had made another trip to Milwaukee and purchased a stove and other indispensable household articles, the family moved into their new home Nov. 11th, exactly six months after their departure from Upsala. Of the toil and the trials of pioneer life these people got their full share. Although coming from the so-called better class in the old country and being as such unaccustomed to hard work and privations, they never lost heart, but labored arduously on, breaking ground, cutting down trees, building fences, patching up their dwelling, and building a shed for their yoke of oxen and one cow. The settlers celebrated their first Christmas in America with joy and contentment over the things already accomplished but with tender memories of the old home and those left behind.

The winter was bitterly cold, with severe storms and much snow, and the cultivation of the soil could not begin until late in April. That spring Polman, who had shared the cabin with the others, left them to begin the practice of medicine in a more populous neighborhood a few miles away. He had studied medicine in Sweden and proved quite successful, possessing, as he did, a far greater knowledge of the profession than the average doctor in the West at that time.

The Swedes at Pine Lake gradually formed the acquaintance of surrounding settlers, and in the late spring they had a visit from an American clergyman of the Episcopal Church who had started a mission a few miles distant.

True, these early settlers did not always have food in plenty, nor of the most nourishing kind, but they never suffered actual want. Game was plentiful in the surrounding forests, and occasional hunting trips were made with good results. Fishing in the lake also proved profitable to the family larder. The cow supplied all the milk needed, and through barter and trade with the neighbors several pigs, a quantity of corn, potatoes, rutabagas and other necessaries were procured.

One day the settlers were surprised by some very distinguished visitors viz., Baron Thott from Skåne, Mr. E. Bergvall from Göteborg, and one Wadman, a retired merchant from Norrköping. The baron and Mr. Bergvall each purchased a piece of land in the neighborhood, while Mr. Wadman returned to Milwaukee to seek employment in some line of business. About the same time one B. Peterson, a shoemaker, arrived, obtained lodging with Unonius, and began to ply his trade in the settlement.

New settlers thus kept coming, but the main influx began when Unonius in correspondences to Swedish newspapers described the conditions in Wisconsin, and especially the facilities offered emigrants to acquire their own homes. Not only Swedes, but Norwegians and Danes emigrated and settled there. Among the first to arrive from Sweden was a lieutenant in the army, a good singer, who often cheered the hearts of the colonists by singing the songs and ditties of their fatherland. Ivar Hagberg, his traveling companion, came there for a visit, bought a piece of land, but for some reason was compelled to return to Sweden, and never came back. Among other Swedish visitors to the settlement about this time were one Ihrmark, a man of sixty, who had settled in Illinois, and a man from Göteborg, by the name of O. E. Dreutzer. The latter lived for many years in Wisconsin, attaining a respected position in his community. Another Swede, named Erick Wester, a veritable adventurer, whose true name was supposed to be Westergren, visited the colony in the alleged capacity of a Methodist minister, preaching here and there in the homes, but without note-worthy success. Entirely destitute, he left Wisconsin in 1850 for Illi-nois, settling in Princeton, where he fell into bad repute among his fellow countrymen on account of repeated acts of fraud and dishonesty in business. From Princeton he went to Dallas, Texas, and his career is little known from that time on. This adventurer will reappear in another part of this history.

Some time later, a student from Vestergötland, Björkander by name, and a number of others arrived from Sweden and settled at Pine Lake. Simultaneously, many Norwegians, hardy, industrious folk, but mostly without means, came there directly from their native land. The Swedes settled east and the Norwegians west of the lake, around whose wooded shores thus sprang up a miniature Scandinavia. The two na-tionalities here, as at home, had their petty differences, resulting in frequent disputes and neighborhood quarrels. The Norwegians sur-passed the Swedes both numercially and in point of industry and enter-prise.

As previously indicated, the Swedish settlers were mostly of the bourgeoisie class, such as army officers, college men, and decadent noblemen, all of whom were unaccustomed to work in the old country and, when driven to it by necessity in the new land, soon tired of a task that seemed to them both odius and barren of immediate returns. For these reasons many remained in the colony only a short time, leav-ing for other parts in the hope of better prospects or a change of luck. Carl Groth went to New Orleans, where he established himself as a cigar and news dealer. The old maid-servant Christine became the wife of a Norwegian settler and left the Unonius home to found her own household. In this manner the settlers were dispersed; in a short time the founder of the settlement stood alone with his faithful wife and the children who had grown up in the course of years. Not long after-wards, Unonius himself deserted the colony, and the lands formerly owned by the Swedes came into the possession of Norwegians and Americans.

To complete the story of this historic Swedish settlement, we take pleasure in appending some excerpts from the description given by Fredrika Bremer, the Swedish authoress, of her visit to Pine Lake. It was on a bright, warm Sunday morning, Sept. 29, 1850, that the authoress arrived, accompanied by Captain Lange. The little Swedish colony was already broken up, but a half dozen families still remained, earning their livelihood by farming. During the one day she spent in the settlement, several Swedish families were visited. All seemed to

be in limited circumstances, most of them living in log cabins. Among
the more fortunate ones was a blacksmith and "one Mr. Bergvall, who
had belonged to the genteel class in Sweden, but turned out an excellent
farmer on American soil." He had, continues the authoress, "the
prettiest, most charming and amiable young wife, with cheeks of a
fresh ruddiness, such as one seldom sees in America. This was a happy

Fredrika Bremer

and cheerful home, a good Swedish home in the midst of the American
wilderness. The dinner of which I partook was delicious in all its
simplicity, better than any I had eaten in the big, pretentious American
hotels. Delicious milk, excellent bread and butter, the most toothsome
seafowl, fine cakes, the hearty hospitality, the bright good cheer, and
the Swedish language well spoken by everyone, all these things combined to make the simple meal a veritable feast." The widowed Mrs.
Petterson, mother of Mrs. Bergvall, lived in the oldest house in the Pine
Lake settlement. There Fredrika Bremer passed the evening and the
following night. There were gathered "one and twenty Swedes who
spent the evening with games, songs and dances, in genuine Swedish

fashion. I felt happy to be with these my countrymen, happy to find them true Swedish folk still, although strangers in a strange land. And then I read to the assembled company that pretty little Norse 'Tale of the Pinetree,' by H. C. Andersen, at the conclusion of which I requested them to sing some Swedish folksongs. The fresh Northern voices had lost nothing in clearness in the atmosphere of the New World. My heart filled with tenderness as the men, with strong, clear voices, sang: 'Upp, svear, för konung och fädernesland,' and followed it up with several other old patriotic anthems. Swedish hospitality I found here as genuine, Swedish mirth and song rang as true as ever in our native land. Finally all joined in singing the old hymn: ' Nu hvilar hela jorden,' whereupon all broke up, bidding each other goodbye with firm clasping of hands and hearty good wishes.''

The first Swedish Lutheran clergyman in America since the time of the Delaware colony for a time lived and labored in the Pine Lake settlement. His name was Peter Vilhelm Böckman. He was born Dec. 5, 1806, and was the son of a clergyman in the parish of Söder-Hviddinge, in the province of Skåne. He was graduated from college in 1824 and entered the ministry several years later. With the aid of private persons in Sweden, he came to this country, presumably in 1844, to minister to the spiritual wants of the Scandinavian emigrants, and eventually drifted to the settlement at Pine Lake. Without success, he sought to unite the settlers into one congregation, thereby causing a conflict with Unonius. After having vainly sought admission to the American Episcopal Church, he visited various Swedish settlements as a traveling physician, having studied medicine in his youth. Finally he returned to Sweden, where he died in Göteborg, Oct. 3, 1850. Böckman seems to have been a man actuated by pure motives but lacking in energy and the genius of organization, qualities indispensable to a clergyman, especially in the days of the pioneers.

Before concluding this sketch, we are constrained to add that the letters of Unonius, which appeared in Swedish newspapers, besides inducing emigration by members of the Swedish bourgeoisie, caused a company of fifty persons to emigrate from Haurida, in Småland. The voyage was made in the sailing vessel ''Superior'' which landed them at Boston after ten weeks. All but one traveled from Boston to Sheboygan, Wis., and thence scattered to various parts of the state. Next to that of Unonius, this was the earliest company of Swedish emigrants during the eighteenth century.

Unonius and his family at length removed to Chicago. His further career will be recounted later in connection with the history of the Swedish Episcopal Church in Illinois. We now proceed to tell the story of another member of the Pine Lake colony, one who, like

Unonius, was destined to play a prominent part among the earliest Swedes in Illinois.

P. von Schneidau, First Swedish Vice-Consul in Chicago

Polycarpus von Schneidau was born in 1812, being the son of Major von Schneidau of Kisa, Östergötland. While still a very young man, he was enrolled in the Svea Artillery, and was soon made lieutenant. As such, he served at Fort Vaxholm during the summer of 1833, when he became one of the chief actors in an episode which attracted much attention at the time.

That summer certain naval surveys were carried on in the Baltic sea by the mutual agreement between the Swedish and the Russian governments. The chief of the Russian section, M. Schubert, when the operations brought them near Stockholm, expressed a desire to visit the Swedish capital. King Charles XIV. John granted the request and sent orders to Col. Anders Israel Pancheen, the commander at Fort Vaxholm, to permit the Russian flagship "Hercules" to pass the fort unmolested. The royal orders, however, did not relieve the ship of the ordinary duties of warcraft, such as laying to under the walls of a fort in order to report to its commander and show its papers.

So one day a warship hove in sight in the channel and approached Vaxholm with a full head of steam. The Russian flag designated its nationality, but nothing served to indicate that it was the "Hercules." When the steamer got within reach of the guns of the fort, still going with full speed, it was signaled to stop, but paid no attention to the warning. This was a breach of international naval law and a gratuitous insult to the flag that waved above the ramparts of the Swedish fort. Consequently, the commander ordered Lieutenant von Schneidau to open fire on the foreigner. Two shots were fired as a warning, but without the desired effect. The man of war steamed ahead undisturbed. Then the commander ordered the lieutenant to aim at the wheelhouse of the intruder and fire. The order was carried out to the letter. Lieutenant von Schneidau himself fired the shot, which shattered the wheelhouse of the "Hercules" into smithereens. Consternation reigned on deck, and a few moments later a boat shot out from the side of the damaged ship and made directly for shore under the walls of the fort. An officers stepped ashore, hurried to the commander and explained indignantly that the vessel was the "Hercules," which had permission to pass. Col. Pancheen shrugged his shoulders and expressed regret at not being informed of the fact in the regular way. A quarter of an hour after the Russian officer had returned on board, two boats, one from the fort, the other from the "Hercules," started in a race for Stockholm. In the former was Lieutenant von Schneidau, in the latter the same officer who had carried the message to the fort. The

Swedish lieutenant urged his men to the utmost exertion, and won the race. Arriving in Stockholm, he hastened to Count Magnus Brahe, the king's interpreter and confidential adviser, told his story, and requested the count to repeat it to the king. Count Brahe, greatly excited, at once sought the presence of his majesty. A few moments later, Lieutenant von Schneidau was called in and asked to give a minute account of what had transpired. When he told of the effective shot at the foreigner's wheelhouse, the old monarch showed signs of

Polycarpus von Schneidau

pleasure and requested the narrator to carry back a royal greeting to Col. Pancheen and tell him that he had acted like a man and that the king was entirely satisfied with the affair. When von Schneidau left the royal palace, he met the Russian minister, accompanied by the officer from the "Hercules," hurrying to lodge their complaints with the same high tribunal.

Lieutenant von Schneidau was a gallant officer, eminently fitted for his calling, nevertheless, his military career was soon interrupted. He was compelled to resign and leave his country almost a fugitive, not on account of any crime, but for the mere act of marrying a Jewess below his station in life, and thereby, as it was held, putting a blot on the honor of the military corps. It will be remembered that at this time the Jews did not enjoy the rights and the social position and privileges in Sweden since accorded them. Lieutenant von Schneidau had an early acquaintance with Unonius, and in 1842 joined his little colony, purchasing a piece of land at the south end of the lake. His wife and her mother arrived later and for a time all found a home in the log cabin of Unonius.

The young officer's prospects of success here were scant. He was not fitted for farming, an old injury to one of his legs incapacitating him for physical labor. Circumstances conspired against him, and in 1845 he removed to Chicago, where he hoped more easily to earn a living. His presumption proved correct. Being a skillful civil engineer, he soon obtained profitable employment. When in 1848 work began on the first railroad out of Chicago, the Chicago and Galena Railway, now a branch of the Northwestern system, von Schneidau was made superintendent of construction. On her American tour under the management of P. T. Barnum, in 1850, Jenny Lind, the great singer, furnished von Schneidau the money wherewith to purchase a French daguerreotype apparatus with supplies, and he then established a daguerreotype studio, the first of its kind in Chicago and, doubtless, in the entire West. He thus became the pioneer photographer in this part of the country.

After Swedish and Norwegian immigration to Chicago and vicinity had acquired greater proportions in the early fifties, von Schneidau was appointed Swedish and Norwegian vice consul here in 1854, being the first to hold that office. His official duties he discharged with the greatest efficiency. The numerous immigrants, many of whom were poor or afflicted with sickness, found in him a friend and benefactor. In his work for the welfare of his countrymen he had in his faithful wife an able assistant, who has been described as a loveable and noble-hearted woman.

Von Schneidau's illness was gradually aggravated, and soon he was unable to attend to his consular duties. He consequently resigned the office, to which his old friend Unonius succeeded. On Dec. 28, 1859, von Schneidau died, not quite forty-eight years of age. His wife had passed away the year before. This venerable pair is still cherished in loving remembrance by the early Swedish citizens of Chicago.

As the letters of Unonius, published in the newspapers of the old country, had caused the exodus of a company of emigrants from Småland, so von Schneidau's letters to his father in Kisa, Östergötland, early induced emigration from that part of Sweden. The contents of these letters were reported far and wide throughout the neighborhood, giving rise to much speculation as to the great West and the promises it held out to settlers. Discussion soon ripened into decision with some of the most determined ones, who emigrated under the leadership of one Peter Hassel, a miller. Besides Hassel, the company consisted of Peter Andersson, his brother-in-law, one John Danielson, a Mr. Berg, and an old sailor by the name of Dahlberg, the last two from Stockholm, and one Åkerman, who had served in the American army, making five families all told. They made the voyage in 1845 in the brig "Superb," embarking at Göteborg and landing at New York. Their original intention was to go to Wisconsin, presumably to Pine Lake, but in New York they were told that they could find more suitable soil in Iowa, so they changed their destination. They traveled first to Philadelphia, thence to Pittsburg, where they took passage on a steamer down the Ohio River, and then proceeded up the Mississippi as far as Burlington, Iowa. From that point they journeyed forty-two miles over the country and founded New Sweden, in Jefferson county, the first Swedish settlement in Iowa. During the following years new groups of immigrants from the same part of Sweden kept continually coming; soon there sprang up neighboring settlements known as Swede Point, in Boone county, and Bergholm, in Wapello county. This opened the way to the influx of Swedes into Iowa during the subsequent decades, both directly from the old country and from the earlier settlements in Illinois.

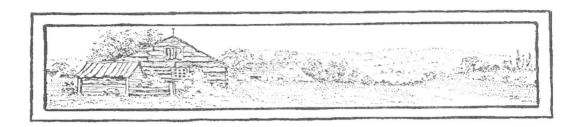

CHAPTER IV.

The Bishop Hill Colony

Early History of Erik Janssonism

BOUT 1840, there arose in Helsingland, Sweden, a peculiar religious sect, named Erik Janssonists from the founder, a farmer by the name of Erik Jansson. In order that the reader may fully understand the origin of the sect, it is necessary to describe briefly the religious conditions in that province just before and at the time of Erik Jansson's public appearance.

At that time spiritual decadence was general throughout Helsingland. Whisky distilling, as yet a lawful business for the peasantry, was carried on at almost every farmhouse, and drunkenness aided in brutalizing the minds and destroying domestic happiness. Particularly were the young people notorious for their unlicensed behavior. Brawls, thefts, and nocturnal orgies were common occurrences. The sturdiness and immutability characteristic of the Helsingland peasantry by no means served to mollify their brutality. Indeed, there were many outwardly pious folk, but their piety consisted primarily in observing certain religious customs, such as attending divine worship and partaking of the Lord's Supper. Many of the ministers were persons who made light of their duties as keepers of the flock. The majority of them lived a life of outward decency, but others showed even in their manners by what spirit they were governed, and not a few were steeped in drunkenness; others were so absorbed in political and municipal affairs or in agricultural pursuits that they neglected the duties of their calling.

In all this spiritual darkness, however, there were certain glimpses of light. For half a century the province had been the field of religious movements of various kinds, and although these had resulted in strife and disruption in many places, yet in a part of the population here and there in the villages they had awakened and sustained a true Christian life. The better class of ministers took an intelligent view of these movements and encouraged them so far as seemed permissible. Here as elsewhere the pietistic movement, or revivalism, resulted in religious gatherings, called conventicles. People began to gather in private houses for mutual edification, devoting themselves to singing and praying, studying the Word of God, and discoursing on religious subjects. These gatherings were styled "samlingar" (meetings), and the participants were nicknamed "läsare" (readers), for their zealous study of religious books. The same name was soon applied to the followers of any revivalist movement in Sweden, no matter what was its origin.

While several of the more earnest and devoted clergymen allied themselves with the "readers," watched over their meetings, and guided them in their Bible studies and their worship, the worldly-minded portion of the clergy took either an indifferent or an inimical position anent the movement. Instead of endeavoring, through instruction and a kindly disposition, to lead aright the souls that felt spiritual hunger and thirst, they looked upon the conventicles as dangerous manifestations of dissension which ought to be suppressed by the aid of the law. In many instances the so-called Conventicle Placard* of 1726 was used as a means to this end. These attempts to assuage by injunctions and fines the thirst for spiritual enlightenment, which the people sought to quench at the fountain of Holy Writ and other religious writings, since the average clergyman offered them no other spiritual nourishment than the ordinary sermons, which the common people found dry and incomprehensible, seemed to the "readers" harsh and unreasonable; and there was justice in their complaint over the fact that while gatherings in private houses for the purpose of gambling, dancing, and other worldly pleasures were left unmolested, it was considered a crime to hold private meetings to praise and worship God.

In defiance of the letter of the law, the "readers" held their private religious meetings, taking the ground that so long as they were not guilty of heresy, the law did not apply. Holding as they did that the preaching of an unregenerate clergy could bear no good fruit, they recognized ministers of proven piety only. Although the conventicle law charged the clergy with the duty of conducting meetings in private houses, yet devout ministers who took the conventicles in their own hands would frequently incur the disfavor of the consistories, and worldly-minded or bigoted clergymen usually led in the persecution of the "readers."

It is not surprising that members of congregations having such ministers sought to satisfy their spiritual cravings by reading such

* A law designed to prevent the spread of heresy by forbidding all religious gatherings not conducted by the clergy, or by parents, employers or heads of households exclusively for their own families and subordinates. Infractions were punishable by fines, imprisonment and banishment.

religious books as they had and by listening to preachers who arose from among the common people and claimed to give that which the clergy was unable to bestow. The bitter attacks made by some of the pietist writers ofttimes begot a fanatical hatred of the established church forms, and their criticisms of the conduct of the clergy frequently gave rise to wholesale denunciations of the state church.

The consequences of these religious movements were not slow to manifest themselves. In the parishes where the clergy had taken active part in the revival and gained the confidence of the "readers" by superintending and participating in the meetings, a considerable portion of the population soon became well versed in the Scriptures and capable of successfully combating any false teachings that self-appointed preachers might attempt to spread; but in many places the peasantry had been left entirely to themselves and had become accustomed to listen to revivalist preachers of various kinds. men of the working class. often without culture or experience, but endowed with a certain readiness of speech and an ample measure of self-assertiveness, who claimed to have become regenerated and to be under the direct guidance of the Holy Spirit. By their hideous depictions of hell and the sufferings of the condemned, and by seathing denunciations of all those whose views differed from their own, they contrived to hold their followers completely in their power, and masses of people followed them untiringly from place to place, from parish to parish. The "readers" possessed a certain amount of scriptural knowledge, but their reading was generally limited to modern religious writings; the Bible, being considered too difficult a book for the unlettered, was read only in exceptional cases or brought out as authority, when, in the meetings, some one sought to clinch some particular assertion or give added force to an admonition. For these reasons the revivalism of the Helsingland parishes was misdirected and became one-sided. It was not always characterized by that spiritual soundness, vitality, self-sacrificing love, kindness and forbearance, inseparable from the true life of faith. but frequently bred bigotry, intolerance, hypocrisy and self-righteousness.

These conditions had paved the way for a lay preacher of extra-ordinary power, who at first taught in full accord with the doctrines, though not the practices, of the state church and the beliefs of the "readers," but soon departed from the tenets of both, headed a new sect, was charged with heresy and presently found himself in open warfare with the authorities of church and state. This religious leader. a rather remarkable character in Swedish church history, was Erik Jansson—farmer, preacher, self-styled prophet, ambassador of God and restorer of the true Christian faith.

Erik Jansson's Youth and First Public Appearance

Erik Jansson was born December 19, 1808, in the village of Landsberga, in Biskopskulla parish, Upland. His parents, Jan Mattsson, a farmer, and his wife Sara Eriksson, lived in Thorstuna, but after their marriage in 1802 they rented a small farm in Landsberga. To them were born four sons, Johan, Erik, Peter and Karl, and one daughter, Anna Katarina. In 1820 they moved back to Thorstuna, and lived there until 1838, when Jan Mattsson, who had improved his condition materially by diligent application, purchased a farm, called Klockaregården, in Österunda parish of the same province, where he lived with his family until his death in November, 1843, the estate then passing to his children. His boyhood and youth Erik Jansson spent at home. As a boy of eight, he was one day engaged in doing some hauling, when the horse took fright and ran away, overturning the wagon and throwing the boy violently to the ground, at which he received so hard a blow on the head that for several weeks he hovered between life and death. For many years after his recovery the boy suffered from severe headaches. This accident seemed to have had a marked effect on his mind. After that he was different from other children of his age, he avoided his former companions, and sought out some secluded spot where he would spend hours in tearful prayer. He claimed to be the most unhappy of children, for he could not, like them, join with zest in games and amusements. At the age of seventeen, he was prepared for admittance to the holy communion. To him this was a period of comparative peace of mind; the youth sought spiritual solace in the reading of the Bible and other religious books. However, he soon ceased, and when his old fears returned he vainly endeavored to dissipate them by joining the young people in dancing parties and similar amusements.

The parents resented the "silly notions" of their son and kept him hard at work, thinking that this would cure him. But the remedy had quite the contrary effect. He continued his melancholy ponderings and, besides, was taken physically ill with a severe attack of rheumatism. Things went on in this way until the summer of 1830, when Erik Jansson experienced his conversion proper. While on his way to the field one day with his father's horse, he had an acute attack of his complaint. Dismounting, he fell to the ground and lay for a while helpless. Then, according to his own assertion, he heard a voice, saying: "It is written, whatsoever ye ask in prayer, believing, that ye shall receive, for all is possible to him that believeth; and when ye cry, I shall answer, saith the Lord." At that he arose to his knees and prayed long and fervently; and from that moment he was entirely rid of his malady.

In another sense, that moment was of still greater significance to Erik Jansson, for then and there his spiritual conversion was accomplished, according to the narrative found in his autobiography. Sorely oppressed by his burden of sin, here in the solitude, he fled to Christ and felt that he had obtained remission of his sins and mental peace.

It is impossible to ascertain how complete was this regeneration, but that it was not a mere sham seems evident from the discourses on divine themes written by him about this time. However, Erik Jansson was not satisfied with the fact that he himself was awakened to spiritual life; he wanted others to be similarly awakened and, therefore, began the very next day after his conversion to preach the gospel to those about him. He continued preaching thus for four years. Meanwhile he sought, by home study, to add to his stock of knowledge, particularly as regards religious topics. Although Erik Jansson spent much time in reading, still he did not neglect his work, since he pursued his studies mostly at night. His favorite studies, aside from the Bible, were the works of Luther, Arndt, Nohrborg, Murbeck and other religious writers, with whom he thus became thoroughly familiar.

These studies, however, imbued Erik Jansson with a true sense of his own insignificance in the field of Lutheran teaching, so he determined to discontinue preaching altogether. It was especially from reading "True Christianity," by Johan Arndt, that he was, at least for a time, cured of his desire to preach, for he found a passage in that work admonishing people to stick to their calling instead of seeking to become the teachers of others.

About this time, Erik Jansson married Maria Kristina Larsson, a servant to his parents, who, like himself, was a devoted student of the Bible. The parents obstinately opposed the match for a long time, until circumstances forced them to permit the union. At this they took still greater offense, and when the son set up his own household they dismissed him curtly, a cow and a pig being the only dower. He was not discouraged, but began life on his own account by renting part of a farm in Vappeby, also going into business in a small way as a grain dealer in company with his oldest brother. He soon earned the reputation of being the best farmer in the neighborhood, and in spite of several crop failures he had done so well that in 1838 he was able to purchase the Lötorp estate, near Sånkarby, in Österunda parish, for one thousand crowns in cash. Here he is said to have lived in quiet seclusion for a time, working diligently on the farm, and trying to live the life of a humble Christian. At times, however, his former desire to preach returned, when he would publicly expound the Scriptures with power and ability, acquired doubtless through his extensive reading.

The Erik Jansson Dissenters

In the year 1840 occurred what Erik Jansson himself has termed his second conversion. Together with his youngest brother, Karl, he went to the October fair in Upsala to sell cattle. The rowdy and ungodly conduct of the people attending the fair impressed him in a manner to awaken anew his desire to preach. Upon his return home, he consulted his pastor, Rev. J. J. Risberg, in the matter and from him received the advice to follow the inner call. About this time he deserted Luther, Arndt, as well as all other religious authors, for which he conceived an intense hatred, and kept to the Bible alone. Then he noted the overwhelming power and simplicity of Holy Writ, as compared with other writings, and he soon acquired the fixed conviction that the Bible alone ought to be read.* In the community where

Fac-Simile of Page from Erik Jansson's Church Prayers

he lived were held meetings at which Erik Jansson often appeared together with Risberg. This man as well as C. C. Estenberg, the adjunct clergyman of the parish, publicly lauded Erik Jansson in the most cordial terms, giving him every encouragement to continue his activity.

---

* It will be noticed that he soon changed his mind on this point, by publishing books of his own. From wholesale condemnation of other printed interpretations of the Bible to the publication of his own, the step was easy for Erik Jansson, on the ground that his was the divine and only true interpretation.

Erik Jansson's religious discourses soon began to show marked divergences from the doctrines of the Church of Sweden. He taught complete freedom from sin on the part of the true believer, maintained the full and complete sanctification of the Christian once and for all, his inability to do wrong and still remain a Christian, and held that the trespasses spoken of in the Lord's Prayer have reference only to the unregenerate. This was Erik Jansson's first serious departure in doctrine. He defended his view by means of an ingenious combination of scriptural passages, an art which he had completely mastered. He further aroused the opposition of the clergy by claiming to be sent as the special messenger of God to restore the true faith.*

By these contentions he aroused much adverse sentiment in Österunda. The rumor that the "readers" were very numerous in Helsingland gave him the idea that there he might find a more receptive field of operation than at home. For the alleged purpose of selling wheat flour, but really to gain a better knowledge of the religious movements in those parts, he made a trip to Helsingland in January, 1843.† accompanied by a hired man. Arriving at Söderala socken, at that time one of the hotbeds of revivalism, he first made inquiries whether there were any prominent religious teachers in that locality and was promptly referred to the peasant Jonas Olsson of Ina, who, together with his brother Olof Olsson of Kingsta, was a revivalist leader in the parish. Erik Jansson and his companion obtained lodging at the house of the former over night. They arrived on a Saturday evening. Erik Jansson at once declared himself one of the faithful, receiving, nevertheless, a somewhat cool reception at the hands of the devout Jonas Olsson. The following morning the married sister of the host came to purchase some flour, but Erik Jansson refused to do business on the Sabbath. This Jonas Olsson accepted as proof positive that the visitor was a true "reader," and adopted a more amiable manner toward the stranger. Such was the first meeting between these two men, who soon were to have so many weighty interests in common.

That Sunday morning Erik Jansson accompanied the host and his family to church, and in the evening they attended a meeting held in the neighborhood. Although requested by Jonas Olsson to rise and speak to the assemblage, Erik Jansson sat quiet in his seat. After their return home, the two men had a conversation regarding the meeting, which the stranger said was not at all to his liking, because he had

---

* His usual public declarations on this point were these: "The new doctrine I teach is of God; I am sent by God; since the time of the Apostles there has been no true preacher before me."

† This accords with all writers consulted. except Eric Johnson and C. F. Peterson, who say, "in the spring of 1842." If a trip was made prior to 1843, it was of no apparent consequence.

detected that the participants did not hold themselves to the Bible alone. At the meeting a portion had been read out of a postil and subsequently expounded. "What kind of Christianity is this you have?" Erik Jansson inquired sternly. The next morning he reprimanded Jonas Olsson for not conducting household worship. Hereby Erik Jansson made a profound impression on his host, and from that time the latter and his brother Olof became stanch supporters of Erik Jansson and pillars of his sect. From his own diary it appears that Erik Jansson felt great inner satisfaction at having got even with Jonas Olsson for the haughty manner in which he was received at his first meeting with the peasant preacher.

Erik Jansson now continued his journey northward. In the next parish, Norrala, he met Per Norin, a blacksmith, who was the virtual leader of the "readers" in that locality. His first conversation with Erik Jansson convinced him that the latter was an impostor. When they parted he exacted a promise from him never to return. This exasperated Erik Jansson to such an extent that he broke forth in execrations over the community of Norrala. Erik Jansson now journeyed on through Enånger, Njutånger, Hudiksvall and Helsingtuna, preaching everywhere and generally winning large numbers over to his views. This may be accounted for partly by the fact that he deviated only slightly from the tenets held by the "readers" in these parts, but what mostly impressed the multitudes was his ability to speak for four or five hours without signs of exhaustion, his abnormal memory, enabling him to quote almost any passage of the Bible at will, and his forcible advocacy of the Bible as the only source from which truth may be derived. For the time being, he shrewdly concealed his antipathy to the writings of Luther, Arndt, Nohrborg and others. After visiting Helsingtuna he returned home, Jonas Olsson accompanying him as far as Gefle. Here several meetings were held, at which Jonas Olsson invariably was loud in his praise of Erik Jansson. When in the middle of February he arrived home to Österunda, he was warmly received by Risberg, who, however, warned him against spiritual arrogance.

Erik Jansson's impressions of conditions in Helsingland were so favorable that he returned there in the latter part of February the same year. From Söderala he journeyed northward together with Jonas Olsson to Enånger, Njutånger and Hudiksvall, but did not meet with the same degree of success as on his former visit. His explanation of this was that the "readers" in Norrala were opposing him, but the real reason was found in his more open departures from the teachings of the state church and his bitter attacks upon the revivalism of the "readers" and the clergymen who upheld it. Disgusted with his meager success, he determined to seek other fields for his labors, and, with a girl from Delsbo, Karin Ersson of Nyåker, acting as his guide, he went to Forssa. From there he went to Bjuråker, where at first he was well received by A. G. Sefström, the parson. But this friendship did not last, so Erik Jansson soon returned to Forssa, where he was carrying on a vigorous propaganda during the latter part of March.

Jonas Olson, Trustee and Preacher, in his Later Years

Accompanied by the girl Karin and a few other women followers he went from place to place, preaching many times a day. The audiences grew apace. His fiery invectives against the general indifference on the part of the spiritual guardians of the people mightily increased his popularity. Yet there were those who opposed him, the principal opponent being a woman, Karin Jonsson from Utnäs, who traveled from village to village antagonizing and disproving Erik Jansson's statements. As a result there arose a vast amount of controversy over the question of Erik Jansson's divine mission. His vindictiveness gained the day, however, convincing the majority of the zealots that he was the special messenger of God.

Late in March Erik Jansson left Forssa. After a brief stay in Söderala, which brought him many converts, he reached Österunda at the end of April. During his absence the "readers" had gained so great accessions that the king's bailiff of the district was moved to have an announcement read in the Österunda church threatening the instigators of the movement with arrest and fines, did they not discontinue their meetings. Risberg, who had encouraged these gatherings, was warned to desist and urged to counteract the movement by means of special biblical exegeses in church and the introduction of private worship in the homes. These warnings were not given without cause, for tumults had actually occurred in connection with the numerous meetings. Erik Jansson was also met by the news that in his absence part of his personal property had been carried away by thieves and that his wife had been harshly treated by his parents. To add to his misfortunes, Risberg, in consequence of warnings received, had now turned against him.

Erik Jansson now staid at home for two months, attending to the spring work on his farm. About midsummer, he claimed to have received the same kind of a revelation that King Solomon had, according to I. Kings 3 : 5. Like King Solomon, Erik Jansson then prayed for "an understanding heart to judge thy (God's) people, that I may distinguish good from bad," and claimed to have been given, like Solomon of old, an understanding heart in response to his prayer.

Shortly after midsummer, Erik Jansson made another journey to Helsingland. This time he traveled through Hanebo, Bollnäs and Jerfsö to Delsbo and Forssa, in which latter locality he went about holding meetings in the pasture fields. In these parishes he spoke with great assurance, claiming, as a result of the new revelation, "greater light than ever before." At a meeting in Delsbo he announced that he and Rev. Estenberg from Österunda were collaborating on a new translation of the Bible, for which he was now taking subscriptions.

He had unbounded confidence in himself. In order to command still greater respect among his followers, he attempted to imitate the Savior and his apostles by performing miracles. In Svedja, Delsbo parish, there was an old maid-servant who had been bedridden for years. When Erik Jansson learned of this he at once went to her bedside in order to cure her. Standing close to the sickbed he commanded the woman to take him by the hand and repeat the words, "I believe," when she would be instantly cured. She did as she was told, but without any effect whatever; nevertheless Erik Jansson turned to the bystanders praising God for what had been done, saying he had driven out the devil and quoting the words, "Today hath salvation come unto this household."

In Kälkbo, Forssa parish, there was a young man aged twenty-nine, a cripple who had been bedridden from his childhood. After having made the house his headquarters for some time, Erik Jansson attempted to heal him in a miraculous manner. He predicted that on midsummer day (1844) the young man, suddenly cured of the malady, would "leap like a young deer." The invalid and his family firmly believed this, and clothes were ordered for him, but when the day arrived, there was no perceptible change in his condition. The failure cost Erik Jansson a number of adherents, and the house was closed to him from that day.*

During a drouth in the early summer of 1845 Erik Jansson gave it out that there would be no rain for three years and six months, as a result of his prayers to that effect. When in July the drouth was broken by rain, Erik Jansson attempted to save his reputation as a prophet by explaining that out of pity for the people he had averted the wrath of God with a new prayer.

On his return to Österunda, he was met by opposition in many quarters. Then he determined to sell his farm and remove to Helsingland to remain permanently among his followers there. He sacrificed Lötorp for 900 crowns for that purpose, but his father having died, he went to live on the paternal estate until April, 1844, before removing permanently to Helsingland. On this journey he went to Bollnäs and thence to Delsbo and Forssa. About this time Erik Jansson began his so-called "apostolic pilgrimages." At first he was followed only by women, but soon men also joined him at the meetings, sitting in a semi-circle around him as a kind of jury, testifying to the truth of everything he said. Urged by several of his followers, Erik Jansson now extended his operations to Alfta parish, in western Helsingland. Here he discovered a very grateful field for his labors, it having been prepared beforehand by traveling evangelists, who had held meetings of a Methodist character, so that Erik Jansson's doctrine of freedom from sin was not entirely new to the people. Besides, license and contempt for the clergy were prevalent in the localities where the so-called "readers" were numerous.

Under such circumstances it was but natural that the inhabitants of Alfta would be impressed by Erik Jansson's spirited antagonism of the established church. They were influenced all the more easily by his strong insistence on their reading the Bible to the exclusion of all other religious books. Step by step marked his departure from the established faith. Gradually he began to pose among them as being especially

* This and the following instance are cited by Landgren.

inspired by the Holy Spirit and set up his claim as the restorer of the pure Christian faith.

Having gained the greatest number of followers in northern Helsingland, he decided to make his home there. With his wife and two children, Erik and Mathilda, he moved to Forssa in April, 1844, shortly afterward purchasing from Jon Olsson of Stenbo the right of homestead at Lumnäs, a torp, or tenancy, subject to Stenbo. This marked a new epoch in the career of Erik Jansson. Prior to this, he had merely been preaching to his followers, who were scattered throughout the different parishes. Now these began to form a party or sect of their own, known as the Erik Janssonists, their leader simultaneously adopting the title of Prophet and assuming the authority of dictator and lawmaker for his faithful. One of his first mandates was to prohibit them from attending the regular church services, commanding them, instead, to be present at the meetings now regularly conducted by him.

The clergy and the civil authorities, considering the attitude now assumed by Erik Jansson all too defiant, called a meeting of the parishioners of Forssa. It was resolved to petition the provincial governmen to have him arrested as a vagrant and brought back to his home parish. Meanwhile, Erik Jansson went to the southern part of the province, operating mostly in Alfta, with brief excursions to Ofvanåker, Bollnäs and Söderala. He held meetings everywhere, posing as the "God-sent prophet," "the greatest light since the time of the Apostles," "the restorer of the true faith," etc. Almost everywhere he was received with high enthusiasm, and great masses, especially the "readers," believed him blindly. He had now entirely abandoned the caution observed earlier in his career, and when charged with preaching doctrines different from his earlier teachings, he replied in the words of St. Paul, that he had "desired to win them over by cunning." The theory of sinlessness was all along the central theme in his doctrine. To anyone who ventured to protest against the teaching or to dispute the divine mission of the teacher, he had the set retort: "Thou art of the devil," or, "Thy faith is of the devil," proving the statement by the assertion: "It is written in the Scriptures, the devils believe likewise, with fear." The way of salvation as pointed out by Erik Jansson grew the more free and easy according as the number of proselytes increased. Reduced to its simplest terms it was to confess one's belief in the prophet. Hardened sinners, who showed no sign of repentance, are said to have been shriven in this manner: at the meetings he embraced the new converts, with the query, "Wouldst thou be saved?" If the answer was, "Yes," he gave the immediate assurance, "Thou art saved," and wrote the name of the convert in a book.

The suppressive measures of the authorities were like an attempt to fight fire with oil. They served to increase the ardor of his adherents and caused them to gather all the closer around their leader, declaring that no evil should ever befall him. They loudly protested that he was sent by God and threatened blodshed, should the authorities violate his person. So far did they go in their devotion that they promised to follow him in death and even into hell, should that be his ultimate goal.

The alleged sinless state of the believers gave them great latitude in the matter of behavior. The prophet permitted himself the utmost freedom of conduct, and his relations with his women followers were not always above reproach. In the spring and summer of 1843 the aforesaid Karin Ersson traveled about with him, moved by religious infatuation. She had implicit confidence in this "man of God" until he began to pay her such attentions as seemed to her improper in a married man. When she upbraided him, he would own to being tempted and pray for deliverance from temptation, only to repeat the indecency with growing boldness. When at length he made her a shameless proposition outright and was promptly repulsed, he made the insidious reply: "Yes, but as a true believer in my Savior, Jesus Christ, I might do this without sinning." He adjured her not to say a word about the incident, as that would be committing a grievous sin, and the girl kept the matter secret for some time. When she finally made known his conduct, the prophet broke into a towering wrath and publicly denounced her as a liar and a vixen, praying that God might "add iniquity unto her iniquity." Some time in the winter of 1844, in the presence of one Isak Rudolphi and five women, one a follower of the prophet, Erik Jansson admitted the truth of the charge made by Karin Ersson, as attested by the six witnesses in a signed document dated at Delsbo, May 6, 1844.* Subsequently the prophet alternately denied the confession, charged that the girl had been the guilty party, that he had merely wished to put her to a test, or that his own evil desire had been sent as a punishment from God.

In March, 1844, Erik Jansson visited Alfta at the invitation of certain women, including an unmarried woman of Broddlägret, Bollnäs, who also had been his traveling companion. During his sojourn here the prophet, his former companion and another woman from Bollnäs shared the same room at night. The villagers led a simple life and were no sticklers on decorum, but this could not pass without comment. One woman, who with her husband was then devoted to the prophet,

* Landgren: Erik-Jansismen, p. 29.

afterwards said of Erik Jansson and the Bollnäs girl: "Their wanton and unchaste behavior made me blush on behalf of our sex."

At Hamre, Forssa parish, Erik Jansson one morning just before opening a meeting had a frolic with two or three girls, who had accompanied him from Alfta. His wife, who was present, took offense and a disagreement ensued, witnessed by a number of the worshipers. Before these the prophet justified himself in this wise, "Because ye lack faith, all this befalls me; faith is not in you, therefore Satan hath been empowered to winnow her like wheat."

Erik Jansson's moral character once stained, his enemies sought to paint the man entirely black. Other rumors were set afloat impeaching his private and public conduct, but they are branded as false by the same authority upon which the above incidents have been quoted. The latter were enough to bring the prophet into ill repute with the general public, but the faith of his adherents remained unshaken. He declared himself perfect and holy, like God himself, and they took him at his word. Even granting the truth of the damaging evidence, some still held him blameless, maintaining that the heart had no part in the doings of the flesh.

Many iniquities were committed against the prophet and his adherents in the name of the law. One of the most flagrant outrages was perpetrated in August, 1844, at Klockaregården, Österunda, by the parish vicar, N. A. Arenander, one of Erik Jansson's bitterest enemies. Shortly after the return of the latter from his fourth apostolic pilgrimage to Helsingland, his adherents in Österunda met one night in Klockaregården, the house of Olof Stenberg. Sophia Sjön, an ardent believer in the prophet, was staying there. At midnight Arenander arrived, with a number of men, and demanded entry. This being refused, the door was forced. On the pretense of searching for Erik Jansson the minister, who is said to have been drunk at the time, entered the bedchamber, where Sofia Sjön and Anna Maria Stråle slept. He pulled the former out of bed, tore handfuls of hair from her head, pushed her out to the men in her night garment, and after finishing his vain search through the house, brought the woman half dressed as a prisoner to the sheriff's house in Thorstuna, a neighboring village. To justify his action, the parson charged the woman with vagrancy, but the officer promptly ordered her release. The injured woman brought suit against the vicar for disturbing the peace, assault and battery, false arrest, and sundry minor offenses, for all of which crimes and misdemeanors she sought damages and urged one year's imprisonment and fines. At the preliminary hearing the charges were fully substantiated by five witnesses. The defendant impeached the witnesses on the ground that they belonged to the "readers" and were not church members in good standing, and accordingly the court declared two of the witnesses incompetent. The case was continued, and during preparation for the exodus to America it seems to have been dropped. This same Arenander was a tireless prosecutor of the "readers" and Erik Janssonists, but according to an official report of the magistracy the cases in that district were all dismissed 'for want of equity.

One explanation of the great influence Erik Jansson wielded over his followers lay in the hypnotism of his eye, which few were able to withstand. Thereby he controlled his people with a power and personal influence that was irresistible. In personal appearance, Erik Jansson was of medium stature, with brown hair, blue eyes, pale, thin face, with high cheek-bones, and thin lips, uncommonly long and broad teeth, especially in the upper jaw; the last joint of the right index finger was lacking, having been severed with an ax by his elder brother, Johan, in their boyhood. His voice was harsh and disagreeable in tone, and his speech rather indistinct, as though he had something in his mouth while speaking. In meeting he habitually overexerted himself, when his voice was transformed to a piercing shriek. A constant grin, which may have been the result of involuntary muscular contraction, gave him a repulsive look. Furthermore, he had frequent recourse to tears, the abundant flow of which did not tend to make his appearance more attractive. A portrait of Erik Jansson cannot be given, he having never sat for his picture, either in photograph or on canvas.

Book Pyres and Consequent Arrest of Erik Jansson

As we have seen, Erik Jansson ever since his so-called "second conversion" had a bitter aversion to the writings of Luther and Arndt. By and by, he conceived a plan to rid himself, once and for all, of these hated authorities which were continually quoted in rebuttal of his views by both prospective proselytes and outright antagonists. He would have liked to make short shrift with the Lutheran catechism and psalmbook, but these were still held in so high esteem among his own followers that he dared not as yet do violence to them directly, but confined himself to scathing denunciations in his sermons, applying to them such terms as, "an empty barrel with both ends closed" and the "wails of Satan." The beasts of the Book of Revelation, he claimed, were the prototypes of these "false and devilish teachers, Luther, the demigod, and Arndt, the murderer of souls." The following excerpt is quoted to give some idea of the tone of the sermons preached by Erik Jansson at this time:

"The Word of God has lain fallow from generation to generation. There is no salvation in the sermons usually preached in times past. If ye believe my words, ye shall be saved; if ye mistrust me, ye also mistrust God. Once a man set himself up against my teachings, but what happened? Within three days he was taken hence and thrust into eternity. Ye would read the idolatrous books of the accursed Luther and the devilish Arndt. But hear ye! Mark well my words! It was not the Gospel of the Lord, but of the devil; it was with the waters of hell that he deluged the whole world. Hear ye! Since ye will not believe the pure gospel that I preach unto you, the Lord shall pour out his cups of burning wrath over you, and ye shall be thrust into nethermost hell!''

These rantings soon took effect. All that was necessary to set his followers to destroying their Lutheran books was for the prophet to point to the words of the 19th verse of the 19th chapter of Acts: ''And not a few of them that practiced magical arts brought their books together and burned them in the sight of all.'' A like scene was enacted on the 11th of June, 1844, in the village of Tranberg, in Alfta parish. People in great numbers from Alfta, Söderala, Ofvanåker and Bollnäs for several days had been engaged in lugging sacks filled with books down to the banks of the lake where they were piled into a great pyre near Fiskragården. Erik Jansson was present in person, encouraging the people in this wise: ''Satan celebrated a jubilee, when the works of Luther were first published; when we now burn them, it will be his turn to grieve''; or, ''Those who take part shall feel a heavenly joy when they see the smoke rise.'' A person who warned them of the consequence of their act was told by Olof Olsson of Kingsta that so fixed were they in their determination that blood would flow, ere a single book would be exempt from the pyre. Some would save the covers of their books, but Erik Jansson declared in a loud voice, ''Whosoever saves the coverings of his idols shall be damned!''

The pyre was lighted, and books to the value of about 975 crowns, including the postils of Luther, Nohrborg, Linderoth, Pettersson and others, ''True Christianity,'' by Arndt, and great masses of temperance tracts, were consumed by the flames.

''Behold, how Satan opens his jaws!'' the fanatics exclaimed when the books would open from the heat and draft. To the vast assemblage Erik Jansson read the 18th chapter of Revelations, whereupon two hired men chanted: ''Give thanks and praise unto the Lord,'' to which the crowd sang the response: ''Glory be unto the Lord.''

The heavenly joy predicted by the prophet did not materialize, however; instead, evil forebodings seemed to haunt the minds of the spectators as the last flicker of the pyre died out.

The cup of fanaticism was now brimming over and the authorities could no longer watch Erik Jansson's operations with indifference. Two days after the burning of the books, he was arrested after a bloody encounter between the deputies and the followers of the prophet. Erik

Jansson himself was near being killed in the fray. He was imprisoned first at Gefle, then at Vesterås, until July 12th, when he was released after a hearing before the provincial governor in the latter city. Together with some of his friends, Erik Jansson then went to Stockholm and obtained an audience before the king. From the capital he wrote letters to his disciples in Helsingland, admonishing some of their number to go out and proclaim his doctrines, which they did. After a second hearing before the governor at Vesterås Sept. 21st, when Erik Jansson put up a clever defense, he was entirely cleared of the charges and at once returned to Helsingland.

If he had heretofore been a prophet in the eyes of his followers, his arrest and the mistreatment to which they thought him subjected, crowned him with the halo of martyrdom. He went so far as to liken his sufferings to those of the Savior himself. Surrounded by eleven men, corresponding to the apostles of Christ, and a great number of women, he went from village to village, holding meetings at which "the Passion of Erik Jansson" was recited, including all his acts and sufferings from the time of his arrest. He claimed to be in high favor with the king after his visit to the royal palace; and all things contributed towards making his fame greater than ever before. In the height of his arrogance, he now began to grant forgiveness of sin to all who at the meetings announced themselves as believers in him.

On Oct. 28th of that year, at Lynäs, Söderala parish, he arranged a second pyre of theological books, this time including the catechism and the Lutheran hymnal, with the promise that a new catechism and hymnal, written by himself, would soon be published. Following the ceremony of burning, a thanksgiving service was held in a neighboring farmhouse.

Not quite a month afterwards, Erik Jansson had intended to arrange still another auto-da-fé, especially for the Forssa and Delsbo parishes, but he was again arrested, this time by order of a royal letter, instructing the Upsala chapter to administer a warning. The provincial authorities at Gefle, where he was again brought, placed him under medical surveillance, on the supposition that he was demented. In the meantime, Erik Jansson was writing hymns, founded largely on the books of Ezra and Nehemiah; he also sent his wife instructions to have his early writings copied and prepared for publication. Having been found of sound mind, he was sent to Upsala, where on December 18th he was officially warned by the chapter against propagating false doctrines, and then set free.

Three days later he was back in Söderala, conducting meetings as before. A meeting was held Sunday, December 22nd, during the time of high mass, but the audience was dispersed by the king's bailiff, who appeared on the scene with a number of deputies. A great tumult arose in which several persons, among whom the wife of Erik Jansson, received bodily injuries. He was now taken back to the Gefle prison and kept there till April 18th the following year.

Erik Jansson's Flight to Dalarne and Norway

While Erik Jansson was in prison, his disciples carried on his work. Their meetings were now generally held simultaneously with the regular services in the churches. In expectation of the new catechism and hymnal promised by Erik Jansson, his followers refused to send their children to the common schools. Wherever Erik Janssonism gained a foothold it created more or less disturbance in the parishes. Disagreements were provoked between husband and wife, parents and children, masters and servants, and naturally those who suffered persecution had nothing but contempt for the civil and ecclesiastical authorities.

At Forssa occurred a third burning of books in the early morning of Dec. 7, 1844, when the perpetrators had the audacity to include a copy of "Sveriges Rikes Lag," the code of the realm. This, however, was saved in the last moment, as were a number of the other books doomed to destruction. A trial followed, resulting in the conviction and fining of the fifteen participants. To illustrate the feeling towards the clergy: an Erik Janssonist peasant of Delsbo is said to have offered to have all his timber cut down and made into headsman's blocks and gallows for the men of the cloth. Equally fanatical were they in their adoration of the new religious leader. For instance, a subscription was started in Ofvanåker for the purpose of purchasing his liberty, his deluded friends believing that the authorities could be bribed to release him from prison. In Alfta his followers went from village to village, holding meetings at which the established church and the clergy were roundly abused, the tenor of the denunciations being that all churches ought to be burned and all clergymen hanged, or, leastwise, their tongues cut out. They appropriated two per cent. of their property "for the restoration of the crumbling church of Christ." In other Helsingland parishes where the movement had gained a foothold similar operations were carried on, extending also into Österunda and Thorstuna parishes in Upland, everywhere resulting in more or less violent clashes with the civil authorities.

Immediately after his arrest, Erik Jansson lodged a plea with the provincial governor's office demanding his release, which was denied. He appealed to the king's court, which on March 17th found the charges insufficient to warrant his detention in prison, whereupon the prison authorities returned him to Forssa on April 23rd.

Having been enjoined from leaving Forssa parish, "the Savior at Stenbo," as Erik Jansson was nicknamed by the local population, continued his work there more aggressively than before, and the people flocked in ever increasing numbers to listen to this "voice in the wilderness." He also proceeded to ordain and send out apostles, to whom he solemnly delivered the keys of the Kingdom of Heaven.

On midsummer day he conducted a largely attended meeting at Stenbo. J. M. Åström, the king's bailiff, determined to arrest Erik Jansson and break up the meeting, ordered out a number of parishioners to assist him. They were told to provide themselves with clubs. Thus armed, they moved on to Stenbo, where they found the prophet preaching from the doorstep to the crowd outside. In the act of making the arrest, the officer was pulled down from the doorstep by a woman, and Erik Jansson escaped through the crowd and fled, but those of his believers who remained were terribly beaten and otherwise mistreated, while defending themselves as best they could. The next day the bailiff again appeared, now accompanied by the parson and a large crowd of people, and again ordered the assemblage at Stenbo to disperse. As soon as the king's officer had left, a desperate fight ensued between the Erik Janssonists and their antagonists, in which knives were flourished, windows and doors broken, and much household goods destroyed. Erik Jansson's wife, who had taken refuge in the cow-barn, was discovered by some young fellows just in the act of disappearing through a dung-trap in the floor and was then and there treated to a thorough bastinado.

Erik Jansson sought refuge in the home of Jonas Olsson in Ina, Söderala, then escaped to Österunda and Thorstuna, and lay in hiding for five weeks under the floor of a cow-barn in Thorstuna and then for several weeks more in an attic in the same parish.

These disturbances could not pass unnoticed. A royal decree of Feb. 17, 1845, had ordered a legal investigation and definite charges preferred. July 21st, the day set for the trial, came, but the accused was nowhere to be found. Summons for his capture were again issued, and in September he voluntarily made known his whereabouts. Service was at once had, citing him to appear at the county court at Forssa, Oct. 11th. Erik Jansson then pleaded that, having been driven into hiding by threats against his life, he had received no summons and consequently had failed to appear in court on the day aforesaid. This trial was not concerned with the recent disturbances, but dealt with certain heterodox statements made by Erik Jansson at a meeting in Hamre, Forssa parish, on Nov. 3rd, the year before. On this as on prior occasions Erik Jansson's friends and sympathizers were barred from testifying, being declared incompetent and untrustworthy on account of their faith, and the witnesses for the prosecution only were heard. From this resolution of the jury the judge dissented. After an order for Erik Jansson's detention in prison pending a verdict had been denied by the court, the case was continued until Oct. 30th and change of venue then taken to the county court at Delsbo, which convened in extra session Nov. 18th. The disposition of the case was that Erik Jansson be sent to the Gefle prison pending a new trial. The jury rendered this verdict, overriding the judge, who was for acquittal and is said to have imposed a fine on each of the jurors for contempt.

His followers had begun to suspect that there was a secret plan to put him out of the way during imprisonment; for that reason they decided to deliver him from jail at all hazards. Therefore, when the transport reached the road to Lynäs, in Söderala, four men rushed from ambush, halted the conveyance, cut the reins and, overpowering the guard, set the prisoner free. This happened Nov. 21st. A rumor was at once circulated that Erik Jansson had been murdered, and for the evident purpose of lending credibility to the story, his wife appeared in widow's weeds at Gefle, making inquiries for her dead husband. In addition, a woman at Lynäs had poured the blood of a kid in the road, in further support of the rumor. It soon became evident, however, that this was a pure fabrication to aid in keeping the prophet in concealment.

After the rescue, Erik Jansson was in hiding at various points in western Helsingland, or went about in the guise of a woman. This incognito gave his apostles occasion to liken him to Christ after the resurrection. His first hiding place was in the house of Peter Källman at the Voxna Mills. After having been discovered holding a secret meeting there one night, when he narrowly escaped being taken, he was transferred to Ofvanåker, where he was hid for seven weeks under a barn-floor. Threatened with discovery, he was soon after brought to the home of one of his followers, Sven Olsson, in Alfta. While under the influence of liquor, this man divulged the whereabouts of the prophet, who, being warned, fled to Dalarne. There he found refuge among his believers, principally in the home of a well to do peasant, Linjo Gabriel Larsson in Östra Fors, Malung parish. In the meantime, his teachings spread quite extensively in Dalarne, particularly in Malung and Mora parishes, but also to Lima parish and the city of Falun. In Herjedalen Erik Jansson also succeeded in gaining a few proselytes, among whom Olof Jonsson and Sven Jonsson, two peasants in the village of Långå, Hede parish. These arranged book pyres patterned after those in Helsingland. At one of these occasions a copy of the Bible was included in the mass of books consigned to the flames, but it was snatched from the fire in the last minute by a female relative of the man who arranged the auto-da-fé. Long after the prophet had deserted his own country, his disciples continued to spread his

Fac-Simile of Page from Erik Jansson's Church Prayers

doctrines and gain proselytes in the provinces of Helsingland, Gestrikland and Upland.

This same winter and spring the promised catechism and hymnal were published, entitled, "Commentaries to the Holy Scriptures, or Catechism, Arranged in Questions and Answers, by Erik Jansson," and, "Sundry Songs and Prayers, Composed by Erik Jansson." These books were printed at a shop established in violation of the law by a pay-sergeant, named C. G. Blombergsson, in the village of Ina, Söderala parish, just outside of Söderhamn. The language used in this catechism, like that of his other writings, is verbose and incongruous. The ever-recurring theme is the divine mission of Erik Jansson and the spiritual perfection of his faithful followers, claims which he seeks to establish by references to Old Testament narratives and prophecies. In point of diction and rhythm, his hymns are faulty in the extreme.* Besides these works, several other writings of Erik Jansson were issued in print, such as his "Farewell Address," "A Glorious Description of the Growth of Man," "A Few Words to God's People," "Timely Words," and "Farewell Speech to all the Inhabitants of Sweden, who have despised me, whom Jesus hath sent; or rejected the name of Erik Jansson."

From Erik Jansson's catechism, embodying his principal teachings, a few excerpts may properly be made by way of defining this religious movement in the words of the founder himself. We translate literally from a reprint published at Galva, Ill., in 1903.

In the foreword we read this authoritative declaration: "Thou, who taketh this precious treasure in thy hand in order to accept every word of it as if spoken by God, or as though God himself stood before thee in visible form and spake to thee all that is herein written—and everything is written as the Word of God—I pray thee to consider well the import of certain expressions."

On page 22 we find his views on education thus expressed: "It is not unbeknown to us that all the schools of the times are founded by the devil, yet they are of some use in teaching that which pertains to a knowledge, sanctioned by God, of those figures (things) from which the prophets drew their parables, etc."

On page 24 the author speaks of himself in this wise:

"Question. But how canst thou know that God now shall send a certain person, when we have God's word in abundance amongst us, without (need of) any more teachings, by untutored laymen?

"Answer. As regards this, that the canonical books of the Bible are sufficient to instruct us about the way of salvation, it has already been said that all other writings and books are needless and devilish and cannot be considered (in ascertaining) whether the Word of God, without the faulty interpretations of others, is and shall ever be the only foundation, on which the one sent by God shall build. But in regard to this, that Jesus will send some one, who shall restore that

---

* "So tedious, repugnant and impious a collection of songs no other religious body has ever had foisted upon it. Among the rudest products of versification in any literature one will search in vain for anything to match it." (WIESELGREN.)

which long hath lain fallow, we know by all the signs of the times that he hath already been sent, for everyone who believeth, may see that the same miracles that Jesus wrought are also being performed by him whom God has sent. Further, we find that the signs of Jonah, the Prophet, have come to pass in all lands and are being fulfilled in all the nations under the sun. Therefore I may be sure that Jesus has sent the one who gives his life for that which is right, or alone for the salvation of his brethren.''

The first commandment is commented thus on page 35:

''Q. Mayst thou have other gods besides God, when thou disbelievest him whom God hath sent as the light of the world?

''A. Not to believe in him whom God has sent is the worst idolatry of which the Bible speaks; for whosoever toucheth him toucheth the apple of God's eye.''

The eighth (ninth) commandment is thus interpreted (p. 75):

''Q. Since thy brethren in the faith alone are thy neighbors, mayst thou bear false witness against the unbelievers?

''A. Whenever it is required to bear such witness as to promote the eternal welfare of my neighbor, I cannot but bear witness free from falsehood. But should I, like Judas, be asked where he, whom I am sure God has sent, is (hidden), then I cannot testify truthfully, being convinced that I would thereby bear false witness against my neighbor.'' The next two pages are devoted to proving that lying is not only permissible but praiseworthy; quoting Scripture to show that the Lord's servants often have lied to the glory of God. We are told (p. 77) that ''when the faithful speak falsely and lie before men for the sake of truth and right, they do so in order to destroy falsehood and eradicate the tares.''

On page 103 Erik Jansson gets down to the bedrock of his doctrine in these words:

''Q. You believe, then, that the coming of Christ has not been fulfilled until Erik Jansson came with the true light, just as God in the beginning created light in the midst of darkness?

''A. It is to be remarked that all prophecies have reference, first, to Christ, the first-born, secondly, to his believers or those of whom Jesus says that they shall perform the same miracles that He wrought, etc. 2. It follows, that we must consider the words of Jesus Christ himself on this point, namely, that according to the Prophets the last house shall surpass the first, i. e., as the second glory (of the) Temple of Jerusalem surpassed the glory built by the son of David and placed in said temple—a sorry tangle of words for a prophet—so also it now shall come to pass that the glory restored by Erik Jansson in Christ's stead shall surpass that of Jesus and his Apostles in all lands; for now Jesus Christ hath been made manifest in the flesh to all those who believe in the name of the Son of God, and hence it is plain that the coming of Christ is fully realized through Erik Jansson's obedience to God.'' —.— There is much more of this, with frequent repetition of the name Erik Jansson, which we forbear to quote.

The above excerpts are given as characteristic of Erik Jansson's mode of thought and literary style as well as of his teachings, but they do not by far cover all the points on which he was charged with heresy by the state church.

Emigration of the Erik Janssonists to America

In his arrogance Erik Jansson had prophesied that within two years the world would be converted and all his antagonists annihilated. The prediction seemed all the more unlikely to come true now that the prophet himself was in dire peril. He had fled to escape punishment and, when reached by the arm of the law, would face conviction and banishment for heresy and repeated attempts at proselyting in violation of the law. When it became manifest that the Erik Janssonists could no longer operate without constant clashes with the authorities and the populace, and when the novelty of religious martyrdom had worn off, they began to look about for a place of refuge, and their eyes and hopes were directed to the United States. Gustaf Flack, mentioned in the foregoing chapter, had highly commended America in letters to his relatives in Alfta parish, especially dwelling on the religious liberty enjoyed in the new world. Hence the Erik Janssonists resolved to transplant the whole movement to this country, or, in their own phrase, "to turn to the heathen, inasmuch as the inhabitants of their own country refused to accept the truth and believe in it."

In order to make needed preparations for their coming, Olof Olsson of Kingsta turned his property into ready money at public auction and left for America in the summer of 1845, accompanied by his wife, their two children and a couple of other persons. He and all the other leaders, including Erik Jansson himself, who from his hidingplaces sent numerous letters to his faithful, were untiring in their efforts to paint in the most glowing colors the future that the promised land had in store for the chosen people. One of the promises held out to them was that there they would have their fill of "figs, white bread and pork, hogs being so plentiful that one only had to shoot, butcher and eat them." They need have no fear for the language, it was claimed, for upon their arrival it would be given unto them to speak with tongues. Furthermore, the heathen were to build for them walls and cities. All the glories of the millennium were to be realized; all were to be as one large family; snakes and dragons would be powerless to injure any of God's chosen seed; the lions were to graze together with the cattle of the fields,—these were some of the alluring pictures held up to the prospective emigrants.

Upon his arrival in New York, Olof Olsson encountered Rev. O. G. Hedström, the founder of Swedish Methodism in America, who received him with the utmost cordiality. Rev. Hedström endeavored to win his guest over to Methodism, and had no difficulty in so doing, owing partly to the similarity between that creed and the teachings of Erik Jansson, partly to Olof Olsson's previous acquaintance with Methodist doctrines, acquired through the visit in Helsingland of Rev. George Scott, a Methodist preacher stationed at Stockholm. To Rev. Hedström Olof Olsson confided the purpose of his trip, stating that he had come to find a suitable place of settlement for the oppressed Erik Janssonists; and the former was not slow to recommend Victoria, Ill., the home of his younger brother Jonas Hedström. After a short stay in New York, Olof Olsson came on to Illinois in the fall, provided with a letter of recommendation from Rev. Hedström to his brother, looked him up and enjoyed the same cordial reception accorded him by the elder brother. From Victoria Olof Olsson early in the spring of 1846, after having made a prospecting tour of Illinois, Wisconsin and Minnesota, wrote back to Sweden, recommending settlement in Illinois.

Among the Erik Janssonists at home this aroused great eagerness for an early start for the new land of Canaan, the sentiment being in every way encouraged by the prophet and his apostles. At this juncture Erik Janssonism might have had a backset but for the proposed exodus which, as an adjunct to their religious fanaticism, aroused the spirit of adventure and held out the most alluring prospects of the blessed land beyond the Atlantic. But it was not easy to get from Sweden to America in those days. In the first place, the Erik Janssonists had some difficulty in obtaining the necessary passports. In the second place, vessels suited to the purpose of the emigrants were scarce. The few Swedish vessels engaged in American trade carried cargoes of iron and lacked accommodations for passengers. Some of these were remodeled for the convenience of the emigrants, but proved very inconvenient at best. Besides, several of the ships were old and hardly seaworthy.

Erik Jansson had made up his own plan of emigration and decided to adopt absolute communism.* Accordingly, the members of the sect sold their real and personal property and formed a general treasury out of which the expenses of the passage were to be defrayed for all

* On this point authorities differ. "In this plan did not enter *** those socialistic or communistic principles of society, which were enforced after the colony was well established. — — Upon leaving Sweden necessity prompted the emigrants to put their money into a common fund and to have everything in common. This community of property they chose to maintain after their arrival but there was no intention of founding the colony on a socialistic basis. Erik

alike. As preparations were going forward, many difficulties arose.
Thus many were in debt, and their affairs had to be cleared up; others
were soldiers and had to pay large sums for their release from military
service; still others had difficulty in finding buyers and were forced to
sell their property at great sacrifice. Nevertheless, the common fund
grew quite large. Linjo Gabriel Larsson of Östra Fors, Malung parish,
one of Erik Jansson's chief followers in Dalarne, made the very
substantial contribution of 24,000 crowns; others added twelve, nine,
five or one thousand crowns to the general fund. Even the clothing
not needed for daily use was sold, for all were to be dressed alike. The
prophet appointed four persons as so-called "princes," who were to
keep and administer the general fund, viz., Jonas Olsson and Olof Jansson (afterwards known as Johnson) from Söderala, Olof Jonsson (in
America he changed his name to Stenberg or Stoneberg) from Forssa,
and Anders Berglund from Alfta.* Anyone who wavered in his allegiance to the prophet was expelled without getting back his contribution
to the general fund or any share of it.

While his faithful followers were preparing for the general exodus,
Erik Jansson left the country.† Equipped with the passport of another
family, he set out with his wife and two children and several other
persons. He himself, being a fugitive, traveled secretly at night,
remaining hid by day at the homes of his believers. When he had left
the parts where these lived, he traveled on skis, generally ahead of his
party, and slept in vacant woodchopper's huts or wherever he could
find shelter. After crossing the fjelds into Norway he traveled openly
with the party to Christiania.

Other members of the party were, Olof Norlund, who, to make the
passport tally in Sweden, traveled as Mrs. Jansson's husband, and three

Jansson spoke of it as a temporary arrangement and it was his purpose, as also
that of the other leading men, to make a change as soon as conditions permitted."
(JOHNSON and PETERSON.)

"It is safe to say, that into his colonization plan did not enter any of those
communistic or socialistic principles, which afterwards found a practical application in the colony. These were the fruits of necessity." (SWAINSON.)

"That communism in the Bishop Hill colony originated in this way is quite
likely; but even if no distinctly communistic plan was framed prior to emigration,
yet I recollect that the doctrine of Christian communism was at the time strongly
urged by the Janssonists, and therein lay the seed of the communism that subsequently sprung up at Bishop Hill." (NORELIUS.)

Hiram Bigelow's assumption that Erik Jansson had come under the influence
of the French socialists and adopted their communistic views is not supported by
any known facts.

So much is certain, that the plan was patterned after that of the earlier
Christians, and there is nothing to show that it was to apply only during emigration.

* The number is sometimes given as seven, but the names of the other three
are nowhere recorded.

† The statement that he left Sweden in January, 1846, does not tally with
other data, which seem to place the event well toward the spring. Capt. Johnson,
who avers that his father "left for America before Christmas, 1845," counts from
his start from Helsingland.

women. When Norlund was no longer needed, he returned, as did also Linjo Lars Gabrielson, who saw Erik Jansson safely out of the country and is said to have paid the passage to America for the entire party. From Christiania the party crossed over to Copenhagen and proceeded via Kiel, Hamburg, Hull and Liverpool to New York.

The rest of the Erik Janssonists took passage on vessels in the ports of Stockholm, Söderhamn, Göteborg, Christiania, but principally Gefle. In the latter city they gathered in large numbers and held public meetings. They likened themselves to the children of Israel departing from Egypt. As Moses had destroyed the Egyptians in the Red Sea, so the prophet and messenger Erik Jansson would by the power of God lay waste all Sweden, that accursed hell-hole, with fire and sword. In their eagerness to join in the exodus, wives deserted their husbands and infants, children their parents, and servants their employers. The journey was one of severe hardships to most of the emigrants. The lords of the exchequer, appointed by Erik Jansson, were to supply provisions and other necessaries, but their inexperience entailed much illness and suffering. To this was added seasickness. True, Erik Jansson had assured them of immunity from that nauseous affliction if they were steadfast in the faith, but subsequent events showed that either they were misled on that point or else there was a very general wavering among the faithful.

Many of the emigrants were exposed to great peril. One ship, which set sail from Söderhamn in October, 1845, and was the first to carry any considerable number of Erik Janssonists, was wrecked off Öregrund, but all the passengers—there were sixteen or seventeen in the Janssonist party—were saved and returned to their homes. They re-embarked on a ship which left Gefle in March the following year. Another of the emigrant vessels, commanded by one Captain Rönning, went down with fifty emigrants on board, not one of whom was saved. A third ship foundered off New Foundland, the passengers saving their lives but losing all their property. When the ship "Vilhelmina" reached New York, in September, 1846, twenty-two children had died on the voyage. In this and subsequent years altogether one hundred and seventy Erik Janssonists perished on the way.

Founding of the Bishop Hill Colony, the First Swedish Settlement in Illinois

Erik Jansson and his family reached New York in June, 1846. His wife having just given birth to a son, they were delayed in that city several weeks. In the interval, Erik Jansson preached to the Methodists on board their Bethel ship. As soon as his wife was restored to health, they started for Illinois, accompanied by an American family named Pollock of New York and two Swedish women. In the early part of July they reached Victoria, where Erik Jansson met Olof Olsson, who had gone to America the year before. The latter lived on a forty acre farm in section 22, Copley township, and made a home for himself and family in a log cabin. In this same cabin the first Swedish Methodist congregation in America was afterwards organized on December 15, 1846. The shelter was far from satisfactory, but in the absence of better accommodations it had to do. Rain poured through the leaky roof, and snakes crawled in through the holes in the walls, subjecting the inhabitants to discomfort and danger.

The first meeting in America between Erik Jansson and Olof Olsson was not a pleasant affair. As before stated, the latter had been converted to Methodism by Rev. O. G. Hedström of New York, and when Erik Jansson learned of this, there was a hot encounter between the two men.

Eric Jansson and family shared the log cabin occupied by Olof Olsson. They had no more than become fairly settled when this same log cabin was transformed into a theological forum, says Capt. Eric Johnson, in relating this reminiscence of his early boyhood. Theological discussions were served up for breakfast, dinner and supper. Between meals the combatants would sit in the shade of a tree, continuing the debate, and worst of all for the non-combatants, the wordy battle raged long after all had gone to bed. The only truce was during morning and evening prayers. This religious combat had been going on for days, if not weeks, when one night after retiring the war grew fiercer than ever. After a rapid exchange of redhot religious broadsides, Olsson finally lost his temper and threatened to get out of bed and throw Erik Jansson and his family out of the house. This proved the turning point in the affray, for next morning the two men were friends and looked at religion from the same point of view—Olof Olsson had become a Janssonist again.

A few days after the arrival of Erik Jansson came the first party of his followers. They were people from Dalecarlia province who, under the leadership of Linjo Gabriel Larsson, had left Malung April 9th and 10th for America, via Christiania. From New York they had taken the route which was used by the great mass of Swedish and other immigrants for almost a decade before the first railroad was built to Chicago, viz., up the Hudson to Albany by steamer, thence by canal to Buffalo, and again by steamer over the Great Lakes from that point to Chicago. From the latter point, most of the adults traveled on foot to Victoria, while children and invalids rode on pack horses and in wagons purchased for transportation purposes. Later parties took the canal route to Henry or Peru, whence they walked or rode. The very last comers traveled by railroad the entire distance from New York to

Galva. This was in 1854 after the completion of the C. B. & Q. road to the latter point.

For the sum of $250 out of the common treasury Olof Olsson purchased a sixty acre farm at Red Oak Grove, in sections 9 and 17, with a loghouse and a few acres of ground under cultivation. On August 21st, after the first party of immigrants had arrived, 156 acres of section 8, in the same township, was purchased for $1,100. The party at once moved upon the land, managing as best they could. There was a log cabin, a piece of cultivated ground, and some timber. They now began to plan a small town or colony for those that were to follow, and after looking over the neighborhood they decided to locate at Hoop Pole Grove, comprising the southwest corner of section 14, Weller township. Here Erik Jansson bought 160 acres directly from the government on Sept. 26th, for $200. The same day a tract of 320 acres in sections 23 and 24 was purchased for $400. It was a fine locality, with a small bluff, a spring of water, clumps of oak-trees and a small stream, known as South Edward's Creek. The place was named Bishop Hill, after Biskopskulla, the birthplace of Erik Jansson. Olof Olsson had accompanied the others to Red Oak Grove, and before the end of the year he and his wife, together with two of their children, were claimed by death.

In readiness for a numerous party that was expected soon, two log houses were hurriedly put up, also four large tents and one so-called church tent, built of logs in the form of a cross and covered with canvas. The entrance and the pulpit were at the north end, while the south end was occupied by a fireplace and a gallery. This tabernacle had a capacity of 800 to 1,000 persons. A laudable trait of the colonists was this, that immediately upon their arrival they built a house in which to give praise and thanks to God, whom they would serve and for whose sake they believed themselves persecuted and martyred.

On Oct. 28th Jonas Olsson arrived with a large party, including Erik Jansson's two brothers, Johan, or Jan, and Peter. His mother, who was in the party, died during the voyage. Many members of this as well as subsequent parties deserted in New York, the hardships endured on the voyage creating in their minds a doubt as to the divine mission of the alleged prophet. There is good ground for the belief, however, that many of the deserters probably had never professed an abiding faith in him, having merely taken advantage of the movement to get rid of their debts and obtain free passage to America. Many stopped in Chicago, among whom Jan Jansson, one of Erik Jansson's own brothers.

At the approach of cold weather, another party arrived, raising the total number of colonists to three hundred. The existing buildings now proved entirely inadequate, and many additional loghouses were hastily built, also a large sodhouse which served as kitchen and dining hall, or, according to the recollection of some, three sod kitchens were built, one by one, as needed, and later replaced by one large adobe kitchen in three sections. But even at that, the demand for shelter was not fully met. In addition no less than twelve so-called dugouts were constructed, by the process of digging holes, or cellars, in the side of the hill, the partial earthen walls being completed by a superstructure of logs. The hut was covered with a layer of thin boards on which was placed a thatch of sod. The door was at the front end, flanked by a couple of small windows, and the fireplace at the back wall. These unsanitary dwellings were 25 to 30 feet long and 18 feet wide and housed from twenty-five to thirty persons each. These slept in berths built in two tiers along the side walls, each berth with a capacity of three persons. During the first winter no less than fifty-two unmarried women are said to have lived together in a rude wooden structure.

Late in the fall still another company of Erik Janssonists arrived, swelling the total number to four hundred. Of these seventy lived at Red Oak Grove. Fortunately the winter proved exceptionally mild, the ground being frozen for a period of only eight weeks. At times, however, the cold was so bitter as to prevent outdoor work.

Before undertaking a more detailed description of the Bishop Hill Colony, some account must be given of subsequent parties of Erik Janssonists that kept coming from time to time. In June, 1847, there were added to the settlement four hundred men and women and a large number of children. One hundred and eighty were brought over from Gefle on the ship "New York." The voyage had taken five months, the ship having been delayed by storms and laid up for repairs in an English port for six weeks. Not until March 12th did the passengers reach New York, much fatigued by sickness and famine. There they found another party of Erik Janssonists who had set sail from Göteborg. Even after reaching New York the members of these two parties were subjected to indescribable hardships. The effects of their subsisting for so long a time on unwholesome food now became apparent, and conditions were still further aggravated by the necessity of crowding the emigrants together like cattle into small and unsanitary quarters. They were attacked by scurvy in its most loathsome form; in many instances the flesh rotted from the bones and joint was severed from joint, the poor victims writhing with pain at the slightest touch or movement. Within a fortnight thirty persons died. The dead were placed by twos or threes into rough boxes and buried without ceremony. The most afflicted ones were sorted out and placed in a subterranean room where scant beds were prepared on the floor. Instead of providing suitable food and medical attention for the patients, the leaders prescribed fasting, while they went out in the city and provided themselves amply with food and drink, maintaining that such a course could be taken without prejudice to their faith. Instead of giving comfort and solace to the sick and dying, they preached to them for two hours every morning and night, harshly denouncing them for their unbelief, which they declared was the chief cause of their sufferings. The leaders made daily attempts at performing miracles in the way of healing the sick; they compelled the patients to arise and ordered them to believe that they were healed, invoking dire punishment upon them, when they fell back powerless on their beds.

Several of the healthy members of the party, moved to compassion by the sufferings witnessed on every hand and revolting at the ignorance, hypocrisy and hardheartedness of the leaders, bade their companions farewell, declaring they could no longer endure the sight of the misery. These deserters the leaders took care to deprive of everything of value that they possessed.*

On April 26th, when the spring sun had melted the ice from the waterways, the survivors of the two parties were finally able to leave New York on their way to Illinois, taking the same route as their predecessors. The leaders of the combined parties were Anders Andersson from Thorstuna and a blacksmith by the name of Hammarbäck. All who were able had to travel on foot from Chicago to Bishop Hill. This slow mode of travel consumed ten days. To house the newcomers five new dugouts were built for the people, and additional ones for the horses and cattle, while to shut out the rain, the house of worship was provided with a solid roof of oak shingling.

The sixth party of emigrants reached Bishop Hill in the summer of 1849 under the leadership of Jonas Nylund from Delsbo, a papermaker's apprentice. He had gone to Norway and there induced a number of people to emigrate and join the new colony. Between Chicago and La Salle cholera broke out in this party, which the aforesaid Anders Andersson found on his return from a business trip to Chicago in a deplorable condition and, with good intent but lack of forethought, brought them to Bishop Hill, where the dreaded pest broke out forthwith.

A seventh party came over in 1850, under the joint leadership of Olof Johnson and Olof Stoneberg, who had returned to Sweden in order to collect moneys due and inheritances of minors, as also to gather up the remainder of the sect. The sum they brought back is said to have amounted to $6,000. The emigrant party was composed of 160 persons, who under Stoneberg's supervision embarked at Söderhamn. On the ocean ten persons died. At Buffalo the whole company was taken on board an old propeller steamer bound for Milwaukee. Owing to bad weather and breakage in the machinery, the trip took two weeks,

* The accuracy of this narrative is doubted or denied by certain survivors.

and their provisions gave out. In Michigan, where the steamer touched, cholera added to their miseries, carrying off fifty to sixty of the party before Milwaukee was reached. A Swedish-American of that city, C. Blanxius by name, learning by chance that a party of his countrymen had arrived, at once provided care and medical service for the sick. Upon learning afterwards that Stoneberg had several thousand dollars in his possession, he compelled him to pay the bills.

Later in the autumn of that year one Jöns Andersson brought over the eighth party, numbering eighty colonists who sailed from Gefle on the ship "Condor." They had one loss by death during the passage. In 1854 the ninth and last party of Erik Janssonists arrived, numbering seventy. This ended the actual exodus of the sect.

According to the ecclesiastical records, the Erik Janssonists in the provinces of Gestrikland and Helsingland numbered 913, all but 36 of whom lived in the last named province. Of the total number 649 were adults and 264 children; 409 were recruited from the so-called "readers." The greatest exodus of Erik Janssonists occurred in 1846, when 823 persons emigrated from the two provinces, Alfta alone furnishing 346, Ofvanåker 44, Voxna 40, etc. From the province of Dalarne 99 people emigrated, from Upland an equal number, and from Herjedalen 10 to 15.

Individual immigration to Bishop Hill continued throughout the period, 1846—1854, swelling the total to about 1,500. While the early emigrants were actuated solely by a desire for freedom of worship, the latter presumably were led by mercenary motives, awakened by the rumored prosperity of the colony.

In Sweden, Erik Janssonism was thus almost entirely eradicated, those of his converts who did not follow him to America returning to the established church or going over to other sects almost to a man. But even to this day persons in these parts have been known to persevere in their belief in Erik Jansson as "the new light sent by God." Erik Janssonism was also transplanted to Denmark, but gained only a mere handful of converts in that country.

Daily Life in the Colony

The daily life in the colony offered many peculiarities, the religious phase being the most pronounced. That the Erik Janssonists, who had emigrated in order to gain freedom to worship according to their own dictates, made sedulous use of their newfound liberty was but natural. During their first fall and winter in the new land, they held religious services twice every week-day and thrice on Sundays. Erik Jansson arose every morning at five and roused his people for matins. Half an hour later he made a second round, when all were required to gather immediately in the tabernacle for the morning services, consisting of a sermon and prayers, often consuming two hours' time. At Christmas, 1846, a church bell was procured, which served the double purpose of calling the people to worship and to their meals. The second religious service of each day was held in the evening. Along in the spring of 1847, when work in the fields began, the morning and evening services were replaced by a short noon meeting, held in a shady spot in the woods adjoining Bishop Hill on the north. These meetings were generally conducted by Erik Jansson in person, sometimes by the assistance of Jonas Olsson, Anders Berglund, Nils Hedin or some other leader. Erik Jansson's own hymnbook was used, and in his sermons

Bishop Hill—The Old Colony Church

he dwelt incessantly on his God-given mission, the sinless state of his faithful followers, and similar doctrines.

For the propagation and perpetuation of Erik Janssonism twelve of the most gifted young men of the colony were selected in 1847 and given special instruction in the doctrines of the sect by the prophet himself and the most enlightened of his assistants. The prophet's prediction about the gift of speaking with tongues still remaining unfulfilled, the English language was made one of the studies. The classes generally met in the shadow of a great oaktree, but a dugout was also used for school purposes.

In the summer of 1848 the tabernacle, or church tent, was destroyed by fire, and the colonists at once began to build the edifice now known as the Old Colony Church, which is still one of the landmarks of Bishop Hill. It was completed in 1849, being built in three stories, the third forming the sanctuary while the first and second were partitioned off into dwelling rooms, there being also a couple of such rooms in the third story.

Erik Jansson continued preaching to his faithful flock as long as he lived, though with some difficulty in his later years, owing to the loss of his teeth. The set of false teeth used by him after that formed such an impediment in his speech that his hearers had to strain themselves to the utmost in order to catch his meaning.

Provision was also made for the education of the young. During the first winter, Mrs. Margareta Hebbe instructed the illiterate elders in reading and writing, the school sessions being held in the tabernacle. After Mrs. Hebbe left the colony, Peter Hellström succeeded her as instructor. A similar school was opened at Red Oak Grove, where Karin Pettersson and a Mrs. Rönnquist acted as teachers. In January, 1847, an English kindergarden was established in one of the dugouts, and conducted by an American clergyman by the name of Talbot, assisted by Mrs. Sophia Pollock.

It was with the utmost difficulty that the colonists could procure flour for bread. The nearest flour mill was at Green River, twenty-eight miles away, the second nearest at Camden, the present village of Milan, a short distance from where the Rock River empties into the Mississippi. To these two points they sent their grain from time to time, but frequently the mills would be out of repair, necessitating still longer trips. In the meantime, the supply at home would give out, a real calamity in those days, when there were no neighbors from whom to borrow in an emergency. Then some substitute for bread had to be produced, and a couple of primitive hand mills were procured in which corn was ground into a coarse meal requiring 10 to 12 hours of cooking to make it palatable. The colonists were many and the capacity of the mills was small, so they had to grind by shifts all night in order to produce meal sufficient for the next day. In the large common refectory all dined together on food which was often insufficient and generally unpalatable. The situation was relieved to a great extent, when in 1847 a flour mill was built on Edward's Creek, but this stream would sometimes run dry, closing down the mill. In these emergencies the colonists would be called into requisition to tread the mill wheel, this arduous task falling principally to the lot of the twelve apostles to be. This method, however, proved too laborious, and man power was soon replaced by horse power. When this mill nevertheless proved unable to supply the demand, a windmill with two pairs of mill stones was built in January, 1848. The following year preparations were made for the erection of a steam power flour mill, which was completed in July, 1851. This establishment at once proved highly profitable, the farmers from near and far bringing their grain, while all the surplus grain of the colony was made into flour for the market.

Bishop Hill—Bakery and Brewery Building—"The Big Brick," Dining Hall, Kitchen and Dwelling

In the spring of 1847 the colony began to manufacture sun-dried brick, and several buildings of that material were put up; about the same time a saw-mill was built at Red Oak Grove, where there was a tract of oak timber. The saw-mill was later traded for a parcel of land and another saw-mill, located on a small stream in Clover township. This mill was moved to Bishop Hill and located on Edward's Creek in 1848. In May the same year, eighty acres of timber land, with a saw-mill, in Weller township, was purchased from Cramer and Wilsey for $1,500. Thenceforth the colony was well supplied with lumber. Limestone was found in a ravine within the domain of the colony, and a man by the name of Philip Mauk taught the settlers the art of burning lime, yet large quantities of lime had to be bought. Brick kilns were also constructed, and gradually large and comfortable dwelling houses began to supplant the stuffy and unsanitary dugouts.

The rapid increase in population by immigration made the purchase of more land peremptory. Nov. 18, 1847, a quarter of section 17, in Weller township, was purchased of W. H. Griffin for $380, and before the end of the year other purchases were made as follows: 80 acres in section 17, 240 acres in section 16, and 39 acres additionally. Moreover, pieces of land were rented here and there in the neighborhood, some as far away as present Woodhull. Farming was carried on with great energy. Part of the lands bought were already planted to corn; other portions were turned into wheat fields. After the last-named land purchases no less than 350 acres were under cultivation. During that and the following years the colonists surrounded their domain on three sides with an earthen wall or fence.

The grain crop of the first year (1847) was cut with scythes in Swedish fashion; the next year so-called cradles came into use. In 1849, during harvest time, thirty cradles were kept working night and day, but on finding the dews injurious to the health of the harvest hands night work was discontinued. Each cradle had a capacity of six acres per day. Women generally worked in the field binding the grain, while young boys and girls were employed to gather the sheaves and the aged to do the shocking. The last named year a reaper was procured from La Grange, but it was sent back as unsatisfactory and the cradles again brought into use, several of the men having acquired great skill in handling this implement. Anders Kilström and Hans Dahlgren, for instance, each cradled 14 acres of wheat from sunrise to sundown.

The harvest over for the season, a pleasant spectacle was enacted. The two hundred laborers formed in a double line, with the men in the lead, the women following, and the children bringing up the rear, and marched back to the village to the tune of merry folksongs. Arriving home, the reapers arranged themselves around the long tables in the largest dining hall, where a feast was spread, and thus was celebrated their first harvest festival with merrymaking and thanksgiving.

In the year 1852 improved reapers were introduced, replacing the inferior cradle and giving a different character to the work of harvesting the crops.

The threshing of the crop of 1847 was left to one Broderick, who used a very simple and imperfect threshing contrivance. The machine afterwards became the property of the colonists who proceeded to build a new one of the same type but with many improvements.

The colonists did not, however, confine themselves to the cultivation of wheat and corn. Flax was raised, especially at first, with still greater success, owing to the fact that this was one of the staple products of Helsingland from time out of mind, and the emigrants from that province were experts in flax culture. The flax was prepared and woven by the colonists themselves and the linen products found a ready sale in the neighborhood. From the flax crop of 1847 12,473 yards of linen was woven and sold. The production increased yearly, reaching 28,322 yards of linen cloth and 3,257 yards of carpets in 1851. The linen industry was continued until 1860, but it was reduced in 1857 on account of competition with the eastern factories, who dominated the western market as soon as shipping facilities were improved. Up to that time the colony had produced for the general market a total of 130,309 yards of linen goods and 22,569 yards of carpets, together with all goods needed for domestic use. From these figures it appears that this industry was an important source of income to the colony during its first decade. After 1857 flax was raised only for home consumption. The total, including 1860, was 169,386 yards.

To the women and children, as well as to the men, belonged the credit for this flourishing industry. The latter cultivated the flax and prepared it, but the women did the spinning and weaving, while children were employed in the spooling and other minor processes. The first few years, while the number of looms was very limited, the weavers were divided into shifts who kept the looms going day and night. Thus the women were employed during the winter months. In summer the women, as they were accustomed from the old country, took part in the outdoor work with an endurance equal to that of the men.

Though zealots in the matter of religion, the colonists were no temperance fanatics. Whisky was used to some extent among them, and in order to supply the growing demand a still was established. Their indulgence in liquor, however, was repugnant to the neighbors and brought the colonists into ill repute.

For the sake of greater variety in the matter of food, and possibly with an eye to extra profit, Erik Jansson in 1848 established a fishing camp on Rock Island, in the Mississippi, near the present site of the city of Rock Island, and placed it in charge of N. J. Hollander and a half dozen other colonists. Fish was also obtained from the Illinois River.

The lack of wholesome food, especially during the first year, combined with the unhealthy conditions in the overcrowded dugouts, caused a very high death rate. Fevers, ague and diarrhea, the most prevalent diseases, claimed many victims. In Red Oak alone 50 persons died during the winter of 1846 and the winter months of 1847 claimed no less than 96 lives in Bishop Hill. The dead bodies were loaded into wagons and buried without any ritual or ceremony whatever. Many corpses were not even provided with coffins. These grewsome conditions drove many of the healthy colonists from Bishop Hill in spite of Erik Jansson's efforts to prevent desertions by posting armed pickets at night. The sick were not permitted to call in a physician: they were to be healed by faith alone. Those who did not believe, the prophet condemned to "the stones of hell." Jonas Hedström of Victoria was so shocked by the brutality and stolidity of Erik Jansson towards his people that he threatened legal proceedings, unless medical attendance was provided. Thereby Erik Jansson was ultimately induced to engage an American physician, whom he also consulted in his own behalf. When the people were famished from lack of nourishment, the prophet evinced the same stolid indifference to their wants and sufferings. He sought to relieve their hunger not by supplying food, but by imposing repeated fasts. To their prayers and complaints he replied that if they had faith they could very well subsist on an eighth less than the rations they had been accustomed to in the old country, arguing that their lack of faith was the primary cause of their maladies.

The continued misery of the colonists again moved Jonas Hedström to protest. He called the attention of the colonists, and rightly so, to the fact that there was absolutely no necessity for all the suffering and privation to which they were subjected at the behest of Erik Jansson. The country was large, he argued, land was to be had almost for nothing; settlers in other localities were prospering on their well-kept farms, and the same opportunity was open to all. In the fall of 1848 these representations resulted in probably two hundred persons leaving the colony, mostly joining the Methodists, a step which led to long and bitter religious warfare between the Erik Janssonists and the Methodists. The deserters settled at Victoria, Galesburg, and neighboring localities. The great majority of the colonists, however, were not to be shaken in their faith, but continued under the harsh rule of the prophet with remarkable patience and forbearance.

Another decree of Erik Jansson in the early stages of the colony, causing much adverse comment, was one forbidding marriage.* This interdict soon had very damaging results, many young persons who desired to get married simply leaving the colony for other parts, where they were free to establish a home and family. When the prophet saw how his ban on matrimony worked, he declared that it had been dictated by "present need," meaning the lack of individual dwellings and other untoward conditions. He now alleged that he had received a new revelation to the effect "that the sons and daughters of Israel should marry and take in marriage, multiply and fill the earth." Now, therefore, all those that God had given a desire to marry should enter wedlock without delay, on peril of being condemned to "the stones of hell." Erik Jansson himself and all the subordinate leaders became extremely active as matchmakers among the young people, causing a veritable marriage epidemic throughout the colony. On several successive Sundays between 20 and 30 marriages were solemnized, but the fever ultimately subsided and normal conditions were restored.

The material as well as the spiritual interests of the colony were looked after by Erik Jansson personally. He exercised the same arbitrary despotism in the one field as in the other. This man's chief ambition was to rule and govern, no matter how. In the administration of the colonial affairs he was supremely arbitrary, his incompetence and recklessness bringing the community to the verge of ruin, as will be presently shown.

When it had been decided to call in a physician, an Englishman by the name of Robert D. Foster made application for the place and was accepted, but afterwards discharged by the colonists. Erik Jansson then made a secret agreement with Foster to this effect: he was to be the body physician of the prophet at a compensation of $2,000 per annum, with the privilege of extra charges for services rendered other members of the colony.

Foster, who seems to have been a sharp and crafty fellow, in a short time won the unlimited confidence of Erik Jansson. At La Grange, in Western township, 18 miles from Bishop Hill, he owned a tract of 1,116 acres of land, only a small part of which was under cultivation. This he desired to dispose of to Erik Jansson, but at first offered for sale only the growing wheat crop. Without making a thorough investigation Erik Jansson closed the deal at all too high a price. The harvesting and threshing of the wheat had to be done by the colonists without compensation. But Erik Jansson did not stop at this. Before he knew whether he had gained or lost by the deal, he bought the land itself for $3,000. These transactions as well as the

---

* Landgren quotes testimony to the effect that Erik Jansson from the outset urged strict sexual abstinence in wedlock.

previous agreement with Foster were made without a word to the colonists, and the same secrecy was observed in the matter of payments. The money in the treasury not sufficing, Erik Jansson turned over to Foster much of the property of the colony, consisting of horses, oxen, cows, hogs and calves, together with wagons, implements, clothing, bedding, grain, provisions, etc., leaving the people almost destitute of what they needed for their subsistence and by which to cultivate the soil. Actual want resulted for all but Erik Jansson, who maintained his own household and took about all that was left for his own use.

This disastrous deal was made, and its consequences were felt, in the summer of 1849. About the same time the colony was visited with another and greater affliction, but not even that could touch the impervious heart and shake the imperturbable selfassurance of Erik Jansson. The sixth immigrant party, under the leadership of Jonas Nylund, had just arrived. Cholera had broken out among them en route, and they brought the contagion to the colony. The pest began to spread July 22nd and raged till the middle of September, sometimes craving as high as twelve victims per day. Dr. Foster was totally helpless. This man, who had boasted his ability to cure ninety-nine out of a hundred cholera patients, failed to save a single life. The prophet himself now proved lacking in that firm faith which he had demanded of others by fleeing with his family to La Grange. After a short stay, he ordered those colonists still immune from the pest to follow him thither, but these brought the contagion, resulting in the death here of seventy cholera victims.

No longer safe in La Grange, Erik Jansson took his family and several women to the fishery camp he had established on Rock Island, in the Mississippi, but even here the plague pursued him, carrying off his wife and two children. In spite of his incompetence, Dr. Foster still enjoyed the full confidence of Erik Jansson and was permitted to accompany him to Rock Island. As an instance of the blind faith he reposed in this impostor and his cool indifference in the midst of dire misfortune, it may be stated that while his wife lay in the death-throes which a few hours later put an end to her untold sufferings, Erik Jansson offered to wager $10,000 with certain physicians of the city of Rock Island that Dr. Foster would save her.

Just after his wife's death, Erik Jansson began to plan a new marital union, "in order to give a new spiritual mother to the children of Israel," as he put it. On a Sunday some three weeks after her demise, the prophet in his sermon made known his purpose without reserve. The inner testimony of all the faithful, said he, was to determine the choice of this new "spiritual mother," and she also was to receive such assurance within her own heart. After services, all should come to him and make known what the inner voice had spoken. The general verdict is not known, but this much is true, that two women appeared as claimants for the vacant place. Sophia Pollock, who had accompanied Erik Jansson and his family from New York, was the successful candidate, and the same day she assumed the management of the domestic work of the colony. She also acted as Erik Jansson's secretary. A week later the wedding was solemnized with joy and hilarity on the part of the prophet but with a feeling of uneasiness among the guests, who were unable to forget that only a month had elapsed since his first wife died.

Sophia Pollock, the second wife of Erik Jansson, was the daughter of a merchant of Göteborg and was born in that city. Her father having become bankrupt, she was adopted by a well to do family that moved to New York, where she was married at an early age to a sailor, who soon after went to sea and never returned. She was remarried to one Pollock of New York, principal of a private school, who after giving her an education, engaged her as his assistant. When Erik Jansson arrived in New York the couple made his acquaintance and afterwards accompanied him to Victoria. The Pollocks were prominent in Rev. Hedström's flock in New York and her going over to Erik Jansson was no small triumph for the latter. At the founding of Bishop Hill Mrs. Pollock joined the colony against the wishes of her husband.* Being widowed for the second time shortly afterwards, she subsequently married Linjo Lars Gabrielsson, who after a brief union succumbed to the cholera. She is said to have been a personable and gifted woman, and proved an invaluable helpmeet to Erik Jansson during the remainder of his life.

In the meantime, the straits to which Erik Jansson's rash business transactions had brought the colonists opened the eyes of the prudent, who contemplated with fears and misgivings the desperate state of affairs. The day after his wedding, Erik Jansson had a visit from three persons, Jonas Olsson, Nils Hedin, and E. U. Norberg, the latter remonstrating with him on his reckless extravagance in the management of their common property. The people, said he, had toiled beyond their power of endurance in order to accumulate wealth for the common good, but their wishes and opinions as to the disposal of it had not once been consulted. Instead of being treated as friends and brothers, they were held as slaves, bound to obey blindly his every beck and nod, Norberg concluded. ·

The lecture, however, had not the slightest effect on the despotic

---

* Her husband, who loved her as he did his life, went with her and tried to persuade her to return. But for the sake of her soul she dared not, for Jansson preached that there was no salvation outside of his New Jerusalem, and her husband died in Victoria, of a broken heart. Mrs. Pollock lost her reason over her husband's death, but shortly recovered. (MIKKELSEN.)

Bishop Hill—The Steeple Building

prophet. He replied briefly that he simply acted in accordance with his "inner testimony," meaning the dictates of his conscience, and that all who complained of his actions were the dupes of the devil.

Norberg was from Ullervad, Vestergötland, where he had held the office of king's bailiff, and had preceded Erik Jansson to America. Being a just and clearsighted man, he appeared time and again as the spokesman of the oppressed colonists and the defender of their rights as against the tyranny of those in power. Had they taken his advice, the colony doubtless would have met a better fate.

John Ruth, the Adventurer, and the Assassination of Erik Jansson

In the autumn of 1848 there came to the colony a trio af adventurers, viz., the aforementioned Erik Wester, one Zimmerman and John Ruth, alias Root, the latter destined to figure prominently in a tragic episode in the history of Bishop Hill.

John Ruth was born in Stockholm, supposedly of a family from Norrland, and served there as sergeant in the army. He emigrated to America, presumably on account of some crime or breach of discipline, enlisted in the United States army and served in the Mexican War. When Ruth and his confreres arrived at Bishop Hill the aforesaid "marriage epidemic" was at its height, and he took advantage of the situation by marrying Charlotta Lovisa Jansson, a cousin of the prophet. Being of a rowdyish disposition and an unruly temperament, he presently had a disagreement with Dr. Foster. Erik Jansson sided with the latter, giving rise to a feud between himself and Ruth, which brought disaster to both. Not more than a month after his marriage, Ruth wished to leave and take his wife with him, but Erik Jansson would not permit it, basing his prohibition on a written agreement, drawn up and signed by the contracting parties at their marriage, requiring the husband to obtain a divorce and let his wife remain, should he ever desire to leave the colony. She dared not desert the colony contrary to the prophet's wishes, fearing thereby to incur the wrath of God, for so Erik Jansson had taught. When all his persuasions proved in vain, Ruth went his way alone, but remained for several months in the neighborhood in the hope of ultimately inducing his wife to accompany him.

At the end of that time he returned to his wife, who had given birth to a son in the interval. When at the prophet's behest she still refused to come away with him, Ruth became enraged, making dire threats against them both, and resolved to force his wife into obedience. In order to give the act an appearance of legality he engaged a couple of county officers and, accompanied by a fourth person, a man from

Cambridge by the name of Stanley, he appeared one Sunday in the fall of 1849 to claim his wife, who agreed to follow him, fearing to offer resistance. Ruth departed at once, with his wife and child, Stanley accompanying them, while the two county officers went another way. He left Bishop Hill just as the people came from church and sat down to their common meal. He had been detected, however, and less than two miles off a number of armed pursuers caught up with him, barred further progress, and commanded him to give up the woman and child to be returned to the colony. Ruth drew his revolver and threatened to shoot, but Stanley dissuaded him, deeming it the part of discretion to bow to a superior force.* In a special conveyance, which soon reached the spot, the wife and child were brought back to Bishop Hill.

Thus thwarted in his attempt to carry off his wife, Ruth on the very next day swore out warrants for the arrest of Erik Jansson and others and had his wife summoned as a witness at the trial, which was to take place at Cambridge. She was brought there by a county officer who had a secret understanding with Ruth, and confined in a room in the hotel, where she was not permitted to see any of her friends. Neither Erik Jansson nor Ruth were present at the trial. The latter was represented by his counsel. That night Ruth took his wife away to the home of some friends in the Rock River settlement. Several Erik Janssonists stated under oath that Ruth had violated the right of domicile during the hour of worship and secured a warrant for his arrest. When this was to be served, the friends of Ruth interfered in his behalf, preventing the arrest.

At Bishop Hill various plans for the rescue of the abducted woman were evolved. Erik Jansson asserted that this must be done, even though half of Bishop Hill should be sacrificed. Not to be taken by surprise, Ruth secretly left Rock River with his wife and went first to Davenport and from there to Chicago, where they arrived on March 15th, 1850, the woman finding asylum for herself and child in the home of a married sister. By stealth, Erik Jansson succeeded in discovering her whereabouts and sent five trusty henchmen to bring her back. The scheme succeeded: the woman and child were returned to Bishop Hill and so carefully concealed that few knew her hidingplace.

Deprived of his wife a second time, Ruth broke into a furious rage and swore to wreak bloody vengeance on Erik Jansson and his colony. He proceeded to Green River, and, by describing the Erik Janssonists as a band of criminals that ought to be annihilated, he

---

* Another version of the story has it that while Ruth was holding down his wife in the bottom of the rig, his revolver, which he had placed beside him, was snatched by one of the colonists (who were unarmed) and leveled at his head, when Ruth surrendered the woman, who, upon being given her choice, accompanied her rescuers back to Bishop Hill.

succeeded in raising an armed posse of about 70 men, with which he advanced on Bishop Hill in order to capture Erik Jansson and rescue his wife. A thorough search was instituted, yet neither was to be found. The posse then gave the colonists one week in which to deliver the wife of Ruth to them, under penalty of having Bishop Hill burned to the ground. Frightened by this threat, Erik Jansson did not dare to remain at Bishop Hill, where he had been in hiding, but went to St. Louis with his family, Mrs. Ruth and several others.

The economic state of Bishop Hill continuing desperate, the colonists conceived the idea of relieving the situation at one stroke by fitting out an expedition of goldseekers for California, where rich gold fields had been discovered two years before. As members of the expedition the following nine men were selected: Jonas Olson,* P. O. Blomberg, P. N. Blom, Peter Jansson, E. O. Lind, C. M. Myrtengren, C. G. Blombergson, Sven Norlin and Lars Stålberg. A number of these having taken part in the rescue expedition to Chicago, and fearing the revenge of that dangerous man Ruth, they arranged to leave the colony simultaneously with Erik Jansson, starting for California on March 28th.† After a journey replete with perils and hardships, they reached Hanktown, Cal., Aug. 12th, hale and hearty, except Blombergson, who died after two weeks. Of the other eight, all but Stålberg, who remained in California, returned home in the course of the year 1851, having found barely enough of the precious metal to pay the cost of the expedition. The plan to put the colony on its feet again by means of Californian gold thus fell through. Nothing now remained for the colonists to do but to continue work in the fields, in house and yard, at sawmill and brickyard, and by redoubled energy repair the losses.

About this time Jon Olsson Stenberg of Stenbo removed from Moline to Bishop Hill and upon joining the colony is said to have contributed a substantial amount of money to the community.‡

Late in the evening of April 1st, Ruth returned at the head of the same armed posse and demanded the surrender of his wife. Her absence making that impossible, a respite of several days was again given, coupled with a renewed threat of burning the village, should the colonists fail to fulfill the condition. When the time was up, the crowd

* This and similar names are henceforth given in the form their bearers wrote them in this country.

† According to the diary of Jonas Olson, three of the men set out March 23rd, going via Rock Island, through Iowa, etc., the others apparently on March 29th, going by way of St. Louis. The two parties joined on the way and reached Hanktown (Placerville), Cal., Aug. 12th, according to Olson.

‡ In "Sverige i Amerika" Peterson, writing about Jonas Olson, illustrates that man's great persuasive powers with a story of how he "discovered" Stenberg and "dug up" $50,000 in gold, while the California party were in the gold fields and found nothing. Stenberg's fortune, it is safe to say, could not have reached such a figure. Besides, the author apparently forgets that Jonas Olson himself was the leader of the party of goldseekers.

again appeared, with reinforcements, evidently with a grim determination to carry out the threat. The Mormon colony at Nauvoo had been wiped out by fire three and a half years earlier, and that event was still fresh in the memory of all. The passions of the incendiaries were keyed to a high pitch, but fortunately the catastrophe was averted just as they were about to throw out the firebrands. Norberg, who had been driven from the colony by the odium heaped upon him by Erik Jansson, got word of the intended outrage and the day set for it, and, quickly mustering another posse of well armed men, he marched to Bishop Hill and in a parley with the mob dissuaded them from violence.

Again thwarted in his plans, Ruth swore vengeance on Erik Jansson personally and sent him word that he would shoot him down at the first opportunity.. The prophet was living high at St. Louis while his deluded followers at Bishop Hill were haggard from hunger and privation. Erik Jansson succeeded in obtaining considerable loans on the strength of ingenious newspaper articles setting forth the flourishing condition of his colony and putting himself in the most favorable light. For the evident purpose of strengthening his credit, he subscribed for $50,000 worth of railway stock at this juncture.

His fear of Ruth was somewhat allayed on hearing that the attack on Bishop Hill, planned by that desperado, had failed, so he returned home on May 11th. He arrived on a Saturday, and while preaching his sermon the following day in the colonial church, he seemed agitated by fear, as evidenced by his quoting II. Timothy 4: 6-8 and at the subsequent communion service Matthew 26: 29 in reference to himself. A large number of law suits had been entered against him in the county circuit court during his absence, and in order to defend his interests he went to Cambridge the following Monday, May 13th.* That morning he seems to have had a definite presentiment of danger, for on starting from home he is said to have asked his driver, one Mr. Mascall, "Well, will you stop the bullet for me today?" About one o'clock p. m., during the noon recess of the court, Erik Jansson stood near a window in the court room, conversing with Attorney Samuel P. Brainerd. Suddenly Ruth appeared outside the window and put the question to Erik Jansson, whether he would give him back his wife and child.† The prophet retorted that a sow would be a more fit companion for Ruth than a woman. Maddened by the insult, Ruth rushed into the building and the next instant stood in the doorway leading to the courtroom, loudly calling Erik Jansson by name. When the prophet turned to look, Ruth fired a pistol shot directly at

* An examination of the clerk's record disproves the assertion made by almost every writer on this subject that the case of Ruth vs. Jansson was before the court on that day.

† According to Mikkelsen, friends of Erik Jansson claim no words were exchanged between the slayer and his victim prior to the firing of the shot.

him, the bullet piercing the chest of Erik Jansson, who fell backwards and expired in a few minutes. As his victim fell, Ruth fired a second shot, which only tore a hole in the wounded man's clothing. Such was the tragic end of the checkered and peculiar career of Erik Jansson, the Prophet.

His death created a tremendous sensation and deep sorrow in the colony. Nils Hedin and Jacob Jacobson, who had witnessed the tragedy in the courtroom, brought the dead body to Bishop Hill, where it was interred several days later. Many of the simple-minded colonists could scarcely believe that their master was really dead, some even hoped that he would rise forthwith from the grave. A simple wooden cross at first marked the last restingplace of Erik Jansson, the self-appointed ambassador of God on earth. This was replaced later by a handsome monument of white marble.

At the time of the assassination, the courtroom was filled with people, who had no difficulty in catching the assassin. He was arrested and, after a trial pending two years, convicted and sentenced to three years in the penitentiary. After having served half of his term he was released in response to the numerous petitions for his pardon that were sent to Governor Joel A. Matteson. Ruth then went to Chicago where he spent the remainder of his life among the scum of the city. His stormy life ended in a revolting tragedy. While engaged in a drunken brawl with two other ruffians in a saloon, he was badly bruised and finally knocked to the floor, when one of his assailants jumped upon his chest and broke several ribs, the injuries causing his death shortly afterwards. Among the few Erik Janssonists in the old country the belief was general, however, that the murderer of the prophet was "consumed by worms" while in prison.

The Incorporation of Bishop Hill and the Administration of Jonas Olson and Olof Johnson.

After the murder of Erik Jansson the property of the colony, which was all in the leader's name, devolved upon his widow. Mrs. Sophia Pollock Jansson knew more about the colony's affairs than any other person and took the reins of government into her own hands. But women were not allowed to speak in public, therefore Andrew Berglund, one of the assistant preachers, was appointed the spiritual leader, as also guardian of Erik Jansson's son, who, according to the expressed wish of the prophet, was to become his successor. At the funeral Mrs. Jansson stepped forward and placed her hand on Berglund's bowed head, creating him guardian of the heir to the leadership of God's chosen people until the boy should have attained his majority. Berglund thus became nominally both the temporal and spiritual head of the community, but in matters of business no important step was taken without the knowledge and consent of Mrs. Jansson. The affairs of the colony were very much involved, and the creditors caused the new management much worry. The situation was somewhat relieved when Olof Johnson and Olof Stoneberg returned from Sweden with the aforesaid $6,000 in inheritances collected. Then the farming and industries of Bishop Hill were pursued with renewed vigor.

Berglund was not permitted long to exercise leadership. A rival soon appeared in the person of Jonas Olson, who was on his way to

Andrew Berglund
Preacher and Leader

Jacob Jacobson
Colony Trustee

the gold country at the time, and did not learn of the death of Erik Jansson till after his arrival in California. Actuated by a desire to succeed to the leadership he decided to return forthwith. He abandoned the expedition, having had no faith in it from the outset, and started back home with a couple of the men, leaving the rest to follow at their leisure. Arriving in Bishop Hill in February, 1851, he at once began to set matters right. He persuaded several of his friends that Erik Jansson's prophetic dignity was not to be handed down as a heritage, for the reason that no other man could receive the Holy Spirit in like measure; consequently, he argued, the present leadership ought to be abolished for a complete equality of rights. His friends were easily won over, and his views gained ground, being disseminated guardedly at first, but soon without any pretense of secrecy.

The guardians of Erik Jansson's son could not claim infallibility of judgment, and many were dissatisfied to be governed by a woman. A respectable minority, while admitting Jansson's other claims, were not disposed to recognize those in behalf of his heir. It was this growing sentiment of dissatisfaction, which Jonas Olson voiced when he denounced Berglund as a usurper and demanded his abdication. Jonas Olson's standing added weight to his words, and ere long the democratic spirit which he represented prevailed. The movement also gained strength from the operation of another circumstance. The affairs of the community were in such a condition that a strong and able man was needed to conduct it through the pending crisis. Jonas Olson was such a man, and to him the people instinctively looked for guidance. Thus it happened that, although no formal election or transfer of power took place, the leadership passed from the guardians of Erik Jansson's son into the hands of Jonas Olson. With his advent into power the claims of the family of Jansson retreat into the background until, upon the adoption of the charter in 1853, they practically disappear. In the struggle between autocracy and democracy the latter prevailed, but it carried with it the supremacy of Jonas Olson in spiritual and temporal affairs for years to come. This man's ambition to rule was probably as great as that of Erik Jansson, but it must be said to his credit that in general he made more discreet use of his power.

During the troublous times of religious persecution in Sweden Jonas Olson's knowledge of men and affairs had more than once rescued the sinking cause of the Erik Janssonists. After the flight of their leader he had been the chief agent in bringing about their emigration. Now his gifts and attainments, which latter were not inconsiderable in an untutored farmer, once more came to be of service to the people—and to himself.

A democratic form of government was now established, quite different from that to which the Erik Janssonists had been accustomed. Special superintendents or foremen were appointed for the various departments of work, these to be discharged at the discretion of the colonists themselves. These foremen, who also constituted the governing body, met at brief intervals to deliberate and act on matters of common concern. Important questions were referred to the people for their decision. This form of government proved beneficial in every respect. Agriculture and manufacture flourished, the most pressing debts were paid, want was followed by plenty, and the future looked bright and full of promise. The cultivation of broomcorn, begun in

1851, under the direction of an American named Davenport, proved particularly profitable. One large brick structure after another was built, and maples and other shade trees were planted to beautify the landscape. Many of the colonists were expert artisans, whose products found a ready sale.

Although the colony was governed by the will of the majority, Jonas Olson was the controlling spirit. This man did not flaunt his ambition, but gained favor with the people by showing great zeal for the common welfare.

From the first the colonists had owned all property in common; not even the arbitrary conduct of Erik Jansson had suggested the necessity of a change in that respect. But the more the wealth of the community increased, the more evident was the need of specific regulations governing the ownership of property. The only way to obtain a satisfactory basis seemed to be to incorporate the community under the laws of the state. Under the existing order, the colony could not legally own property in its own name; in every instance property was acquired through purchase made in the name of some individual, at whose death the transfer to the community would meet with legal obstacles and entail trouble and expense. This fact Jonas Olson made to serve his ends. In conjunction with a few intimates, he drafter a charter for the Bishop Hill Colony, for passage by the state legislature. Signatures to this document were obtained from the majority of the adult members of the colony without any explanation save that the list of names was to be appended to a petition asking the legislature to grant the charter.

Two of the colonists, the aforementioned E. U. Norberg and August Bandholtz, a German, who had married into the colony, being more prudent than the others, asked to see the proposed charter before affixing their signatures. After some hesitation, the draft was shown to Norberg, who made the pertinent objection that the trustees therein nominated had not been duly elected by the colonists but had arbitrarily placed themselves at the head; furthermore, a number of them were interrelated by blood or marriage, a circumstance presaging the rise of a family autocracy prejudicial to the rights of the individual. These objections, publicly made, caused the colonists to rise in protest against the proposed charter, which for the moment seemed doomed to defeat.

Jonas Olson, however, was master of the situation. After being closeted with Olof Johnson for several hours of secret deliberation, he declared to the assembled colonists that the proposed charter ought by no means to be changed. He insisted that the trustees would need all the power it conveyed, but suggested that the colonists might restrict this power and control their acts by passing special rules. Norberg protested that no special rules could be enforced at variance with a constitution once ratified. Jonas Olson maintained his point, adding that, after all, the charter would be a mere formality, inasmuch as the colonists were God's people, with the divine precepts inscribed in their hearts and consciences and with the Holy Writ for their fundamental law, making all temporal laws superfluous. So convincing arguments by the foremost leader silenced the opposition—all but the obstreperous and heretical Norberg, who continued to object.

Olof Stoneberg   Peter Johnson
Trustees of the Bishop Hill Colony

The proposed charter, together with a petition for its passage, was sent to the legislature, and, after some pressure from the trustees to be, it was granted on Jan. 17, 1853. The seven self-appointed trustees, who were named in the articles of incorporation and whose appointment was thus ratified by the legislature, were the following: Jonas Olson, Olof Johnson, Jonas Erickson, Jacob Jacobson, Swan Swanson, Peter Johnson, a brother of the prophet, and Jonas Kronberg. The first five were from Söderala and were all related by blood; Kronberg was from Alfta. Peter Johnson was succeeded in 1859 by Olof Stoneberg, one of the colony preachers. According to the wording of the charter, they were to hold their positions for life, or during good behavior. They were removable by a majority vote of the male members of the colony.

The conduct of affairs by the seven trustees for the first few years offered no ground for complaint. They seemed desirous of convincing the colonists that their mistrust had been entirely groundless, and the people were thus led to repose the fullest confidence in the trustees. The danger of arbitrary action, implied in the charter, was entirely forgotten, being obscured by incessant preaching of the theocratic doctrine. The members of the community were persuaded to adopt, on May 6, 1854, a set of by-laws, providing for the holding of an annual business meeting, when the trustees were to submit a full and complete report of the past year's business, but in no sense limiting the authority of the trustees or extending the privileges of the colonists. A draft previously submitted by Norberg and Jonas Olson had been rejected by the trustees for the good and sufficient reason that it would have had the opposite effect. The principal necessity for the early adoption of by-laws lay in the fact that the charter contained no provision for the admittance and expulsion of members of the colony. On this point the by-laws stipulated that insubordination in faith, teaching or living was punishable by expulsion with no compensation to banished members, except as the trustees might see fit to make. By this time it could be easily perceived that the popularization of the form of government had been more apparent than real. The colonists were unaccustomed to self-government. Their leaders hardly looked upon themselves as servants of the people, but rather as authoritative interpreters of the will of God. The seven self-constituted trustees were all persons who had been appointed to positions of trust under Erik Jansson and who considered that they had a perfect right to formal recognition of the power which they already virtually enjoyed. In reality the distribution of authority remained very much the same as before. Through the tireless industry of the colonists, the wealth of the community was materially increased during the first years of the administration of the trustees. All realty (except the Foster tract) owned by the colony in the time of Erik Jansson, but subsequently sold, was re-purchased and new extensive tracts of land were added to the colony's holdings. The reputation of the colony and its financial credit also improved.

According to the annual report submitted by the trustees on Jan. 21, 1855, the colony owned 8,028 acres of land, improved and unimproved, 50 building lots in Galva, valued at $10,000, and ten shares of stock in the Central Military Tract Railroad, valued at $1,000. The live stock numbered 109 horses and mules, 586 head of cattle, and 1,000 hogs. All other assets such as wheat, flax, broom corn, provisions and general merchandise, were valued at $49,570.

While the colony enjoyed marked material progress, it suffered spiritual decadence. The former religious zeal had apparently cooled, while the material interests pressed to the fore and engrossed the minds of the people. The Erik Janssonists formerly had sharply criticised the state church for its formalism and lack of spiritual ardor. Now that their own zeal had subsided, they were guilty of the same faults. Nevertheless, regular divine services were held, the principal preachers being Jonas Olson, Anders Berglund, Nils Hedin, Olof Osberg and Olof Stoneberg. Yet, any member who so desired had the right to preach. The services consisted of prayers, singing and the reading and expounding of passages from the Scriptures.

Olof Johnson   Swan Swanson
Trustees of the Bishop Hill Colony

Under Jonas Olson's leadership the religious tendency was in some measure one of conservative retrogression. He eliminated some of the excesses of the Janssonist theology and effected a partial return to the devotionalism of the Pietists and Readers, abolishing Erik Jansson's catechism by degrees and thoroughly revising his hymnbook in 1857. As modified, the religion of the colony had a close resemblance to Methodism. The singing at divine service was particularly beautiful and inspiring, owing to the fervor evinced by the young people. The spoken language used in the sermons, however, was not always the best, being sometimes a mixture of provincial Swedish and bad English. Many colonists had learned to speak the latter language fluently, and a school was maintained, where instruction was given in the subjects of reading, writing, ciphering, and other branches.* Higher education was odious to the colonists; they feared that "learning might tend to vanity." Several of the trustees and spiritual leaders, however, realizing their ignorance, began to acquire knowledge on their own account. A large schoolhouse was built in 1860, that being the last structure erected by the colony as such. From principle, the trustees were opposed to newspapers, yet a weekly Swedish paper called "The Swedish Republican" was started by them at Galva, in July, 1856, with S. Cronsioe as editor. The paper ceased publication after a short period.

Success and prosperity made Jonas Olson and Olof Johnson vain and led them to believe and to proclaim openly that the material welfare of the colony was the result of the wise administration and successful speculations of the board of trustees, rather than the fruit of the labors of the people themselves. As their ambition grew, so did their independence. Great enterprises would be started and large contracts entered into without previous notice to the colonists, often, it is claimed, without the knowledge of any one besides Jonas Olson and Olof Johnson. Should any one inquire into the common affairs, he would be sharply rebuked for his mistrust of the administration.

The despotism of the trustees, like that of Erik Jansson, showed itself in a proclamation forbidding marriages for a certain period. This prohibition provoked constant irritation and eventually proved one of the chief factors of disintegration. The edict was brought about in the following manner: Nils Hedin, the only one of Erik Jansson's twelve apostles who possessed the ability of propagating his master's teachings, had made missionary journeys to Hopedale, N. Y., to the Perfectionists in Oneida, N. Y., and to the Rappists in Economy, Pa., and persuaded 25 or 30 persons in Hopedale to move to Bishop Hill. In 1854 he made a trip to the Shaker Colony at Pleasant Hill, Ky., and there also succeeded in gaining many converts. His visit to the latter settlement had convinced Hedin of the advantages of celibacy. This conviction he succeeded in imparting to Jonas Olson, who thereupon issued a marriage interdict on alleged moral grounds and on the further plea that if all young women became wives much of the outdoor work performed by them would be left undone to the detriment of economic progress. After the edict had been in force for about a year, arousing strong resentment, Jonas Olson began to preach against the marriage institution as belonging solely to the Old

---

* Mikkelsen states that Swedish was not one of the subjects taught in the school, its study being limited to the meager instruction given in the home. In the early fifties Capt. Wickstrum is said to have plugged the keyhole so as not to be detected burning the midnight oil over his English books.

Testament period. It is a union, based entirely on the lust of the flesh, he held, therefore, those who already were married ought to abstain from connubial intercourse.

Before the promulgation of the celibacy edict, ten members, among whom the widow of Eric Jansson, had left the colony and joined the Shakers. When it became a law without being submitted to a general vote, many others deserted Bishop Hill to settle elsewhere. Discontent was general among those who remained; but should any one dare to give vent to his disapproval, he would be summarily dismissed from the colony, according to the fifth article of the by-laws. On this ground eleven persons were expelled on May 7, 1855. Of the remaining colonists a number formed a secret league under the leadership of Norberg with a view to oppose the new doctrine and, whenever the organization should become sufficiently strong, to depose the administration. Certain ones weakened and betrayed the movement, and a rigorous investigation followed. Many of the conspirators were induced by threats again to accept the views of the leaders. Only Norberg himself remained steadfast in his opposition. For the leaders Norberg had long been a thorn in the flesh, and by continued vigorous opposition to their measures, he was largely instrumental in undermining their power.

In the meantime, the temporal and spiritual leaders sought to conceal from outsiders both the doctrines of the sect and the conditions obtaining in the colony. At the annual meeting held in 1856, it was resolved on motion of Jonas Olson that all persons visiting relatives or friends at Bishop Hill should put up at the hotel. In case of over-crowding, lodging was to be provided by the trustees, no member being permitted to house an outsider except by their permission. In spite of all this secrecy, the true condition became known to the neighboring American population, many of whom spoke their mind to the leaders without reserve. One of the points of comment was the fact that the women whose husbands, willingly or by expulsion, left the colony, neither dared nor desired to accompany them, having been persuaded that to leave Bishop Hill, the only place where religion was being preached pure and unalloyed, were to commit a mortal sin. In order to clear themselves, Jonas Olson and Olof Johnson invited their American neighbors to appoint a committee to institute a thorough investigation. This was done, but the report of that committee was far from complimentary to the leaders. Besides substantiating the charges made, it laid bare the prevailing social conditions. Not even by these disclosures could the leaders be persuaded to change their policy. On the contrary, they renewed their efforts still further to alienate the wives from their banished husbands.

Bishop Hill—Colony Store and Post Office and Other Colony Buildings

The drastic marriage interdict, which not only prohibited new marriages but forbade conjugal relations between man and wife, created much strife and caused irreparable damage to the reputation of the colony. Scandal followed upon scandal, heaping opprobrium on the Erik Janssonists and Bishop Hill. In sheer exasperation, a number of colonists determined to come out in open warfare against the leaders and their tenets. These persons were Sven Johan Nordin, Olof Molin, and Hans Nordström, headed by the intrepid Erik U. Norberg. Fearing that their antagonists might eventually bring about a dissolution of the colony, the leaders decided to call a public meeting at which the boldest of the disturbers were to be publicly excommunicated for their own punishment and as an example to other malcontents. This meeting was held October 31, 1856. In direct violation of the express stipulation in the by-laws, it was resolved, on motion of Olof Johnson, to give every woman and child a vote. Then a resolution was passed directing members desiring to marry to obtain permission from the board of trustees. That being granted, the contracting parties were to leave the colony for other parts before consummating their union. Persons entering wedlock without asking permission in due order were to be summarily expelled. Norberg and three others positively refused to submit, and in consequence were banished from the colony. Furthermore, all members were strictly forbidden to have any intercourse whatever with them. No one of those expelled had any part of his property returned to him, although they had toiled from eight to ten years for the common good.

The actions of the leaders were sharply attacked in the public press; a number of Americans took the part of Norberg and his friends and proposed to get justice for them by force if no other means availed. It was proposed to invade Bishop Hill with an armed posse and force the trustees at the point of the musket to grant restitution to the men they had banished. Norberg, however, objected to this method and proposed a settlement by legal process. His plan was to petition the legislature for the revocation of the charter of the Bishop Hill Colony and the appointment of a committee to distribute its property equitably among the colonists. Thereby the dissatisfied members would receive their just portion, and be left free to leave the colony, while those who so desired might remain loyal to the leaders, reorganize the corporation and change its laws to suit themselves. The Americans approved this as a wise and equitable solution of the mooted question. A petition was drawn up and circulated, receiving no less than 1,500 signatures, and was then submitted to the legislature. Norberg appeared in person and by the assistance of Senator Graham urged the granting of the petition. The Bishop Hill leaders were represented by Attorney Ramsay and Senator Henderson. After three weeks the matter had been brought to the point where the fate of the Bishop Hill charter hung on the vote of a single senator. That senator had the matter postponed from time to time, demanding more time for consideration. Meanwhile Senator Graham began to waver. One day he inquired in guarded terms whether Norberg would withdraw his petition for a consideration of one thousand dollars. Suspecting foul play, Norberg refused the money

Jonas Kronberg   Jonas Erickson
Trustees of the Bishop Hill Colony

point-blank. A few days after, Graham stated that urgent private business made a trip home necessary, adding the assurance that he would soon return to push the matter through. The same day Graham left the capital, Olof Johnson arrived in response to a telegram, and the matter was hurriedly disposed of in the legislature to the entire satisfaction of the trustees. That bribery had been resorted to was patent to all.*

This victory, though a rather costly one, raised the courage and enterprising spirit of the leaders to a high pitch. They persuaded the colonists that, God being on their side, all opposition was doomed to failure. The one man who was not to be imposed upon by these fine phrases was Norberg. Assisted by the dissatisfied element, he strove energetically for a division of the property. This was a thing worth while, for in the year 1857 the property held in common doubtless aggregated over $700,000 in value. The individualization of the property, however, did not take place until great losses had been

* It is reported that the thing was done by judicious use of the sum of $8,000.

sustained in the panic of 1857 and through unfortunate business ventures.

Olof Johnson's Business Ventures and the Downfall of the Colony

As has been shown, Jonas Olson was the dominant spirit in the council of seven, but at his side stood Olof Johnson, whose power and influence was ever on the increase, undoubtedly with the approval of his chief. These two men were each the complement of the other. Jonas Olson was shrewd, but conservative, and cautious in the extreme; Olof Johnson, on the other hand, bold and enterprising. The administrative work they divided between them in accordance with natural gifts and capabilities. All matters pertaining to worship and the administration of domestic affairs were in the hands of Jonas Olson, who laid particular stress on the development of the extensive agricultural pursuits, while Olof Johnson looked after the business affairs of the colony, his activities in this line dating back to about the time of the change in the administrative system.

The opportunities for speculative enterprise were very favorable. In 1854 the town of Galva was founded five miles from Bishop Hill. When the Chicago, Burlington and Quincy Railway was completed in 1855, giving Galva a railway station, the little town had a great boom, which Olof Johnson took advantage of. He started a number of business enterprises there, under the auspices of the Bishop Hill Colony, calculated to bring sure and abundant profit. In a short time he sat in his office at Galva and directed practically the whole economic machinery of the colony, all the more easily done since he controlled four of the seven votes in the board of trustees. At first he had the most pronounced success. The Crimean War had caused a sharp rise in the price of such commodities as wheat, corn, and other produce. But his reckless passion for speculation grew even more rapidly than his successful business enterprises. Overspeculation was epidemic at this time, and Johnson was soon drawn into a veritable whirl of diverse ventures, such as dealing in grain, lumber and general merchandise, meat packing, coal mining, banking, railroad building, etc. Together with several other persons he signed a contract to grade the roadbed for the Western Air Line Railroad for the sum of five million dollars, and pledged the Bishop Hill Colony to take stock for one million in the road. This was his most extensive undertaking. Ere long, Olof Johnson found himself in too deep water, and when the panic of 1857 came, the colony suffered loss upon loss, rapidly reducing the wealth which the colonists had produced in the sweat of their brow and sweeping away the earnings of the successful business ventures. The period was marked by great financial disasters, and the Bishop Hill Colony was early drawn into the vortex, heavy losses compelling the colonists to submit to some sacrifice in order to raise money to stand off the creditors. Attempts made to start new enterprises invariably failed, owing to the prevailing hard times.

All too late, the colonists now began to realize whither the speculations of Olof Johnson had carried them, and they urged measures wherewith to control the actions of the board. That body obstinately refused to surrender a single prerogative. The only man on the board who was willing to admit the justice of the demand was Peter Johnson, who resigned as trustee in 1859 and was succeeded by Olof Stoneberg. The involved financial affairs added to the general discontent, and all things conspired to bring about the collapse of the whole system of religious and economic communism. Conditions grew still worse in the latter half of the year 1859, when it leaked out that the trustees had negotiated large loans to cover business losses. Questioned on this point at a public assemblage, the trustees laid the blame on Olof Johnson, who had sole charge of the finances. He finally admitted that he had borrowed $40,000 from one Mr. Studwell of New York, but protested that this was a private transaction of his, not in the least affecting the interests of the other colonists.*

Under the circumstances, the division of the property proposed by Norberg in 1857 naturally came to be favored by many. Evidently the only avenue of escape from complete ruin was to be found in amending the by-laws and repealing the communist pact. At the annual meeting held in January, 1860, a resolution to this effect was passed. The annual report rendered showed that the colony owned between 13,000 and 14,000 acres of land, partly improved, real estate in Galva, stocks and credits in various enterprises, and other resources. making a total of $846,270, while the liabilities amounted to $75,644 all told. This report aroused suspicion, and the colonists demanded that the books be audited. The trustees refused to show their accounts, and a storm of indignation was about to break, when Jonas Olson quieted the murmur of the people by declaring that their demand was just, whereupon he had an auditing committee appointed, with the proviso that the accounts of the lasts two years were to be submitted to them after a period of three weeks.

On the 7th day of February, new by-laws were adopted at a

----

* The official statement of colony debts in 1861, included in the "Answer of the Defendants," recognized as a corporate liability a mortgage loan of $40,000 obtained from Alexander Studwell in February, 1858. When in 1861 the loan was renewed, this debt exceeded $50,000. This fact seems to account for a statement that at about that time Johnson borrowed such a sum from Studwell.

meeting, the legality of which the trustees denied. These by-laws deprived them of the right to buy and sell realty, make contracts or incur debts on the general account, except upon formal resolution of the colonists and with their express sanction. After much strife and discord, a resolution to divide the property was carried into effect on Feb. 14th, each of the 415 colonists receiving one share of stock in approximately two-thirds of the total resources. This portion

Mrs. Mary (Malmgren) Olson,
First Child Born in Bishop Hill

of the property consisted of nearly 10,000 acres of land, valued at $400,000, buildings and realty in Bishop Hill, worth $123,208, and personal property, worth $69,585, making a total of $592,793. The undivided property was estimated at $248,861. The stockholders split up into two groups, the Olson and Johnson parties, the former representing 265, the latter 150 shares. But Olof Johnson managed to get control of the stock of Olson's friends as well as of his own, and soon directed the entire business.

The audit of the accounts of the corporation had a disheartening effect. Among the disclosures made was the fact that the trustees, during the three weeks' respite given them, had opened an entire new set of books, and that, according to the "corrected" accounts, the colony owed $42,759 over and above the reported indebtedness of $75,647, or a total of $118,403. The discoveries made shook the confidence of the colonists in their trustees and hastened the end. Olof Johnson was in a sorry plight. By a resolution of Nov. 13, 1860, he was deposed from the office of trustee for arrogating to himself the management and control of the colony's affairs, violating the bylaws and betraying his trust. By intrigue he managed to get himself reinstated as trustee on May 24, 1861, and proved himself almost indispensable to the board in the work of clearing up the muddle. In a short time he was again almost solely in charge of affairs. He was clothed with power of attorney to make the best bargains possible with the creditors of the corporation and served as attorney in fact until 1870.

Shortly after the division of property had taken place, the

remainder of the common estate, valued at $248,861, was placed in the hands of the trustees with instructions to use it to clear the colony of debt. They were given five years in which to clear up the affairs, with instructions to report annually. Part of the assets being found valueless the amount proved inadequate and a lot of cattle, broomcorn, etc., to the value of $52,762 was subsequently set aside to make up for the deficit.

In the spring of 1861 the Johnson party divided up their holdings so that each got his or her share of the property. To every person,

Major Eric Bergland   Capt. Eric Johnson
Well-known Descendants of Bishop Hill Leaders

male or female, who had attained the age of thirty-five years, was given one full share, comprising 22 acres of farm land, one timber lot of nearly two acres, one town lot and an equitable share of all barns, horses, cattle, hogs, sheep and other domestic animals and of all farm implements and household furniture and utensils. All under this age received a share corresponding to the age of the individual, the smallest being 8 acres of land and other property in proportion. After another year's trial the Olson party, now split up into three groups, known respectively as the Olson, Stoneberg and Martin Johnson groups, took similar action, the shares received by their members being somewhat smaller. Thereby all economic community of interest had ceased, and each colonist could dispose of his property as he saw fit. This new order of things for a time made Bishop Hill flourish as never before. Handsome residences and other buildings sprang up in rapid succession, and the colonists seemed hopeful and confident of the future. If not now relieved of the debt, for the payment of which they had already made so great sacrifices, they firmly hoped to be rid of the burden inside of five years. But their hopes were to be rudely shattered. At the end of the period, the trustees came in with a request for an additional $100,000 to satisfy the creditors. An assessment was levied. The majority being prosperous, they decided to pay rather than go to law, but about half refused or neglected to pay. The sum of $54,858, or $56,163, was raised and turned over to the trustees. Those who refused to pay their assessments held the former appropriation ample. That, however, had been decreased about $100,000 by assets found worthless, making the total appropriation for debt-paying purposes, inclusive of the receipts from the last levy, about $260,000.

The years passed by; the people toiled on as before, and their labors were blessed with rich returns. The trustees also labored on in a way, but as no reports were forthcoming, the people were left in the dark as to what progress they made in paying off the debt. Finally, when in 1868 the trustees again requested a large sum of money—$123,835—the sorely tried patience of the people gave out. At a public meeting on May 11th, the malcontents appointed a committee, composed of Norberg and five others, to bring the trustees to an accounting, and on July 27th, legal proceedings were instituted. A special master in chancery was appointed who, after due examination of the books, certified that the trustees since 1860 had received money and property to the value of $249,763 and paid out on account of the colony $140,144, the sum of $109,619 remaining to be accounted for.

The Bishop Hill Colony Case

In this famous lawsuit, renowned among the legal fraternity of Illinois as the "Colony Case," there were many facts brought out, favorable to the defendants, which are usually ignored by writers who have dealt with the history of Bishop Hill. While the trustees as a body cannot be exonerated from blame for the sins of commission and omission charged to their executive head, Olof Johnson, printer's ink has tended to make them out rather blacker than they deserve. It is only common fairness to assume that the truth in this case was not all on one side.

When the Erik Jansson family ceased to dominate the colony's affairs. it naturally went over to the opposition, and thus we find Erik Jansson's son making common cause with Norberg, his father's old antagonist, against those in control. The suit against the trustees was filed by Erik U. Norberg, Eric Johnson, Olof Olson, Andrew Norberg, Lars Lindbeck and Andrew Johnson, complainants, acting for themselves and in behalf of other persons dissatisfied with the manner in which the trustees were winding up the common affairs. Being a party to the suit and one who thereby sought redress for old grievances, Eric Johnson was not free from bias, and his published account of the case, though quite generally accepted without question, cannot be considered impartial.

The bill of complaint charged the trustees with malfeasance on a large number of counts, such as, exercising undue and improper influence over the legislature in securing the passage of the charter and coercing the colonists into joining the corporation; illegal construction of the charter and by-laws; diverting colony property to their own use; violating the revised by-laws; sinister purposes in subdividing the property; failure to make the required reports; collusion in fraudulent lawsuits to waive just defense, procure judgment and decree against the colony and deprive it of money and property under color of judicial proceedings; gross neglect of duty; misuse, waste and unlawful disposition of corporate funds; concealment of the true state of the colony's pecuniary affairs; unlawful use of the corporate funds for private speculation; mortgaging property without good and sufficient consideration—on all of which and other grounds the complainants asked for a writ enjoining the trustees from further exercise of their authority.

In answer, the trustees urged a formidable array of facts, allegations and denials, many of them well-grounded. Without this admission, the progress of the case can hardly be understood. In fairness to the memory of those of the trustees who did act in good faith and whose principal fault was lack of vigilance, the chief points in their defense, touching the various charges of maladministration, are here outlined. As to the diversion of real estate to private uses, reference was had to the county records to show that all colony lands, formerly vested in individuals, had been duly conveyed to the colony upon its incorporation, no real estate being illegally retained by or conveyed to any trustee individually for his private use and enjoyment prior to or after the general subdivision; and it does not appear from available accounts that this specific charge was substantiated.

The individualization of the property was stated to have been planned and carried out on a just and fair basis, without any other motive than a desire to meet the wishes and subserve the interests of all concerned, the express condition being that the corporation should not be dissolved until after the payment of all corporate debts. The debt was understood at the time to be $100,000 and upward, and the individuals were to remain charged with the lien of this debt, the deeds to their respective pieces of land not to be given until they had paid their proportionate share of the same.

After the sub-division had been made, and certain property had been exempted to apply on the payment of the debt, part of this property, to the value of $40,000 or thereabouts, was destroyed by fire in September, 1861, the available capital being thereby reduced so much, that, too, at a time of pressing want to meet corporate obligations and to equip the colonists for individual farming the next year.

· From the year 1861 on the colonists cultivated their respective tracts, enjoying the issues and profits therefrom. As they needed all the fruits of their labors, the corporation determined to procure extensions from the creditors until the members should be better able to contribute their share toward the payment of the debt. In August, 1865, the trustees levied an assessment of $200 per share, and deeds were made out and placed in escrow, to be delivered to the shareholders upon completing payment of the assessment. The trustees stated that if those assessments had been promptly met, it would have enabled them to avoid costs, save the sacrifice of property and nearly or quite discharge the colony debt. But only a part of the required amount was realized, namely the sum of $54,858, which was disbursed by Olof Johnson, as attorney in fact, in part payment of debt.

The defendants, further answering, stated that since the chartering of the colony, it had been engaged in many lawsuits and was especially so involved after proceedings were inaugurated for a sub-division of the property; creditors then became restive and outsiders sought by legal strategy to take advantage of the corporation and speculate upon its misfortune. The rights of the colonists, they averred, had been defended to the utmost, and against the charge of collusive and fraudulent lawsuits, defaults, combinations to waive just defense and other legal strategies, entailing losses to the colony, they entered positive denial. A schedule of some 120 lawsuits was given, not including many suits before justices of the peace and other inferior courts, nor all of the cases brought before courts in Chicago—and it is a safe inference that these suits cost the corporation a large amount of money.

The loans negotiated are stated to have been solely for the benefit of the colony, in time of pressing need; the mortgages in every instance having been given for good and sufficient consideration, and the money thus secured turned into the common treasury to be disbursed for the common good, wherefore, the trustees averred, to attempt to avoid these just obligations, as suggested by the complainants, would be bald repudiation and dishonesty.

In March, 1868, the trustees, desiring to complete the individualization, pay all obligations and dissolve the corporation, levied a new assessment, aggregating $123,835, which sum, together with remaining assets, was thought adequate for the payment in full of the colony debt, now amounting to about $158,000. But the majority of the members were unable to pay their pro rata share without hardship. The trustees therefore made an arrangement with Elias Greenebaum of Chicago whereby he was to loan them the respective amounts, on mortgage security, giving such terms as to prevent sacrifice of property. Had all availed themselves of this arrangement, which they did not, the debt might have been fully liquidated, the trustees asserted, and each member would have obtained clear title to his or her allotment of property.

The trustees accounted for the size of the debt of 1868 in the following manner: To the amount due in 1861, estimated at $112,000, should be added interest at 10%, commissions, costs incurred in litigation, sums paid in compromise, in cases where legal advantage had been obtained over the colony, payment of taxes, and other legitimate causes of increase of corporate debts; it would then be readily seen why the debt had become the debt of 1868, although $54,858 had been paid thereon. Furthermore, a claim of about $60,000 against the Western Air Line Railroad, counted as an asset in 1860 and 1865, had been found worthless, except as to the sum of $6,500, which had been received in settlement. It was further estimated that undivided property remaining unsold would bring at most $20,000.

As to contracting, banking and other enterprises, into which the trustees engaged on the initiative of Olof Johnson, they offered a plausible defense of their acts. In 1854 they contracted for the grading of part of the roadbed of the Chicago, Burlington and Quincy and earned $37,000 under that contract. Two years later the colony was awarded a contract to grade the projected Western Air Line Railroad, and a large sum of money ($60,000) had been earned, when the railway company failed as a result of the panic. As the failure could not be foreseen at the time when the contract was made and labor thereon performed, and as the claim was watched for some ten years prior to its settlement for $6,500, the trustees disclaimed responsibility for the loss sustained. This contract, which involved no less than five million dollars, and promised to yield the colony a very handsome profit, was by no means a bad speculation, as has been freely admitted even by Eric Johnson himself.*

In 1856-1858 Olof Johnson represented the colony in a copartnership with Samuel Remington, in a bank at Galva, known as the Nebraska Western Exchange Bank, through the failure of which as a

* See "Svenskarne i Illinois," page 66.

result of the panic the colony incurred losses. The trustees, while admitting this, declared that the undertaking had been reported to the members of the colony and approved by them, adding that a settlement was had in 1860 with Olof Johnson, who was then discharged from liability for the failure.

While on many points the defense of their acts offered by the trustees seems valid, the manner of handling the accounts of the colony by them does not appear equally defensible. In 1849 Olof Johnson had raised in Sweden about $6,000 for the colony. In the schedule of debt submitted in 1868, we find this item, "Notes and interest due parties in Sweden for money loaned, etc., $12,000." This was either a part of the same item or another loan, which through neglect had been allowed to accumulate, notwithstanding intervening years of prosperity, one of which alone showed an increase of $238,334 in the value of personal property, according to the trustees' report. The Studwell loan of $40,000 in 1858, which three years later represented a liability of $66,570, is another case in point, though the prevailing financial stringency no less than lack of vigilance may account for this increase. The summary of accounts submitted by the trustees in 1868, showing receipts of $171,964 and disbursements of $195,837, was not convincing, and Olof Johnson's claim for reimbursement in the sum of $23,873 for money paid out in excess of receipts was naturally viewed with suspicion.

From the answer of the defendants we gather, in conclusion, that the complainants were not all legal members of the corporation, and that they had in almost every instance failed to assist in paying off corporate obligations, while the trustees, with a single exception, paid both assessments, amounting in the case of Jonas Olson to as much as $3,120. The revised by-laws were, the trustees declared, illegally passed and therefore could not be binding upon their acts, and they were in fact never so held by them.

After a long and aggravating legal contest stretching over five years, the case was left to the judge, who delayed his decision for a like period. Finally in 1879 some sort of settlement of the case was effected. The trustees were not held accountable for the $109,619; Olof Johnson's claims of $23,873 and salary for the years he had acted as attorney in fact were disallowed; all other claims against the corporation were held valid and ordered paid, in addition to which $57,782 in new obligations, including a contingent fund of $16,000 and costs on both sides, were saddled on the colonists. This "so-called decree," like others caustically referred to in like terms by the Supreme Court at a later occasion, was the result of a compromise between the attorneys in the case and was doubtless signed by the judge merely as a matter of form. Under the decree, entered April 25 and July 28, 1879, many tracts of land were sold by the special master in chancery (William H. Gest), the owners of which were not parties to the suit. The most of the lands were not redeemed from the sale, and deeds were made out to the purchasers, who had been notified at the sale that possession would not be voluntarily yielded by the owners. Petitions were filed by the grantees in some of the deeds for writs of assistance to put them in possession of the lands, among them the lands of John Root, a son of the man who killed Erik Jansson, now a prominent attorney. This proved the test case, on the outcome of which hung the fate of the entire colony case. Root's land had been sold for $2,868.50 and was purchased for the benefit of Charles C. Bonney, the attorney who prosecuted the suit against the trustees. The judge who tried the case granted a writ of assistance directing the sheriff of Henry county to put the petitioner, Lyman M. Payne, acting for Bonney, in possession of the land. Root appealed the case to the Appellate Court, where the judgment of the lower court was reversed. Payne appealed his case to the Supreme Court, where the judgment of the Appellate Court was affirmed. The opinion of the Supreme Court, rendered May 12, 1887, by Mr. Justice Mulkey, reads in part as follows:

"Numerous orders and so-called decrees were, from time to time, entered in the cause, even a cursory examination of which, we think, fully justifies the claim of appellant that it is 'a case sui generis.' Under the compendious title of The Bishop Hill Colony Case, after the manner of Dickens' celebrated case of Jarndyce and Jarndyce, it has been 'dragging its slow length along' for a period of over eighteen years, and, as far as we are able to perceive, those who have been chiefly benefited by it are the immediate parties to the suit, their counsel and the officers of the court—notably the master in chancery, who has received some $9,000 out of the fund, as fees in the case... The conclusion sought to be drawn from the circumstances pointed out as sustaining the claim (against Root) find no sanction in law and just as little in reason or logic. Viewed from a legal aspect, or, indeed, from any other aspect, we have seldom, if ever, seen a case so entirely destitute of merit."

The law governing the remaining cases being thus determined, the cases were dismissed and never resurrected. The original Bishop Hill case then remained, deserted by those who brought it and by their attorney. When the clerk of the Circuit Court of Henry county was making up the docket for the February term, 1888, a member of the bar of the county suggested to him that the case be omitted from the docket, which was done, and thus the last remnant of the Bishop Hill Colony was given a quiet burial.

To estimate the losses to the colonists incurred by Olof Johnson's

Old Settlers Monument at Bishop Hill, Erected in 1896, in Memory of the Founders of the Colony

administration and through the resultant litigation is not possible, in the absence of reliable figures. Up to and including the year 1879 there seems to have been an expenditure in money and property, to pay debt, aggregating $300,000, and a loss of more than $100,000 in bad accounts, worthless notes and other doubtful assets.* What remained of the old corporate debt was paid with the proceeds from the subsequent land sales. After the death of Olof Johnson in 1870, the affairs were managed by Jonas Olson, with the assistance of Swanson and Jacobson, Stoneberg and Kronberg taking little part.

The Final Fate of Erik Janssonism

The decisive steps in the dissolution of the colony having been taken in the years 1860 to 1862, many of the Erik Janssonists left Bishop Hill and settled elsewhere. Jonas Olson sought to form a congregation that would remain true to the doctrines of Erik Jansson, but failed in the attempt, the colonists already having been divided in the matter of creed. In 1867 the Seventh Day Adventists made a successful effort at proselyting among them, establishing a church in 1870 with 150 members, among whom was Jonas Olson. Shortly afterwards, the congregation was divided on certain doctrinal points, the one faction being headed by Jonas Olson and Martin Johnson, the other by John Hellsen, Peter Wexell and others. The rupture was not permanent and the members have worshiped together for many years. Not a few of the former colonists have gone over to Methodism. A Methodist Church was organized as early as 1864 with fifteen members, which number rapidly increased. Olof Stoneberg and Anders Berglund became the local preachers of this flock. A small number accepted Swedenborgianism; beyond that the colonists largely preferred to remain outside of all denominational pales.

Sept. 23—24, 1896, the fiftieth anniversary of the founding of Bishop Hill was commemorated. Over two thousand people were in attendance, among whom were no less than ninety-nine of the incorporators of 1853. Of the trustees two were still living, Jonas Olson, aged ninety-four, and Swan Swanson.

A granite monument had been erected bearing this inscription:

1846
Dedicated to the Memory of the Hardy Pioneers
who, in order to secure
RELIGIOUS LIBERTY,
left Sweden, their native land, with all the endearments
of home and kindred, and founded
BISHOP HILL COLONY,
on the uninhabited prairies of
ILLINOIS
Erected by surviving members and descendants
on the 50th Anniversary, September twenty-third
1896

* A statement in "Svenskarne i Illinois," p. 51, that by 1879 it had cost the colonists $672,910.61 to pay their debt of $118,406.33 is clearly erroneous, the enormous total having been reached by duplicating items aggregating a quarter of a million.

The Sixtieth Anniversary Celebration in 1906, Held in the Village Park, Bishop Hill

At the present time Bishop Hill is a small village with a population somewhat in excess of three hundred. The large buildings erected at the time of its greatest prosperity are still occupied, though somewhat dilapidated. But few of the early colonists now remain alive. Berglund, Norberg, Hedin, Stoneberg, Olof Johnson, and Jonas Olson, all these leaders have passed away and the second generation sprung from them and their contemporaries is already growing old. Sophia Jansson, the widow of the prophet, died in the Henry County infirmary in 1888; Erik Jansson's son, Captain Eric Johnson, is now living in California, and the daughter, who was married to Captain A. G. Warner, a veteran of the Civil War, and later became Mrs. Rutherford, also survives.

In the evening of his life Jonas Olson, although confined to his invalid's chair by decrepitude, continued to preach. His eyes were dim, and it was better so, for his flock had grown pitifully small and looked grotesquely out of place in so capacious a house of worship as the old colony church. In 1871 he lost his first wife, whose maiden name was Katrina Wexell. The following year, at the age of seventy, he obtained a second helpmeet in Miss Katrina Johnson, a girl of twenty-eight. He passed away at his home in Bishop Hill on Nov. 18, 1898, at the ripe age of ninety-six years.

Olof Johnson, born in Söderala parish, Helsingland, June 30, 1820, died at Galva, July 18, 1870, in the midst of difficulties attending the famous lawsuit. He left an insolvent estate, and but for his life insurance, it is claimed, it would have fared hard with his family.

Andrew Berglund, born in Alfta parish, Helsingland, Jan. 10, 1814, departed this life at Bishop Hill, Aug. 17, 1896. In 1867 he joined the newly organized Swedish Methodist Church at Bishop Hill, which he served as local preacher until his death. His son, Major Eric Bergland, U. S. A., retired, of Baltimore, Md., is one of several descendants of the original colonists, who have attained eminence.

Olof Stoneberg, elected colony trustee in 1859 to succeed Peter Johnson, joined the local Methodist church in 1868 and became local preacher and an eminent member of the denomination. At his death, which occurred Jan. 8, 1892, he left a generous bequest to the Swedish M. E. Theological Seminary at Evanston, Ill., on whose board of directors he had served for many years. Stoneberg was a native of Helsingland, born in Forssa parish on Feb. 17, 1818.

Swan Swanson, the last surviving trustee of the colony, died in Bishop Hill Mar. 24, 1907. He was born May 25, 1825, in Söderala, Helsingland. Swanson served as colony bookkeeper and storekeeper prior to 1860 and subsequently with Jacob Jacobson became joint owner of the store. He was for many years postmaster of the village.

Eric Ulric Norberg, whose conspicuous connection with the Bishop Hill Colony has been shown in the preceding pages, was born June 22, 1813, at Ullervad, Vestergötland, Sweden, and graduated from the college at Skara at the age of eighteen, after which he became private secretary to the provincial governor, serving until the age of twenty-

Eric U. Norberg in Old Age

three, when he was appointed "länsman" for Skaraborg and one other "län." This office he held until 1842, when with his sister he emigrated to America, settling first in Michigan, then moved to Wisconsin and afterwards to Minnesota. This region at that time was scarcely inhabited by any white people, and he lived near the Indians and had very friendly relations with them. In 1847 he joined the colonists at Bishop Hill, where he married and lived in the colony off and on for about ten years, then left and came to Chicago, where he lived for some two years, but returned about the time that the colony broke up and the division of property took place. Part of the time he was with the colony, he was secretary and kept the records of the meetings of the corporation. He also had charge of the colony warehouse at Galva. Prior to that time he also had charge of the warehouse at Henry on the Illinois River, where the colonists did a large portion of their shipping. In 1863 he moved with his family on a farm near Toulon, where he lived for a number of years until he moved to Galva, with his daughter, Mrs. Carrie N. Jones, where he died at the age of nearly 86 years. A son of Eric Norberg is Gustaf Norberg, an attorney, of Holdrege, Neb.

CHAPTER V.

Other Early Settlements

Character and Condition of Settlers

N the latter forties and the early fifties, when Swedish immigration to the West showed a marked increase, these immigrants either settled in communities already established by Americans from the East or founded new settlements of their own. All who were able to do so purchased a piece of land and some live stock. The others had to hire out for work until they had saved up enough money to buy land. Simple dwellings, mostly log cabins, were built. One of the first cares of the immigrants was to organize a congregation and build a church edifice in which to worship God in the manner of their fathers. After having provided for these most urgent temporal and spiritual wants, they began to acquaint themselves more thoroughly with the new country and to prepare themselves for the proper exercise of the rights and duties of citizenship.

These settlements flourished rapidly, their progress largely due to the industry and hardiness of the settlers. The fertile prairie soil, under careful cultivation, yielded rich harvests; large herds of cattle soon grazed on the green bottoms; the rude little loghouses gradually gave way to larger and more commodious dwellings; the small, struggling congregations grew to be a great factor in the mental culture of the settlers; the settlements grew steadily more extensive and populous, due partly to their own enterprise, partly to continued immigration. In many of these settlements agriculture, combined with the raising of live stock, was then, and continues to be, the principal occupation, while in others industrial plants were established which have since developed so as to rank with the largest of their class.

At that time the American settlers in Illinois, composed largely of New England yankees, had purchased tracts of land, not so much from a desire to become farmers as from a penchant for speculation. When Swedes in any considerable numbers flocked to a certain spot, these original settlers usually retreated, leaving the newcomers as lords of all they surveyed. Hence, certain settlements, almost from the outset, became exclusively populated by Swedes, and have retained that character. In others there was a mixture of Americans and Swedes, the two nationalities getting on well together and making united efforts for the development of their communities. In still others the Americans were numerically stronger, yet the Swedes pushed to the front in various lines, thus forming an important factor in the community.

Although it is not our present purpose to write the local history of the Swedish settlements in Illinois, yet, for the sake of obtaining a connected story and a survey of the historical field, brief sketches of the rise and development of the principal early settlements, founded prior to the outbreak of the Civil War, are here given, commencing with Andover, in Henry county, next to Bishop Hill the oldest Swedish settlement in the state.

ANDOVER, HENRY COUNTY

The first white settler in Andover was a Dr. Barker, who arrived May 6, 1835, remaining there only a short time. In June of the same year three other Americans, viz., Rev. Pillsbury, Mr. Slaughter and Mr. Pike, came there for the purpose of looking up a site for a colony that was being organized in New York. They selected an extensive tract, part of which was platted as a town site. Streets, alleys and a public square were laid out, and the place was named Andover, after the Massachusetts city where the renowned Congregational theological seminary is located. The land company in New York evidently worked with the pious intention of building up a Christian community, and making money incidentally, but the plan was not realized as originally framed, for in the place of a strong colony of American Puritans there sprang up a populous settlement of Swedish Lutherans.

One of the first buildings erected in the place was a flour mill. During the first few years the population was small, and the settlers experienced all the hardships of pioneering. The nearest post office was at Knoxville, thirty odd miles distant. The letter postage at that time was 25 cents.

The first Swede in Andover and Henry county at large was Sven Nilsson, a sailor, who arrived as early as 1840. The next arrival of Swedish descent was Miss Johanna Sofia Lundqvist, born Jan. 15, 1824, at the paper mill Perioden, near Jönköping, her parents being J. E. Lundqvist, a paper manufacturer, and his wife Brita Maria, née Flodén. The factory having been destroyed by fire, Lundqvist in 1842 moved with his wife and four children to Helsingland, where he purchased the Lund paper mill in Forssa parish. Together with many others, Lundqvist and his wife were drawn into the religious movement started by Erik Jansson. Mrs. Lundqvist appears to have been a particularly zealous member of the sect, judging from the fact that she was one of the fifteen persons who on Dec. 7, 1844, made a bonfire of Lutheran books, near Stenbo, in Forssa parish. For this alleged sacrilege these persons were tried at Forssa Feb. 24, 1845, and fined each 16 crowns, 32 shillings banco. The verdict no doubt had something to do with Lundqvist's determination to emigrate to America with his family in company with Erik Jansson's followers. He sold the paper mill and with wife and three children, including the oldest daughter, joined a company of Erik Janssonists who emigrated in 1846. The youngest daughter, Mathilda Gustafva, remained in Sweden to clear up the estate.

While the parents settled at Bishop Hill, the oldest daughter early in 1847 hired out as a domestic in the family of a Mr. Townsend in Andover. She was the first Swedish woman to live in Andover. The year of her arrival she formed the acquaintance of P. W. Wirström, a Swedish sea captain, whom she married. This was the first Swedish family in Andover. Captain Wirström, born at Waxholm in 1816, seems to have emigrated at an early date. The year of his arrival is not known, but it is known to a certainty that he was here as early as 1846, when he sailed on the Great Lakes. In the fall of that year he learned that a company of his fellow countrymen had arrived at Buffalo, N. Y. Going there, he found that the emigrants were Erik Janssonists headed by Nils Hedin. At their request he accompanied them as interpreter on their journey to Bishop Hill. After their arrival he became almost indispensable in the capacity of physician, possessing, as he did, a smattering of medical learning. He remained there till July, 1847, when he removed to Andover.

After his marriage to Johanna Sofia Lundqvist, they made their home in a log cabin in Andover until the fall of the same year, when they removed to New Orleans, where Captain Wirström hired out as a slave driver. The following spring the couple returned to Andover, but went back to New Orleans in the fall, Wirström returning to his former occupation there. One day, in weighing up the cotton on the plantation where he was employed, it was discovered that the day's harvest was too small, and Wirström got orders to urge the slaves to still greater exertions. This he refused to do, and, having already had enough of the slave driver's job, he once more returned to Andover in 1849. The same summer the cholera epidemic ravaged Andover as well as Bishop Hill, and Lundqvist's two sons were among its victims.

This was also the year of the great California gold fever. Among those who went west to seek their fortune in the newly discovered gold fields were Captain Wirström and his young wife. In company with a number of others from Andover, they set out April 6, 1850, on their long journey across the prairie wilderness to the golden land. They traveled mostly on foot, and many were their sufferings en route. For Mrs. Wirström, who had to do the cooking for eight men in the company, the journey was especially hard and toilsome. She stood it manfully, however, and late in August all arrived safe and sound at Beadville's Bear. A few weeks later, the Wirströms bought a hotel. Adversities now came in rapid succession. Their only child died, and an attack of consumption compelled Captain Wirström to return to Illinois in 1854. He died Feb. 25, 1855, at Bishop Hill. Then Mrs. Wirström sold the hotel in California for $8,000 and removed to Bishop Hill.

Nov. 4, 1856, Mrs. Wirström was wedded to an American by the name of M. B. Ogden, of Galva, and they settled on a farm which she purchased at Victoria, living there for more than twenty years. In 1881 they removed to Riverside, California, where she resided until her death, June 10, 1904.

The younger sister, who had been left behind when the Lundqvist family emigrated, came over in 1850, was married to one J. W. Florine and moved to Andover in 1855 with her husband, who became the first physician, druggist and photographer of that place. Florine served as second lieutenant in Company H, 43rd Illinois Volunteers in the early part of the Civil War, but asked for his discharge Feb. 4, 1862, and died the same year. His wife, born at Nyköping in 1829, is still living.

Returning to the early settlers of Andover, we meet here the aforementioned Peter Kassel, who emigrated from Kisa, Östergötland, to Iowa in 1845, and corresponded with friends in the old country with the result that another company emigrated in 1847 from the same part of Sweden. They arrived in New York with the fixed intention of going to New Sweden, Iowa, but Rev. O. G. Hedström succeeded in persuading them to go by way of Victoria, Illinois, where his brother Jonas Hedström was located, and investigate conditions in that locality. Jonas Hedström referred them to Andover, where they went to live. In the company were N. J. Johnson with wife and an adopted daughter, all from Järeda, Småland, and Anders Johansson with wife and three children, from Linneberga in the same province. Johnson and his family obtained temporary lodging in the home of Rev. Pillsbury, later on moving into a loghouse that stood on the present site of the Andover orphanage.

At the same time, or possibly somewhat later, came a family by the name of Friberg, one Nils Nilsson, a family named Hurtig, and in 1848 John A. Larson from Oppeby, Östergötland, who was to play a prominent part in the public affairs of Andover and vicinity.

N. J. Johnson and Nils Nilsson were the first Swedish landowners in Andover. As early as 1848, they each purchased ten acres of land at $1.25 per acre. Johnson's rude hut, the first Swedish home in the settlement, stood as a landmark for many years and may have been preserved to this day.

Anders Johansson died in 1849, but his widow was married again, to Samuel Johnson of Orion. In her younger days she was a strong and sturdy woman, in physical prowess the match of any man. N. J. Johnson and his wife were still living in the year 1880, and Nils Nilsson in the latter part of the eighties. Friberg removed to Colfax, Iowa; Hurtig, who lived south of "Deacon Buck's place," died in 1849, his wife surviving him by many years. In 1880 she was residing in Polk county, Neb., where she had moved in 1875. John A. Larson did not long remain at Andover, but went to Galesburg and there learned the wagonmaker's trade. In 1850 he went to California in search of gold, of which he found little or none, whereupon he returned in 1851, taking up his former trade in Galesburg two years later, and shortly afterwards removing to Andover, where he built a carriage shop of his own and was engaged in that trade for fifteen years. During that time he purchased the homestead of Rev. Pillsbury, which he made his home. Having early acquired a knowledge of the English language, he was of great assistance to his countrymen in legal or business matters and thus earned their lasting gratitude. In time he became a large landowner. In 1880 he owned no less than 587 acres of fertile land. His wife, who died in 1879 after a union lasting twenty-six years, bore him eight children. This honored and distinguished pioneer passed away at Andover in April, 1903.

The little Swedish settlement was reinforced in 1848 by two unmarried men, Gabriel Johnson and Gustaf Johnson, and five families, viz., Samuel Johnson from Södra Vi, Småland, with wife and three sons; Halland Elm from Gammalskil, Östergötland, with wife, one son and two daughters; Erik Peter Andersson from Kisa, Östergötland, with wife, two sons and three daughters; Samuel Samuelsson, also from Kisa, with wife and four children, and Måns Johnsson from the same place, with wife and one son.

These five families were part of a party of 75 emigrants who left Sweden in 1846, embarking at Göteborg on the sailing vessel "Virginia," Captain Johnson, for New York. The entire company were bound for New Sweden, Iowa, but their plans were frustrated. In Albany, N. Y., the modest sum set aside for their traveling expenses was stolen, and all the way to Buffalo, N. Y., the emigrants had to subsist on wild plums growing on the banks of the canal, and anything edible that they could pick up. Reaching Buffalo, they were unable to proceed farther, but remained in that city for two years in order to earn the money needed for reaching their final destination. In the meantime, friends and kindred at Andover had learned of their whereabouts and their sorry predicament, and sent letters urging them to come to their settlement. The five families just enumerated obeyed the call. One of the party, Måns Johnsson, had died during their stay in Buffalo.

The balance of the party proceeded to Sugar Grove, Warren county, Pa., and became the pioneer Swedish settlers there and in the vicinity of Jamestown, N. Y. The aforementioned Samuel Johnson, who eventually settled at Orion, Henry county, died in 1887. Erik Peter Andersson passed away in 1854 and his wife in the latter seventies. Samuel Samuelsson and his wife removed to Galesburg, Ill.

In 1849 Andover received a substantial addition to its population. That summer a party arrived from Östergötland and northern Småland, originally consisting of 300 persons who had left Göteborg in the spring on the sailing vessel ''Charles Tottie,'' Captain Bäckman. After seven weeks and four days they arrived in New York, whence they were carried by three canalboats to Buffalo. On board one of the boats cholera broke out. At Buffalo they took passage on a steamer for Chicago. There they met Captain Wirström, who escorted them to Andover, their final destination. The trip was made by canal from Chicago to Peru, from which point the emigrants and their effects were carried across the country in nine wagon loads at $18 per load, arriving at Andover July 31st. Their original intention also had been to look up Peter Kassel at New Sweden, Ia., but the cholera epidemic and other diseases in the party cut short their trip and compelled them to stop at Andover and neighboring points. Among the members of the party were the following: Nils Magnus Kihlberg and family, from Kisa, who settled at Swedona, where Kihlberg was still living in 1890; the brothers Carl Johan Samuelsson and Johannes Samuelsson from Vestra Eneby, Östergötland, who with their families settled at Hickory Grove, Lynn township, south of Andover township. When the railroad was built through that country a station was located at Hickory Grove and named Ophiem, after Johannes Samuelsson's old home, Opphem in Tjärstad parish, Östergötland. The two brothers had great success in farming and accumulated considerable wealth. In 1880 their combined estates were valued at $130,000. Both were earnest churchmen, contributing liberally, to churches, schools and benevolent institutions. Johannes Samuelsson died June 11, 1887, at the age of 72, the younger brother Apr. 23, 1900, nearly 78 years old. He bequeathed to Augustana College and Theological Seminary a sum amounting to nearly $15,000. The same year, on August 20th, his wife Carolina, née Persson, whom he had married in Sweden, followed him in death and was buried at his side in the Swedish cemetery at Ophiem.

The same year that the last named party of immigrants came to Andover, there arrived also the following: Nils P. Petersson and wife, from Lönneberga, Småland; Anders Peter Larsson; A. P. Petersson; Pehr Svensson from Djursdala, Småland, with his wife, son and daughter. The daughter died of cholera at Princeton, while en route to Andover, and shortly afterward the mother fell a victim to the same disease. The first wheeled vehicle made in Henry county was constructed by Svensson. It was an extremely primitive affair, drawn by a yoke of oxen. In it Svensson and his son were often seen riding to the little church of a Sunday morning.

Still another party of immigrants from Sweden arrived in Andover in 1849. This consisted of 140 persons from the provinces of Gestrikland and Helsingland, headed by Rev. L. P. Esbjörn, a man destined to play a prominent part in the history of the Swedes in America. The party left Gefle on board the sailing vessel "Cobden" June 29, 1849, and arrived in Andover in the late summer. The majority of these people were soon induced by Rev. Jonas Hedström to go to Victoria.

Among those in Esbjörn's party who remained in Andover were, Jonas Andersson, with wife and three children; Matts Ersson and Olof Nordin with families, all from Hille. Jonas Andersson and Matts Ersson were members of the party of goldseekers that left Andover for California, returning in 1851, short on gold but long on experience. Andersson later engaged in the merchandise business in partnership with G. E. Peterson, but was forced into liquidation by the panic of 1857. Two years later he removed to Colorado with his sons, his wife and daughter remaining in Andover. Olof Nordin and his family also left shortly afterward and their fate is not known. Matts Ersson lived in Andover until 1901 and died June 3, 1905, at the Bethany Home in Chicago, an old folks' home supported by the Swedish Methodists, where he spent the last four years of his life. Among the new arrivals from Sweden in 1849, not members of the Esbjörn party, were, S. P. Strid, an old soldier from Östergötland, and Åke Olsson from Ofvansjö, Gestrikland, the last-named having accompanied a party of Erik Janssonists to America in 1846, but separated from them in New York, remaining three years in the state of New York before proceeding farther west.

Disease was prevalent in many forms, the worst of which was the cholera. That dreaded epidemic made annual visitations from 1849 to 1854, making great inroads on the population. As an example of its ravages may be mentioned that in 1849 one John Elm worked with two different harvesting gangs of sixteen men each, and of the thirty-two all but Elm and two others were stricken down and died of the pest.

To obtain profitable employment at this time was no easy matter. A day's wages varied from 35 cents to 50 cents, and in many instances it had to be taken out in the form of pork and other provisions, cattle or anything of value. On the other hand, live stock and merchandise were very cheap. A good cow could be bought for $8, and a first class working horse for $40. The price of pork was 1½ cents, and potatoes were to be had for the trouble of digging them. This was the golden age of topers, whisky selling at 12½ to 15 cents per gallon. These prices ruled until 1853, when railway building began in western Illinois. This brought more money into circulation, increased the demand for labor, and raised the price of agricultural products. Economic conditions thus kept improving up to 1857, when the panic struck the Andover settlement as it did the country at large.

Better times came about 1862 when the Civil War put large amounts of money into circulation and farm products began to command enormous prices. At this juncture, many of the Andover Swedes became independent farmers. They bought farms, often on time, but generally the returns from the first year's crops would suffice to clear them of debt. The more provident ones continued similar purchases until they became the owners of many hundreds of acres. The less enterprising ones were contented with farms of ten to eighty acres. The soil was carefully tilled; even the small farmers made more than a living off their acres and had no need of going farther west in search of larger farms. Thus Andover early became a well-to-do Swedish-American community, whose prosperity has been on the increase ever since.

What has been said of the prosperity of the farmers applies in like measure to the artisan and the tradesman. By industry and thrift they also have acquired economic independence. The first Swede who obtained a deed to a building lot in the village—the place never reached the dignity of a city—was C. Larsson, the paper being dated Dec. 15, 1849. The first Swedish mechanic was the aforesaid John A. Larson, who in 1853 built a blacksmith and wagon shop. The first Swedish merchants were Jonas Andersson and Georg(e) E. Petersson, who in 1854, under the firm name of Andersson & Petersson, opened a general store, which they conducted until 1857.

The name of Andover early became known in many parts of Sweden, and the place long continued to be the destination of Swedish emigrants westward bound. The conceptions of its size and importance were highly exaggerated. It is told of the emigrants of the forties and fifties that when they came to Chicago and noticed the bustle and activity of that progressive city they would give vent to their surprise by exclaiming, ''If Chicago is so large, just think what a place Andover must be!'' There must have been a fresh surprise in store for them when, on their arrival in Andover, they found neither a city nor a town, nor even a village. Nevertheless, the early Swedish emigrants bound for other points than Andover were comparatively few. From there, however, they soon scattered over the state in every direction. Although they did not leave Andover in great numbers at any time, yet from various aspects that settlement must be considered the second mother colony in Illinois, Bishop Hill holding first place.

Andover early became known as a conservative and reliable Swedish-American community, a reputation which has followed it to this day. The reasons for this conservatism are doubtless to be found in the teachings imparted to the settlers by their early pastors, principally Revs. L. P. Esbjörn, Jonas Swensson and Erland Carlsson, who labored in this field for a long term· of years. The first two, in particular, exercised a very marked influence on the character of the settlers.

As stated before, a Swedish Lutheran congregation was organized here as early as 1850. This was the first regularly organized Swedish Lutheran church in America since the days of the Delaware Swedes. Two years previously, pastoral work had been begun in New Sweden, Iowa, but no fully organized church was established there until a later date. Also a Swedish Methodist church was very early established in Andover, but the year of its founding is in dispute. Some claim 1848, others 1849, and still others 1850 as the correct date. The Baptists and the Mission Friends, on the contrary, have not deemed it worth while entering this old community, nor has any fraternal organization met with encouragement in Andover.

At the close of the year 1905, the total Swedish population in the Andover settlement, extending over three townships, was roughly estimated at from 1,500 to 2,000 persons.

VICTORIA, KNOX COUNTY

Victoria is located on a rolling prairie in the northeastern part of Knox county. Its first white inhabitants were Edward Brown, John Essex, and one Mr. Frazier, all of whom settled there in 1835. The first marriage solemnized there took place in 1838, between Peter Sonberger and Phebe Wilbur. The first house was built in 1837 on a plain near the subsequent site of the town. The first sermon was preached in Victoria in 1836 by Rev. Charles Bostie, a Methodist minister.

In course of time, a number of other settlers arrived, the first Swede among them being Jonas Hedström, the Methodist preacher. He came in 1838, from Farmington, Fulton county, his first place of residence on Illinois soil. For several years Hedström was the only Swede in Victoria, but after the Erik Janssonists began to settle at Bishop Hill, a number of these were by him attracted to Victoria. We have already related how Olof Olsson, their first envoy, with his family came there in 1845 and was housed in a rude hut of logs situated in Copley township; also how Erik Jansson himself and his kindred found shelter in the same log cabin the following year. Not long afterwards, Sven Larsson, Olof Norlund, and Jonas Jansson arrived from Söderala, Helsingland, and Jonas Hedin from Hede, Herjedalen. Norlund and Jansson soon succumbed to the cholera, and the others left Victoria for Red Oak Grove after a stay of only a few weeks.

Among the earliest settlers here may be mentioned Olof Olsson from Ofvanåker, Helsingland, who came to Bishop Hill in 1846, but after three months bade farewell to the prophet and his colony and moved to Victoria, where he bought a small farm. Olsson also died shortly after his arrival. Jonas Hellström, a tailor, left Bishop Hill in 1847 and opened a tailor shop at Victoria, where he plied his trade until 1850, when he caught the gold fever and went to California. After a year he returned to his old trade at Victoria. At the outbreak of the Civil War, he enlisted as sergeant in Company C, 83rd Illinois Volunteers, being advanced in 1864 to the rank of first lieutenant in the 8th U. S. Artillery. He died shortly afterward, leaving a wife and one son. "Old Man Bäck" from Bollnäs, Helsingland, an eccentric character, was another of the Bishop Hill settlers who moved to Victoria, where he purchased a small farm in Copley township. He is said to have considered himself the most important personage in the entire community. Olof Olsson from Alfta, another Erik Janssonist, simultaneously with Bäck moved to Copley township and became one of Victoria's first landowners. Then came in rapid succession Hillberg, Hans Hansson, Carl Magnus Pettersson, Sven Larsson, Lars Larsson, and Peter Källman. The last named accompanied the first party of Erik Janssonists to Chicago, remaining in that city a few years, subsequently living three years in Galesburg, finally settling in Victoria in 1853. He died in 1877, leaving a family. Furthermore, we find among the Swedish pioneers at Victoria Charles Pettersson from Österunda, Upland, who also came with the first Erik Janssonist party, remaining two years in New York, and coming to Victoria in 1848. He also went to California in 1850 as a gold seeker, and eventually settled on the coast. John E. Seline was another Erik Janssonist who deserted Bishop Hill, going to Galesburg in 1849, whence he moved to Victoria, where he was employed as a building contractor until 1856, when he purchased a farm. This man was one of Erik Jansson's twelve apostles. Seline later in life became an agnostic and a stanch follower of Robert G. Ingersoll. One Petter Skoglund, who came over with the Esbjörn party of emigrants, settled down in Victoria as a tailor, but later went to farming. He was still living in 1880, in comfortable circumstances. Peter Dahlgren from Österunda severed his allegiance to Erik Jansson after half a year's stay in the colony and established himself in Victoria township as a farmer in 1853. He was accidentally killed in 1856 by falling earth.

The Town of Victoria was organized May 11, 1849, by John Becker, John W. Spalding, G. F. Reynolds, A. Arnold, Jonas Hedström, W. L. Shurtleff, Jonas Hellström, Joseph Freed and J. J. Knopp. The site then selected was not the same as the present one, being a mile and a half southeast, where Hedström had a blacksmith shop, Becker a general store, and Reynolds a hotel. The present village of Victoria slowly grew up to one side of this starting-point.

The large Swedish settlement of which Victoria forms the center early grew to be one of the most flourishing localities in the state. Prosperity was general owing partly to the fact that the Swedes almost from the start became owners of the soil, partly to the circumstance that Methodism gained a firm foothold there from the first, making for industry, temperance and good morals. Furthermore, this settlement is the most Americanized Swedish community in the whole state, resulting from early stoppage of immigration, the great majority of its present inhabitants having been born and reared in this country. From the very start Methodism became a power in that community and is still firmly rooted there. The Swedish Methodist church is the only house of worship in the place and almost the entire population of the village and the surrounding country are members of that congregation. Neither Lutherans, Baptists, nor Mission Friends have sought to establish missions there, and encroachment by secular organizations in this stronghold of Methodism is out of the question.

The population of the town of Victoria in 1900 was 329. The number of Swedish-Americans in the village proper together wih the surrounding settlement we have been unable to ascertain.

GALESBURG, KNOX COUNTY

The city of Galesburg is situated on a rolling plain, 164 miles southwest of Chicago, on the Chicago, Burlington and Quincy railway line. It was named from George W. Gale, who, together with several others, came there from Oneida county, N. Y., in 1836 and purchased 11,000 acres of land in Knox county. On this tract he laid out a town site, the sale of lots and the building of houses progressing nicely at first. In one year the population increased to 232. From 1837 to 1850 progress was slow, owing to lack of communications. The outlook for a railroad line through the place brightened during the latter year, however, causing increased business activity in the little town.

During the first decade of its existence Galesburg had a formidable rival in the neighboring town of Henderson, now Knoxville, which had certain advantages through permitting the sale of liquors, a traffic absolutely prohibited in Galesburg. So strict were the authorities in this respect that they inserted in every deed to property sold within the town limits a clause specifically prohibiting the sale of spirituous liquors on the premises. In the meantime, the liquor traffic flourished in Henderson, where the Galesburg people also had to go when in need of the cup that cheers. The rapid growth of the town

Galesburg—Main Street

soon inspired dreams of greatness in the Hendersonites, mingled with pity for Galesburg, which town seemed doomed to perpetual stagnation. A certain Swede, who was particularly hopeful for the future of Henderson, bought two building lots there for $200, although he might have got them in Galesburg at a much lower figure. Only a few years later, he sold his two lots for $20. The slump in realty values in Henderson came when Galesburg got its railroad. On Dec. 7, 1854, the first locomotive steamed into Galesburg over the Chicago, Burlington and Quincy road, which was then almost completed. On Jan. 1, 1849, the town got its first newspaper, "The Knox Intelligencer." In 1873 it became the county seat of Knox county.

The Galesburg of today is a live, wide-awake and somewhat aristocratic city, whose population of 18,607 at the census of 1900 had reached 20,000 at the close of 1905. It is one of the chief railway centers of the state, being the intersection of the main line of the Burlington, with several branches, and the Atchison, Topeka and Santa Fé railways. The city has several beautiful parks, and its streets are shaded by avenues of trees giving to the entire city the aspect of a park. The pavements are of brick throughout. The city has a splendid street railway system, excellent waterworks, is well lighted, and has an efficient fire department. Although not a factory center, yet Galesburg has a number of manufacturing plants, including two foundries, an agricultural implement factory, flour mills, wagon factories and a broom factory. The railway shops of the Burlington road are located here, also extensive stock yards. Coal mines are found in the vicinity. Galesburg has a handsome opera house, five banks, nineteen churches, several of them Swedish, and ten public schools, including one high school. It is also a notable educational center, having several higher institutions of learning, namely, Knox College, Lombard University, and one or two Catholic schools. The courthouse, which is the seat of the Knox county government, is one of the largest and handsomest buildings of its class in the state. The city is situated in the center of one of the most fertile and prosperous farming districts in Illinois, with which it stands in direct and intimate communication. The townspeople as well as the farmers of the surrounding country are well-to-do, and, taken all in all, Galesburg is as fortunately situated and as prosperous as any of the smaller cities of the state.

The first Swedish settlers in Galesburg arrived about the middle of the forties. In 1847, as far as known, the only Swedes there were the following: John Youngberg and family, one of the early Bishop Hill colonists, who later removed to Galva, but returned to Galesburg and went from there to California in 1860; Nils Hedström, a tailor by trade, who afterwards settled in the Victoria colony; Anders Thorsell, a shoemaker from Djursby, Vestmanland, who came over in 1846 with one of the first parties of Erik Janssonists; a family by the name of Modin; Kristina Muhr, a widow, and Olof Nilsson, a shoemaker. Thorsell, who is said to have been a very skillful workman, plied his trade for some time with so great success that he accumulated a small fortune. Had he stuck to the last and shunned the bottle, he would have become the wealthiest Swede in Galesburg, but unfortunately he became a slave to the liquor habit. He died in 1870 leaving a widow and one child.

The majority of Swedes who settled in Galesburg earlier than 1854 were such as had deserted Bishop Hill, having become dissatisfied with conditions in that colony. In the year last named, however, the influx of immigrants brought many Swedish settlers directly to Galesburg, and from that day its Swedish population has constantly grown, numbering at the close of 1905 about 5,000, American born descendants included.   That this numerous element has made itself felt in the development of the city and set its impress on its general character goes without saying.   In every line of activity in Galesburg Swedes are engaged.   We find them as city and county officials, as merchants, and in all the various trades.   They are employed in considerable numbers on the railroads and at the Burlington shops.

In the Swedish colony here different denominations early began missionary work.   As early as 1850 Swedish Methodist class meetings were held, and the following year Jonas Hedström organized a Swedish Methodist congregation.   Simultaneously, Rev. L. P. Esbjörn, the Swedish Lutheran pastor at Andover, began work in this field, and a church was established in 1851.   This, the First Swedish Lutheran Church of Galesburg, in 1853 secured as its pastor Rev. T. N. Hasselquist, another pioneer of Swedish Lutheranism in America.   The Swedish Baptists in 1857 organized a church, which had dwindled down to seven members in 1880; a few years later, however, work was pushed with renewed vigor, resulting in a reorganization in 1888. In 1868 a second Swedish Lutheran church was organized, composed of former members of the first church, and other persons.   We are creditably informed that the present Mission Church was formed from its membership.   A third Swedish Lutheran congregation in Galesburg was organized several years ago, which now seems to have disbanded. . There is also a Swedish Episcopal church in the city.

The fraternal movement was started among the Galesburg Swedes in 1866 when a sick benefit society, named Skandia, was organized. The society was soon forced out of existence by church opposition.   A lodge of Good Templars, organized the following year under the name of Svea, was almost equally shortlived.   In 1871 a Scandinavian lodge of Odd Fellows was formed.   Among the present Swedish population of Galesburg we find no great interest in fraternal movements based on nationality.

In local politics the Swedes of Galesburg have taken aggressive part, many having served the city or county in various capacities.   At least one of their number, M. O. Williamson, has been honored with a high state office, having served as state treasurer for the term of 1901-1903.

Galesburg has the distinction of being the cradle of the Swedish-American press.   Here was started in 1854, by Rev. Hasselquist, the first Swedish-American newspaper of permanence, viz., "Hemlandet," its first number being issued Jan. 3, 1855.   This paper was published at Galesburg, until the close of 1858, when it was removed to Chicago. In the early part of 1859, "Frihetsvännen," another Swedish paper, was launched in Galesburg, but was discontinued in 1861. This journal was started to champion the cause of the Baptist denomination, which was the object of continuous attacks by "Hemlandet." A third Swedish organ, "Galesburgs Veckoblad," started in 1868, shared the fate of "Frihetsvännen," being discontinued after a short time. A couple of religious papers in the Swedish language have also been published here for short periods, and after the great fire in 1871, "Nya Verlden," a Swedish weekly newspaper of Chicago, was published for five months in Galesburg.

The Swedish colony of Galesburg furnished a proportionate number of recruits to the Union army during the Civil War. Company C, 43rd Illinois Volunteers, was made up exclusively of Swedish-Americans from Galesburg and vicinity.

These data establish Galesburg's claim to an eminent place in the history of the Swedes not only of Illinois but of the country at large.

MOLINE, ROCK ISLAND COUNTY

This community dates back to the year 1843, when the first houses were built on the site of the present city of Moline. The place made little progress until the late forties, when John Deere and others laid the foundation for the local plow and agricultural implement manufacturing industry which caused the place to develop with enormous strides during the next few decades and which has given the city world-wide fame. The plow works of Deere and Company are said to be the largest in the world and their products are sent annually to the uttermost parts of the earth. The Moline Plow Company is the name of a younger concern which manufactures plows and other agricultural implements on a large scale. Besides these, Moline has a large number of industrial plants, making it one of the greatest manufacturing cities in the state. The chief reasons for the subsequent location of so many factories at Moline were its water power facilities, its location on the border of two of the most flourishing agricultural states in the Union, and its unexcelled communications by land and water with all parts of the country.

As an industrial city, Moline naturally has a large population of laborers. A large percentage of its many thousands of workingmen are Swedes, many of whom have established economic independence and a respected station in the community by their traditional industry, thrift and good habits. The greater number have homes of their own and some are quite wealthy. The Swedes of Moline are a power in the community not merely by dint of numbers but owing to their splendid citizenship. While conscientiously fulfilling their duties as citizen, they cautiously guard their rights as such, and as a result they will obtain the majority in the city government from time to time. A large number of them belong to one church or another. Almost every religious denomination pursuing work among the Swedish people is here represented. The fraternity movement also has made great accessions. The neighboring Augustana College has exerted considerable influence on the numerous Swedish population of Moline, giving out powerful impulses to religious and intellectual endeavor.

Moline—Bird's Eye View from City Hospital

While the great mass of the Swedish workmen are common factory hands, not a few of them have forged ahead by skill and competence to become foremen, superintendents and mechanical experts in the works, and in rare instances they have gone so far as to found their own industrial establishments.

The earliest Swedish settlers in Moline were Olaus Bengtsson and Carl Johansson, the former coming over from Sweden in 1847, the latter in 1848. Bengtsson landed with wife and children in Chicago and, being unable to find work, left his eldest son there and came on to Moline on foot, accompanied by his wife and three of the children, the parents taking turns in carrying the smaller ones when their strength gave out. The family settled on a farm in Moline township, near the Rock River, and did well at farming. Olaus Bengtsson died before the eighties. The son left behind in Chicago after three years rejoined the family, when he had to learn his mother tongue anew, having completely forgotten it while living exclusively among English-speaking people.

Carl Johansson, a tailor by trade, came from Kämpestad, Östergötland, to Andover in 1847 and from there to Moline the next year. The place was at that time a bit of a village with a grocery and sundry other little stores where the farmers of the neighborhood exchanged their farm products for merchandise and provisions. A flour and saw mill combined was located on the river bank, and from the Illinois side, stretching across the south branch of the Mississippi to the island opposite, was a wooden dam which served until 1858. A large portion of the present site of the city was under cultivation, and at the foot of the hills which now comprise a fine part of its residence district grew thick woods from which the early inhabitants derived their fuel supply.

During the years 1840 to 1850 came the following Swedish settlers: Sven Jacobsson, a carpenter from Vermland, with family, who subsequently moved to Vasa, Minn., but returned to Moline after a few years; Carl Petter Andersson, who purchased land on the bluffs where he was still engaged in farming thirty years later; Gustaf Johnson, with family, he and Jacobsson dying before the eighties; Erik Forsse with family, who later joined the Bishop Hill colony, was a major in the 57th Illinois Regiment during the war, removing to Falun, Salina county, Kansas, some time after the close of the war; Jonas Westberg, who died prior to 1880; M. P. Petersson, who began farming on the bluffs, then conducted a small store, removed to Altona, thence to Iowa, where he was still living in 1880; Petter Söderström, who moved to Minnesota and from there to Swede Bend, Ia.; Sven J. Johnson, who for thirteen years ran the ferryboat across the Mississippi between Rock Island and Davenport; Abraham Andersson from Gnarp, Helsingland, a hired man who bought a small property in Moline and at his death in the early fifties willed to the Swedish Lutheran Church a house and lot as a parsonage for its future pastor.

A unique character among the immigrants was Jon Olsson from Stenbo, Forssa parish, Helsingland, who came to Moline in 1850. In the old country he had lived like a peasant king on a fine, well cultivated estate. When Erik Jansson, the prophet, came to Forssa and began preaching, the "Old Man of Stenbo," as he was commonly called, was among the first to embrace the doctrines of the prophet and open his home for his meetings. His sons also early affiliated with the new sect, one of them, Olof Stenberg, or Stoneberg, which was the American form of his name, becoming one of its leaders. During the winter of 1849-50 he and Olof Johnson went back to Sweden in order to gather together the remaining followers of Erik

Jansson and bring them to America. Then it was arranged that the old man, who was now a widower, also should emigrate, but he did not accompany his son, preferring to travel alone. After having sold his estate, he chartered a steamer at Hudiksvall, took a cargo of iron and, in addition, all his household goods and utensils, down to the dough-troughs and wooden bowls and spoons. The voyage across the Atlantic was successful. He took with him a small party of emigrants, part of whom, at least, were not Erik Janssonists. In New York he sold his cargo, but brought with him inland the whole odd collection

Moline—Fifteenth Street

of partly worthless wares, which no doubt cost him a pretty penny in freightage.

He made straight for Bishop Hill, but apparently did not take a fancy to the locality and its prospects. Besides, he probably hesitated to turn over his considerable fortune to the common exchequer. Be this as it may, he made his appearance in Moline early in January, 1851, having already purchased two houses there, one a brick, the other a frame building, with large lots appertaining. It was rumored that he deposited $20,000 in gold in a bank in Rock Island; whether or not, he was looked upon as a mighty rich man.

"The Old Man of Stenbo" was an odd character in every respect. He stuck religiously to the manners and customs of his old home.

He wore an old fashioned coat, its skirts reaching almost to his heels, and a leathern apron of nearly the same length. Dressed in this fashion, he circulated about the streets of the little village with an agility quite unusual for a man of his years. If he found a chunk of coal, an old shoe, a broken dish or a stick of wood he would pick it up, carry it home and place it on a pile of similar rubbish in the middle of the floor of the living room. In the basement he had arranged the appurtenances of a blacksmith shop brought over from Sweden, and the smoke from the smithy, which penetrated the whole house, did not bother him in the least. In the basement he also had an oven of masonry in the Swedish style, where he baked thin loaves of hard bread in the manner of the Helsingland peasantry.

The old man practiced genuine old time hospitality, and would always urge his friends to partake of his repast, were it only a pot of cabbage soup served in wooden bowls. Having broken the thin bread into the bowl he would invariably dust the flour from his hands into the bowl so as not to waste any of his God-given substance.

At length, the old man was lured back to Bishop Hill. Though advanced in years, he was hankering after another matrimonial venture, and what induced him to go was the assurance of friends that a suitable bride had been picked out for him. The match was made, and so he moved to Bishop Hill with all his earthly belongings, which presumably went the way of all other small fortunes invested in that enterprise. A few years after his removal the "Old Man of Stenbo" breathed his last.

While he was still in Moline, there lived with him for some time Per Andersson from Hassela and Per Berg from Hög, Helsingland. These men went to Minnesota in the spring of 1851 and there founded the Chisago Lake settlement. One Peter Viklund from Ångermanland, who also lived in Moline at the time, accompanied them, settling in the vicinity of Taylor's Falls, where he died. Another of the early Swedish settlers in Moline was Daniel Nilsson from Norrbro, Helsingland, who about the same time founded the settlement of Marine, near Marine Mills. Along in the summer of 1851 Hans Smith and his family moved to Moline from Princeton. He also left for Minnesota, going to Chisago Lake.

The first attempt at organization among the Swedish population of Moline was the founding of the Swedish Lutheran Church, which still prospers. The founder was Rev. L. P. Esbjörn of Andover. The organization meeting was held in the home of Carl Johansson, the tailor, this being a small room, 14 by 10 feet, in which those interested in the movement had habitually met to worship. But Esbjörn was not long to be alone in the field of religious endeavor among the Moline

Swedes. Shortly after his first visit, the enterprising Rev. Jonas Hedström appeared and, being cordially received by the other pioneer Swedish resident, Olaus Bengtsson, at once began to hold Methodist meetings in the equally primitive home of that pioneer. In the latter part of the year 1850 or the beginning of 1851, he organized here a little Swedish Methodist church, which, like the Lutheran, grew and prospered apace with the influx of Swedish immigrants.

A third Swedish church, called Gustaf Adolf, now a part of the Swedish Mission Covenant, was organized in 1875, and in the following

Moline—Third Avenue

year a fourth one, the Swedish Baptist Church. A little flock of Swedish Episcopalians, formed in recent years, worked with but scant success, and soon disbanded.

The fraternal orders have operated very successfully in Moline, ever since the latter sixties. The first Swedish fraternal society organized there was Freja, in 1869, which flourished for a number of years. During the seventies a couple of other fraternal bodies came into existence, and during the last two decades a number of different societies have been formed, including a Swedish singing club, the Svea Male Chorus.

Three secular newspapers in the Swedish language have been published at Moline, viz., "Skandia," issued from December 1876 to April

1878, "Nya Pressen," from 1891 to 1897, and "Vikingen," published for a short time in the early nineties. At the present time, the city has no Swedish newspaper. In the seventies and eighties, the firm of Wistrand and Thulin published a number of books and papers in the interest of the work of the Augustana Synod.

The Swedes in Moline in 1880 numbered 2,589; at the close of 1905 their number was approximately 8,000. The total population according to the census of 1900, was 17,240, succeeding years showing a substantial increase.

ROCK ISLAND, ROCK ISLAND COUNTY

The prosperous city of Rock Island had its origin in 1816, when the national government planted a fort on the island of the same name, known as Fort Armstrong. As its commander was appointed Col. George Davenport, who, together with his wife and the garrison, for thirteen years were the only white inhabitants of the locality. The arrival in 1823 of the steamer "Virginia," with a cargo of provisions, from Prairie du Chien, Wisconsin, made a welcome interruption in the monotony of frontier life. This vessel was the first to traverse this portion of the Mississippi. In 1825 Col. Davenport was appointed postmaster on the island and about the same time formed a co-partnership with Russell Farnham, a fresh arrival, to engage in fur trading with the Indians. For the purpose the partners put up a building which afterwards was occupied as the first court-house of Rock Island county. In 1828 a few whites, among whom was John M. Spencer, arrived and settled there. Oct. 19, 1829, Davenport and Farnham purchased a tract of land in the present county of Rock Island, that being the first realty transaction in the county.

In 1831 the little settlement had grown sufficiently strong to equip a troop of 58 men to engage in fighting the Indian chief Black Hawk and his tribe. Two years later, or 1833, Rock Island county was organized and on July 5th of the same year its first county election was held. After another two years Stephenson, as the place was then called, was selected as the county seat. Its name was subsequently changed to Rock Island. The first prison, a two story blockhouse, was erected in 1836. The same year work was begun on a county courthouse, which was completed the following year. The first incorporation of Rock Island was effected in 1841. Late in the sixties the federal government established on the adjacent island a large arsenal together with factories for small arms, the plant having since reached an extensive development. During the Civil War a large number of prisoners taken from the Confederates were kept on the island, and a burial ground for soldiers dates from that time. The entire island, together with extensive establishments, is under the control and strict surveillance of the federal government, and the buildings and well-kept grounds are among the interesting sights in this part of the United States.

The west arm of the Mississippi at this point is navigable while the east and smaller arm is closed by a dam which furnishes water power for industrial plants in Moline and Rock Island and for the government works. A combination railroad and public highway bridge facilitates traffic between Rock Island and the city of Davenport, situated on the Iowa side, directly opposite, and named after the

View of Rock River from Black Hawk Watch Tower

first commander of Fort Armstrong, who together with several others in 1835 purchased the land on which the city was built.

Rock Island is at the present day a lively manufacturing and business center. Here are located large lumber mills, an agricultural implement factory, a glass factory, iron works, wagon factories, etc. The city has several banks and four newspapers, two of which are published daily. A new courthouse, one of the largest and most imposing structures in this part of the state, was erected a few years ago. In the surrounding public square stands a monument in honor of the men from Rock Island who fought in the Civil War. In a pretty park in the western part of the city is a statue of Black Hawk, the Indian chief, whose name is intimately combined with the early history of the city and its surrounding country. A charming point of vantage south of the city bears the name of Black Hawk Watch Tower. It is a high bluff rising steeply from the Rock River and crowned with a pavilion, the verandas of which afford a charming panorama of the vicinity, northwest over the Mississippi and the wooded bluffs disappearing in the blue distance, southward and eastward over the fertile valley drained by the winding Rock River and cut at this point by a section of the Hennepin Canal. This prominence Chief Black Hawk is said to have often sought at the head of his warriors when on the lookout for the hated palefaces who took possession of the rich hunting grounds of his tribe. The census of 1900 gives the city of Rock Island 19,493 inhabitants.

The beginning of Swedish immigration to Rock Island was in 1848, when the founder of the Bishop Hill colony established a fishing camp on the island, managed by the aforementioned N. J. Hollander as foreman for a half dozen colonists. At this point Erik Jansson's wife and the youngest two of their children, together with several other persons, succumbed to the cholera in 1849.

Among the earliest Swedish settlers at Rock Island was A. J. Swanson, who came there in 1850 and made a small fortune in the boot and shoe business. Swanson, or Svensson, hailed from Ödeshög, Östergötland. When he died, Jan. 8, 1880, at the age of fifty-one, he left an estate worth $40,000. Other Swedish settlers about this time were: J. Bäck and Peter Söderström, both sons-in-law of Rev. J. Rolin of Hassela, Helsingland; Jonas Strand, Jonas Norell, and Erik Thomasson, all from Northern Sweden; A. T. Manké, and Fredrika Boberg. Manké is supposed to have been among those who perished at the burning of the steamer "Austria" on the Atlantic Sept. 13, 1858. Petter Söderström and Fredrika Boberg moved to Iowa before the eighties. In the fifties came August Linder, a tailor, Erik Åkerberg, a jeweler, N. J. Rundquist, a wagonmaker by the name of Envall, Israel Johansson, a shoemaker, one Hofflund, the brothers Carl and Peter Stjernström, the one a tailor, the other a day laborer. Hofflund moved to Osco township, and the Stjernström brothers to Iowa previous to 1880. Not until the sixties and more especially in the seventies, however, did the Swedish immigrants come to settle in Rock Island in any great number.

The little colony of Swedes that existed there in the fifties is noteworthy in this that it was the origin of the first Swedish Baptist Church in America, organized there Sept. 26, 1852. The founder was Gustaf Palmquist, a former school teacher from Stockholm who had joined the American Baptists in Galesburg in June of that year, and its first members were: A. T. Manké, A. Boberg and Fredrika, his wife, Petter Söderström, Carl Johansson, mentioned among the Moline pioneers, and Anders Norelius, a brother of Eric Norelius who later became a pastor of the Swedish Lutheran Church in America and is now president of the Augustana Synod.

The few Swedish Lutherans in Rock Island at first belonged to the church in Moline, but in 1870 they tired of going to the neighboring city to worship, and that year an independent congregation was organized, with a membership of only twenty-eight. The few Swedish Methodists and Mission Friends who reside in Rock Island are members of their respective church organizations in Moline. Rock Island has little or nothing in the way of Swedish fraternal societies.

The oldest and principal Swedish-American educational institution, Augustana College and Theological Seminary, is located at Rock Island, having been removed there from Paxton in 1875. Under the

Rock Island—Spencer Square

guidance of zealous and competent educators, the institution has developed far beyond the aspirations of its founders. Besides being a complete college and a theological seminary, Augustana embraces an academic department, a normal school, a commercial school, a musical conservatory, and a department of art. For several years past the work of gathering large endowment funds for the institution has been carried on. These and other signs point to a period of new and greater prosperity for this old and venerated institution of learning. In immediate proximity to the institution lies the Augustana Book Concern, the publishing house of the Augustana Synod.

The Swedish-American population of the city of Rock Island at the close of the year 1905 was estimated at 3,500.

PRINCETON, BUREAU COUNTY

On the Chicago, Burlington and Quincy Railway, 105 miles west of Chicago, is situated on a plateau the pretty little city of Princeton. Its history dates from the year 1832, when the site was mapped out and the first houses were erected. A log cabin, here as in most of the other settlements, formed the first human habitation. It was built by one S. D. Cartwright near the spot where the Congregational Church now stands. The sale of lots was not brisk, and it took a number of years to dispose of the entire plat. Bureau county was organized Feb. 28, 1837, when Princeton was made the county seat. The county court held its first sessions there the following August. In 1845 the first courthouse was built, with county jail and sheriff's residence in connection. The structure was remodeled in 1860.

Prior to 1850, only five known Swedes resided in Princeton. Doubtless the first to arrive was a man named Burgeson, who later settled at Andover. He came to Illinois in company with the Rev. Pillsbury mentioned under the head of Andover, and for some time was in his service. Simultaneously, a young Swede was in the employ of Owen Lovejoy, the renowned abolitionist, who in the later forties and early fifties was stationed in Princeton as minister of the Congregational Church and afterwards was elected to Congress. In the city hotel a Swedish girl was employed, supposed to have been Sigrid Norell from Bergsjö, Helsingland, who in 1859 became the wife of A. J. Field from Östergötland. The name of the fourth one is not known to a certainly. It may have been the aforesaid Field.

The fifth one was Captain Erik Wester, the adventurer spoken of in Chapter III. This man's career is of sufficient interest to warrant a fuller account. His right name was Westergren, shortened to Wester for convenience. The year and place of his birth and the date of his arrival in America are not known. It is a matter of record, however, that he emigrated to escape punishment for a crime. Wester, who was employed as guard in the riksbank in Stockholm, was once sent to Helsingör to purchase a large lot of old rags for the Tumba paper mills, where the paper for the Swedish national currency has been turned out for years. Instead of closing the deal, he fled to America with the money entrusted to him. Landing in New Orleans, he remained there for an indefinite period. In the fall of 1848 he made his appearance at Bishop Hill in company with two other adventurers, one being John Ruth, who later became notorious, the other a man by the name of Zimmerman, who, like Ruth, claimed to have a military training from Sweden, and to have served in the French army during the campaign in Algiers. Bishop Hill and its plodding life had no charm for the three soldiers of fortune. Zimmerman soon departed for California, presumably in quest of gold, while Wester went to the Pine Lake settlement in Wisconsin, and Ruth, who had been enamored of a young woman at Bishop Hill, remained there a few months, after which time he resumed his roaming career.

At the outset, Wester masqueraded at Pine Lake as a very devout person, going around preaching in the different homes. Finding that this line of endeavor among the few Swedish settlers yielded but poor returns, he established himself as a barber, securing friends and customers among the more numerous Norwegians, many of whom are said to have been victimized by this smooth stranger.

Having reached the end of his rope in Wisconsin, Wester returned to Illinois. He first appeared in Peru, whence he came to Princeton in the spring of 1850, so utterly destitute that he was unable to pay the freight on his barber's chair. Though short of money, he was enterprising and resourceful in his own peculiar way, and soon found Princeton a splendid field to exploit. A prosperous merchant helped him to a supply of cigars and with that he opened for business in a shanty. When business grew a trifle dull, he turned his cigar store into a grog shop. This attracted more customers, the business grew, and presently Wester had to look around for larger quarters. Soon the place grew to be quite a large department store, considering Princeton's stage of development at the time. He sold goods of every description, such as clothing, eatables, boots and shoes, hardware, tobacco and whisky. Wester subsequently extended his business beyond the limits of Princeton, establishing a branch store at Galesburg.

For a time it appeared as though the quondam bank messenger, evangelist and barber would finish his career as a rich and respected businessman. Such might have been the case, but for wild speculations and a decided decline in general business. In the young neighboring town of Galva, Olof Johnson, the financier of Bishop Hill, was at this time actively engaged in the management of its affairs, and looking forward to a highly roseate future. Why not join with him in one of his numerous enterprises and get rich in a trice? With this object in view, Wester went into partnership with him and Samuel Remington and started the Western Exchange Bank at Galva. No one knows how much money Wester furnished, but it is more than likely that the bulk of the capital was taken out of the Bishop Hill funds. This was in 1857, while the speculative fever, especially in the West, was still at its height. The same year the reaction came—a panic that swept the entire country, wrecking countless business enterprises vastly more solid than those of Olof Johnson and Wester. The latter was caught in the crash, so was his financial institution, and in this failure a large bulk of the money that the Bishop Hill colonists had earned by the sweat of their brow is said to have been lost.

But Wester persevered with dogged tenacity. The next year he made a new start, but failed again. In 1859 he started in business for the third time, but only to court another catastrophe. This time he appears to have made a fraudulent assignment, it being reported that he withheld more than enough property to pay his debts, had he been so inclined. With $1,700 in his pocket and a trunk packed with revolvers—it will be remembered that he also dealt in hardware—Wester left, stating that he was bound for Chicago, but going instead to Dallas, Texas, where he was still living in 1880, but in reduced circumstances. What afterwards became of the adventurer, whether he again got on his feet or went down in the struggle for existence, there are no records to show.

In the summer of 1850, A. P. Anderson came to Princeton from the parish of Horn, Östergötland. He had come over the year before and gone to Peru, whence he came alone to Andover in the hope of finding certain relatives, but on his arrival he learned that they were all dead. He then returned to Peru and moved with his family to Princeton. Anderson still lived in 1880 at the age of seventy-one. His eldest child, a son, had then lived in California for many years.

In the autumn a whole party of Swedish settlers arrived from northern Helsingland and southern Medelpad. They had sailed from Gefle August 17th on the Swedish ship "Oden," Captain Norberg, and arrived in New York October 31st, coming on to Princeton November 21st, after a difficult journey. In the party was Erik Norelius from Hassela, Helsingland, then a mere youth of seventeen, whom Providence had destined to take an eminent part in Swedish-American religious progress. In his valuable work entitled, "The History of the Swedish Lutheran Congregations and of the Swedes of America," he has given a vivid and graphic description of the whole journey.

Of this party of immigrants a few stopped in Princeton while the rest, Norelius among them, proceeded to Andover. Among those remaining at Princeton were: Hans Kamel, Olof Jonsson, Staffan Berglöf, and Anders Nord with their families, all from Bergsjö, Helsingland; Per Söderström from Norrbo or Bjuråker, Helsingland; Hans Smitt from Hassela, Helsingland; Anders Larsson from Torp, Medelpad; Olof Nilsson and one Simeon from Attmar, Medelpad. The Kamel family died out before the eighties, Söderström after a few years moved to Iowa or Minnesota and Simeon went away, leaving no trace. Olof Jonsson became the first Swedish property-holder of Princeton, living and prospering as a farmer for more than twenty-five years, afterwards removing to Humboldt, Kansas, where he is said to have owned large country estates. Anders Larsson also went west in the late seventies.

In 1851 came Lars Magnus Spak and Nils Johan Nilsson from Djursdala, Småland, and Jacob Nyman from Tjärstad, Östergötland, the first and the last named with their families. The Spak family had come to this country in 1849, living for a time in Chicago, where they are said to have taken part in the organization of the Swedish Episcopal Church of St. Ansgar (Ansgarius.) The family head passed away long before 1880, but his widow was then still living, also their elder

Princeton—Main Street Looking North

son, who was engaged in business. The younger son was living in Galesburg, as also the daughter, who was married to one A. J. Andersson. Jacob Nyman also passed away in the late seventies, his widow and their son Johan still living in Princeton after his death. Nils J. Nilsson was also conducting a business of some kind in the eighties.

The year 1852 brought large acquisitions of Swedes to Princeton. Among the new arrivals were the following: C. M. Sköld, a tailor, from Vestra Ryd, unmarried, and Anders P. Damm, with six children, from Åsby, both in Östergötland; Anders Petter Larsson from Vadstena, Östergötland; J. O. Lundblad from an unknown locality in the same province; S. Frid and wife from Wä, Skåne; Åke Nilsson with wife and two children; Nils Lindeblad with wife and son, all from Skåne, but localities unknown; P. Fagercrantz from Brösarp, Skåne;

Lars Andersson från Gingrid and Johan A. Westman from Börstig, both located in Vestergötland; Pehr Christian Andersson, also from Vestergötland, locality unknown; Johan Gabriel Ståhl with wife, son and daughter from Småland, place unknown; Johan Andersson and Henrik Norman from Stockholm. Of these Sköld was still living in 1880; Nilsson lived on his own farm near Wyanet; Pehr Christian Andersson was employed by a railway company since twenty-five years back; also Westman, Ståhl and his wife, Fagercrantz, Anders Petter Larsson, Lars Andersson and J. O. Lundblad, the latter living in Aledo, Mercer county, were among the survivors in 1880. Norman removed to Monmouth in 1856. Damm, who changed his name to Stem, died in 1878, leaving a widow and several children; Frid died before 1880, also Lindeblad, while the wife and son of the latter were still living in Princeton in that year. Johan Andersson, who had been foreman in the printing office of "Stockholms Dagblad" died of the cholera in 1853, his wife returning to Stockholm the following year.

Another Swedish pioneer of Princeton was Jonas Andersson from Färila, Helsingland. He emigrated in 1849, remained a short time in Chicago, spent the following winter in St. Charles, went to Wisconsin in the spring, returning to St. Charles after working a few months in the woods, and remained there until 1853, when he moved to Princeton. Here he settled permanently and became the father of a large family. He was still living in the eighties and was a prosperous building contractor.

Almost simultaneously with Jonas Andersson came A. A. Shenlund. He was born at Toarp, Vestergötland, and was engaged in the merchandise business in his native land. He emigrated in 1853 to Princeton, where he went to work on Rev. Pillsbury's farm, his wife being employed there as housekeeper. Having worked for some time at sawing wood, he next got a situation as bookkeeper with the aforementioned Wester, but disapproving of the loose business methods of his employer, he went into business on his own account, opening a small grocery store near the railway station just two days before the first railway train rumbled into Princeton. A few months later he removed with his stock to Bureau Junction, but moved back to Princeton after five months. When Wester failed in business, the administrators persuaded Shenlund to take charge, and he conducted the business until 1865, when he retired. In 1868 he resumed business in partnership with one Clark who withdrew from the firm in 1876. After that Shenlund ran the business alone for a number of years with so great success that he grew moderately wealthy. He was highly respected by his townsmen, Americans and Swedes alike. Shenlund died many years ago.

Speaking of the early business men of Princeton it may be noted that S. Frid in 1854 established a boot and shoe store, conducting the business for some years, afterwards going into farming. Having no success as a farmer, he soon returned to the last and stuck to it, being successfully engaged in the shoe business to his death. J. O. Lundblad had early left for Missouri, but returned when the Civil War broke out, engaging in the same line of business but soon afterwards removed to Rock Island, going from there to Aledo to live. P. Fagercrantz in 1853 established himself in Princeton as watchmaker and jeweler, conducting

Princeton—Main Street Looking South

the business for a period of twenty-five years, after which he surprised his friends by going bankrupt. Although well advanced in years, he made a new start in business. In the vicinity of Princeton a number of Swedes settled and soon became prosperous farmers.

Religious activity was begun early among the Swedish people of Princeton. A Swedish Lutheran congregation was organized in 1854, a Swedish Mission church in 1870, a Swedish Baptist church being added seven years later.

According to the city directory, there were 1,200 Swedish-Americans in Princeton at the close of 1905, but well informed townsmen believed that figure too low, holding that the actual number was 1,400. The Swedes living in the surrounding locality are about equally numerous. Besides, there are Swedes in considerable numbers living at other points in Bureau county, viz., Wyanet, Tiskilwa, Providence, Spring Valley, Ladd, Seaton, New Bedford, Walnut, and other places, adding about 1,200 more to the Swedish population in the county and bringing the total up to about 4,000.

CHICAGO, COOK COUNTY

There have been Swedish people in Chicago almost from the earliest days of the city, and their number has constantly increased until, at the last general census in 1900, it was 48,836, or greater than the population of Norrköping, the fourth city in Sweden in point of size. The same year there were in Chicago 95,883 persons born of Swedish parents, making a total Swedish-American population of 144,719. Counting as Swedish-Americans 6,707 persons, one of whose parents was born in Sweden and the other in some other foreign country, we would obtain a total of 151,426 Swedish-Americans in the city. During the last seven years this number naturally has grown according to the usual ratio of increase. This is further evidenced by the school census of 1904 which set the number of Chicagoans born in Sweden at 55,991. A comparison of various estimates would indicate a Swedish-American population in Chicago of not less than 170,000 at the close of 1907.

A large proportion of the Swedish-Americans have engaged in business and thereby laid the foundation for prosperity and economic independence. The great mass of their male population, however, is composed of skilled workmen. In almost every trade they are found, and everywhere they have the reputation of being highly intelligent, skillful and conscientious in their work. Not a few have distinguished themselves by making ingenious and practical inventions. Especially in certain trades, like that of the cabinetmaker, the architect and builder, the custom tailor and the mechanical artisan, they are found in the front rank. In many instances they have succeeded in building up comparatively large industrial establishments of their own; others are engaged as engineers and foremen in large industrial plants owned by Americans and men of other nationalities.

The majority of Swedish-American skilled workmen in Chicago doubtless are members of the labor organizations, their coolness and conservatism making them a desirable and wholesome element thereof. The unskilled laborers among them are few in proportion both to the entire number of Swedish-American workmen and to the proportion of unskilled laborers among other nationalities. As a consequence, the Swedish working class in Chicago stands on a higher economic plane than the corresponding class among the average foreign nationality, and is able to lead an existence more in keeping with the American standard of life.

The Swedish workingmen are in the main industrious, orderly, temperate, and thrifty. Generally, their first care is to get a home of their own, and for this purpose they have usually placed their savings in some one of the Swedish building and loan associations, obtained loans, purchased lots and built their own houses. Probably few other nationalities can show so large a proportion of property owners and home builders. Long ago the Swedes of Chicago solved the question of workingmen's homes which is agitating industrial communities everywhere, thus setting an example worthy of emulation in other parts of the world. Many of the Swedish householders have two houses on their lots, the older one a frame structure built during pioneer days; the new one usually a brick building erected after the children grew up and the family began to prosper.

A number of Swedish skilled workmen and men in business and the professions put their earnings into realty; others deposit them in the banks or put them out at interest elsewhere. There are two Swedish banks in the city, viz., the State Bank of Chicago, founded in 1879, and the Union Bank of Chicago, founded in 1905. The majority prefer the latter method of keeping capital growing, as against the more risky one of speculating.

The Scandia Life Insurance Company is a Swedish corporation with head offices in Chicago, and the Swedish Methodists and Baptists each have a mutual life insurance society with headquarters here.

The Chicago Swedes have been criticised for their lack of political activity, and to a certain extent the criticism is deserved. True, they have always cast their votes in great numbers at elections and fulfilled their duties as as citizens in the intervals, yet when nominations and appointments were to be made they have not insisted on the representation due them in consideration of their numbers and their civic standing. This fact possibly is due to the prevailing opinion among them, that the office ought to seek the man and not the reverse. Furthermore, they seem to take greater pride in upbuilding and maintaining the community than in the governing of it. In other words they would rather be producers than consumers. The great mass of the politically interested among them are Republicans. In the wards where they are numerous they form political clubs, and evince great political activity, especially prior to important elections. These ward clubs are combined into a central organization known as the Swedish-American Central Republican Club of Cook County, which in turn forms a part of the Swedish-American Republican League of Illinois. Many Swedish-Americans of Chicago have held political offices in the city and the county, and not a few have represented the community in the state legislature during the past thirty years.

A trait characteristic of the Swedes in Chicago, as elsewhere, is their obedience to law and the high order of their citizenship. While they deprecate the wholesale manufacture of laws, they believe that good laws, dictated by the people's own sense of justice and equity, should be absolutely obeyed.

They believe in education and culture. They keep their children in school regularly, and the great number of prizes and distinctions awarded them from time to time bear witness to the fact that they rank with the best pupils both in point of diligence and of intelligence. Many of them continue their studies from the public to the high school, while others enter commercial schools in order to fit themselves for a business career. Still others in considerable number attend technological institutions, such as the Armour and Lewis institutes, pursuing courses in engineering or other technics, or go to the universities, the medical colleges, the law schools, the dental colleges, the musical conservatories, where they are graduated year by year in ever increasing numbers.

It would seem that so large a Swedish population would be capable of supporting a common institution of learning in the city. The absence of such an institution must be ascribed to the fact that from the first the nationality has been divided into numerous religious and fraternal organizations, each striving in its own way to make the greatest possible acquisitions and accomplish the best results in behalf of its own adherents.

Without exaggeration, it may be said that the traces of Swedish-American activity are most marked in the field of church and fraternal organization. The principal denominations and sects that have gained a foothold among them are the Lutherans, Methodists, Baptists and Mission Friends. Less numerous are the Episcopalians, the Salvationists, the Seventh-Day Adventists, and a few still smaller religious groups.

At the close of the year 1905, there were in Chicago and vicinity 41 Swedish Lutheran congregations having a total membership of 15,000 and owning property to the aggregate value of $517,300. The Swedish Methodists had 18 congregations with 2,520 members and property valued at $249,600; the Swedish Baptists, 11 congregations with 2,588 members and $159,975 worth of property, and the Mission Friends, 12 congregations with 2,036 members and property to the value of $131,940. As to the other denominations there are no statistics at hand.

These denominations carry on a relatively extensive work along educational and charitable lines. The Lutherans control and maintain the Augustana Hospital, one of the prominent institutions of its kind in the city. Martin Luther College, an institution of learning, was founded by them in 1892 but discontinued in 1896. In Evanston the Swedish Methodists have their own theological seminary, and in Chicago they maintain a home for the aged, named Bethany Home. The Swedish Baptists also conduct their own theological institute, located in Morgan Park, and support an old people's home, known as "Fridhem." The Mission Friends not only own a school, North Park College, but a hospital and an old folks' home. In addition to these institutions there is in Englewood a Swedish-American hospital owned and controlled by the people of the various Swedish churches in that part of the city.

As far as it has been possible to ascertain, the Swedish fraternal societies and lodges in Chicago number about one hundred. In the total absence of common statistics exact information concerning them cannot be given. These organizations, designed for the pleasure as well as the pecuniary benefit of its members, annually disburse large sums in the form of sick benefits, funeral expenses and mutual life insurance. Two lodges, "Svithiod" and "Vikingarne," have branched out in recent years so as to form large independent orders, with branch lodges as far west as the Missouri River. The Independent Order of Svithiod now embraces 38 lodges and has 16 ladies' guilds. The Independent Order of Vikings is composed of 30 lodges in addition to which there are 15 ladies' guilds. The Svithiod and the Viking lodges of Chicago are included in the above total. There are 10 lodges of Good Templars, four other temperance societies, and a number of lodges of the Scandinavian Brotherhood of America. Other fraternities, including a couple of lodges each of Free Masons and Odd Fellows, together with nondescript organizations approximate twenty in number. Many churches, moreover, have their own sick benefit and benevolent societies.

A number of different societies have associated themselves for the common purpose of charity and benevolence. One is the Swedish Societies' Old People's Home Association (formerly the Swedish Societies' Central Association), which founded and maintains an old people's home at Park Ridge. The other is the Swedish National Association, which conducts a free employment bureau and carries on charity work in a measure.

A significant movement among Chicago's Swedes is the organization and maintaining of singing societies, chiefly male choruses. Such have existed for several decades and they now number a dozen, exclusive of male or mixed choirs connected with the churches.

They all form a part of the American Union of Swedish Singers and, in order to further their local interests, they have united into a local organization named the Chicago Union of Swedish Singers.

In the field of culture, the Swedish-Americans here have accomplished noteworthy results, aside from the work of their churches, schools and singing organizations, this city being as far back as the '60s the Swedish-American literary producing center and for decades the location of a considerable publishing and bookselling business. At present no less than eight large weekly Swedish newspapers are published in Chicago, four being secular, viz., "Hemlandet", "Svenska Tribunen-Nyheter," "Svenska Amerikanaren," "Svenska Kuriren;" the remaining four religious wholly or in part, viz., "Sändebudet" (Methodist), "Nya Vecko-Posten (Baptist), "Missions-Vännen" (Mission Church), and "Chicago-Bladet" (Free Mission Church). In addition to those mentioned, a large number of monthly church and society papers are issued in this city. A general publishing business was first started in Chicago by the Swedish Lutheran Publication Society and is still continued by The Engberg-Holmberg Publishing Company. In connection with the church paper "Sände-budet" a Methodist Book Concern has more recently been established, in connection with "Missions-Vännen" a book store for the Mission Covenant, and in connection with "Chicago-Bladet" a similar store to meet the needs of the Free Mission churches. To this should be added that the American Baptist Publication Society has established a Swedish book department. Several small book stores are conducted by private persons.

It should not be forgotten that from time to time there have existed in Chicago various Swedish dramatic companies which, although composed largely of amateurs and not to be compared with the standard theatrical companies of Sweden, yet have served to acquaint Swedish-Americans with the Swedish drama of past and modern times.

These various lines of activity pursued by the Swedish people of Chicago are more fully treated in subsequent chapters.

Somewhat later than Flack and Von Schneidau, mention of whom has been made, one Åström came to Chicago from Norrland. In South Water street, not far from the spot where Old Fort Dearborn stood, he and another man from Norrland by the name of Svedberg, who came here from Buffalo, opened a restaurant, conducting that business for several years. This was in the latter forties. In 1850 Svedberg, doubtless smitten with the prevalent gold fever, went to California, and Åström returned to Sweden. He came to America a second time; after that nothing is known of him.

In 1846 the first party of Swedish immigrants to Chicago arrived. There were fifteen families, and the newcomers seem to have had no connection with the emigration movement directed by Erik Jansson. Not one among them understood a word of English, not one had a relative or friend here, all were poor to the verge of destitution. But von Schneidau befriended them, acting as their interpreter and counselor, and soon procured work for the men in the employ of two Americans, W. B. Ogden and A. Smith. They were set to clearing a piece of ground just north of the present Division street, at 50 cents per day, without board, which, nevertheless, they considered fairly good pay. That winter and all the following year (1847) those Swedes are said to have worked at sawing wood for a daily wage of from 50 cents to 62½ cents. The women took washing in American families and thereby earned 10 to 25 cents a day, with board.

Oct. 3, 1846, Jonas Olsson arrived in Chicago at the head of a party of Erik Janssonists bound for Bishop Hill. Many of the emigrants, having begun to doubt the divine mission of Erik Jansson, now refused to go any farther and decided to remain in Chicago. Among these recalcitrants was Jan Jansson, the prophet's own brother. He afterwards became the owner of a fertile farm situated one and one-half miles from Montrose, Cook county. Among the others were, Anders Larsson, John P. Källman, Pehr Ersson, Petter Hessling, A. Thorsell and Källström. They all lived together for a time in a house in Illinois street, between Dearborn avenue and State street.

The year after, forty Swedish immigrants came to the city, and in 1848 one hundred more. Times had now improved noticeably, so that a good laborer could earn 75 cents a day. But the necessaries of life were high, a barrel of flour costing $6 to $7, while pork sold at 6 to 8 cents per pound.

One of the earliest Swedish settlers in Chicago who, like Åström and Svedberg, had a business of his own, was a man from Gotland by the name of Lundblad. He came over in 1847 and the year after started a soda water factory which he ran for some months and then went to Quincy, where he died. His widow returned to Chicago and died here. At the close of the year 1848, the Swedish population of Chicago could not have exceeded 300, all of whom waged a hard fight for existence. In 1849 no less than 400 Swedish immigrants were added to Chicago's population. If conditions had been bad before, things now grew still worse, for the newcomers of that year brought the cholera, the epidemic causing indescribable suffering and misery among them.

In some instances the plague broke out on board the emigrant ships, and many victims were buried at sea. The majority of cases, however, occurred on the tedious journey from the eastern ports to the western points of destination, and after the arrival. The canal-boats were stopped ever and anon to permit the emigrants to go ashore and bury their dead. Conditions grew little better after the railroad from the East to Chicago was completed. Then the emigrants were packed like cattle in uncomfortable cars whose doors were opened seldom, if at all, during the entire journey.

The cholera raged unabated for several years till 1854, inclusive, apparently claiming more victims that year than any foregoing, increasing immigration furnishing a favorable field for its ravages. In 1850 Chicago received 500 Swedish immigrants and in 1851-52 1,000 each year. We quote a few examples of the dreadful effect of the scourge among these people during 1854. One large party from Karlskoga and Bjurtjärn, in Vermland, brought with them six corpses, when the train arrived at the Michigan Central railway station. Seventeen of the party, afflicted with the disease, were brought to the pesthouse, where more than half of their number died before morning. Of the older members of the Immanuel Swedish Lutheran Church, organized the year before, about one-tenth died of the plague, the percentage of deaths among their children being still greater. Among the newcomers the death rate was so great that two-thirds of the immigrants arriving that year are believed to have succumbed to the cholera.

Poverty, unspeakable misery, absolute wretchedness—such was the lot of the families of the deceased. Fortunately, there were charitable people among their fellow countrymen here, who took pity on these victims of pest and penury. Chief among these were Consul von Schneidau, and three clergymen, Gustaf Unonius, Erland Carlsson and Sven Bernhard Newman. The names of these four noble-hearted men shine in the annals of the Swedish pioneers in Chicago like stars in a dismal night. One's heart is warmed and the pulse is quickened in reading the accounts of what these men accomplished in behalf of the suffering immigrants.

Actuated by his goodness of heart as well as by his sense of duty, Consul von Schneidau obtained permission to use the United States Marine Hospital for the accommodation of the plague victims. As soon as they were fairly restored to health, the question of getting work arose. Yet this was sometimes a difficult problem, and if they did obtain employment, being weak and emaciated, they were not always equal to the task. In either event, they turned to von Schneidau for assistance, and he helped them as far as it was in his power to do so. Having exhausted his own resources, he appealed to public benevolence, nor was this done in vain, for donations poured in in such quantities

that the residence was turned into a veritable supply depot, where his
good wife acted as distributor of the accumulated provisions.

Unonius was equally energetic in the cause of charity. In 1849,
the very first year of his residence in Chicago, it fell upon him to
render assistance to the cholera victims. He was untiring in his efforts
to solicit among well-to-do citizens money, clothing and food for the
relief of the sufferers. When the pesthouses could no longer hold the
plague victims he opened the second story of his parsonage as a
temporary hospital. His wife had the welfare of the patients equally
at heart, giving them her service as nurse. When parents died, Unonius
would see to it that their children were cared for, either in some
orphanage or by adoption in private families.

Rev. Carlsson also, immediately upon his arrival in Chicago, became entirely engrossed in relief work among the cholera sufferers.
Not only among the members of his flock, but among the immigrants
as well, his energy proved equal to the emergency. Scarcely an immigrant train arrived but he was at the station to assist and advise his
fellow countrymen. After having spent all that terrible summer of
1854 on a constant mission of relief among the sick, he himself was
attacked by the plague in the fall, but rallied after a few weeks. Even
after the cholera epidemic subsided, Rev. Carlsson continued his mission
of benevolence among the Swedish immigrants.

What has been said of these three, in their relation to the cholera
victims, applied equally to Rev. Newman. Without the slightest fear
of the epidemic he went about ministering to his stricken countrymen,
sat at their bedsides, comforting the sick and dying by word and deed,
buried the dead and gave advice and succor to the survivors.

Sometimes Revs. Carlsson and Newman coöperated in the work.
Thus, one day the former made the suggestion, "Brother Newman,
suppose you take one street and I another, and we solicit for a common
fund." The memory of the unselfish exertions on the part of these
pioneer clergymen in the days of dire calamity will be ever dear to the
hearts of succeeding generations of their countrymen.

Another example of prevalent conditions among the immigrants
of those days may here be given. In 1855 Swedish and Norwegian
paupers cost the city of Chicago and Cook county no less than $6,000,
exclusive of assistance rendered by individuals aggregating a still
larger sum. During the month of October that year, which was by no
means the most unhealthy period, 35 Swedes who had died in private
houses were buried at public expense because of the destitution of
their families. During the same period the county defrayed the expense
for the interment of about double that number of Swedes who died in

hospitals and the poorhouse. Yet health conditions and the death rate were no worse in Chicago than in Milwaukee or other neighboring cities.

The city of Chicago at this period was a mere nucleus for future development, and as yet few, if any, anticipated or dared hope for the enormous progress it was destined to make. The north side being the original location of the Swedish colony in Chicago, that part lays claim to the especial interest of Swedish-Americans.

In 1850 that part of the city was an open, almost uninhabited prairie, the only objects that broke the monotony of the scene being large stumps or individual trees still left standing. The locality was low and swampy, with here and there pools of stagnant water, inhabited by snakes and other reptiles. To the north from the present Division street line stretched an extensive swamp covered with underbrush and vines. Although the district was platted and the streets were laid out on paper, there were in fact no other thoroughfares than Kinzie street, North Clark street and Chicago avenue, if indeed those might be so styled in their almost impassable state. They were practically very badly kept country roads, unworthy of the name of city streets. But what could be expected of the north side at a time when the streets on the south side, in the very heart of the city, were at times little better than quagmires. Ordinarily they were like rough country roads flanked at intervals with narrow planks in lieu of sidewalks. In the fall, winter and spring they were especially wretched, not to say perilous to life. Then the mud would be knee deep throughout, while in places there would be bottomless mudholes. It was no uncommon sight to see, on Clark, Lake and other principal streets, a pole stuck in the middle of the street and on it a cross board bearing the legend: "No Bottom." In the north and west parts of the city as well as to the south of the "down town" district weeds man-high skirted the driveways on both sides, while the vacant blocks were the stamping ground of tethered cows and goats, and flocks of cackling geese, not to mention pigs, chickens and turkeys innumerable. Add to this that dead dogs and cats and other carcasses graced the roadsides and perfumed the air as they lay putrifying in the ditches, and you will have a true picture of Chicago and its immediate environments at this period.

On the north side the buildings were as yet few and primitive. Standing at the Clark street bridge you had an unobstructed view of a two-story house and an adjoining blacksmith shop erected by one Sheldon, a Norwegian, at Ohio street, just west of Market street. From the same point of observation one had a free prospect all the way to Hubbard street, where R. B. Johnson, another Norwegian, had built a house. So few and far apart were the houses in this neighborhood. The price of a building lot in those days was a mere bagatelle in comparison with present day realty values. Traets north of Division street eould then be bought for $100 per aere, which was considered quite high enough. At Chicago avenue lots eould be had for nothing, provided the applicants agreed to put up two-story houses on them, this stipulation being designed to attraet people to the neighborhood and raise the value of realty. A few years before, or in 1847-49, any one could beeome the owner of lots 140 to 150 by 25 feet on the north and west sides, a few blocks from the river, for the mere trouble of sawing a few eords of wood for the owners of the ground. Many of the pioneers took advantage of this offer to proeure cheap building lots. Not many years thereafter the priee of such lots had risen to $1,000 and over. Today an immigrant who desired to earn one of these lots in the same manner would be sawing wood for the better part of his natural life.

The Swedes who had beeome established in Chieago at this time had loeated between Indiana and Erie streets, on an island formed by the two arms of the north branch of the river, the west arm following the present river bed while the eastern came about to present Orleans street. The place was known as "Swedish Town" and formed the nueleus for the populous north side Swedish community. The buildings on this island, as elsewhere in the outskirts of the eity, were small frame houses or primitive log cabins, or shanties built of rough boards set on end. The latter style of arehiteeture was mueh in vogue in the large stretch of swamp between Indiana street and Chicago avenue. The neighborhood was literally filled with these shanties, put up without respeet for eompass or street lines, by poor immigrants who eould afford no better shelter. In these rude huts hundreds of Swedes lived and died during the terrible years of the cholera scourge in the early fifties.

After a few years the east arm of the river was filled in, whereby the island beeame part of the north side district. When the owners of the land on whieh the Swedes were squatters in the years 1853 and 1854 began to assert their property rights, the settlers were forced to move. They then bought lots here and there on the north side, the entire distriet being owned by two men, W. B. Ogden and W. L. Newberry. Both grew immensely rich from the sale of real estate. Mr. Newberry donated a part of his wealth for a library to be established in that part of the city and to bear his name. This was done, the present library building having been completed in the nineties.

The early Swedish colony on the north side embraeed principally that part bounded on the north by Division street, on the south by Indiana street, on the east by Wells street and on the west by the river. Within these limits their first churches, the Ansgarius Episcopal, the

Immanuel Lutheran, and the Methodist-Episcopal, were built. Little by little, the Swedish people, however, scattered over the entire north side, but before that another rapidly growing Swedish colony had been started on the south side. In a short time there were Swedish settlements in all three of the older divisions of the city, while thousands of Swedes poured into the outlying districts or suburbs that grew up in rapid succession. While none of these suburbs bears a distinctively Swedish stamp, still it is only the plain truth to say that the Swedes have taken a leading part in the work of building them up.

Time and change have long since erased every vestige of the aforesaid island and its "Swedish Town," but to following generations of Swedish-Americans it will always retain an historic interest.

The calamity that befell Chicagoans through the great fire of Oct. 9, 1871, probably fell more heavily on the Swedish inhabitants than on any other nationality, from the fact that these still lived almost exclusively in one locality, that being swept by the flames, while other nationalities, being generally distributed over the whole city, partly escaped. It has been estimated that three-fourths of the Swedes that had established homes up to that time were residing on the north side, principally along Market, Sedgwick, Townsend, Bremer, Wesson and Division streets and North avenue. This whole area was swept by the fiery tornado, and Swedish homes were destroyed by the hundreds. Four Swedish churches, as many newspaper offices and numerous shops and stores owned by Swedes were leveled with the ground. Of the 50,000 people who during the nights following the catastrophe slept out of doors with no protection from the cold but the few garments they had snatched from the flames, probably 10,000 were Swedes. True, they were left under the open sky practically destitute, but all was not lost, for they still possessed the power and the will to work and an unflinching trust in the future. Like all the other fire victims, they took up the task of building a new and greater Chicago on the smoking ruins of the old. By industry and thrift they succeeded after a few years in retrieving their fortunes. An instance of the enterprising spirit of the fire sufferers was given by the members of the Immanuel Swedish Lutheran Church who gathered around the still smoking ruins of their fine, newly built house of worship and, in the name of God, decided to continue work and rebuild the edifice as soon as possible, a resolve all the more sacrificial as the members' own homes were in ashes. So promptly was the resolution carried out that the congregation on Christmas Day, 1872, could worship for the first time in the new edifice which, however, was not fully completed until the winter of 1875.

The total loss sustained by Swedes in the Chicago fire was not far from one million dollars. Few of them received any insurance money, most of the local insurance companies being forced to the wall. In this and other countries a relief fund of $7,500,000 was raised, but of this only an insignificant share fell to the modest and unobtrusive Swedes, while less numerous but more aggressive nationalities claimed more than their rightful share. The sums that were sent from Sweden for the relief of their countrymen here were designated for the "Scandinavians," and had to be divided in brotherly fashion among Swedes, Norwegians and Danes alike, although the losses sustained by the last two nationalities were not to be compared to those of the thousands of Swedes. Our countrymen, together with other sufferers, were sheltered in hastily built wooden sheds where they endured great hardships during the severe winter of 1871-72, despite the free distribution of coal and provisions. The free building materials placed at the disposal of those who would avail themselves thereof, enabled many of the Swedes to rebuild at once, their new houses being in many instances larger and more commodious than those burned. Thus the Swedish district on the north side was rebuilt in a short time, the inhabitants gradually resuming their former functions in business and daily life.

ORION, HENRY COUNTY

This flourishing little town is the center of a prosperous farming community in Western township, which was organized in the early days of the Bishop Hill Colony. Erik Jansson visited the locality in 1849 and, finding the soil very fertile, determined to locate an auxiliary colony there. Another point in its favor was its location halfway between Bishop Hill and its fishery and nearest trading station on Rock Island. He purchased a tract embracing 1,116 acres. When the colony built its steam power flour mill, the authorities took a loan of $2,000 from Hall & McNeely of St. Louis, offering this property as collateral. The colony failing to meet payments, the mortgage was foreclosed and the land, together with several primitive buildings, was sold at auction in 1851 to satisfy the creditors.

But before Erik Jansson's visit a Swede named John Johnson is said to have lived there, removing to Iowa in the late seventies. When the cholera broke out at Bishop Hill in 1849 many of the colonists sought refuge in this locality, but were pursued by the plague, which raged here with such fury that as many as sixteen persons died in one day. Fifty cholera victims among the refugees lie buried in the southeast corner of section 25, with nothing to mark the place where these pioneers sleep.

One of the earliest permanent settlers was William A. Anderson, who came over in 1851 and died here in 1858. He is said to have been very helpful and accommodating towards Swedish newcomers. Other pioneers were Anders M. Pettersson, from Södra Vi, Småland, who arrived in 1852, and N. P. Pettersson.

John Samuelsson was one of the prominent Swedish settlers here. From Vestra Eneby, Östergötland, he came as an immigrant to Andover in 1852. During the Civil War he served for three years in the 43rd Illinois Infantry and was in several battles, including Shiloh and the siege of Vicksburg. With the small savings from his pay as a soldier he made the first payment on a small farm which he purchased and kept adding to and improving until in 1880 it comprised 400 acres, with splendid farm buildings.

Peter Westerlund is another prosperous pioneer settler in these parts. He was born at Hassela, Helsingland, Aug. 10, 1839, emigrated in 1850 and settled at Andover. There he lived for seven years, whereupon he made a trip to Pike's Peak, Colo., with a party in search of gold. From there Westerlund and eleven others started on an adventurous expedition to the southwest without a guide, through a territory without roads or trails. Their vehicles were drawn by oxen. They eventually reached the Rio Grande and followed the river to Albuquerque. Here they sold their oxen, built three boats and, contrary to the advice of the townsmen, started to float down the unexplored waterway, ultimately arriving at El Paso. Up to that time the Rio Grande was supposed to be impassable, one reason given being that it ran through a mountain at a certain point. The intrepid Swedes, however, exploded that tradition.

The town of Orion was founded in 1853 by Charles W. Deane, and at first bore the name of Deanington, which was subsequently changed to Orion. Three years later it got railroad communications and entered upon a new stage of development. Orion has a Swedish Lutheran church, organized in 1870.

According to the census of 1900 the town then had a population of 584. At the close of 1905 the number of Swedish-Americans living in and around Orion was 800, of whom 298 were born in Sweden and 522 in this country.

ST. CHARLES, KANE COUNTY

That part of Illinois now comprising Kane county was first settled by whites in 1833 when a party of colonists from Indiana came there to live. The next year another party arrived from New York, and in 1836 the county was organized and named after Elias K. Kane, who became one of the early United States senators from Illinois.

St. Charles, on the Fox River, was one of the first settlements in the county. In 1834 the place had only six houses, but the following year the growth of the population necessitated the building of a school-house. In another year a hotel was erected and a bridge was built across the Fox River.

Almost from the first, the Swedes have formed an important, though not the dominating, element of the community. They were there in the latter forties, it being a matter of record that at least three Swedes, viz., Nils Jansson, who ran a turning lathe, and two storekeepers, Björkman and Baker, settled in St. Charles prior to 1849. The latter, who changed his name to Clark, failed in business and then removed to Chicago.

Nils Jansson, who hailed from Hörby, Skåne, emigrated to America in 1830 as a young man. He was a hard drinker and somewhat of an adventurer, having traveled in Mexico and roamed at large over the western continent for some time before settling down here. When the number of Swedes in St. Charles increased, he assumed a sort of guardianship over them, started raising money for a little church and sometimes tried his ability as a preacher, which was none too great. The church was built in 1852, and Swedish clergymen of different denominations, among them Gustaf Unonius, the Episcopal pastor in Chicago, made occasional visits. The wife of Nils Jansson is said to have been a pious woman who often warned her husband to mend his ways. One morning she took him severely to task, pointing out his fate in the hereafter, if he persisted in his sinful course. To this he replied, it is said, that she need not worry about his soul, for half an hour was all he wanted to prepare for death. That same day Nils Jansson was killed by lightning in the country, a short distance from St. Charles. This seems to have occurred in 1850, though the year is not positively known.

The Jonas Andersson from Färila, Helsingland, who is mentioned among the Princeton pioneers, was one of the first Swedes to settle in St. Charles. He came from Chicago in 1849, remaining over winter, and left for Wisconsin in the spring. After a few months, he returned to St. Charles, lived there till 1853, then removed to Princeton.

Such were the beginnings of the Swedish colony in St. Charles. In 1852 several hundred Swedes arrived directly from the old country. Most of the immigrants came from Vestergötland, being persuaded to come by the glowing accounts of St. Charles and surrounding country given in letters from Anders Andersson, a blacksmith and wagonmaker from Timmelhed, who had emigrated in 1847. Some years later he moved to Taylor's Falls, Minn., where he died. He left two daughters, one of whom was married to Daniel Fredin, living near that place, the other to Dr. Erland Carlsson, one of the pioneer clergymen of the Swedish Lutheran Church in America. Other arrivals in 1852 were,

Lars Frän (Frenn) from Timmelhed and his brothers, Sven Thim, and Anders Larsson, and a half-brother, Carl Larsson; the first-named moved to Wayne Station, a few miles from Geneva, after a year, and from there in 1880 to Vasa, Minn., where he died the same year at the age of eighty-one; Thim died in Geneva; Anders Larsson moved to Red Wing, Minn., in 1855 or 1856, and died at Vasa in 1871, fifty-eight years old. Still others were, a shoemaker named Bowman, who served in the Union Army during the war and died several years thereafter; his stepson, P. G. Boman, who moved first to Chicago, then to Rock-

St. Charles—West Main Street

ford; J. Sannquist; Carl Samuelsson and Carl Sjöman from the Timmelhed neighborhood, the former, who was somewhat of a spiritual leader, moving to Elgin, the latter to the neighborhood of McGregor, Ia.; Abram Swensson and his sister, later removed to Hastings, Minn.; Anders Svensson and his brother-in-law Hedelin from Rångedala, Vestergötland, both removing later to Faribault, Minn. Among the early settlers was also one Jonas Håkanson, thought to have moved from there to Rockford.

These immigrants also brought the cholera, the plague having broken out on shipboard and pursuing them to their destination. Had they taken the necessary precautions upon arrival, such as obtaining clean and airy lodgings, the danger of contagion might have been minimized. Unfortunately, however, few houses were to be had, and the immigrants had to be packed into small and unsanitary rooms that became the hotbeds of the disease. The first case of cholera in St. Charles appeared July 3, the victim being a man. An Irish physician named Crawford, who was called in, advised the immigrants to scatter so as not to give the epidemic a chance to spread to the others, but instead of heeding his counsel, a dozen newcomers occupied a vacant cooper shop, which was turned into a pesthouse, all the occupants being attacked by the epidemic. Immigrants living elsewhere in the place also were taken sick. Dr. Crawford and a volunteer nurse were at the bedsides of the plague victims night and day for one whole week, exerting their utmost power to save the stricken ones. Meanwhile the contagion spread among the older settlers, five of whom died. Among the immigrants the plague at this first outbreak claimed ten lives.

At length the local authorities awoke to the necessity of strenuous and systematic measures to check the ravages of the disease. For that purpose a temporary hospital was hastily erected of boards at a healthy and picturesque spot in the woods north of St. Charles. Several women volunteered as nurses and provided everything needed for the patients. But despite the best efforts of the community the epidemic was not checked until seventy-five persons had succumbed.

A small party of Swedes came to St. Charles in 1853, including Peter Lundgren, from Bottnaryd, Småland, John Carlsson, from Askeryd, in the same province, Peter Lundquist, Fredrik Pettersson, and August Nord. Lundquist afterwards removed to Rockford and Pettersson to Nebraska. In the surrounding country a number of Swedes early settled down as farmers.

In 1853 a Swedish Lutheran congregation was organized in St. Charles, but its growth was deterred by litigation over the question of ownership of the aforesaid church. An Irishman named Marvin took almost forcible possession of the edifice in settlement of claims against the congregation, so that when its members came to celebrate early mass on Christmas morning, 1854, they found the doors of the little church tightly nailed up. One of the intending worshipers, named Jonas Magnusson, broke open the door and let the people in. When the congregation came to worship on Easter Sunday the following year they discovered that the edifice had been moved away on rollers, and from that time Marvin seems to have had undisputed possession.

From this time until 1882 the Swedish Lutherans in St. Charles worshiped together with their brethren in Geneva. That year a new congregation was organized in St. Charles, and a church was built the following year. During 1905 a new and larger edifice was erected.

As early as 1853 S. B. Newman, a Methodist clergyman, organized a small Swedish class in St. Charles, which soon disbanded owing to the prevailing hostility to Methodism among the Swedish settlers. Again in 1890 the Methodists began work, resulting in the organization of a small congregation. A church edifice was erected in 1904.

During the last two decades the Swedish population of St. Charles has slowly but steadily grown, partly by immigration from Sweden, but principally from people moving in from other localities. At the close of 1905 they numbered about 1,500, out of a total population of 2,675.

KNOXVILLE, KNOX COUNTY

Knoxville is the oldest town in Knox County, having been founded in 1831. During the first two years of its existence the place was known as Henderson. For many years it was the county seat until the more prosperous city of Galesburg laid claim to the honor. A bitter fight ensued, Knoxville vigorously defending the right once granted, while Galesburg claimed it as the prerogative of the principal city in the county and was ultimately victorious. One day in 1873, the question having been settled, the archives of the county were removed to Galesburg, where they have since remained. In the fight for the county seat none took a more active part than Sven Pettersson of Knoxville, who sacrificed both time and money in behalf of Knoxville as the seat of the county government. The part played by the liquor traffic in the rivalry between the two communities is described under the head of Galesburg.

Prior to 1849, there were no Swedes in Knoxville, but that year several located there, among whom were two shoemakers, Adolf Andersson and one Boström. The latter left in 1850, Andersson remaining until 1853. Simultaneous with these two were other settlers, among whom one Tinglöf with his family, Kristian Johnson, A. Bergquist, a farmer, and Trued Persson, a schoolmaster from Stoby, Skåne, known as Granville among the Americans of Knoxville and Galesburg. He removed to Vasa, Minn., in November, 1855, where he attained prominence, was elected to the state legislature and held other positions of trust. He died there Dec. 27, 1905. One Daniel J. Ockerson came to Knoxville in 1851, went to California in 1859 and removed to Red Oak, Ia., in 1880. The same year Ockerson came, John Gottrich located in Knoxville and in 1880 was the only one of the early Swedish settlers still living there. The aforesaid Sven Pettersson arrived in 1852 as did a considerable number of Swedes. The influx was steadily on the increase, and in 1854 the Swedes formed a considerable part of the population.

That year the cholera broke out in Knoxville, its ravages being mostly confined to the Swedes, forty of whom died of the pestilence. The fact that the Americans generally escaped is attributed to their more sanitary dwellings. As poor immigrants, the Swedes, on the contrary, had to be satisfied with little stuffy huts; besides, they were unaccustomed to the climate and did not know how to accommodate their diet to the circumstances. The lack of proper sheltering resulted

Knoxville—Street Scene

from the lack of money, for while there was plenty of work to be had, the pay was usually in the form of cows, calves, sheep and pigs.

For a period of about twenty years, from 1852, there was a rapid increase of the Swedish population. But in the latter seventies came a stagnation which has continued to this day. The descendants of the old pioneers, as also the Swedes who have located there in later years, are generally prosperous and belong to the best portion of the Swedish population of the state. During the Civil War the Knoxville Swedes displayed their great loyalty to the flag by enlisting to the number of forty to fight for the perpetuation of the Union.

The city has a Swedish Lutheran church, one of the oldest in the state, founded in 1854. In Knoxville there was printed, in December, 1854, the first issue of "Gamla och Nya Hemlandet," the oldest Swedish newspaper in the West and the next oldest in the United States. The first number was dated Jan. 3, 1855.

From 1873 to 1885, Knoxville had a Swedish institution of learning, the Ansgarius College, owned and controlled by the Ansgarius Synod. The total population of Knoxville in 1900 was 1,857. The number of Swedes cannot be precisely stated. The membership of the Swedish Lutheran Church at the beginning of the year 1905 was 280, and the total number of Swedes in the city will not exceed 850.

WATAGA, KNOX COUNTY

The little town of Wataga is situated in Sparta township, its first white inhabitant having been Hezekiah Buford, who located there in 1834. Two years later came three brothers, Cyrus, Levy and Reuben Robbins, who planted a grove of shade-trees and a large orchard, known as Robbin's Grove.

The first Swedish settlers arrived in 1849. They were: Lars Olsson, with family, from Bollnäs, Helsingland; Peter Ericksson, with wife and two sisters-in-law, from Alfta, Helsingland; Olof Pålsson and Anders Danielsson from Ockelbo, Gestrikland. The first named died in 1864, having lived long enough to reap the fruits of his labors as a pioneer. One of his sons, Wm. H. Olson enlisted as a volunteer in Company I, 102nd Illinois Infantry on Aug. 9, 1862. He was soon promoted to corporal and died March 26, 1865, from wounds received in battle. His brother, L. W. Olson, died in 1907. In 1880 he was a member of the firm of Olson and Bergman. Two of his sisters were also living at that time. Peter Ericksson, his wife and one of her sisters after a few years moved to Bishop Hill, where all died prior to 1880. Olof Pålsson moved first to Minnesota and then to Kansas. Anders Danielsson was still living in Wataga in the early eighties.

In 1850 N. J. Lindbeck came over from Ockelbo and settled two miles east of Wataga; also Jonas Pettersson and his wife from Alfta, the Williamson family from Jerfsö, Helsingland, and Lars Williams from Ljusdal, in the same province. Lindbeck left after nine months' stay, subsequently moving from one place to another, finally settling at Victoria, where he was still living in 1880. Jonas Pettersson died after a few years, but his widow and children, two sons and three daughters, were still living there in 1880. The head of the Williamson family died in 1885. His five sons all became prominent citizens in their respective communities. William Williamson went to farming on a large scale near Wataga, owning over 400 acres of land in 1880, a general merchandise store in Galesburg and a large interest in the grocery store of Nelson Chester & Co., in Moline. Jonas Williamson at that time also owned a large farm near Wataga. The third brother, Peter Williamson, had a valuable farm in Lucas county, Ia. The fourth, John Williamson in 1862 enlisted in Company K, 83rd Illinois Infantry, was wounded and received honorable discharge the following year.

dying shortly after his return home. Moses O. Williamson, the fifth of the brothers, born on the Atlantic during the voyage of the family to America, began his career as a harness-maker and later devoted himself to politics, rising from one position to another until elected to the office of state treasurer. After serving one term, 1901-1904, he retired from public life and established himself in business in Galesburg where he has resided for a long period. A sister of the Williamson brothers married W. C. Olson, who, after many years' residence in Wataga, where he held several public offices, removed to Wakeeney, Kans., some time in the seventies.

Wataga was founded in 1855 by an American by the name of J. M. Holyoke and a Swede named A. P. Cassel, who jointly established a general merchandise store. The next year the place got a railway station and a hotel. Rich coal veins were early discovered in this vicinity and the work of mining began forthwith. The coal mining industry was at its height here about the middle of the fifties, when the mines employed 250 workingmen; after that it declined, causing the floating population, a large percentage being Swedish laborers, to drift away to other localities. Those of the Swedes who had been able to purchase land remained, as a rule, and in time became well-to-do. A few engaged in business with uniform success.

A Swedish Lutheran church was organized here in 1856 and a Swedish Methodist church the year following. Neither church is numerically strong, the former numbering 245 and the latter only 26 members. In 1900 Wataga had 545 inhabitants. The percentage of Swedish-Americans in the town and the surrounding country can only be conjectured.

SWEDONA, MERCER COUNTY

The town of Swedona was first known as Berlin. It is situated on a plateau commanding a view of the plains stretching to the south and drained by the Edward's Creek. The growth of Swedona was stunted from the first by the lack of railway communication, New Windsor, Lynn and other neighboring towns developed at its expense, a number of houses being moved from Swedona to these places. No other factors requisite to development having since came into existence, the place is still but a small village. The country around is populous with successful farmers, largely Swedes.

The first Swede in Swedona, undoubtedly, was Nils Magnus Kihlberg from Kisa, Östergötland, who came over with a party of 300 emigrants on board the sailing vessel "Charles Tottie," in the summer of 1849, after a seven weeks' voyage from Göteborg to New York. Their original destination was New Sweden, Ia., where Peter Cassel had settled, but the cholera and other diseases crossed their purpose and compelled them to stop in Andover and vicinity. Late in the autumn, Kihlberg started for New Sweden, but while in Rock Island awaiting a boat for Burlington he changed his mind and returned to Andover. Shortly afterwards he located at Swedona with his family, consisting of wife and three sons. In 1880 Kihlberg and his wife were still living. The year following the arrival of Kihlberg, other Swedes settled here. They were Gustaf Larsson and Anders Samuelsson from Sund, Östergötland, the former with wife and three daughters. Larsson died in the seventies. Samuelsson later removed to the vicinity of Cambridge, Henry county. In 1857 still another family was added, that of Peter Magnusson from Ydre, Östergötland, with wife and five children. Magnusson died late in the seventies; one of his sons became one of the most prominent farmers in the locality, and two daughters successively married Rev. L. P. Esbjörn.

After 1870, parties of immigrants, mostly from Småland, began to arrive and settle in Swedona. The largest influx seems to have occurred in 1865, or thereabouts, when a number of fairly well-to-do families arrived and made extensive land purchases in the neighborhood.

The Swedish Methodists were on the ground as early as 1855, when a mission was established, but not until 1863 did the congregation get its own pastor.

The Swedish Lutheran Church in Swedona was founded in 1859. Among its early pastors was Rev. A. Andreen, one of the pioneers of the Augustana Synod, and father of Gustav Andreen, president of Augustana College, and Revs. Philip and Alexis Andreen, all ministers of the Augustana Synod.

While Swedona had a population of 111, the Swedish Lutheran Church there numbered 490 at the close of 1905, the majority living in Cable and Sherrard and in the country roundabout Swedona. The Swedish Methodists are 36 in number, some living in New Windsor. In the Swedona neighborhood there were in 1905 approximately 250 people without church connections.

ALTONA, HENRY COUNTY

The first white man in Altona was John Thompson, who came there in 1836. His nearest white neighbor was living in Franker's Grove, eleven miles away. After a few years a number of Mormons located in the neighborhood. Joseph Smith, their prophet, had had a revelation to the effect that here an auxiliary colony of the Latter Day Saints was to be founded, the principal one being at Nauvoo. The branch colony numbered about one hundred persons. The neighbors having given the Mormons due notice that they could not count on security of life and property, the prophet had another revelation with orders to the branch colony to reunite with the main body at Nauvoo, which was done.

The first schoolhouse in this vicinity was built in 1841. When the Chicago, Burlington and Quincy Railway was built through this locality one J. B. Chambers, who furnished the railroad laborers with provisions, built a store on the present site of Altona, which was subsequently platted in 1854 by the heirs of John Thompson, who named the place La Pier, the name of Altona dating from 1863.

Altona—Main Street

The first Swede to settle here was Anders Snygg from Bergsjö, Helsingland, with wife and four children. The family had emigrated in 1849 and settled in Victoria. The year following Snygg bought 40 acres of land three-quarters of a mile north of Altona and moved there with his family. Shortly after the removal, Snygg was taken sick and, after a lingering disease of five years' duration, died. His widow was still living in 1880, at the age of seventy. One son, Anders Peter Snygg, was then living in Dayton, Ia., one daughter was married and lived in Des Moines, and another daughter was married to an American by the name of Shade, in Oneida, Ill.

The first Swedes to settle in Altona next after Snygg were P. Petterson and his brother G. A. Ericksson from Djursdala, Småland. The former had been living for some years in Moline, where he was farming for a time and then engaged in business. These men, who located here in 1850, proved very enterprising, their first concern after arrival being to erect a combined flour mill, sawmill and planing mill run by steam. A little later they built a blacksmith shop, a wagon shop and a cooper shop. Not satisfied with this, they started a large general store, which supplied the neighborhood with all the necessaries. After nine years Ericksson moved to Iowa. His brother Petterson continued all the various lines of business until 1862, when he sold the flour mill to Olof Andersson, shortly afterwards rejoining his brother in Iowa. One Anders Johnson for a time had charge of the wagon shop, which was subsequently removed to Andover. One A. M. Lönner, who later removed to Andover, was bookkeeper for the Petterson brother and Ericksson from 1853 to 1859.

Another early Swedish settler in Altona was Nils J. Lindback, who came in 1854, remaining only a few years and then moving to a farm east of Victoria. The marriage interdict in effect in Bishop Hill at this time caused many young people to desert that colony and settle in surrounding places, including Altona. Among the Erik Janssonists who located in Altona in 1855 were Erik Lindvall and his wife Helena, John Söderström and his wife Louisa, Erik Hart, Hans Lindgren, John Granat and G. E. Rodeen. This party at first engaged in brickmaking near Altona. The two married couples made their homes in Altona proper. In 1858 Lindvall got work in a flour mill, very likely that of Petterson and Eriksson, and afterwards established a wagon shop, which he conducted so successfully that it made him wealthy in a modest way. Söderström for some years had owned and operated a brick yard west of Altona, then moved to the Galva neighborhood and rented a farm, still later removing to Osage county, Kansas, where he was living for many years as one of the most prosperous farmers of the state. Erik Hast went to California; Hans Lindgren moved to a farm near Ulah, Henry county; John Granat went to Galesburg, where he was still living as late as 1880, and G. E. Rodeen died in the Civil War, while serving in Company D, 57th Illinois Infantry.

In 1858 Mr. and Mrs. Youngström moved to Altona from Pleasant Hill, Ky., where they had belonged for a few years to the Shaker sect, after leaving Bishop Hill in 1854. Youngström still lived in Altona in 1880.

The first Swedish church in Altona was the Lutheran, organized in 1854. In the sixties its membership grew very large, but in the seventies a general exodus to the West caused a material decrease which, however, has been more than outweighed by normal growth in the later decades.

A Swedish Baptist church was founded in 1858, and is still extant, according to the records of the denomination, but no statistics are therein given. This church also lost members during the emigration farther westward. In 1887 a Swedish Mission church was organized, but meeting with no success, the little flock soon disbanded.

In the Altona country district there was an early influx of Swedish farmers. The first was George Chalman, who came in 1851 or 1852, and was still living in 1880. Other of the earliest settlers were Peter Newberg, Nils Hedström, L. Carlsson, E. Kraus, P. Olsson and Georg Eriksson. Shortly after 1860 a considerable number of Swedes settled to the north and northwest of Altona.

In 1905 the Swedish Lutheran Church in Altona numbered 450 out of a total Swedish population of 700. Altona's total population was 633 in 1900.

ROCKFORD, WINNEBAGO COUNTY

That portion of the state which is now Winnebago county was, like the whole northern part of Illinois, little known to the whites prior to the Black Hawk War of 1832. The first spot in this territory settled by whites was Galena, then named La Pointe. One Col. Johnson from Kentucky came there in 1824 with a number of miners and opened a coal mine about a mile from the present site of the city. The enterprise proved very successful and when the news spread hundreds, not to say thousands, in 1826-7 flocked there from all parts of Illinois and neighboring states to seek work in the coal mines.

Partly in this way, partly through those who fought in the Black Hawk War, which extended to these parts, the Rock River valley was made known. One of the first white men who set foot on the present site of Rockford was Ira Parker, who came in 1824 with a party of landseekers from Terre Haute, Ind. On their way to Galena, they crossed the Rock River here and at this point found an Indian village with 300 to 400 inhabitants. Only the women and children and a few of the men were found at home, all the others being on the war path. The hills on both sides of the river were covered with thick timber and in the valleys the grass grew to a man's height. The scenery that met the party of whites at this point was inviting and highly picturesque.

But Ira Parker and his party were not the only whites who visited this place before the settlement of Rockford began. Shortly after the Black Hawk War, Abraham Lincoln, possibly in the capacity of surveyor, and a party of government officials camped on the Rock River at this point, and he afterwards said that both he and the party were charmed with the natural beauty of the locality.

In the summer of 1833, one John Phelps resolved to explore the Rock River valley throughout. Accompanied by a Frenchman, he left Mineral Point in a canoe and made a stop on the present site of the city. One of the explorers was in favor of settling on the spot at once, but there being no building material at hand, they proceeded on their way down stream. These two men became the first white settlers at Oregon, in Ogle county.

Several years before Phelps made his tour down the river, the first white had settled in Winnebago county and built a cabin one and one-half miles from the mouth of the Pecatonica River, at a point afterwards known as Bird's Grove. This man was Stephen Mack, a son of an ex-officer in the army who lived in the East and carried on an extensive fur trade. Stephen Mack was born in Vermont, where he received his early education, afterwards entering Dartmouth College at Hanover, N. H. Being a roysterer to whom discipline was irksome, he soon left for home. His father then sent him to the West to superintend his fur trade there. One day while alone in his cabin, he was attacked by Winnebago Indians, and left for dead. He would doubtless have perished, had not the daughter of Chief Ho-no-ne-gah remained and given him the most tender care. She afterward became his wife and bore him four sons and four daughters. Two of the daughters later attended the Rockford Seminary, but their wild disposition and their hatred of the whites soon caused their dismissal from the institution. They then rejoined the Winnebago tribe which had been compelled to withdraw to Minnesota.

Stephen Mack was a tall, stately looking man with the air and manner of the man of the world. His Indian wife died in 1847. The following year he was married to a white woman. She was addicted to drink and made life miserable for her husband. One day, while under the influence of liquor, she set fire to their cabin, which was partially destroyed. These sorrows and perplexities proved too much for Mack, who was laid on a sickbed from which he never arose. He was buried side by side with his first wife in a spot near his cabin.

Among the early settlers here we find Germanicus Rent from Alabama, Thatcher Blake from Maine and Daniel Haight, who lived on what is now known as the east side. A dam constructed across the river by Rent was swept away in January, 1835, but rebuilt the following July. At that time there were only eleven persons living in Midway, as the place was called on account of its location half-way between Chicago and Galena. By fall the number had increased to twenty-seven. Ephraim Wyman, born in Lancaster, Mass., in 1809 was one of the early settlers, coming here Sept. 21, 1835. In the woods on the east side of the river there were living about 750 Pottawatomie Indians and on the Pecatonica River about 700 Winnebagoes. Fortunately for the settlers, these redskins were very quiet and peaceable. The nearest garrison was at Fort Winnebago on the Fox River, in

Wisconsin, and from there assistance could not have been dispatched in time to protect the whites in the event of an uprising.

The number of settlers steadily increased, and in 1836 they were sufficiently numerous to organize the county, which was named Winnebago after the neighboring Indian tribe. For some time afterward, the settlers were subject to hardships and dangers of frontier life here as elsewhere in the western wilderness. A band of outlaws, known as the "Red Robbers," or "Prairie Bandits," operated in these parts from 1836 to 1839, striking terror to the settlers and making the neighborhood generally unsafe. Robberies and other flagrant crimes were of frequent occurrence, travelers between Midway and Galena being especially exposed to outlawry.

The first merchandise store in Rockford was opened by John E. Vance on the east side of the river, not far from the spot where the railway station now stands. Shortly afterward, E. H. Potter and one Preston opened a store in a frame building near the present corner of State and Main streets. These were soon followed by others, mostly located on the east side. Year by year business grew, and in 1848 a bank named the Winnebago Bank was established by the firm of Robertson, Holland and Coleman. Two years later, or only about sixteen years after the arrival of the first white settlers, the place had 1,500 inhabitants, and in the next three years this number was trebled, owing doubtless to the completion to Rockford of the Chicago and Galena Railway, now a part of the Northwestern system. Realty values rose rapidly. A new and larger dam was constructed across the Rock River in the fifties for the generation of water power for mechanical purposes. A couple of saw mills were the first industrial establishments, but gradually various small factories grew up—the modest forerunners of the big industrial plants of modern Rockford. During the first few years the inhabitants wishing to cross the Rock River generally forded the stream, entailing many accidental drownings. Fatalities were not materially decreased by the subsequent system of ferrying. When a bridge was built in 1840 the river could be crossed with some degree of safety, but this bridge was far from satisfactory. The structure was a rickety affair that undulated like thin ice under the feet of passengers and sagged like a hammock under heavier weight. In spite of constant threats to give way, it stood all tests until replaced by a more substantial wooden structure, which in turn gave way to a modern steel bridge.

In 1880 the city had 13,129 inhabitants; in 1890 the number had grown to 23,584 and in 1900 to 31,051. In the last named year the city had 246 industrial establishments of different kinds, with an aggregate capitalization of $7,715,069, 5,223 workingmen and an annual production valued at $8,888,904. The chief products of the Rockford industries are furniture, hosiery, agricultural implements, pianos, sewing machines and machinery and tools. Secondary in order are, paper, flour, grape sugar, matches, plated ware, etc.

To the Swedish-Americans it is a satisfaction to know that of all foreign nationalities represented in Rockford the Swedes have had the greatest share in the rapid development of the city industrially, commercially and otherwise. It is even a question whether they have not surpassed the native Americans in these respects. All the way from the early fifties, Swedes have been living here. During the last three

Rockford—River View

decades they have formed the pith of the working population in the city, and from twenty years back the Swedish-Americans constitute a considerable percentage of the manufacturers and businessmen of Rockford. Industrious and thrifty as a rule, they have generally worked in the employ of others until acquiring a competence, when they have combined into co-operative companies for the purpose of furniture manufacture or carrying on other lines of industry, thereby becoming employers and themselves reaping the profits. Wide-awake and intelligent, as they are, they have made many practical inventions, thereby simplifying processes, reducing the cost of production and increasing the efficiency of labor and machinery. Naturally saving and provident, they have established a building and loan association whereby many have become the owners of comfortable homes. A number of sick benefit and funeral aid societies have been organized, lending economical assistance of no mean importance to families suddenly stricken by misfortune.

The spiritual care of the Rockford Swedes is well provided for. Religious work has been carried on among them ever since pioneer days, and there are now no less than half a dozen Swedish churches, most of these having a large membership and owning valuable property.

They have always evinced a live interest in educational work and given liberal support both to the purely American schools and the specifically Swedish-American institutions of learning. Many are the Swedish young men from Rockford who, after completing the prescribed courses, have entered the service of the church or devoted themselves to the teacher's calling or the learned professions. Several Swedish newspapers have been published in Rockford at different periods. Swedish-song is here cultivated with as much zest as anywhere in the United States. Although not a Swedish-American center of culture in the same sense as Chicago, Minneapolis, New York, and Rock Island, yet Rockford is an eminent factor for Swedish-American progress. Its Swedish colony is more homogeneous than most similar communities, making the Swedish characteristics more pronounced here than elsewhere.

In 1854 the Swedes of Rockford numbered approximately 1,000, in 1862 about 2,000, ten years later about 3,500, and in 1885 about 6,000. At the close of 1905, their estimated number was 16,000. Assuming that the total population increased in the five years of 1901-5 in the same ratio as in the foregoing census period, the Swedes of Rockford would now constitute nearly half the population.

After taking this general survey, we will review the story of the Swedish pioneer settlers of Rockford. About 1852 the first Swedish settlers came here. When John Nelson from Kärråkra, Vestergötland, subsequent inventor of a celebrated knitting machine, came to Rockford from St. Charles that year, he found ahead of him a few Swedish families and single men who had arrived shortly before. Among these were Abraham Andersson with his family and a young man named Clark, possibly the same person mentioned in the early history of St. Charles. Anderson soon left for Minnesota, and Nelson removed to Elgin a few months later, and from there to Chicago in the spring of 1853. The following autumn he formed the acquaintance of Erik Norelius, then a divinity student, lived together with him for several months and attended the private English school taught by him in the winter of 1854. The same year Nelson returned to Rockford, accompanied by Anders Johnson who later removed to New Mexico, where he lived for many years.

During Nelson's absence from Rockford in 1853 a number of Swedes had moved in, including the following: Sven August Johnson from Ving, Vestergötland, who came over in 1852 and subsequently became a prominent business man of Rockford where he is still living, loved and honored by all; C. J. Carlsson, a tailor, and P. Pettersson, with their families, both from Ving; Peter Johansson, or Johnson, and two men, Lindgren and Lundbeck, both from Vestergötland, who died as pioneer settlers in Minnesota; Jonas Larsson and Johan Sparf, with families, both from Ölmestad, Småland; Isak Pettersson, a tailor from Bellö, Småland, all of whom came in one party from the old country.

The Rockford pioneers were beset with the customary trials and hardships on their way to the new country and after their arrival. According to the story told by Jonas Larsson, they left Göteborg in a small, filthy sailing vessel, in which the emigrants were packed together in most uncomfortable quarters. A terrific storm at sea still further aggravated their misfortune, tossing the little vessel about on giant waves, momentarily threatening to swallow up the frail craft. The ship took the route north of Scotland, and the captain asserted that he had never encountered so heavy seas during thirty years of sailing. The ship was driven toward the coast of Ireland, apparently doomed to imminent destruction. So great was the despair on board that the cook ceased to prepare and serve food to the passengers. When they complained, they got the grewsome reply: "You have no further need of food: by tomorrow morning we will all be at the bottom of the sea." There was nothing to do but prepare for death. But the storm subsided, providentially averting shipwreck, and after a voyage of five weeks the ship made port at Cork, Ireland. Here the passengers were detained for two and one-half months while the ship was lightened and repaired. Then they set out anew, on an equally stormy voyage, reaching the American coast after another ten weeks spent on the ocean.

Ultimately the party reached Rockford in the fall, after a journey lasting six months; but even then their hardships were not at an end. Poor food, still poorer dwellings, sickness and lack of work prolonged their misery. Wages were very low, ranging from 25 cents to 50 cents per day. Fortunately, however, the price of commodities was cheap, butter selling at 5 cents per pound, and meat at 3 to 4 cents. Single men could obtain board for $1.50 per week. Even bibulousness was not an expensive habit in those days, when whisky was to be had at 15 cents per gallon.

Larsson and Sparf with their families secured common lodgings at North Second street, near the present public square, at a rental of $3 per month. Larsson went south that fall in search of better employment, but returned in a few months and remained in Rockford. About 1890, he was engaged by the Zion Swedish Lutheran Church as parochial school teacher. Johan Sparf, after living in Rockford for some time, purchased a farm near Davis Junction, where he suffered from crop failures, but ultimately bettered his condition and in 1868 bought a second farm at Cherry Valley, seven miles from Rockford. Now everything went well, and about 1885 Sparf was considered one of the most prosperous farmers of Winnebago county. He died in the nineties.

During the years of 1854-5 many Swedes came to Rockford directly from their native land, others after a brief stay in Chicago. Among others we mention the following: Johannes Anderson, shoemaker, arrived from Chicago in 1854; John Erlander, tailor, arrived

Rockford—River Front

in Rockford in 1855, having emigrated from Slätthög, Småland, the year prior; Peter Lindahl, later a grain dealer; A. P. Petterson, a mechanic, from Vadstena; G. Bergquist, painter, and Gustaf Berglund, dyer, both from Vermland; the former remained in Rockford, the latter removed first to Norwegian Lake, Minn., thence to Water Valley, Miss., where he engaged in manufacture; Anders Hedin, hatter, and Edvard Wallborg, both from Vermland, who accompanied Berglund to Minnesota and from there to Mississippi, where Wallborg was drafted for service in the Confederate army, but escaped to Chicago, going from there to Beloit, Wis., where he died; Gustaf Scott, Johan Abrahamsson and A. Johnson, all of whom removed elsewhere; Adolf Andersson, who lost his life in the war; Peter Håkansson, shoemaker, died in 1880; A. C. Johnson from Törneryd, Blekinge, who came to St. Charles in 1854 and to Rockford the following year, becoming the pioneer furniture manufacturer of the city; Gustaf Lundgren from

Småland and Isak Lindgren, who removed to Andover, still living there in 1880.

In the fifties Rockford, like Chicago, was a stopping-place for Swedish immigrants going west to buy land and establish- homes. This was especially the case in the years 1852 to 1856. The greatest influx of Swedes to Rockford occurred in the decade of 1856-66.

Here, as elsewhere, the immigrants were subject to disease, chiefly the cholera, which claimed most of its victims in 1854. A few examples of the ravages of this messenger of death may be here noted. At this time Inga Christina Persson from Vernamo, who later married John Erlander, was a domestic in an American family. One day she saw a cholera victim carried past the house on the way to the grave. It was the body of her own mother. She had not been notified of her death for fear that she would hasten to the deathbed, contract the disease and spread it to others. Her father also died of the plague about the same time, no notice being given the daughter, who learned of his death accidentally, when a friend called to express her sympathies for the orphaned girl. The daughter herself had a slight attack of the cholera, from which she soon rallied. Johannes Andersson, the aforesaid shoemaker, one morning visited a woman engaged in doing the family washing. That very evening he was requested to order a casket for her, she having been suddenly stricken down by the pestilence. An aged immigrant one day brought home a piece of pork and placed it in the frying-pan, with the remark: "Now that we are in America, I reckon we'll have some pork." That was his last meal. The next morning he was carried to the grave, having died of cholera in the night.

Fortunately there were in the city many charitable people whose hearts went out to the sick and the suffering. Among those who in this dark hour showed themselves most sympathetic and self-sacrificing, Sven August Johnson, John Nelson and Clark, then young men, deserve special mention. Among the Swedish settlers, they were the most proficient in the English language. Without fear of contagion, they went from house to house, bringing help and comfort to their stricken countrymen. Clark is said to have solicited means among the Americans for the support of the sick and the destitute. The Americans, too, showed great kindness toward the unfortunate newcomers. An old schoolhouse, situated near the present public square on the east side, was turned into an emergency hospital, and one Col. Marsh had a barn adapted to the same purpose.

Along in the late autumn of 1854 the epidemic began to subside, and conditions generally improved. Though nearly all poor, the Swedes were industrious and saving, enabling them not only to earn a bare living, but to lay by something for future use. By their capacity for work and their integrity they soon gained the full confidence of their American neighbors.

At first the Swedish settlers had no means of common worship in their mother tongue, but this want was supplied without great delay. The first Swedish preacher to visit Rockford was doubtless Gustaf Unonius of Chicago, but the year is not known. Most probably his visit took place in the late summer of 1852, for in September of that year he took a trip to Minnesota and very likely went by way of Rockford.

The first Christmas matin services celebrated by the Swedes of Rockford were described by survivors in the eighties as having been

Rockford—Seventh Street

extremely impressive. There was no house of worship, where the gospel was preached in the Swedish language, no bells chiming out the hour of worship, yet the settlers desired to celebrate the "julotta" as best they could. Before daylight, a little company of them gathered in a small cabin, where a Christmas tree had been provided and tallow candles placed in the windows. The order of worship was gone through somehow, but simple and unassuming as was this service, it made so powerful an impression on those present that at its conclusion they embraced one another amid tears. The solemnity of the occasion forcibly brought home to them the fact that they were children of a common land and a common faith.

In October, 1853, Rev. Erland Carlsson made his first visit to Rockford and formed the acquaintance of the Swedish settlers there. He returned the following January and then organized the congregation known as the First Swedish Lutheran Church of Rockford, now one of the largest Swedish churches in the United States. In 1882 members who left this church organized another, the Emanuel Church, which uses the English language in its public worship and for some time belonged to the English Lutheran General Synod, but is now a part of the Swedish Augustana Synod. In 1883 there was a second withdrawal from the First Church to form another Swedish congregation, named the Zion Church.

About 1854 or 1855 a Methodist preacher by the name of P. Challman visited Rockford, preaching to his countrymen there. S. B. Newman, another Methodist preacher, also made a visit, forming a class, which, however, disbanded shortly after. Not until 1861 was a permanent Swedish Methodist church organized.

In 1875 the Mission Friends of Rockford had become sufficiently numerous to form a congregation of their own. Still later the Free Mission Church was added, and in 1880 the Swedish Baptist Church. The independent Swedish Evangelical Church, which was founded in 1882, dissolved after a few years.

Among the Swedish population of Rockford a large number of fraternal societies and lodges have sprung up in the course of years.

It is but natural that the energetic and aggressive Swedish people of Rockford should play an influential part in local and state politics, and a number of them should attain to high positions of public trust, as numerous instances have shown.

GENEVA, KANE COUNTY

The city of Geneva is situated in the township of the same name, only two miles from Batavia and the same distance from St. Charles, the three cities being of nearly the same age. In 1836 a party of colonists from the East settled on the site of Geneva. The year after, a town site was laid out and the first courthouse was built. The first bridge across the Fox River was constructed in 1836, the year of first settlement.

Swedes came to Geneva somewhat later than to St. Charles. When the first Swede settled here is not known, but in 1832 several came here, viz., D. Lindström, who later removed to Paxton, his son John P. Lindström, who removed to Moline, and his grandson, A. P. Lindström, who became a minister of the Augustana Synod and died in 1895. These came from Böne, Vestergötland. In 1854 the following Swedes were living in Geneva: G. Lindgren, Samuel Pettersson, who subsequently removed to Aurora; John Ryström, removed to Oregon, Ill.; Göran Svensson, removed to DeKalb; Gustaf Pettersson, removed to Chicago; B. Kindblad and A. P. Andersson, who located in Batavia later; Julius Esping, an anchor smith, who removed later to Fremont,

Kans.; Carl Samuelsson and Sven Andersson, both subsequently removed to Elgin; Ericksson and C. P. Grönberg, removed to Watertown, Wis.; Jonas M. Pettersson, removed to Galesburg, and Olof Svensson, who remained in Geneva to his death.

In 1880 John Pettersson was the oldest living Swedish inhabitant of Geneva. He came over in 1854 from Gällaryd, Småland, and spent several years in Chicago, working at the shoemaker's trade. In 1856 he came to Geneva, establishing himself as a shoemaker, with a branch shop at St. Charles. After seven years on the shoemaker's bench, he tired of the awl and last, and changed to the watchmaker's trade.

Geneva—State Street

In 1853 a Swedish Lutheran church was organized in Geneva. Not long afterward, a parochial school was opened to give the children religious instruction in their mother tongue. The first schoolmaster was John Pehrson, subsequently a clergyman in the Augustana Synod. He was succeeded by M. Munter, a schoolmaster of the olden type from Sweden, who flogged his pupils mercilessly for every offense, while his ability to impart instruction was questionable. The interest he took in the work of teaching may be illustrated with the following incident of Swedish-American pioneer life. One day the schoolmaster, wishing to kill a sheep, brought the animal with him to the schoolroom and then and there, before the eyes of the pupils, went through the uncanny process of butchering and quartering the sheep, all the while continuing to hear the classes in a perfunctory manner. This same Munter later went to Wapello county, Ia., where he became one of the founders of a settlement named after him Munterville. There he died some time in the eighties. About 1870 a Swedish Methodist church was organized in Geneva, and in 1894 a Swedish Baptist church.

During the last twenty or thirty years Swedes in large numbers have moved into Geneva and the neighboring cities on the Fox River. The Swedes of Geneva in 1905 were estimated at 1,200, the enumeration of 1900 giving a total population of 2,446.

GENESEO, HENRY COUNTY

Like Andover, Geneseo was founded by American colonizers from the state of New York, with headquarters at Genesee, from which place the new settlement was named. In 1836 a company sent three men west to look up a locality suitable for a settlement, and this was the choice of the emissaries. A tract of land, embracing the present site of Geneseo, was purchased, whereupon the committee returned home to report the results of their expedition. Fifty settlers immediately started for the new colony site, arriving in the middle of winter, subject to many hardships. Two thousand acres of land were bought up and parceled out among the settlers, who provided their own dwellings according to their means. In the spring they began tilling the soil, gathering their first harvests the following summer and fall.

Geneseo dates back to 1837, when the first houses were erected there. The place did not receive a postoffice until 1839. Its growth was slow until 1853, when the Chicago, Rock Island and Pacific Railway was built through the place, stimulating a more rapid development for the next few years.

In the early fifties Swedes began settling in Geneseo. In 1852 John Gustus, Lewis Johnson and Carl Johnson were living there The first named, who was from Opphem, Östergötland, first had a shoemaker's shop, then opened a store, and in 1862 sold this business to N. P. Rosenstone. In the late seventies he removed to Iowa, where he was not particularly favored by fortune. Lewis Johnson came from Småland and Carl Johnson from Vermland; the latter settled on a farm just outside the town.

In 1853 Lars Jönsson came over from Skärstad, Småland, and bought a farm of 80 acres north of Green River. Carl Toline, who served as a volunteer in Company D, 57th Illinois Infantry, was among the early Swedish settlers here, and was still living in Geneseo in 1880. Another pioneer was Adolf Säfström from Östergötland who lived on a farm not far from Geneseo.

Most of the Swedes who came to Geneseo to farm were poor and, in consequence, had to be satisfied with the low, badly drained lands. the early colonists having picked out the most desirable tracts. Nevertheless, the Swedish farmers in this neighborhood have been doing well. The Swedish people in Geneseo engaged in business and the trades also have prospered and have as a class attained a respected and prominent place in the community.

In the spring of 1855 Swedish Lutheran mission work was begun in Geneseo but not until 1859 was a church organized. Five years later, a Swedish Methodist church was established. This congregation began to decline in the eighties, and is now dissolved.

At the close of 1905, there were approximately 560 Swedish-Americans living in Geneseo and vicinity. The total population at the last census was 3,356.

DEKALB, DEKALB COUNTY

In. 1853 DeKalb consisted of merely a couple of stores, a small hotel and a blacksmith shop. But at that time a railroad was built through, and the town began to grow apace. Building after building was erected and changes were made, so rapidly that farmers who visited the town only once a month would hardly recognize the place. "An enterprise that contributed largely to the development of the town was the location there of a barbed wire factory, which has since grown to be the largest industrial plant in this locality, employing thousands of workmen, a large percentage of whom are Swedes. In 1873 DeKalb got its village charter.

The first Swede in DeKalb was one Jonas Olsson, who came there from Dixon, where he had owned a farm. He was soon followed by his brother and two young men, the sons of a clergyman by the name of P. Bark. Of the Olsson brothers, who came from Slätthög, Småland, the former was still living there in 1880 while the latter had farmed for twenty years near Sterling. In 1853 three more emigrants from Slätthög came over and settled here, namely: Nils Magnus Johnson, Johan Johansson and Jonas Johnson. All three were well-to-do farmers near DeKalb in 1880. Simultaneously with these, came John Olsson from Hjortsberga, Småland. These four were poor emigrants who at first were employed by Americans as day laborers.

In 1854 Peter Månsson came with his family from Vislanda, Småland. He became the first Swedish householder in DeKalb, whence he moved to Salina, Kans., in 1879. Simultaneously with Månsson came Peter Jönsson, also from Vislanda, with a party of eleven others, all of whom settled in this vicinity, Jönsson and several of the others still living there in 1880.

The Göran Svensson mentioned among the early settlers of Geneva was also one of the early Swedes in DeKalb. He was born in the city of Ulricehamn, emigrated in 1852, coming to Chicago, where he lived for three years before removing to Geneva and establishing himself there as a shoemaker. In the early sixties he came to DeKalb, where he plied his trade for many years.

In 1858 a Swedish Lutheran church was organized in DeKalb, and thirty years later a Swedish Baptist church. There is also a Swedish Mission church of more recent date. The Lutheran congregation is numerically one of the strongest of its kind in the state while the latter

De Kalb—Main Street

two are quite small. The city has a number of Swedish fraternal organizations. The Swedish population of DeKalb and vicinity is now approximately 3,500, the total population in 1900 being 5,904.

GALVA, HENRY COUNTY

Of the origin of Galva, which dates back to the fifties, the following is told. In 1853 two Americans, J. M. and Wm. L. Wiley, took a trip from Peoria to Rock Island, passing through this locality. Pleased with the natural prospect, they decided to pitch their camps here, selecting for that purpose a grove which was afterward named College Park. As they reached the top of the hill one of the men, standing erect in the wagon and surveying the surrounding country, exclaimed, ''What a glorious country! Let us buy the land and found a town here!'' Said and done. Negotiations for the purchase were opened at once and soon the land was theirs. But some time elapsed before any sign of the future town appeared, there being but three human dwellings in the neighborhood, and these small and far apart. The thing needed to give the place a start was a railroad, and the Chicago, Burlington and Quincy Railway company in the fall of 1853 agreed to build its line through that point and locate a station there, provided land for that purpose was donated. This the owners agreed to, and the following autumn its trains thundered through the town of Galva, which then existed only on paper.

This was at the time when the Bishop Hill Colony five miles away was at the height of its prosperity. The Wileys had purchased forty acres of land just south of the new town site and subsequently sold part of it to the colonists and another part of it to one Jacob Emery. In this wise the Bishop Hill people obtained a voice in the affairs of the new town, which they named Gefle, after the capital of the Swedish province of Gestrikland, from which they came. The name is said to have been first suggested by Olof Johnson, one of the leaders of the colonists. The Americans of the neighborhood, however, corrupted this to Galva, which was retained as the permanent form.

Galva was developed with a rapidity almost without precedent among the booming towns springing up in the new country. Three years after its founding, the place had 1,500 inhabitants, a large number being Swedes, whose industry and enterprise contributed to its development. The largest share toward its upbuilding in the first few years was contributed by Bishop Hill. As soon as the railway had been completed, the colony erected a large warehouse at Galva, and shortly afterward a large business block of brick. Other business buildings followed, one of which was first used as a bank but was later turned into a hotel. The first comfortable dwelling house in the place was also erected by the colony.

In the foregoing chapter the extensive business enterprises of Olof Johnson have been described. The large warehouse was used to store grain which was bought up and shipped in large quantities, making Galva, at least for a time, one of the principal grain shipping centers in the state. The other large structure was used as a packing house for pork. It is related that at one time when the colony had $60,000 worth of pork from hogs raised at Bishop Hill stored here, the whole stock spoiled from careless packing, and was carted away and buried in a lot purchased for that purpose, together with many barrels of pork returned from eastern markets. The colony also carried on a general merchandise business and banking at Galva, and had a lumber yard there. Most of these enterprises, if not all, proved failures, entailing great loss to the colonists instead of being, as they ought to have been, great sources of income to their community.

Among the early Swedish business men of Galva were one Youngberg, who owned a small store, and Erik Quick, a watchmaker, who tinkered with innumerable side lines of business. Both of these men later went to California. Afterwards the number of Swedes in business increased, so as to make them predominant in many lines.

Among the more notable men who have resided in Galva are, Jonas W. Olson, son of the aforesaid Olof Olsson, and John Root, son

Galva—Central Park

of John Ruth, the assassin of Erik Jansson; both these men are lawyers and still live in Galva.

In Galva was founded one of the first Swedish-American newspapers, the full title of which was "Svenska Republikanen i Norra Amerika." It was first issued in the spring of 1856 and discontinued in the summer of 1858, after having been moved to Chicago that year. Late in the following decade, or in 1869, a Swedish and English newspaper, "The Illinois Swede," was started at Galva. Simultaneously an all-English newspaper, "The Galva Republican," was published by the same firm. Late in 1870 "The Illinois Swede" was re-christened "Nya Verlden" and published exclusively in the Swedish language. The paper was moved to Chicago early in 1871, and in the fall of 1877 it was combined with "Nya Svenska Amerikanaren," resulting in a new paper, entitled "Svenska Tribunen."

In 1867 Galva obtained its village charter. The town had 2,682 inhabitants in 1900. There are three Swedish churches, the Methodist-Episcopal, founded in 1867, the Lutheran, founded in 1869, and a church of the Mission Covenant. In 1905 the first-named church had 175 members, the second 420 and the last 14 members. It has not been possible to ascertain the number of Swedish-Americans in Galva, but with the aid of the above figures it may be stated with a reasonable degree of accuracy that at least half of the population is of the Swedish nationality.

ONEIDA, KNOX COUNTY

The little town of Oneida is situated in the most fertile part of Knox county. Although not among the first settlers there, the Swedes have had a large share in the development of the locality. The first

Oneida

white settler in Ontario township, where Oneida is situated, was Alexander Williams, who came there in 1833. The same year G. W. Melton settled there and built the log cabin which was the first permanent human habitation in the locality. The first schoolhouse was erected in 1839 and the first church edifice, a Presbyterian one, in 1840.

The town of Oneida was founded in 1854 by C. F. Camp and B. S. West, who built a hotel in the place. At Christmas time the same year the railroad came through, giving the place its real impetus for growth.

The first Swedish settler in the township was Georg Boström, who came to America as a boy and was reared in an American family. The year of his arrival in Ontario township is not known, but that he removed from there to Wataga in the seventies is a certainty. After Boström came D. Danielsson and his wife from Ockelbo, Gestrikland. They had come to Bishop Hill as young unmarried people, and were there subjected to bitter persecution on account of a love correspondence carried on in defiance of the drastic rule against marriage and every form of courtship. Disgusted with the petty annoyances following their innocent correspondence, they removed to Oneida in 1855 and were married. A few years later the pair located in Clay county, Kansas. Simultaneously with Danielsson, E. J. Pettersson from Tjärstad, Östergötland, settled in Oneida, after living for five years in various parts of the United States. He established himself as a watchmaker and jeweler and was engaged in that business for at least twenty-five years. A number of Swedes early moved into the surrounding neighborhood, where they have become successful farmers and added materially to the wealth of the community. The population of Oneida was 785 at the last census. No Swedish church has been organized here.

BATAVIA, KANE COUNTY

The Swedish colony of Batavia is of a later date than those of the neighboring towns of St. Charles and Geneva, but its members are numerous and active, and the place amply deserves a mention among important Swedish communities.

The very first settler in Batavia was Christopher Payne, who came in the summer of 1833. He was soon followed by other settlers who came in such numbers that a school was built and a merchandise store opened the next year. In 1844 settlement of the opposite bank of the Fox River was begun after a bridge had been constructed. The splendid water power afforded by the rapids at this place was gradually exploited for manufacturing purposes and thus this bustling little manufacturing center came into existence.

One of the early Swedish settlers here was A. P. Andersson, who figured also among the pioneers of Geneva. He came from Böne, Vestergötland, and was a tailor by trade. In 1854 he removed to Batavia, where he established a tailor shop of his own in the middle sixties. Andersson, however, found several Swedes ahead of him, men engaged in cutting timber for a railroad company. Following

A. P. Andersson came August Andersson, from Halland, who removed to DeKalb after a short stay. A little later Gustaf Svensson, a moulder, joined the Swedish settlement. By 1880 he had made himself known as the inventor of a new kind of fence which was used extensively in the West.

In the late sixties there was a considerable influx of Swedes to Batavia, most of the newcomers obtaining work in the stone quarries situated just outside of the town. Since then Swedes have constantly kept moving in. A large number are employed in the factories, while not a few are in business for themselves. Several have gone to farming in the immediate neighborhood.

Batavia

Until 1872 the Swedish Lutherans of Batavia had belonged to the church in Geneva, but that year they withdrew and organized a local congregation, now one of the largest in the Illinois Conference. In 1870 a Swedish Mission church was founded and about the same time a Swedish M. E. church. There is considerable activity in the matter of fraternal organizations in Swedish circles here. Batavia had a population of 3,871 in 1900 and at the close of 1905 the Swedish-Americans of the city numbered about 1,600.

MONMOUTH, WARREN COUNTY

The city of Monmouth was founded in 1852, but made little progress up to 1855, when it got its railroad. The following year the Presbyterians founded Monmouth College, an institution which grew to be largely attended. The Swedes have been on the ground since the early fifties, but never in such numbers as to cut much of a figure in the municipality.

The first Swede in Monmouth was, it is believed, Johan Lund from Helsingland, who came here in 1853, but soon moved away and is known to have died somewhere in Missouri while on a journey to Pike's Peak, Colo. In 1854 came J. O. Lundblad, from Oppeby, Östergötland, who was also among the pioneer settlers of Princeton, and Erik Engvall. The two were for a time partners in the shoe business, and after the firm dissolved Engvall, who died in 1876, conducted a shoe store of his own for a number of years, prospering in the business.

Monmouth—South Main Street

The brothers Håkan and Lewis Nelson from Skåne arrived the same year and a year later Måns Cassell, also from Skåne. In 1855 John Johnson came from Helsingland and Jakob Söderström from Visby. The former left for Iowa in 1879, while the latter continued into the eighties as a shoe dealer in Monmouth. Carl Lundgren from Nyköping located here in 1856 and served in a Minnesota regiment in the Civil War. One year after Lundgren came Jonas Larsson from Skåne, who moved out to Iowa in 1871. One Holmberg, who had a military education from the old country, settled in Monmouth in 1859, enlisted in the Union Army at the outbreak of the war, and the last that was heard of him was his promotion to the rank of major.

So few were the Swedes in Monmouth that a Swedish Lutheran congregation could not be organized here until 1868, and then there was only a very small flock, which, however, has increased materially in the last twenty years. In 1888 a Swedish Baptist church was established with a limited membership, which has grown but little since.

In 1900 the population of Monmouth was 7,460. At the end of 1905 the Swedes in Monmouth proper were about 450 and in the surrounding country about 2,000.

KEWANEE, HENRY COUNTY

The first white settlers in Kewanee township were John Kilvington, Robert Coustes and Cornelius Bryant, who came there in 1836. Through the efforts of these men and others the Chicago, Burlington and Quincy Railway Company was induced to build through the little village of Kewanee, which then developed greatly to the detriment of the neighboring village of Wethersfield, whose inhabitants had the mortification of seeing building after building placed on rollers and hauled to Kewanee. Within eighteen months, the place had 1,500 inhabitants. After rich coal veins were discovered in the vicinity and mining had begun, the young city grew still more rapidly. Several factories sprang up as the beginning of industrial plants which have been growing larger year by year.

Erik Eriksson from Nora parish, Upland, is believed to have been the first Swedish settler in Kewanee. As a member of the Bishop Hill Colony he had grown weary of the irksome yoke laid upon the shoulders of the faithful and removed to Kewanee in 1855, setting up a saddlery shop which he conducted for ten years, whereupon he removed to Altona. From there he went to Nekoma. Quite a number of Bishop Hill colonists located in Kewanee in 1856, among whom another Erik Eriksson from Nora, with his two sons, Erik and Petter, Erik Bengtsson, Anders Barlow and Hans Lindgren. About the same time there came from other localities Petter Berglund, John Hedberg, Petter Vestlund, hailing from Gestrikland, and John Carlsson and John Pettersson from Småland, who were followed the year after by A. Johnson from Gestrikland.

The last named of the two Erikssons returned to Sweden in 1867 where he died a year later. His two sons in 1857 went to California where they worked for several years digging for gold without success. From there they went to British Columbia, where fortune smiled upon them so lavishly that in a year and a half they could return to Sweden with 100,000 crowns. They chose for their wives the two daughters of Erik Eriksson of Nekoma, and made their homes, the one in Upsala, the other in Nora. Barlow later became a storekeeper at Bishop Hill. Of the early Swedish settlers, A. Johnson, Petter Berglund, Petter

Vestlund and John Petterson were mentioned in 1880 as still living in Kewanee.

In the early seventies, when coal mining had been fully developed, there was a generous influx of Swedes to Kewanee. Many of them subsequently removed to Bloomington and vicinity, but in later years immigration has brought others who more than make good the loss, and at present the Swedish population is quite large in proportion to the total.

Kewanee—Tremont Street

The city has a vigorous Swedish Lutheran congregation, organized in 1869. The Swedish Methodist Church was founded twenty years after. Such a church was organized here as early as 1859, but before 1880 its membership was decimated by removals to the point where the field had to be abandoned and the church property sold. Later the Swedish Methodists got a new foothold in Kewanee, the result being the organization of the second church. There is also a small Swedish Baptist church which has been in existence since 1901.

The census of 1900 gave 8,382 as the total population of Kewanee. The Swedish-Americans there at the close of 1905 were from 2,000 to 3,000 in number.

PAXTON, FORD COUNTY

Ford county was organized in 1859. Two years before there arrived the first Swedish settler, Sven Hedenskog, superintendent of a large country estate in Halland, Sweden, who emigrated in 1857, settling a few miles west of the site of Paxton. Being a poor man, he was obliged to undergo the severest hardships, but his fortitude stood the test and he had succeeded in accumulating considerable property before removing in the latter seventies to Nebraska, where he died not long after.

In 1859 a sailor by the name of Carl Andersson and one Anders Olsson, both from Helsingland, settled in the vicinity of Paxton. Andersson in the seventies removed to Colorado, leaving a daughter in Paxton. Olsson was still living on a farm three miles south of the city in 1880 and was then in comfortable circumstances. There was no great influx of Swedes to Paxton until 1863, when they began to settle here in considerable numbers, for reasons presented in the following.

In 1860, the year of its organization, the Augustana Synod established in Chicago the Augustana Theological Seminary for the purpose of preparing young men for the ministry. While the synod was still small, its members few and there was difficulty in raising the money needed for the support of the seminary by free contributions, some of the leading men conceived the idea of purchasing a large tract of land and by selling farms to prospective settlers procure the funds needed to secure the permanence of the institution. The directors of the seminary, who were authorized to look up a suitable tract, after visiting a couple of states for that purpose, without arriving at any conclusion, received from the Illinois Central Railway Company an offer of a suitable tract of land at Paxton. The offer was accepted and an agreement signed by both parties in February, 1863. This brought quite a number of settlers to the place, yet they did not come in such numbers as to insure the success of the plan, causing the authorities after a few years to cast about for a new location for the school. A more detailed account of these transaction will be found in the historical sketch of Augustana College and Theological Seminary.

Among the settlers was Erik Rasmusson from Gammalstorp, Blekinge province, who had emigrated ten years before, locating near Galesburg in 1853. Other contemporary settlers of Paxton were, Carl Larsson, Erik Carlsson, John Andersson and A. M. Hansson, who all bought farms and located there permanently. In 1864 J. H. Wistrand came to Paxton and was in business there until 1875, when he removed to Moline and opened a store in that city. Simultaneously with Wistrand came Petter Hedberg from Attica, Ind., who established a lumber yard. He became justice of the peace and later was elected tax collector. Ill health compelled him to remove to Denver, Colorado, in 1873, where we find him serving as Swedish-Norwegian vice consul in 1880.

From Attica, Ind., where Swedes had settled in the early fifties, a number of these removed to Paxton in 1865, among whom Fredrik Björklund, Carl Fager, John Svan, John Johnson, Carl Pettersson, Petter Larsson, Carl Johnson, Adolph Johnson and John Nelson, all farmers, except Larsson and Nelson, who were merchants.

Paxton—Market Street

The influx of Swedish settlers continued steadily until 1870, but not on so large a scale as the Synod and the directors of the institution had hoped. The removal of the institution to Rock Island in the seventies naturally worked to the detriment of the Paxton colony, many of the Swedish settlers leaving for other places farther west. During the next few years, however, the exodus was partly counterbalanced by an increased immigration from Sweden.

The Swedish element in Paxton has predominated in many respects from the first. This is especially true with respect to local politics and business pursuits. Around Paxton Swedish farmers are living in great numbers, most of them being in very comfortable circumstances.

In church matters the Swedes of Paxton have taken a prominent part. The Swedish Lutheran congregation there dates back to 1863. In 1878 a Swedish Mission church was organized, but the Methodists and Baptists have not seen fit to enter this field.

In 1900 the population of Paxton was 3,036, and in 1905 there were approximately 3,000 Swedish-Americans living in and around the city.

SYCAMORE, DEKALB COUNTY

The city of Sycamore, county seat of DeKalb county, is situated on a plain at some elevation over the surrounding country and is the center of one of the most fertile regions in Illinois, if not in the entire country. The plain, or plateau, which at its highest point has an elevation of 772 feet above sea level, constitutes the watershead between the Fox and Rock rivers and slopes quite abruptly toward the Kishwaukee River, an insignificant stream which bends around the north and east side of the city at a distance of half a mile.

DeKalb county was organized in 1837 and named after Baron John DeKalb from Alsace, who was a general in the Revolutionary War and fell in the battle of Camden. Three years before organization, the area had a population of 1,697. The land was not opened to settlers until 1843, being comprised in an Indian reservation, but landseekers were on the ground as early as 1835 selecting their claims. But in those lawless times to defend one's right to his claim was far from easy. Quarrels and fights were the order of the day throughout that period, followed by protracted lawsuits after definite property rights had been established.

In the early days of the county, the neighborhood was infested by a numerous, well organized band of outlaws, who made a specialty of stealing horses and saddles, not, however, disdaining to carry away other personal property. So great was the general uncertainty, that for a period of four years the settlers were compelled to keep their places guarded by night. Ultimately, when conditions had grown altogether intolerable, they organized themselves into vigilance committees for their own protection and for the summary punishment of the outlaws. The settlers acted with such vigor and promptness that the county was cleared of horse-thieves and robbers in a very short time.

The early history of Sycamore does not differ much from that of other towns. The first white man to settle there arrived in 1835; his name was Lysander Darling. The same year a Norwegian physician named Norbo took possession of a tract of timber land which is known as Norwegian Grove to this day. Simultaneously, a Frenchman settled here, giving his name to the place known as Chartres Grove. A year later a New York land company took possession of a tract in this neighborhood, comprising two square miles. The same company laid out the site of Sycamore, built a dam across the Kishwaukee River and erected a flour mill.

The original Sycamore settlement consisted of a group of three loghuts on the north side of the Kishwaukee. With that, building was discontinued on account of the unsanitary location, and the new site was laid out, the first house to be erected there being built by Captain Eli Barney at the southeast corner of the present courthouse square.

Sycamore—State Street

The first courthouse was erected in 1839. At the end of one year the little village consisted of about a dozen rude dwellings scattered over a large area.

The early growth of the place is shown by the following figures: in 1848 Sycamore had 262 inhabitants; in 1849, 320; in 1850, 390 and in 1851, 435. From 1855 on its growth was more rapid. In 1858 it received its town charter, and in 1869 it became a city with Reuben Ellwood as its first mayor.

Sycamore has a picturesque, healthful location. It has unusually wide streets and large building lots and, especially in summer, the comfort of the inhabitants is enhanced by the double or treble rows of shade trees that surround the houses or skirt the streets and walks, giving to the entire city a park-like appearance. Here and there above the masses of foliage a church steeple points toward the sky, giving mute evidence that the inhabitants are devoted to other than merely material interests. Persons familiar with many different localities in the state say that Sycamore is one of the prettiest of the smaller cities of Illinois.

The city has three large industrial establishments and a number of smaller ones. The former are the Sycamore Foundry and Machine Company, the Chicago Insulated Wire Company and the Sycamore Preserve Works. The first named employs about 100 men, the second an equal number, while the third during the summer season gives work to 200 to 300 persons. Among the smaller plants are a cigar factory, dairies, stone quarries, wagon and agricultural implement factories, flour mills, brick yards, a soap factory, a varnish factory, a furniture factory and others. The city has water works and electric lighting systems. Eleven churches, three public schools and one girls' seminary are located here.

In 1880 the population of Sycamore was 3,028, in 1890 it had been reduced to 2,987 and in 1900 again increased, the census giving 3,653 as the total number.

The citizens carry on various lines of business, liberally patronized by the prosperous population of the surrounding country. The city has excellent communications, the North-Western and Great Western railways crossing each other at this point. The distance from Chicago is 56 miles.

The first Swedes in Sycamore were Peter Johnson from Mjellby, Blekinge, and Andrew Johnson and Anna Carlsson, a widow, both from Skatelöf, Småland. Somewhat later came the brothers Daniel and Sven Gustafsson and Anna Andersson, a widow whose husband had lost his life while serving in the Civil War. Peter Johnson was still living in 1898, a venerated member of the Swedish Lutheran church. His wife and a daughter died in 1897. Andrew Johnson, who was a brother-in-law of Peter Johnson, removed to Colorado in the late seventies and died there as the owner of a goldmine. His widow, née Anna Carlsson, who returned to Sweden, was still living there in 1898, and Daniel Gustafsson was then living in Iowa. His brother Sven died prior to that time.

When the Civil War broke out there lived in Sycamore a Swedish ex-artillery officer by the name of C. J. Ståhlbrand, engaged in the business of abstract examiner. He obtained a commission from Governor Yates to recruit a battery of artillery, was chosen captain of the battalion formed by this and a couple of other batteries, was promoted major and then brigadier general for bravery, served in the army for about a year after the close of the war, then made his home in Beaufort, S. C., died in Charleston Feb. 3, 1894, and was buried in Columbia, in the same state. To this prominent Swedish-American citizen we will revert in a subsequent chapter, dealing with the Illinois Swedes who took part in the Civil War.

In front of the courthouse in Sycamore the people of DeKalb county in 1896 erected an imposing monument in memory of the men from this county who fought and died for the Union cause on Southern battlefields. Among these men were a number of Swedish-Americans.

Another early Swedish settler here was Carl Carlson from Moheda, Småland, arrived in 1869 and subsequently the most successful and prosperous Swedish farmer in the county. He was still living here in 1898, enjoying a considerable fortune accumulated during a life of

Sycamore—Court House and Soldiers' Monument

toil and prudent husbandry. During the period covered by the late sixties and early seventies the number of Swedish inhabitants was substantially increased through direct immigration from Sweden. In 1870 they were strong enough to organize a Lutheran church, which was for a time the only Swedish church in the place, being followed in 1888 by a Baptist church, which, however, has made but small acquisitions. The Swedes of Sycamore have taken active part in local politics, and several of them have held public office. In the matter of fraternal orders the Sycamore Swedes will not bear comparison with other Swedish-American centers.

In the year 1880 there were in Sycamore and vicinity about 1,000 Swedish people and in 1905 some 1,500. Those living in the city are engaged in various commercial pursuits, many of them being in business for themselves. A number of the retired farmers of the neighborhood are now residing in town, enjoying in their old age the fruits of their labors in earlier years.

Before closing this brief historical sketch of the Swedish colony at Sycamore, we desire to give an account of the interesting visit paid to Sycamore years ago by Christina Nilsson, the renowned Swedish singer. In December, 1870, the Swedish nightingale appeared in Chicago, captivating the moneyed aristocracy of the city at a grand concert, and being herself feted at a splendid banquet given by Swedish-Americans headed by the Svea Society. The Swedes in Sycamore, hearing of these affairs, were seized with a natural desire to see and hear the prima donna. This desire was strengthened by the fact that relatives of the great singer were living in Sycamore, as well as other persons who knew her from the time when, as "Stina from Snugge," she traveled around singing at country fairs in Småland.

But there was still another reason why they wished to have her visit Sycamore, and that a weighty one. Twenty years before, Jenny Lind had given a handsome sum to the fund for the building of the St. Ansgarius Church of Chicago and subsequently donated a valuable communion service to the same church. Why, then, they reasoned, should not Christina Nilsson visit her own people at Sycamore and by her voice assist in raising the money needed for a church for the congregation organized that same year? They met and counseled, resulting in the appointment of a committee to go to Chicago and make their wishes known to the singer. In order to make assurance doubly sure, they appointed on this committee Anders Ingemansson, a man whom Christina Nilsson well knew. In former days while Anders was living at Löfhult, a part of the property belonging to the iron works at Huseby, Småland, he often hauled loads of ironware from the factory to Vexiö or Ljungby, and many a time the little flaxen-haired violin player from Snugge got a ride with him to and from the fairs held in these towns. Would she have the heart to refuse a request made by him? Hardly.

The other two members of the committee were one Gustafsson and Andrew Johnson. Through the kind offices of Rev. Erland Carlsson they obtained an audience with the singer, who consented instantly. Certainly she would come and sing for them! But Strakosch, her impresario, said no. Suppose she would catch a cold and become indisposed but for one evening—it would entail the loss of thousands of dollars. Or if there should be a train wreck and she would break an arm or a leg, what a dilemma they would all be in! Such was his reasoning, concluding with a repeated refusal to let her go.

But the singer made light of the objections of her manager, mildly ridiculing his foolish arguments, until he had to submit. Not wanting to break her engagement in Chicago, Christina Nilsson was compelled to go to Sycamore on Christmas Day, which fell on a Sunday. She was accompanied by the singers and musicians of her company, a number of prominent Swedish citizens of Chicago and, last but not least, Strakosch himself, who went in order to see that no harm came to his Swedish nightingale.

The concert in Sycamore was given in the American Methodist church. Christina Nilsson, as usual, made an absolute conquest. Probably never before had she sung Gounod's "Ave Maria" with such profound feeling as at this occasion. She gave two other numbers, besides. Her American hearers were as charmed as her own countrymen. But the concert given in the church, to which an admission fee of three dollars was charged, had to be supplemented by a popular concert, in order to give the poorer classes an opportunity to hear her. At this concert, held in Wilkins Hall, she again sang "Ave Maria" and, in order to get into complete touch with her audience, now almost exclusively Swedish, rendered several Swedish ballads in the most approved style of little "Stina from Snugge." The net profit of these two concerts amounted to about $1,000. The amount appropriated to the church building fund we cannot exactly state.

Ingemansson, the old friend of Christina Nilsson, who had engaged in the carpenter's trade in Sycamore, died there about 1890. Her relatives, who doubtless are still living there, are Anna, Magni, Gustaf, Emil, Ida and Oscar Nilsson, the children of Petter Nilsson and Eva, his wife, now deceased. She was a cousin of the great singer. Another relative of the latter is Mrs. Carrie Bohlin, who bears the same relationship to the singer as the children of Petter and Eva Nilsson.

MISCELLANEOUS SETTLEMENTS

The previous sketches deal with the history of only the older and larger Swedish settlements in Illinois. But there are quite a number of later ones, large and small, many of which, especially those of recent date, by reason of rapid growth and the importance attained, would deserve a place in this series. But we are constrained to limit ourselves to the bare mention of their name and the time of founding. In many cases it has been possible to give the year with absolute certainty, while in many others the time can only be approximated. In the latter instances, the year stated is the earliest in which Swedes are definitely known to have lived in the respective localities, not, however, precluding the possibility of earlier settlement by individual Swedes.

Following are the older of the smaller Swedish settlements of which the time of first settlement is positively known:

Settlement.	County	Founded
Lafayette	Stark	1846
Henderson Grove	Knox	1849
Beaver,	Iroquois	1853
Pecatonica	Winnebago	1854
Avon	Fulton	1854
Toulon	Stark	1855
Wyanet	Bureau	1855
New Windsor	Mercer	1859
New Boston,	Mercer	1859

Following are the smaller Swedish settlements of more recent date, the year of first settlement being definitely known:

Settlement.	County	Founded
Coal Valley	Rock Island	1863
Farmersville	McLean	1863
Bloomington	McLean	1865
Woodhull	Henry	1865
Aledo	Mercer	1866
Roseville	Warren	1867
Nekoma	Henry	1867
Evanston	Cook	1868
Lockport	Will	1768
Danville	Vermillion	1869
Ophiem	Henry	1870
Lynn	Henry	1870
Osco	Henry	1870
Cambridge	Henry	1870
Donovan	Iroquois	1872

Earlier Swedish settlements where the year of founding is doubtful are:

Elgin, Kane County		1852
Aurora, Kane County		1857

More recent Swedish settlements of doubtful date are as follows:

Settlement	County	Founded
Neoga	Cumberland	1862
Varna	Marshall	1868
Joliet	Will	1870
Biggsville	Henderson	1872
Lemont	Cook	1872
Kirkland,	DeKalb	1872
Highwood	Lake	1874
New Bedford	Bureau	1874
Rankin	Ford	1875
Port Byron	Rock Island	1875
Prophetstown	Whiteside	1875
Morrison	Whiteside	1875
Oregon	Ogle	1876

Settlement	County	Founded
Sibley	Ford	1879
Gibson City	Ford	1881
Peoria,	Peoria	1883
Streator	La Salle	1884
Putnam,	Putnam	1885
La Grange	Cook	1887
Clarence	Ford	1887
Morris	Grundy	1889
Gladstone	Henderson	1889
Canton	Fulton	1890
Stronghurst	Henderson	1892
Waukegan	Lake	1892
Wenona	Marshall	1892
Lily Lake	Kane	1894
Belvidere	Boone	1894
Cable	Mercer	1895
Utica	Fulton	1900
Granville	Putnam	1902
Sandwich	DeKalb	1904

Beyond this individual Swedes with or without families are to be found in almost every part of the state.

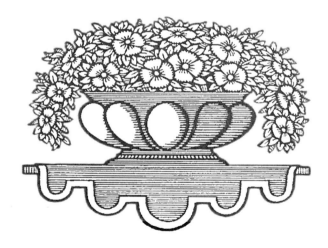

CHAPTER VI.

The Swedish Methodist-Episcopal Church

Preparatory Work

IT was through Olof G. Hedström that Methodism first was introduced among the Swedes and other Scandinavians in New York and later by his brother Jonas Hedström among the Swedish settlers in Illinois. A sketch of the life and work of Jonas Hedström has been given among those of the first Swedes in Illinois. We proceed to give a brief account of the church founded by these two brothers, the earliest Swedish religious denomination in America.

Jonas Hedström preached his first Swedish sermon December 15, 1846, in a little blockhouse in the woods about three miles southwest of Victoria, the same house where Olof Olsson, the advance representative of Erik Jansson, and later Erik Jansson himself, received the first shelter after arriving at their destination in the West. At this same occasion the first Swedish Methodist congregation was organized, consisting of five members, namely, Hedström and his wife, Andrew Hjelm and wife, and Peter Newberg. At Christmas time, a couple of weeks later, the first Swedish Methodist quarterly meeting was held in the same cabin, when several new members were welcomed. For some time Jonas Hedström continued as the spiritual leader of the little group of Swedish Methodists, meanwhile pursuing his blacksmith's trade. But as the flock grew larger, he gave way to the urgings of the members to devote his whole time to gospel work.

In August, 1848, he was received on probation into the American Rock River Conference and appointed missionary among the Swedish settlers. Thereafter he devoted himself almost exclusively to preaching and soon had ample opportunity to display his great capacity as an organizer. After making a few visits to a certain place he would proceed to organize a congregation there, and soon had to divide his time among a number of places. He labored with such untiring energy that within the year he had founded churches at Andover and Galesburg and was able to report to the Conference in 1849 no less than six charges, viz., Victoria, Andover, Galesburg, Lafayette, Moline and Rock Island, aggregating sixty members in full connection and thirty-three on probation.

At first Jonas Hedström was entirely alone in the work in this mission field. Until the arrival of L. P. Esbjörn, the Lutheran minister, in 1849, he was also the only Swedish clergyman in the entire West. Soon afterward he received his first assistant in John Brown, who became itinerant preacher among the widely scattered settlers. In the autumn of 1849 Hedström got a second assistant, C. P. Agrelius, who came on from New York with a letter of recommendation from the

The Log Cabin in which the First Swedish M. E. Church
in America was Organized

elder Hedström. In the spring of 1850, this man was sent to a Norwegian Methodist mission in Wisconsin, but the same year he received new reinforcements in the persons of Andrew Ericson and A. G. Swedberg, who soon after their arrival from Sweden in the late fall of 1849 joined the Methodist Church and subsequently became traveling missionaries. In May, 1850, a new mission field was opened in New Sweden, Jefferson county, Iowa. The records of the conference meeting of 1850 show that the Swedish mission in connection with the Rock River Conference at that early date comprised four circuits with six preachers and 195 church members. The preachers were the five already mentioned, together with Peter Cassel, who was stationed at New Sweden, Ia.

In 1852 two more preachers were added, viz., Peter Challman, or Källman, and Erik Shogren, or Sjögren, who at the behest of Hedström devoted themselves to church work after having returned from a gold-seeking excursion to California late in the summer of 1851, but were not accepted on probation by the Rock River Conference until September, 1853. In January of that year the number of workers was again increased by the addition of S. B. Newman, who for two years had been assistant to Rev. O. G. Hedström on the Bethel ship in New York harbor. Now he was sent to Chicago to take charge of the Swedish Methodist Church which had been organized there the previous month, December, 1852. The next addition was made in 1854, when Peter Newberg, Hedström's former helper in the blacksmith shop at Victoria, where he had been under the spiritual influence of his employer, exchanged the anvil for the pulpit. The following year the corps of preachers received in Victor Witting a very valuable member who, after diverse experiences in this country, was won over to Methodism while on a visit to New York, having become familiar with the church during his previous residence in Illinois. All these preachers labored principally within the state, but incidentally extended their operations to Indiana and Iowa.

In spite of these reinforcements, the work of Hedström himself rather increased than lightened, as the enlargement of the field compelled him to make frequent long journeys to the widely scattered churches in order to exercise proper supervision of the work. His field now extended from Chicago west as far as New Sweden, Ia. Opposing forces notwithstanding, the progress of Methodism among the Swedish settlers was continuous. In 1856, at the conference meeting held in Peoria, all the Swedish churches of Illinois, Indiana and Iowa were combined into a special district with Jonas Hedström as its presiding elder. However, he was not long to hold this position, for in his work as pioneer missionary and on the long, difficult journeys he was constantly compelled to make, his health had been undermined to such an extent that he was forced to retire after one year. On May 11, 1859, less than two years later, death ended his career.

The Co-Workers of Jonas Hedström—John Brown

The first assistant of Jonas Hedström in the missionary field was John Brown. He was of Danish descent, born on the island of Als Dec. 23, 1813, but having been brought up among German-speaking people, he acquired that language and spoke Danish or Swedish with a marked German brogue.

Brown came to America as a sailor prior to May 14, 1843, when he was married in New York city to Johanna Baden, a German woman from Altona, who proved a true helpmeet to him.

In New York, presumably, he came in contact with one of the early emigrant parties of Erik Janssonists, joined the sect, and in 1847 we find him in Bishop Hill. Dissatisfied with the prophet and his colony, Brown soon left, together with a number of others, the deserters settling at Lafayette, Stark county, eight miles east of Victoria, where they obtained employment from an American named Hodgeson. The energetic sailor at once joined the Methodists, whose tenets he favored. His slight acquaintance with Hedström, formed during the visits of the latter to Bishop Hill, was now deepened by more intimate intercourse with him. Finding Brown suitable timber for the ministry, Hedström lost no time in urging him to enter that vocation.

Ere long, Brown was in the field as a missionary, preaching first in and around Lafayette and Victoria, then in Andover and Rock Island. In the last-named place his efforts were especially successful. After having been received into the Conference in 1852, he was sent to labor among the Norwegians in Leland and Fox River, LaSalle county. As a consequence of overwork and privations his health soon broke down, compelling him to retire from active service after three years. He was subsequently employed as bridge tender at Freedom, halfway between Leland and Ottawa, having charge of the local church in the meantime. Some time later he removed to Iowa, locating in the little town of Nevada, Storey county. Despite ill health he traveled about the country preaching in English, German and Swedish in the new settlements, even now gathering many into the Methodist fold. Brown was a man of great zeal, a live, vivid and warmhearted preacher, and a very successful revivalist. When he got especially warmed up, both by his text and the summer heat on the prairies, he would throw off his coat and neckwear, and sometimes his vest, and go on preaching with a vim that was overpowering. Although sincerely devoted to Methodism, he was not fanatical or intolerant. "Let others stand by their flag; I'll stand by mine," was his motto, expressed in his bluff seaman's vernacular.

While engaged one day in painting a fence at his home in Nevada, he suffered an apoplectic stroke which ended his life. This was in 1875, presumably in the month of September.

Rev. Carl Petter Agrelius

The second in order of the ten assistants of Hedström during the first decade was Carl Petter Agrelius, in temperament, energy and mental make-up a complete contrast to Brown. He also had been assistant to Rev. O. G. Hedström on the Bethel ship in New York, serving there 1848-49, and subsequently as Jonas Hedström's assistant in the Victoria circuit. He became the first Swedish Methodist preacher among the Scandinavian population in Wisconsin. Agrelius was born in Östergötland Oct. 22, 1798, studied at the University of Upsala and was ordained to the ministry, very likely in 1822. After serving for twenty-six years as a minister of the state church of Sweden, during the latter years as curate of the parish of Pelarne, in northern Småland, he felt an inner call to go to America and take up Lutheran missionary work among the growing masses of emigrants. Together with a large party, he arrived in New York in 1848, probably in the month of October. Rev. Hedström and his alert assistant, Peter Bergner, who were constantly on the lookout for Swedes, went on board at once to bid the newcomers welcome, give advice and assistance and invite them to attend the service on board the Bethel ship that evening. By his dress and general appearance Agrelius at once attracted their attention, and on addressing him they learned that he was a minister of the Swedish state church.

Agrelius stopped in New York, where he attempted to build up a Swedish Lutheran congregation, an enterprise which, however, proved for too great for his capacity. He was devout, forsooth, and had the best of intentions, but lacked energy, enthusiasm and other qualities requisite to leadership. To him it was more natural to be led than to lead. Finding himself unable to organize a Lutheran church, he began to associate more intimately with Hedström, attended class meetings and services on board the missionary ship and preached there occasionally, at the request of Hedström. Before long he was a Methodist, heart and soul, joined their church, was licensed as local preacher a short time afterward and was engaged as Hedström's assistant on the Bethel ship for a year, or till the fall of 1849, when he was sent to Victoria to assist the younger Hedström. Together with E. Shogren and other recent arrivals from Sweden who, upon Hedström's advice, decided to settle at Victoria, he left New York, arriving at his destination in October. During the following six months he went from place to place in the surrounding circuit, preaching in the houses of the settlers.

At the solicitation of an influential American Methodist in Chicago or Evanston, who took a great interest in the Scandinavians and guaranteed support to the preacher for one year, Agrelius was sent to Spring Prairie, Wis., in the early part of 1850 in order to begin work among the Norwegian settlements thereabout. In July, 1851, he was received into the Wisconsin Conference on probation and sent as missionary to the Norwegians in Primrose, in that state. Here he remained for three years, till the fall of 1854, when he was sent to the Swedish Methodist mission in St. Paul and, a year later, to Marine, Chisago county, Minn. At this place he built a log cabin for himself on a piece of land he had purchased near Big Lake, and remained here for a number of years, preaching to his countrymen in the large surrounding settlements.

In the spring of 1860 he moved back to Wisconsin and served the churches of Coon Prairie, Hart Prairie, Primrose and Highland; in 1866 he was declared superannuated, but continued for another year in charge of the Norwegian Methodist church of Willow River, whereupon his pastoral career ended. He now went back to live in retirement on his little farm in Marine, Minn., remaining there until 1878, when he removed to the home of his youngest son at Deer Park, St. Croix county, Wis. At that place he died August 18, 1881, at the mature age of eighty-three. On the same date twelve years after, his widow, Anna Elisabet, died at the age of eighty-four.

Agrelius was a man of tractable and peaceful disposition. Among his associates he was talkative, benign and social. Hospitable almost to a fault, he was ready to entertain in his little log cabin every wayfarer who passed, whether stranger or friend. He was a man of thorough education but limited executive ability. His sermons were dry and wearisome to listen to, their contents being in substance good, but lacking in depth.

Rev. Andrew Ericson

The third in order of Hedström's co-laborers was Andrew Ericson. Born at Röste, Bollnäs parish, Helsingland, July 8, 1815, he was converted in early youth and soon thereafter began to preach. He and his wife were among those who accompanied Rev. L. P. Esbjörn to America in 1849 and came with him to Andover. Ericson did not long remain there. Urged by Rev. Hedström, who soon after their arrival visited Andover, he, together with a number of other newcomers, decided to locate at Victoria. Almost immediately he joined the Methodist Church and became a faithful and ever willing assistant in whom Rev. Hedström reposed implicit trust. Though not naturally brilliant, he proved a very able preacher. The partisanship so prevalent in those early days did not enter into his mental make-up.

After laboring for a few years in Illinois, he was sent to New Sweden, Ia., in 1854, to assume charge of the Swedish Methodist congregation at that place and to exercise general supervision of the surrounding field, which at first was very large, extending from Burlington west to Swede Bend, a distance of two hundred miles. It is doubtful whether any other Swedish Methodist clergyman ever kept up services at points so far apart as those regularly visited by Andrew Ericson during the first part of the time he labored in this field.

At the close of April, 1854, the year of his coming to the state, a church had been organized in Swede Bend, Webster county, 175 miles west of New Sweden. No less than thirteen times in two years he traveled from New Sweden to Swede Bend, a distance both ways of more than three hundred miles through wild and for the most part unsettled country. Not infrequently his own countrymen would refuse to shelter him, compelling him to spend the nights under the open sky— all because he was a Methodist preacher. Such was the partisan zeal among the church people at that time.

In 1856 Ericson was sent to Swede Bend and labored there exclusively until 1860, when he was sent back to Illinois and stationed at the Norwegian settlement in Leland. The following year he was minister in charge at Andover, which position he held for two years. At the conference of 1863, he requested that he be placed on the retired list, which being done he returned to Swede Bend, Ia., where he owned a farm. Here he spent his last days. Sept. 11, 1878, he was found dead just outside of his house, evidently struck down by apoplexy.

Andrew Ericson was a plain man of the people, with little book learning, his opportunities for study having been limited. Yet by dint of zeal and great devotion to his calling his labors were richly blessed. He was a man of peaceful and benign disposition, who made no enemies.

Rev. Anders Gustaf Swedberg

Anders Gustaf Swedberg, the fourth of Rev. Jonas Hedström's auxiliary workers, was born in 1827 or 1828 in the city of Hudiksvall or near there. In early age he joined the so-called "Luther Readers," or Hedbergians, and occasionally appeared as exhorter at their meetings. He accompanied Rev. L. P. Esbjörn to this country in 1849. When they arrived at Andover, an epidemic of sickness was raging there, and lodging could not be secured, so Swedberg and others proceeded to Galesburg. There he at once came in contact with the Methodists and soon came to feel at home among them. In the spring of 1850 he joined the Methodist Church and became exhorter and subsequently local preacher. The following year he was received on probation into the Rock River Conference. It was then resolved that Swedberg and Andrew Ericson should alternately have charge of the congregations of the Victoria-Galesburg circuit, principally that of Galesburg, where Swedberg resided.

At this time Swedberg was a young man, only twenty-one years of age; he possessed a good education, was a gifted speaker, had a pleasing manner, was full of fire and enthusiasm, qualities by which he won the hearts of all. It was the general opinion that in him Rev. Hedström had obtained one of his most valuable aids. But these expectations were not fulfilled. –In the spring of 1852 an American Baptist clergyman by the name of Barry, a very eloquent man, came to Galesburg and by his sermons on the doctrine of baptism quickly stirred up the whole community. Among quite a number of Swedes who were converted to the Baptist faith was Swedberg. He left the Methodist Church, was baptized anew and in 1853 was appointed minister of a newly organized church at Village Creek, Ia. He at first served for two years, or until 1855, when the church was left without a preacher until the autumn of 1856; then Swedberg was again called there, accepting the charge. In 1864 he was still in charge of this church, but since that time little is known of him and it is not known whether he is still among the living.

Rev. Peter Cassel

Peter Cassel, to whom frequent reference has been made, also was one of Rev. Hedström's co-workers. He was born in Åsbo parish, Östergötland, Oct. 13, 1790. In his native place he was a miller and afterwards foreman on a large country estate. From 1825 to 1830 this locality experienced a general revivalist movement in which Cassel joined. Cassel later became the leader of a party of emigrants who left Kisa, Östergötland, in 1845, destined for Pine Lake, Wis., but on reaching New York decided to change their route and went to Iowa, where they founded New Sweden, the first Swedish settlement in that state.

When in November, 1850, the Swedish Methodist Church in New Sweden was organized, Cassel was one of the first, if not the very first, to sign for membership. He soon became local preacher. The following year he was appointed minister in charge, serving in that capacity for three years, till the fall of 1854. Two years later he was ordained deacon of the Methodist Church. His strength soon failed, however, compelling him to resign. Cassel died March 4, 1857.

"Father" Cassel, as he was reverently styled by the people of New Sweden, was a man of the old stock, honest and true. He was the soul of the church as well as of the community, and was looked up to by all with respect and confidence.

Rev. Peter Challman

Among all the co-workers and assistants of Hedström, Peter Challman, or Källman, both as a revivalist and a pioneer preacher, took foremost rank. Being a man of exceptional energy, he would undoubtedly have attained still greater prominence under more favorable circumstances. He was born at the Voxna factory, in Helsingland, 1823. In the fall of 1844 he joined the Erik Janssonists and the following spring began to conduct religious meetings, preaching in accordance with the tenets of the sect. He was soon chosen one of Erik Jansson's apostles and sent out by him to preach. By Källman's preaching many were won over. But to preach Erik Janssonism was fraught with grave peril. Källman was twice mobbed by the enraged populace; once he was near being killed, another time he was arrested and brought to the Gefle prison, the trial however, resulting in his release. These experiences impelled him to leave the country. With a party of other Erik Janssonists he left Stockholm for America June 26, 1846, arriving at Bishop Hill Oct. 28th, four months later.

Here he found conditions altogether at variance with the claims of the prophet and others, and in June, 1847, he left the colony in disgust, taking up a temporary abode in Lafayette. There he became acquainted with Hedström and other Methodists. In the fall of 1847 he removed to Galesburg, where he worked as a carpenter for two years, preaching occasionally to his fellow countrymen at the request of Hedström. It was at this time that the gold fever was at its height. Following the discovery of gold in California in 1848, the newspapers were filled daily with wonderful stories of marvelously rich strikes. The air was full of wild rumors. Wherever people met, whether in the street, in their homes or in church, they talked of gold, nothing but gold. Everywhere, people were seized with an irresistible longing for the glittering gold fields.

Many Swedes were among those smitten by the epidemic. We have noted that a Swedish party of goldseekers set out from Andover. In Galesburg another similar party was organized under the leadership of the energetic Challman. This party of twelve young Swedes, formed in January, 1850, started on March 14th on the 2,000 mile journey to the gold country. Following are the names of the men composing the party: Peter Challman, Erik Shogren, Jonas Hellström, George Challman, Victor Witting, Louis Larson, Peter Newberg, Charles Peterson, Olof Hedström, C. Alexander, Peter Magnus (surname unknown) and one Gustafson. On Sundays the party rested, Peter Challman, the leader, conducting divine services for his men. On July 14th the party reached their destination in California.

The result of the adventurous trip fell far short of expectations. Gold was found, to be sure, but not in such quantities as they had hoped for and far from sufficient to repay them for the hardships and perils of their long journey. Victor Witting remained until 1852, and Charles Peterson and Gustafson staid permanently, but the main party returned in July, 1851, after one year's work in the gold mines. In Chagres, now Aspinwall, on the return trip Alexander lost all his money in gambling and then disappeared. In despair over the unsatisfactory result of the trip, Peter Magnus drowned himself by jumping overboard shortly before the steamer by which the party returned reached Chicago. Charles Peterson died in Los Angeles in 1898 at the age of eighty. He was a member of the Swedish Methodist Church of that city. George Challman is still living in Galesburg. Olof Hedström died in 1904, near Victoria. Erik Shogren died Jan. 2, 1906. Of him and Newberg we will speak later. Upon his return Hellström located at Victoria, engaging in business, from which, proving unprofitable, he soon retired. He enlisted at the outbreak of the Civil War, served in the Union army as a non-commissioned officer for a time and succumbed in the Arkansas campaign at a time and place unknown. Gustafson was taken ill after working in the diggings that summer and remained in California until his death. Louis Larson separated from the party at Salt Lake City, but proceeded to California, whence he returned to Victoria after a few months, bought land and became a prosperous farmer. He married Christin Olson, who bore him four sons and one daughter. He died a few years ago at his old homestead, about a mile from Victoria, where his son Just. A. Larson now lives with his wife, Nancy Elizabeth, a daughter of George Challman. The Larson family were worthy and respected members of the Methodist Church in Victoria.

Peter Challman returned via Panama and New York to Illinois, settling in Victoria, where he was at first employed as a house builder. The Methodist mission work among the local Swedes having grown quite extensive, Rev. Hedström, who knew Challman both from Lafayette and Galesburg, requested him to devote himself exclusively to this work, although Challman was not even a member of the Methodist Church. Challman acceded and began preaching. On Dec. 31, 1851, he joined the church at Victoria on probation, was later accredited as local minister, was accepted into the Rock River Conference on probation in 1853, at Chicago, and ordained deacon, was for a year itinerant preacher, then served the churches at Andover and Rock Island in 1854-5 and during the next two years preached in Victoria, Galesburg and the neighboring district. Together with Shogren he took a trip to Minnesota in 1854 or 1855 to visit the Swedish settlements there.

When all hope that Hedström would recover sufficiently to resume work was at an end, Challman was appointed presiding elder of the Swedish district in 1857, at the recommendation of Hedström himself. In this capacity Challman served with credit until 1865, when he was assigned to Bishop Hill. Here he labored for a year until the fall of 1866, when he undertook a trip to Sweden, "not for Christ, but in his own interest," he explained.

On his return to America he settled on his farm in Knox county, left the Methodist Episcopal Church for the Free Methodists and began missionary work in and about Victoria in behalf of the latter denomination. He remained with the Free Methodists for four years, preaching and laboring at his own expense. During this time he built a Free Methodist church for the Swedes at Center Prairie, seven miles southwest of Victoria. When the Swedish congregation was dissolved, this edifice passed into the hands of an American congregation. Subsequently Challman gradually transferred his interests from the mission field to the corn field. In his ambition to acquire large tracts of land, he incurred heavy debts which, during and after the panic of the early seventies, he had great difficulty in paying.

In 1884 he removed to northwestern Iowa. He now regretted that he ever deserted his pastoral calling and the "old Methodist Church," as he styled it. In order to correct his error, in part at least, he joined the American M. E. Church at Galva, Ia., in 1890, subsequently taking part in several annual meetings of the Iowa Conference. A severe siege of influenza undermined his health, and after having been confined to the sickbed for half a year, he died in Challer, Ia., July 8, 1900, aged 77 years. His remains were borne to the grave by his six sons.

In several respects Peter Challman was a remarkable man. He seemed a born leader. He was a man of imposing personality, designed to attract attention in any company. Picture to yourself a man broad of shoulder and of powerful build, massive head, wide forehead, a bushy head of hair, lively dark-blue eyes, heavy eyebrows, a beardless face, the expression of which indicated energy, resoluteness and fearlessness, add to this a powerful bass voice that easily filled the largest edifice, and you have a fair image of Peter Challman in his prime. To those who did not know him well he appeared somewhat coarse and lacking in the finer sensibilities. But this was far from true. Under the rough surface of the man there beat a warm, sympathetic, benevolent heart. He was a forceful speaker, though not a finished orator, and knew better than most preachers how to deal with hardened hearts. Among the Methodists stories are still being told of the revivals that followed upon his strenuous preaching. During his clerical career Challman is said to have taken part in the organization of no less than twenty-two churches. In the course of a single year, it is said, he gained 800 converts to the Methodist belief. It was while he was presiding elder that the Swedish denominational organ, known as "Sändebudet," was established.

Rev. Erik Shogren

In Erik Shogren Jonas Hedström obtained one of his most eloquent and popular co-workers. There was something about his manner of resenting the gospel truths that appealed irresistibly to his hearers. This pioneer among Swedish Methodists doubtless was instrumental

Rev. Erik Shogren

in gaining large numbers for the church during his long period of activity.

Shogren was born Jan. 26, 1824, at Gnarp, Helsingland. As a boy he attended the village school and at the age of fourteen became a blacksmith's apprentice, afterward following that trade for many years. In the summer of 1849 he left Gefle on board the brig "Solide," bound for America, arriving at New York sixty-three days later. Here he was met by Peter Bergner, assistant to Hedström, and invited to attend services on board the Bethel ship. Hedström conducted the meeting with his usual vivacity. Shogren, being one of the "readers" from the old country, had attended many of their conventicles, but this was something altogether different. Notwithstanding the strange method of preaching, Shogren felt strongly drawn to Methodism, and Rev. Hedström easily persuaded him to join his brother, the younger Hedström, at Victoria. On his arrival he was unfavorably impressed with the primitive appearance of the settlement. He had expected to find something quite different, and soon left in disappointment, departing for Galesburg after a few weeks and remaining there for three months. In February, 1850, he joined the Methodist Church, becoming a member of the congregation there organized by Hedström the foregoing autumn. In March he joined the party of goldseekers organized in Galesburg and made the trip to California, returning the following year. He then settled in Victoria and began to conduct meetings and preach throughout that circuit, which then embraced Victoria, Galesburg, Andover, Rock Island, Moline and many other points.

At Hedström's suggestion he abandoned his trade and devoted himself wholly to ministerial work. The following year he was received on probation into the Rock River Conference, to which the Swedish missions in Illinois and Iowa belonged at that time. In 1854 he was ordained deacon and was made elder the year following. During the first two years he lived at Victoria while spending almost all his time traveling about the extensive circuit. In 1855 he was sent to preach in Chicago, where, despite stubborn opposition, he met with splendid success. In 1859 he was transferred to the Minnesota Conference, acting as minister in charge at St. Paul the first year and subsequently for three years as presiding elder of the Scandinavian district. In 1864-5 he served in Chicago, going from there to Boston, where, as assistant at the Seamen's Mission, he endeavored to organize a Swedish Methodist church, a task cut short by an illness which compelled him to return to Minnesota. During the years 1866-9 he had charge of the little church at Marine, then took a rest for one year, subsequently going back to Illinois. He was stationed at Bishop Hill until 1876, when he was transferred to the California Conference and placed in charge of the newly organized church at San Francisco. There he remained for over five years, and was then at his own request transferred to the Swedish Northwestern Conference and sent to Beaver.

In this field he labored for only a year, subsequently serving the church at Galesburg in 1883-4 and the one at Rockford in 1884-5. Having been made presiding elder for the Chicago district the latter year, he served as such for two years and afterward as pastor in South Chicago, his last charge, for the same length of time.

In 1889 age and illness compelled him to retire from active work. He withdrew to his little country place near Red Wing, Minn., where he resided until 1903, when with his wife he removed to Napa, Cal., joining their youngest daughter, Mrs. Emma Farman, who is living there. He died in Napa on Jan. 2, 1906, after a short illness.

Like most other pioneers of Swedish Methodism in America, Shogren was a self-taught man. By assiduous studies and self-culture he sought to fill the gaps in his education. His favorite study was history, and from its pages he often drew valuable lessons for himself and his hearers. By nature eloquent, and possessing a pleasing voice, he trained himself year by year until attaining a high degree of skill and finish as a public speaker. This together with his rare affability gave him his remarkable power and influence over those who heard him.

Rev. Sven Bernhard Newman

In January, 1845, the same year that Rev. O. G. Hedström, on Whitsunday, May 25th, preached his first sermon in broken English on board the Bethel ship in New York harbor, a young Swede appeared for the first time at a place near Mobile, Ala., and preached Methodism in equally faltering English to the Americans of that place. This Swedish pioneer preacher in the sunny south, who later became one of the pathfinders and standard-bearers of Methodism, both east and west, was Rev. Sven Bernhard Newman.

Newman was born Sept. 15, 1812, at Höganäs, Skåne, had a careful bringing up and obtained employment as salesman with one of his brothers, a merchant of Landskrona. After working there eight years, he returned to his birthplace and taught private school several years. Another of his brothers had emigrated long before and established himself in business at Mobile. Sven followed in 1842 and for two years dealt in clothing and groceries not without success. Through his brother he was brought in contact with the Methodists, whom he joined in 1844. Without much knowledge of English, he shortly afterward began speaking at Methodist meetings. Friends who thought they detected in the young man more than ordinary ability urged him to consecrate his life to the pastoral calling. After some hesitation he took the advice and began to study theology under the guidance of an American Methodist clergyman. In 1845 he was received on probation into the Alabama Conference, was ordained deacon in 1847 and elder in 1849.

Newman's first field of labor was the Campbelltown circuit in Florida, where he was stationed from 1845 to 1847. Subsequently assigned to another field, with headquarters at Milton, a pleasant little town not far from Pensacola, he labored zealously there for two years until transferred to Landerdale, Miss. In 1851 Newman was called to assist Rev. O. G. Hedström on the Bethel ship at New York, this

Rev. Sven Bernhard Newman

being the beginning of his work among Swedish people, a work which he pursued with untiring zeal as long as his physical strength permitted. After spending two years in New York, he was assigned to Chicago in 1853 to gather the scattered members of the Swedish Methodist Church organized several years before by the Hedström brothers. With his characteristic zeal and energy he took up the task, succeeding not only in collecting the dispersed flock but also in having a house of worship erected. The edifice was built at Illinois street and dedicated in 1854. Part of the building funds were solicited in his former fields in the South. With headquarters in Chicago, he made regular trips to other points, both in Indiana and Illinois, founding churches in Poolsville and Attica in the former state, and St.

Charles and Beaver in the latter. In Chicago, together with Consul Schneidau and Revs. Unonius and Carlsson, Newman labored arduously among poor plague-stricken Swedish immigrants, a task trying indeed, but productive of blessed results.

In September, 1855, Newman was again assigned to New York to assist Rev. Hedström on board the Bethel mission ship. After four years he was sent to Jamestown, N. Y., where he was placed in charge of an extensive circuit, comprising the neighboring points Sugar Grove, Wrightsville, Frewsbury and others. He remained in Jamestown for seven years, 1859-66, afterwards going to the Central Illinois Conference on assignment to Galesburg, where he was stationed for two years. At the conference of 1868, he was appointed presiding elder of the Chicago district, then including Indiana, Illinois, Iowa and Kansas. He held this position for five years, in the meantime acting as solicitor for the Swedish Methodist Theological Seminary at Evanston, for whose benefit he raised a considerable amount.

Rev. Newman's subsequent assignments were: Rockford, 1873-5; Wataga and Peoria, 1875-7; Batavia and Geneva, 1877-9; Evanston, 1879-82; Moline, 1882-4; Omaha, 1884-5; Chicago, as city missionary, 1885-8; Evanston, as solicitor for the seminary, 1888-90.

In 1890 he was declared superannuated, but continued to serve until 1899, preaching at Moreland, in the Emanuel Church of Chicago, at Austin and, lastly, at Ottawa. Having lost his first wife in 1885, he remarried in old age. In the early nineties, at the request of the Swedish Northwestern Conference, he published his autobiography, a very minute account of his life and labors. Enfeebled by the burden of years, he died in his home in Chicago on Oct. 27, 1902, at the mature age of ninety.

In his years of activity Newman was a faithful laborer in the Lord's vineyard. While not an orator in the common acceptance of the term, yet his words left a deep and lasting impression. What he lacked in brilliancy and scholarly attainments was amply made up in zeal and devotion to his calling.

Rev. Peter Newberg

One of the first five members of the first Swedish Methodist church was Peter Newberg, afterward one of Jonas Hedström's most faithful and reliable fellow workers. Newberg was born at Luleå, Jan. 7, 1818. At the age of eight he lost his father, a sailor, and as a boy of fourteen he also went to sea, driven by the necessity of contributing to the support of his widowed mother. For fifteen years he shipped with merchantmen under various flags.

In the spring of 1846 he mustered at Gefle as ship's carpenter on a vessel bound for New York carrying a large party of Eric Janssonists. On reaching harbor he left the vessel and accompanied the emigrants to Bishop Hill, but soon left the colony in disappointment, going first to Lafayette and then to Victoria, where he remained with Hedström over winter as his helper in making plows. The following spring he left for Peoria, where he was employed for some time in the building trade, working for a Swedish contractor or architect named Ulricson, who had lived there for so many years that he had forgotten his mother tongue. In the fall he returned to Victoria and was there married.

Rev. Peter Newberg

In the spring of 1850 he joined the aforementioned party of goldseekers and went to California. Returning in 1857, he located at Victoria, where he had a farm, and also engaged in house building in partnership with Peter Challman. In 1853, when the latter left his trade to devote himself exclusively to preaching, Newberg continued as building contractor on his own account. Among other buildings erected by him was the Swedish Methodist Church edifice at Victoria, dedicated at midsummer, 1854.

While en route to America, he was subject to the religious influence of his fellow travelers, the Erik Janssonists; upon his arrival he came under the influence of Hedström, and at a camp meeting in the Victoria grove, in the summer of 1853, he was converted and accepted the Methodist faith. Thereafter he began to take turns with the other preachers in making circuit visits, and in 1856 he was received on probation by the Peoria Conference and assigned to New Sweden, Ia., as minister in charge. There he labored for two years, besides establishing a small congregation in the country just west of Burlington. For a year, 1858-9, he served the Andover circuit and the following year, 1859-60, that of Galesburg. His ordination as deacon took place in 1857, and in 1860 he was promoted to the office of elder. From Galesburg he was transferred to Victoria, where he served for two years, until 1862. His subsequent fields were: New Sweden, Ia., 1864-5, Rockford 1865-6, Victoria 1866-72, Swedona 1872-3. After that he was not directly in charge of any church, but lived on his farm at Victoria. When occasion required, however, he would assist the other preachers in their work. Thus, in 1881, he went to Texas to aid Rev. Victor Witting in the mission field. He died Jan. 13, 1882, at Austin, aged 64 years.

Newberg was a man of but mediocre mental equipment, lacked education and mastery of speech, yet was a rather popular preacher withal. The secret of it lay in his originality, his art of presenting old truths in new garb and of drawing striking applications from his own varied experience. He was a devout man, who lived in strict accordance with his teaching.

Rev. Victor Witting

The tenth, and last, of the co-workers of Hedström, was Victor Witting. This man was to play a prominent and many-sided part in the work and progress of the Swedish-American Methodist denomination. Alike as an eminent preacher, a skillful organizer, a journalist and author, this venerable pioneer has made himself a name that will ever rank with the foremost in the history of Swedish Methodism.

Witting was born in Malmö on March 7, 1825. His father, Anders Johan Witting, captain of the Vendes artillery regiment, was a descendant of a Finnish family, which had originally immigrated from Livonia and in the seventeenth century had been raised to noble rank. His mother, Gustafva Helena Rydberg, was a daughter of Postmaster Rydberg in Malmö. In the early thirties, Captain Witting removed to Landskrona, having been made chief officer of a battery of his regiment assigned to service in that ctiy. His son Victor now entered the Latin school there, and in 1836, when his father retired from military service and moved back to Malmö, Victor entered the collegiate school there. He left this school intending to prepare for college graduation and admittance to the university of Lund, but instead of carrying out this plan he obtained a position with an apothecary and began to study pharmacy. In his early youth he had acquired some knowledge and more admiration of this country through reading the

history of the United States and the novels of James Fenimore
Cooper and other writers, and when in the summer of 1841 the newspapers related that an Upsala student by the name of Gustaf Unonius,
heading a small party, had departed for the new and wonderful western
world to found a settlement there, young Witting's longing for America
became stronger than ever and he began devising plans of his own for
reaching the New World. To him the only possible way was to become
a sailor. He brooded over the matter incessantly for two years, until
one day, Easter morning, 1843, just as his apprenticeship was at an end
and he was about to take the apothecary's examination, he suddenly
deserted the drug store with its pills and powders and went across to
Helsingör, whence he hoped to ship as a sailor. For want of a passport
the plan miscarried and he was obliged to return home. Having
obtained his father's permission to go to sea, he soon afterward shipped
from Malmö, making several trips to England in the next two years,
after which he entered the school of navigation at Malmö and passed
the shipmaster's examination in 1845. In May he went to Gefle hoping
to be commissioned for a long trip on some large merchant vessel.
After making a short summer trip to England with the bark "Fama,"
when he formed the acquaintance of the aforesaid Peter Newberg,
who was the ship's carpenter, he engaged to take the ship "Ceres,"
with a cargo of iron, from Söderhamn to New York. Thus at last his
long cherished desire to get to America was to be fulfilled.

On board this vessel was a small party of Erik Janssonists, forerunners of the subsequent exodus of that sect. Off Öregrund, during
a dark and stormy night, the ship grounded and all on board probably
would have perished but for the fact that the vessel was so firmly
wedged between two rocks that the heavy seas which broke over it
could not dislodge it. The passengers and crew spent the night in the
forecastle amid indescribable horrors. That night young Witting
received impressions that gave to his life a different course. Profoundly
impressed with the resignation and Christian fortitude shown by the
Erik Janssonists in the very face of death, he made a resolve to become
a Christian, should he survive that dreadful night, and, if he ever
reached America, to look up these people.

The following day they were taken off the wreck, and Witting
went to Gefle, where he mustered on the ship "Gustaf Vasa," bound
for the Mediterranean. Returning, he sailed for two years between
Gefle and other ports. While at Stockholm in the summer of 1847,
he heard that a brig was about to sail for America with a party of
Erik Janssonists. Witting engaged to earn his passage by acting as
steward to the passengers. In October, after a voyage of six or seven

weeks, they reached New York, and the one chief goal of his longing had been reached at last.

He accompanied the Erik Janssonists westward. At Chicago Witting was taken sick and brought to a hospital. After having been restored to health, he obtained work in a drug store and formed the acquaintance of his fellow countrymen in that city. Late in the summer of 1848, he accompanied a newly arrived party of Erik Janssonists to Bishop Hill, thereby fulfilling his solemn promise on the night of the shipwreck. With the very best opinion of the Erik Janssonists and with high expectations of their colony, Witting arrived at Bishop Hill. He had supposed that all was harmony there, and that the colonists "lived secure in dwellings of peace," but he found quite the reverse—strife and discontent over Erik Jansson's despotic rule and the miserable state of affairs. Witting therefore remained only about a year and a half. In the late fall of 1849 he began planning for his departure and left on Christmas Eve, leaving behind him his young wife, whom he had wedded in the colony. He repaired to Victoria, and through Rev. Hedström obtained a position with a druggist in Galesburg, where he began work on New Year's day, 1850.

At that time there were in Galesburg about twenty Swedish families and quite a number of unmarried Swedes of both sexes, probably a total of a hundred persons, nearly all of them former Erik Janssonists. Not a few already had been won over to Methodism. Hedström and Challman in turn conducted the meetings. Witting and his wife attended regularly, joining the little Swedish Methodist Church in February. It was in the days of the gold fever, and Witting joined the party of Swedish goldseekers. The journey as well as the stay in California was rich in adventures and novel experiences. Reaching the gold country he went to digging like everybody else and once was about to "strike it rich" but failed on account of the irresolution of his comrade. From the diggings which they abandoned a Scotchman and his two sons subsequently took out a small fortune in a few weeks.

Tired and disappointed with life in the gold fields, Witting left California in April, 1852, with just enough gold to pay his way back, arriving in Galesburg just before midsummer. In July he removed to Victoria, where he and Erik Shogren attempted to make a fortune by cultivating medicinal herbs. After two years they gave it up as a failure. The first year a shipment of herbs to Cincinnati was lost in transit; the second year Witting, who was now alone in the enterprise, had to sell a large New York shipment at great sacrifice, leaving him without money enough to get home. These reverses almost drove the sanguine and energetic young man to despair. But when all his plans failed, he sought comfort in religion. A few visits to an American Methodist church in New York set his troubled mind at ease and inspired him with new courage. Having obtained a sum of money from the kindhearted Rev. O. G. Hedström, he returned to Illinois.

His trip to New York proved the turning-point in Witting's life. Almost immediately after his return to Victoria, he began to preach at small Methodist gatherings in private houses and was shortly afterwards appointed class leader. In the fall he obtained employment in a drug store in Peoria and began preaching to the handful of Swedes then found in that city. At the suggestion of Presiding Elder Henry Summers he now resolved to devote himself wholly to pastoral work and, having been admitted to the Rock River Conference on probation, in September, 1855, was stationed at Andover. Thus, after a varied career on land and sea, he finally found his proper sphere and settled down to his life's work, spending a long term of years in fruitful labor in behalf of the Methodist Church.

From now on Witting devoted himself unsparingly to his calling. In 1858 he was appointed to the charge at Victoria and in 1860 transferred to Rockford. In 1859 the idea of establishing a seminary for the education of ministers and founding a newspaper as the organ of the Swedish Methodists was advanced, but not until the spring of 1862 did the latter plan materialize, and then chiefly through the efforts of Witting. At a meeting of ministers in Chicago he volunteered, if a paper were started, to edit it for one year without salary. It was unanimously resolved to launch the enterprise and Witting's offer was gratefully accepted. This paper was named "Sändebudet" (The Messenger) and was published at Rockford, the first number appearing July 18th of that year. After occupying the editor's chair for some two and one-half years, having resigned from his pastoral charge in 1863, Witting left the paper, which in November, 1864, was moved to Chicago. The foregoing year he had taken up the school question for discussion in its columns and was gratified to find his plan so generally favored that during the year 1866, the centenary of Methodism, a school fund was subscribed. The school was not opened until New Year's, 1870, Witting serving meanwhile partly as the financial agent of the school project, partly again as editor of "Sändebudet."

In 1865 the Methodists began missionary work in Sweden, but their efforts met with little success. Witting was the first to put life into that work. After having obtained leave of absence, Witting went to Sweden in May, 1867, at the expense of a private individual. He soon attracted large audiences there. and in a short time Methodism became firmly rooted, especially in the capital. At the instance of Bishop Kingsley of the Methodist Episcopal Church, who was then visiting Sweden, Witting resolved to remain to prosecute the work which he successfully started. He hurried back to America to bring his family over, returning to Göteborg in November.

Rev. Victor Witting

It would carry us far out of our way to describe in detail Witting's mission in Sweden. Suffice it to say that with him as superintendent the work was prosecuted with great energy, several congregations being organized and churches built. But it was not all smooth sailing.

The authorities made trouble for the Methodist workers, several of whom were fined for disregarding the injunctions of church councils against public preaching by dissenters. But these obstacles were removed by the passage of the Dissenters Law of 1873, proposed by the government, passed by the riksdag with certain modifications relating to obligatory religious instruction of the young, and finally sanctioned by the king, its effect being materially to extend religious liberty in the country. The following year the Methodists of Sweden resolved to avail themselves of the right granted by that law to leave the state church and organize a denomination of their own, with government sanction. In February, 1875, a delegation of ten Methodist clergymen and laymen had an audience with the king, laying before him a petition with about 1,200 signatures, asking the privilege of uniting into a separate church body. The petition was granted March 10, 1876, that act securing forever the rights of the Methodist Church in Sweden. As may be readily understood, this was a day of triumph for Witting himself. On the 22nd of August following the Methodist missions were combined in a conference.

After ten years' work in Sweden, during which period Methodism made headway and gained permanence, Witting in 1877 returned to the United States. After preaching for a short time in Chicago, he was sent back to Sweden in the capacity of superintendent of the Methodist Church of Sweden. His term of service was, however, cut short by his leaving the Methodist Church, for reasons unexplained, and returning to America in the spring of 1879. The following year he founded a devotional monthly, entitled "Stilla Stunder," which was published in Chicago for two years. This breach between him and the church he had served for a quarter of a century was of brief duration. Having again joined the church, he was for the third time made editor of its organ, "Sändebudet," serving as such from 1883 to 1889. In the latter year he was appointed pastor of the Swedish Methodist Church at Quinsigamond, Mass., where he resumed publication of "Stilla Stunder." The following Christmas he published an annual entitled, "Bethlehemsstjernan," which never again appeared. In 1895, at the age of more than seventy, he was made editor of a weekly, known as "Österns Sändebud." While laboring as pastor and editor, Witting found time for quite extensive literary pursuits. As a writer and translator of religious songs he has undoubtedly rendered his church greater service than any other Swedish clergyman. The hymnal used by the Methodists of Sweden for many years contains a large number of hymns written or translated by him, and it is generally conceded that the best Swedish translations of the well-known songs of Charles Wesley have been made by Witting. He has published at his own expense several excellent collections of songs for prayer meetings, and for home devotion, which are still extensively used. His chief literary work, however, comprises his memoirs, embodied in a volume entitled, "Minnen från mitt lif som sjöman, immigrant och predikant." The first edition of this work was published in 1901, followed in 1904 by a second edition, revised and augmented. This work is especially valuable for its rich contributions to the early chapters of Swedish-American history.

Witting, who spent his later years at his home in Quincy, Mass., died July 2, 1906, his wife having passed away a few years earlier. Two of his daughters are married to Methodist ministers.

Other pioneers of the Swedish Methodist Church of America are Olof Hamrén, whose field of labor was western New York, and Samuel Anderson and John Fridlund, both of Minnesota.

The Early Swedish Methodist Churches

At the period here dealt with the preacher's calling was no sinecure. The country was sparsely settled, with small settlements from ten to twenty miles apart, the settlers were poor, dwelling in small, stuffy huts or dugouts, and the absence of roads and bridges made traveling difficult. The daily routine of a frontier preacher was somewhat on this order: a wearisome journey, mostly on horseback, but often afoot; arriving towards nightfall at some lone settler's cabin, a blockhouse at best, with a single room; preaching in the evening to a score of persons, children included; sharing with the inmates their only bed; breakfasting on cornbread and molasses; then proceeding on his way to the next settlement, there to repeat the selfsame experience, and so on for weeks and months. Owing to the suspicion, not to say hostility, anent the Methodists prevailing among the Swedish settlers, they would ofttimes shut their doors in the face of the itinerant preachers, who were thus compelled to spend their nights in the woods or on the open prairie. With Christian fortitude they submitted to all this, looking upon their calling as a work of love, not a means of livelihood. The majority of them sustained serious financial losses from chosing the minister's calling, being able to earn more at their respective trades than afterwards in the ministry. The highest annual salary received by any of them did not exceed $400. Some got only $100 to $150 a year. A certain preacher with a wife and three children had to get along on $90 for the first year, averaging 25 cents a day. With this modest competence went the duty of serving an entire circuit, viz., Moline-New Boston, involving monthly trips of some two hundred miles with horse and buggy. He was able to make only an occasional visit to his family, living in a blockhouse forty miles away.

During these early days it was customary for a clergyman to preach three times every Sunday and three or four times on week days, going from place to place, stops being made five to eight miles apart. In the spring and fall in particular, the roads would be extremely heavy, in fact impassable for vehicles, and then horseback riding was the only possible mode of travel. Sometimes the deep, sticky mud proved too much even for the saddle horses, and as a last resort the preacher, with his trousers tucked into his boot-tops, had to foot it through miles of mud and water. Under such strenuous conditions a Methodist minister naturally did not put on flesh, but these daily constitutionals kept his body agile and his spirits fresh and buoyant.

Such was the preacher's life in those days. All the Methodist ministers traveled about in like manner the year around. That was quite different from present conditions, which permit the preachers to remain for at least two years in each place, enjoying comfortable homes and other advantages.

The First Swedish Methodist Church in America

It was during the period just described that the first Swedish Methodist churches were organized in Illinois. As stated in foregoing pages, the very first was that at Victoria, founded Dec. 15, 1846, by Jonas Hedström, who on that occasion preached his first sermon. The first members were five all told. This was the small beginning of a movement which soon extended to all the surrounding towns and settlements, wherever Swedes were living, and from these districts came many of the pioneer clergymen. The early settlers at Victoria, with few exceptions, had been Erik Janssonists. Possessing more than ordinary knowledge of the Scriptures, they soon became firmly rooted in the Methodist faith. They took religion seriously, these pioneer settlers. The entire settlement of Victoria became so thoroughly imbued with Methodism that to this day all attempts of other denominations to gain a foothold there have proved futile.

The little church after two years numbered ninety members. At first the meetings were held either in a schoolhouse or in private houses. In the latter instance, it was customary for those attending the meetings to bring their own chairs and candles. In the late summer of 1853 the church building was begun, and it was completed and dedicated the following spring. This, the first Swedish Methodist church in the state, still stands as a landmark and reminder of Swedish pioneer days in Illinois. A steeple was added to the structure in later years. In the late fall of 1858 the adjoining parsonage was built. In 1857 the large Victoria circuit was divided into three, Victoria, Galesburg and Andover forming independent congregations, each with its own pastor. A year later three new fields were taken up, viz., Kewanee, Nekoma and Oneida. The mother church at Victoria in 1905 numbered 105 adult members. The baptized children are not counted as members in Methodist statistics as the case is in some other churches.

The Work at Andover

The second in point of age among the Swedish Methodist churches of Illinois is that of Andover. The date of Jonas Hedström's first visit

The Swedish M. E. Church in Victoria

to the Swedes of Andover is not known, but it might well have been as early as 1847, while the settlers were still few in number. When in 1849 Rev. Gustaf Unonius visited Andover he found cause for complaint in the fact that "a large part of the people had been converted to Methodism and much religious strife and disorder prevailed." In the latter part of July the same year, Jonas Hedström was in Andover to meet a party of immigrants ravaged by cholera. After having distributed food and medicines among the sick and emaciated newcomers, he was kept busy night and day procuring lodgings for them. On Sunday, Aug. 12th, he preached a touching funeral sermon at the biers of the latest victims of the pest, and two weeks later, Sunday, Aug. 26th, while the hearts of the immigrants were still pliant from suffering, he chose as the opportune time to organize a Methodist congregation. Those who joined were, Anna Lovisa Gustafsson, who had just lost both her parents, her husband, three children and a brother; Nils J. Johansson and wife; one Fröberg and wife; Helena Hurtig, a widow whose husband also had recently died of the cholera; Marta Olsson; Nils Olsson and wife; Åke Olsson and wife; E. P. Andersson and, on the following day, Mrs. H. Alm.

The congregation was organized at "Captain Mix's place," a large farm with good buildings, located near the southeast corner of the

The Swedish M. E. Church in Andover

village. This was now purchased by the widow Gustafsson, on the advice of Hedström, and became the home of herself, her daughter Mary, a girl of seven, her sisters Caroline and Mary and her brother John M. Ericksson. She was born in Hägerstad, Östergötland, April 13, 1821; at twenty she married Gustaf Gustafsson and in the summer of 1849 they emigrated to America, with the aforesaid party. Being widowed shortly after reaching Andover, she remarried in 1851, becoming the wife of Otto Lobeck, a Pomeranian, removed with him to Omaha, Neb., in 1884, became a widow again in 1890, and died in Fremont, Neb., March 30, 1903. At her home in Andover also the Swedish Lutheran Church of that place was organized March 18, 1850. Mrs. Lobeck to her death remained faithful to the Swedish Methodist Church by which she was regarded as a venerable mother and held in high esteem.

The Swedish Methodist flock of Andover increased rapidly, numbering in 1850 no less than 74 members, mostly residents of that place. A church edifice was begun and almost completed in 1854 and the following year the parsonage was erected. In August, 1855, the first Swedish Methodist camp meeting held in this country took place here. Two years later Rev. Hedström, at the annual camp meeting in Andover, preached his farewell sermon to his Methodist brethren, it being probably the most stirring address ever made by that fiery leader and organizer. During this early period the Andover minister had pastoral charge of eight other places, namely, Rock Island, Moline, Berlin (now Swedona), Hickory Grove (now Ophiem), LaGrange (now Orion), Geneseo, Pope Creek (now Ontario) and New Boston. In 1862 Moline was made a separate charge, as was Swedona in 1864. In 1905 the Andover church numbered 117 members.

The Galesburg Church

The third oldest Swedish Methodist congregation is that of Galesburg. As early as 1848 Rev. Hedström began his visits there and in September the following year he organized a church, despite religious indifference on the one hand and direct opposition on the other. Its first members were, Linde, a shoemaker, and his wife, Erik Grip and wife, Gustaf Berglund and wife, Mrs. Thorsell, widow of a shoemaker, Christina Muhr, married later to A. Cassel of Wataga, Nils Hedström and wife, besides others. The opposition grew still more bitter when half a year later a Swedish Lutheran church also was organized in Galesburg. In the spring of 1852, a powerful Baptist movement arose to shake the little Methodist church in its very foundations. Several of its members were re-baptized. Even its young pastor, Rev. A. G. Swedberg, was converted to Baptism and took the sacrament of immersion. This movement, however, was of short duration and so superficial that several of the converts soon returned to their former church.

In spite of continued opposition both from Swedes and Americans —the latter being chiefly the Presbyterians and the Congregationalists, who thought their own churches sufficient for the needs of the community—the struggling little church continued to grow, making a house of worship a necessity. In 1850 a subscription was started for that purpose. Jonas Hedström's most formidable opponent was Jonathan Blanchard, president of Knox College. Through his influence, it was said, many Americans withdrew their subscriptions to the Swedish Methodist church building fund. As a side light on Hedström's character the following instance may be quoted. During a hot set-to between Blanchard and Hedström, the latter is reported to have said to his opponent, "Do you see the sun in the heavens? You might as well try to stop him in his course as to attempt to shut the Methodists out of Galesburg. We have come here to stay."

The Swedish Methodists could not be made to abandon their plan to build a church. At the suggestion of some of the leading men in the American Methodist Church, which was not much larger than the Swedish one, it was decided in the fall of 1851 that the two congregations should erect a common edifice, in which both should worship in turn, according to specific agreement, so that on the days when the Americans held their services in the morning, the Swedes were to hold theirs in the afternoon or evening, and vice versa. The edifice was built and dedicated the following year. It was a light and cheerful sanctuary, with a seating capacity of about 200. Great was the joy of the Swedes over the new house of worship, which they justly considered theirs in part. But their joy was soon spoiled. Some sharp individual among the members of the American congregation soon made the "discovery" that, according to the wording of the papers, the Swedish people legally had no claim to ownership whatever. This caused much friction, and at a subsequent meeting of the trustees, two of whom were Swedes and three Americans, it was resolved, in the presence of Hedström, and over the vigorous protests of himself and the Swedish trustees, that the church was the exclusive property of the American Methodist congregation, and that the Swedes had no more property right in it than any other people who, by subscription or other efforts, had assisted in its erection. By that decision the Swedish congregation was ousted and again stood without a church home.

This misfortune befell the church at the time when its pastor, Rev. Swedberg, and about half of its membership, twelve to fifteen young and energetic persons, deserted the flock and joined the Baptists. The remaining ones, however, continued the work, hoping for better days to dawn, and their hopes were not in vain. New members were added, and nearly all of the deserters returned to the fold. In the surrounding country missionary work was begun in the years 1855-7 at the following points, Knoxville, Wataga, Abingdon, Monmouth and Oquawka. Late in the year 1856 a small church was erected which was dedicated New Year's Day, 1857. That same year the congregation was made independent, then numbering 69 members. In 1863 the little church building was moved to a larger lot in a more desirable location, and two years later an addition was built at a cost of a little over $1,300. In 1872 the present large and imposing edifice was erected at a cost of $18,000. In the middle sixties an independent church was formed at Wataga, decreasing the membership by fifty. In 1905 the Galesburg church had a total membership of 300.

Operations in Moline and Rock Island

Swedish immigration to Moline and Rock Island had scarcely begun when the wide-awake Rev. Hedström went there to preach to his

The Old Swedish M. E. Church in Moline

countrymen. The first man that took kindly to him was Olaus Bengtsson, one of Moline's Swedish pioneers. Rev. Hedström lived in his house whenever he visited Moline, and in that same house the Swedish

Methodist Church was organized, presumably in September, 1849, and held its meetings there during the first ten years of its existence. Only seven persons joined the church at its organization, these being Olaus Bengtsson and his wife, three other persons in Moline and two from Rock Island. During the first few years the growth was very slow, the total number of members in 1855 being only 18 or 20, and three years later showing only a slight increase over that figure. The chief reason for this slow progress lay in the energetic work done by the newly arrived Swedish Lutheran pastor, Rev. O. C. T. Andrén, causing the majority of immigrants with religious interests to join his church. In 1859-61, after immigrants had arrived in great numbers, things began to look brighter for the Methodists in Moline, their services were better attended, and in 1860 they could dedicate a little church which had just been erected.

In 1862 the Moline Swedish Methodists were organized into a separate congregation, independent of the Andover church, and with a pastor of their own. The subsequent year, Moline was combined with Swedona, and in 1867 Geneseo was also added to the circuit, a small congregation having been organized in the latter place in 1864 and a little church erected. In 1871 the Moline congregation sold its church building, which was now inadequate, and purchased from an American congregation a larger building which was moved to a new location, where it was used until 1889, the year of the erection of the present still more commodious temple of worship. In 1871 a parsonage was built which four years later was rebuilt and enlarged. The total membership in 1905 reached 202.

During the years 1852-5 there existed in Rock Island a small but vigorous congregation of Swedish Methodists, consisting largely of girls in the employ of American families, but soon most of these girls left the city, almost depleting the church as early as 1856. In 1854 this congregation is said to have owned a small church building which seems to have been disposed of long ago.

The Chicago Field

Swedish Methodism in Chicago dates back to 1852. In the fall of that year Rev. O. G. Hedström of New York visited that city on his way to his brother in Victoria. Here he had an opportunity to preach for several successive days in the Norwegian, subsequently Swedish Lutheran church on Superior street. Large crowds went to hear him, and Hedström is said to have preached with such power that "there was weeping throughout the church, from the pulpit down to the last pew." In December, on his return to New York, he again visited

Chicago, accompanied by his brother Jonas. Here they stopped a couple of weeks. The Superior street church being now closed to them, they conducted their meetings in the Bethel Chapel, or Seamen's Mission, on Wells street, between Michigan and Illinois streets, and here, in December, 1852, the foundation was laid for a Swedish, or rather Scandinavian, Methodist church in Chicago. There is no doubt that this work tended to hurry the organization of the Swedish Lutheran Immanuel Church of Chicago, which took place in January, 1853. Rev. Jonas Hedström remained in the city a few days after his brother had left for New York, in order to encourage the little flock, and give it a good start, services doubtless well needed in a congregation made up of many heterogeneous elements. The membership at the beginning is said to have reached 75, but hardly had Jonas Hedström left the city before more than two-thirds of these deserted and joined the Swedish Lutheran Church just then in process of organization. A mere handful of them remained in the Methodist fold.

In order to save the wreckage, Rev. O. G. Hedström, shortly after his return to New York, sent his assistant, S. B. Newman, to Chicago. His task consisted in gathering the remnant of the church and, with that as a nucleus, form a practically new congregation. In the latter part of January, Rev. Jonas Hedström returned from Victoria, and the two worked so earnestly that in February the number of new members received on probation reached 65. In September of the same year this number had grown to 123, this, however, including a few in St. Charles, Ill., and about 30 in Poolsville, Ind., where a church had been organized in August.

Captain Charles Magnus Lindgren

Among those joining the congregation that year was C. M. Lindgren, a sea captain, who almost immediately became one of the chief supports of Swedish Methodism in Chicago. Lindgren was born in Dragsmark, Bohuslän, Nov. 28, 1819, went to sea at the age of 14, and sailed until 1849, when he went to California, remaining there for three years, first as a goldwasher and later engaged in the freight traffic. In the spring of 1852 he returned to his native land, was there married to Johanna Andersson, returned to America in September and arrived in Chicago in November of the same year. Here he opened a livery stable on Illinois street, but, finding this unprofitable, entered into a railway project together with the Erik Janssonists of Bishop Hill and settled in 1854 at Toulon, Henry county, a few miles from Galva. In the spring of 1856 he came back to Chicago, bought a couple of freight vessels and contracted with a lumber company for shipping lumber from Michigan to Chicago. At first this proved exceedingly profitable, but suddenly the company failed, involving Lindgren in heavy losses. Subsequently he removed to Montgomery, a small town on the Burlington railroad, about fifty miles from Chicago, where he set up as a manufacturer of machinery, but soon failed. In the fall of 1860 he again came to Chicago and engaged in shipping, first with a good-sized freighter with which he succeeded so well that he was soon able to

Capt. Charles Magnus Lindgren

exchange it for a still larger vessel. Fortune now steadily favored him, and he gradually added vessel after vessel until in 1870 he owned half a dozen ships with a combined tonnage of 4,500. Several of these were among the largest in the lake trade at that time. The following year he had three more large freighters built at Manitowoc, Wis., one of which was named "Christina Nilsson," after the great Swedish singer who visited America that year.

Failing health in 1877 compelled his retirement from business. That summer he took a trip to the old country. His condition, however, grew worse and on September 1, 1879; he died at his home in Evanston, aged 60 years.

Captain Lindgren was a man of extraordinary activity and a kind and philanthropic man withal, who did much for his less fortunate fellow countrymen.. His wife was equally kind-hearted. Lindgren was particularly liberal toward the struggling little Swedish Methodist Church in Chicago. Without his aid it would not have accomplished what it did. When in later years the Swedish Methodist Theological Seminary was founded here, Lindgren contributed generously toward its erection and maintenance.

In the spring of 1854 the young Methodist congregation decided to build a church of their own. During the summer Rev. Newman made a trip to his former field of labor in the South to solicit funds for that purpose, and met with great success. The edifice, which was erected on Illinois street, near Market, was completed in the fall and dedicated in October or November, by Rev. O. G. Hedström. The back part of the structure constituted the parsonage.

In those days it was a common occurrence that the meetings of the Swedish Methodists in Chicago and elsewhere were disturbed by drunken rowdies. Frequently the preacher would be interrupted in the midst of his discourse by hideous yells or by the hurling of stones or other missiles, aimed at the speaker, through the windows. After services, crowds of hoodlums would gather outside the sanctuary, jeering and molesting the worshipers as they were coming out. Time and again, these people, both ministers and laymen, were the objects not only of threats, but of open attacks. The aforesaid Captain Lindgren, who was a man possessed of both courage and physical strength, was often obliged to act as a sort of special policeman at the meetings. On one occasion, when he undertook to escort the leader of a gang of disturbers out of the church, the culprit drew a knife, seriously wounding Captain Lindgren. This brutal crime, committed in the house of God, was brought to trial and the perpetrator was severely punished, while several other disturbers were arrested and fined. This example had a wholesome effect, disturbances became less frequent, and soon the Swedish Methodists were permitted to worship unmolested.

The summer of 1854, when the cholera broke out in Chicago, was fraught with many trials for Rev. Newman and his flock. The noble work of relief accomplished by Newman and other Swedish pastors of Chicago is recounted elsewhere in these pages. About this time, also, his field was widened by work being begun in Beaver, St. Charles and Rockford, Ill., and at Attica, LaFayette, LaPorte and other points in Indiana.

In September, 1855, Newman returned to his former place in New

York as assistant to Rev. O. G. Hedström, Rev. Erik Shogren succeeding him in Chicago, where he labored for four years, until 1859, when he, in turn, was succeeded by Jakob Bredberg. At this time two young and gifted men, A. J. Anderson and N. O. Westergreen, joined the church, both of whom in later years became prominent clergymen in the Swedish Methodist Church.

Rev. Jacob Bredberg

The aforesaid Jakob Bredberg was in some respects one of the notable men in the Swedish Methodist clergy. He was born in the city of Alingsås, Sweden, May 1, 1808, completed his college course at twenty-one and was ordained minister in 1832. Having served for twenty years as curate in Sweden, he emigrated in 1853. Like his former colleague, Rev. C. P. Agrelius, a few years earlier, Bredberg became acquainted with Rev. Hedström in New York and joined the Methodists, was subsequently in charge of the Swedish Methodist Church at Jamestown, N. Y., for four years, until 1859, when he came to Chicago. During his first year here the work progressed nicely, Rev. Bredberg's eloquence and his reputation for great learning attracting good audiences. But the second year marked a complete change. Then it was discovered that he was indifferent to the interests of his church even to the extent of planning to leave the Methodists and join another denomination. This lost him the confidence of the parishioners and caused a falling off in attendance and a gloomy outlook generally. In the fall of 1861 the anticipated flop took place, when Bredberg went over to the Episcopalians and became pastor of the St. Ansgarius Church in Chicago, occupying that pulpit until 1877, when old age and sickness compelled his retirement. Alongside of his pastoral work, Rev. Bredberg engaged to some extent in literary pursuits, such as editing a Swedish Methodist hymnal, the contents of which were partly compiled, partly translated by him, and later translating the English Episcopal ritual and a number of English, French and Bohemian tracts into Swedish.

In the condition just described A. J. Anderson found the Swedish Methodist Church when he took charge of it in the fall of 1861. The church edifice was in so bad repair as to be almost condemnable. Sunday school had been discontinued, class meetings, prayer meetings and the customary forms of Christian activity had been abandoned. Furthermore, the congregation was still heavily in debt from the time the church was built. Rev. Anderson succeeded, however, in putting new life into the work: the church was rebuilt in 1863, and through his efforts the membership increased by 160 in the period from 1861 to 1864

The First Swedish M.-E. Church of Chicago

making a total of 210. The Sunday school numbered 130 pupils and
the church property, now free of debt, was valued at $8,000.

During the following year, while Rev. Shogren was in charge,
another hundred members were added, and the attendance at services
was so great that the congregation had to choose between securing
a larger house of worship or dividing into two flocks. They chose the
latter alternative; an American Methodist church on the west side was
purchased and moved to the corner of Fourth and Sangamon streets,
and thenceforth regular services were held also in this part of the city.
This was in April, 1865. The next fall Shogren was succeeded by Rev.
N. O. Westergreen, whose three years of service, 1865-8, were characterized by steady progress. Up to 1867 Swedes and Norwegians had
worshiped under one roof as members of the same church, but about
that time it became apparent that it was better for all concerned that
the Norwegians separated and formed a congregation of their own.
This was done and the second church building was turned over to the
Norwegians, most of whom were living on the west side. This marked
the beginning of Norwegian Methodism in Chicago.

During the years 1868 to 1870 Rev. Nils Peterson was pastor of the
church. The congregation at that time purchased the lot at the corner
of Market and Oak street where later its present church was built.
Rev. Peterson was succeeded by Rev. A. J. Anderson, who labored here
for three years up to 1873. In the great fire of 1871 the church on
Illinois street was destroyed, as were the other Swedish churches of the
city. This disaster was the turning-point in the history of the Swedish
Methodists of Chicago. For a time they held their services in the newly
built Norwegian Methodist church on Indiana street. But after the
fire the influx of Swedes to the west side increased, and for that reason
it was found expedient also to make it the religious center. In pursuance of this purpose the lot on Illinois street was traded for one on
May street, where the present Swedish Methodist church on the west
side was then erected. A small dwelling-house situated on the lot was
remodeled into a parsonage. The basement of the church was finished
in 1872 and the entire edifice was not completed until 1878.

On the north side a temporary chapel was built simultaneously. In
the summer of 1875 it was removed to make room for the Swedish
Methodist church, which was not completed until 1879, during the
incumbency of Rev. D. S. Sörlin, when a parsonage also was built.
From 1873 to 1875 its pastor was Rev. E. Shogren, assisted by Rev.
Alfred Anderson, and in 1875-6 Rev. N. O. Westergreen was in charge.
Although there was a church on the west side, Swedish Methodists
living there still belonged to the north side church until 1875, when a
formal division of the congregation took place and the westsiders

formed a separate church and received their own pastor, Rev. D. S. Sörlin, the following year. In 1876 Rev. Witting, just returned from Sweden, was assigned to the north side church, serving it for one year. On the south side work was begun by the Swedish Methodists about this time, resulting in the organization of a congregation in 1876, with Rev. Fredrik Åhgren as its first pastor. The progress of these churches up to the present time can only be indicated here by means of the following statistics of membership for the year 1905, to-wit: the First Swedish Methodist Episcopal Church 425, the west side church 168 and the south side church 200.

The Beaver Settlement

About 75 miles southeast from Chicago, in Iroquois county, a Swedish settlement, named Beaver, was founded in 1853. There a Swedish Methodist church was started May 4, 1854, with nine members. The next year the missions in Indiana were organized into a separate circuit, comprising Attica, Poolsville, LaFayette, Yorktown and Buena Vista, with Attica as the headquarters. To this circuit Beaver was now added. In 1863 the congregation in Attica disbanded, the church was sold. work ceased entirely and the pastor removed to Beaver, which thus became the principal missionary station of the circuit. A church had been built there in 1860. Work at this point grew still more difficult when in 1870 a Swedish Lutheran congregation was founded there, its church edifice and parsonage being built the following year. The Lutherans, however, had little success owing to the fact that their members arrived later to Beaver and consequently had to settle on poorer land, where they hardly could make their living. Therefore they had to sell their farms and move to other parts of the country, their number was gradually decimated, the pastor left and finally the church closed its doors. The field was thus abandoned to the Methodists, who have worked persistently with the result that the Beaver church is now one of their best country congregations. A new church was erected there in 1890, the parsonage has been rebuilt since 1877, and in 1905 the congregation had a total of 165 members.

Methodist Work in Rockford

Methodism was first preached to the Swedes of Rockford in 1854, doubtless in the month of February, by Rev. S. B. Newman, who went there on a visit to the parents of Rev. N. O. Westergreen, they having moved there from Chicago. A class was started, in charge of the elder Westergreen. Early in 1855 the younger Westergreen, at the suggestion of Rev. Newman, began preaching, continuing until the following spring, when the family removed to Evanston in order to give the son an opportunity to study.   In May he visited Rockford only to find the class dissolved, and when Rev. E. Shogren visited the city in 1856

The Swedish M. E. Church in Rockford

the outlook for Swedish Methodism in Rockford was still very dark. No further visits were made by Methodist clergymen until the year 1859, when Westergreen again came there.   The year after, Rockford had visits from Revs. Challman and Erik Carlson.   At that year's conference it was resolved to begin operations in Rockford with Victor

Witting in charge. A little old church owned by the American Presbyterians was rented for the meetings and in October that year Witting began preaching there, at first to audiences of four or five persons, but the attendance steadily increased. Wednesday, Jan. 30, 1861, a congregation with a membership of 12 was organized. Prejudices and active opposition for a time deterred the growth of the church, but when at length the ice was broken more rapid progress was made. A year later, when Rev. Witting began to issue his paper "Sändebudet," there was renewed opposition, but he was not the man to give up in dismay. He stuck to his post of duty, and in 1863 the congregation was able to purchase the little church they had hitherto hired, and renovate it, all without incurring any considerable debt. That year the congregation had 43 members; its pastor was Rev. Albert Ericson, who was also assistant editor of "Sändebudet." The following year N. N. Hill, a local preacher, was in charge. When he resigned in 1865 and was succeeded by P. Newberg the membership had decreased to 40. Subsequently the church was served for two years, 1866-8, by two local preachers, August Westergreen and Oscar Sjögren, each for one year. Meanwhile the membership grew to 68. The last-named year the congregation purchased a lot in a good location on First avenue to which the church was moved.

Rev. O. Gunderson was in charge of the church during the years 1868-71, when there was an increase of thirty members. After Gunderson there was the following succession of ministers: John Linn, 1871-2; A. T. Westergreen, 1872-3; S. B. Newman, 1873-5, and John Wigren, 1875-7. During Rev. Wigren's incumbency the old church, being found inadequate, was replaced in 1877 by a new and larger one. At the conference that year the congregation reported a total of 165 members. In 1905 this church, which at certain periods has been one of the largest in the denomination, numbered 210 members.

The Swedona and Bishop Hill Churches

A Swedish Methodist society, or congregation, was founded in Swedona in 1857, being made up partly of members of the Andover church. An edifice was erected and dedicated in the period of 1859-61, and in 1864 a parsonage was built, this being moved and remodeled in 1874. In 1863 the Swedona church was made entirely independent of the Andover circuit, its membership being then about 50. This church, which embraces also the Swedish Methodists of New Windsor, in 1905 had 36 members.

The Bishop Hill congregation is also numbered among the oldest of the Swedish Methodist churches. It had its inception in the summer of 1860 when A. J. Anderson was asked by Jonas Olson to come and preach in the old colony church. While in Andover, Anderson made regular visits to Bishop Hill. When and by whom the church was organized is not known. It figures in the list of assignments for the first time in the year 1863, apparently having been started that year by Rev. Peter Challman. In 1865 the so-called "Smedjevinden" (Blacksmith's attic) was purchased and turned into a meeting hall. Three years afterward, quite a large church was erected, as also a parsonage.

The Swedish M. E. Church in Bishop Hill

Several of the former leaders of the Erik Janssonists about this time joined the Methodists. Galva and Kewanee, both belonging to the Bishop Hill circuit, were separated in 1860 and given their own pastors. In 1905 the Bishop Hill church numbered 124 members.

Eminent Workers and Leaders—Rev. Anders Johan Anderson

One of the pioneers of Swedish Methodism was Anders Johan Anderson. He was born in Quenneberga, Småland, June 9, 1833, the younger of two brothers. The elder was Carl Anderson, who became known over a large part of Sweden as a prominent lay preacher. Having obtained an elementary education, A. J. Anderson emigrated to America in 1854, at the age of twenty-one. Landing in Quebec, he came on to Chicago, where he was employed for some months in a drug store. Toward winter he went south, remaining in New Orleans until spring, when he returned to Chicago. Here he obtained lodging with a family of Methodists who induced him to attend their church on Illinois street. There he made the acquaintance, first of Rev. S. B. Newman, and later of Rev. Erik Shogren. After attending services for a time, Anderson, in the spring of 1856, joined the church.

He possessed natural talents of a high order, and these, coupled with his newly awakened interest in religious matters, soon attracted the attention of his brethren in the faith, who called him to important positions in the church. Thus he became, in rapid succession, class leader, local preacher, Sunday school teacher and leader of the church

Rev. A. J. Anderson

choir. He preached his first sermon in July, 1856, at a camp meeting in Forest Glen. In 1857, on the advice of Rev. Shogren and after a lengthy consultation with Jonas Hedström, the Methodist patriarch, Anderson resolved to enter the ministry.

His first pastoral charge was at Galesburg, where he labored for two years, till 1859, his subsequent assignments being as follows: Andover, 1859-61; Chicago, 1861-4; Galesburg. 1864-6; Bishop Hill,

1866-70; Chicago, 1870-73; presiding elder of the Swedish district of the Central Illinois Conference, 1873-7; Chicago, 1877-9; Andover, 1879-80; Immanuel Church of Brooklyn, N. Y., 1880-93; Lake View, Chicago, 1893-7; presiding elder of the Chicago district, 1897-1902. He died in this city Dec. 19, 1902.

Anderson was a talented preacher, a successful pastor and a man of unusual executive ability. This latter gift was especially valuable to him during his first and second term of service in Chicago. He was, furthermore, a clear-sighted and experienced church leader, whom his brethren in the work regarded with love and confidence. Few of the Swedish Methodist clergymen in this country can look back on so long and so successful a career as that of Rev. Anderson. His memory will long be cherished among the people whom he so devotedly served. When he was pastor of the church at Lake View, Chicago, he was offered the honorary degree of D. D. from a German Methodist college at St. Paul, Minn., a courtesy which he politely declined.

Rev. John Wigren

John Wigren, another prominent Swedish Methodist pioneer preacher, was born in Grenna parish, Småland, Oct. 1, 1826. He left his childhood home at the age of seventeen to serve a mason's apprenticeship. After seven years, he received his master mason's certificate from the Grenna council. June 19, 1852, he emigrated to America with his wife and two children, reaching New York Aug. 27th. On the day of his arrival he visited the Bethel mission ship and was converted then and there. From New York he went to La Fayette, Ind., to rejoin some acquaintances from his youth. After a short stay here and in Poolsville, he removed to Attica in the spring of 1853 and joined the Swedish Methodist church that was organized there in August of that year by Rev. Newman.

Wigren at once became a zealous church worker, doing everything in his power for the upbuilding of the congregation. In 1885 he was appointed class leader, in 1856 exhorter and in 1857 local preacher. The pastor in charge being unable to visit the place more than every third Sunday, it devolved upon Wigren to conduct most of the services. With this he continued for five years, or until 1863, when he abandoned his trade to devote himself exclusively to the service of the church. He was then assigned to the Beaver-Yorktown circuit, which he served for two years. Soon after his arrival he set to work to have a parsonage built at Beaver.

At the conference in 1865, he was ordained deacon, a year later he was received on probation into the Central Illinois Conference, and in 1868 he was ordained elder. His subsequent assignments were: Swedona-

Moline, 1865-6; Swedona alone, 1866-7; Andover-Swedona, 1867-9; Andover alone, 1869-71; Moline-Geneseo, 1871-3; Swedona 1873-5; May street church in Chicago, also presiding elder of the Chicago district, 1878-81; south side church in Chicago, 1881-2; Bishop Hill, 1882-5; presiding elder of the Burlington district of Iowa, 1885-7, and of the Chicago district, 1887-91; Lake View, 1891-3; Forest Glen, 1893-4; Aurora, 1894-7, and La Grange, 1897-9, after which he retired from active work in the ministry.

Rev. John Wigren

In his prime, Wigren was a very practical man, whose energies were especially directed toward the building of churches and parsonages and soliciting funds for various purposes. Under his direction the church in Rockford was built in 1877, the west side church in Chicago was completed in 1878-81, and the basement of the south side church was built in 1881-2. While he was stationed at Bishop Hill in 1882-5 his executive talents again stood him in good stead when the camp meeting grounds at Hickory Grove, between Bishop Hill and Galva, were purchased.

Rev. Wigren is, moreover, a successful evangelist and has added many new members to the churches he served. Being a man of good judgement and considerable business acumen, he was often put in charge of important undertakings and has always been a dominant figure at the conference meetings. He worked energetically from the very start in behalf of the theological seminary at Evanston and was for nineteen years a member of its board of trustees. Rev. Wigren is living in retirement in Chicago. Three of his sons have followed in his

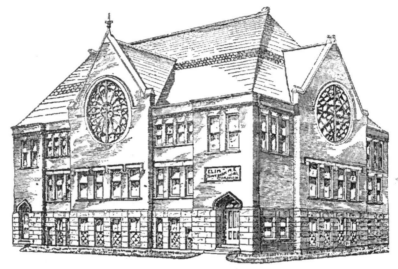

Elim Swedish M. E. Church, Lake View

footsteps and devoted themselves to the ministry in the Swedish Methodist Church.

Rev. N. O. Westergreen

Another of the Swedish Methodist preachers to be numbered with the pioneers is N. O. Westergreen. He was born in Bjäraryd, Blekinge, Sweden, July 25, 1834. Together with his parents and four brothers he came to the United States Sept. 29, 1852. The parents and two of his younger brothers proceeded to Chicago, while he and his two elder brothers remained in the East. The first winter he lived with an American family named Washburn, at Minot, Me., where he attended district school. After spending the spring and summer in Boston he came to Chicago in November, 1853. Here he met Rev. Newman, through whose influence he was converted about Christmas time and embraced the Methodist faith.

Not long afterward Westergreen together with his parents removed to Rockford. He now experienced a desire to enter the ministry, and an opportunity to preach was offered when Rev. Newman, who had

Rev. N. O. Westergreen

begun the work in Rockford, appointed him leader of the meetings. He preached his first sermon in February, 1855, in his parental home. In order to prepare himself for his calling he entered the Garrett Biblical

Institute at Evanston the same year and was enrolled at Knox College,
Galesburg, a year later. In 1859 Westergreen was assigned to the Victoria church. Thence he was sent to serve the Norwegian congregations
in Leland and Norway, and in 1860 he was assigned to Beaver, Ill., and
Attica, Ind. After two years he went back to Leland, whence he was
transferred in 1863 to the Galesburg church. This assignment suited
him all the more as it made it possible for him again to take up studies
at Knox College. After serving a year at Bishop Hill, Wataga and
Kewanee he was in charge of the north side church in Chicago during
the years 1865-8.

The Old Swedish M. E. Tabernacle at Desplaines Camp Grove

In 1870, when the projected theological school was ultimately established, Westergreen became its first teacher, meanwhile having charge
of the church at Galesburg for four years. Having subsequently served
as editor of "Sändebudet" for three years, Westergreen became pastor
of the north side church of Chicago; he was next stationed at Geneva
and Batavia for one year, and at Moline for a like term, acting at the
same time as presiding elder of the Galesburg district. From here he
was sent to the Fifth avenue church in Chicago, where he remained for
three years. After four years' service as presiding elder of the Chicago
district, he was pastor of the Evanston church for a like period, of the
Fifth avenue church one year, at Humboldt Park two years, at Moreland, Melrose and Oak Park one year and at Ravenswood one year. In
1895, at his own request, Westergreen was declared superannuated,
but still continued to serve the small congregations at Waukegan and
Lake Forest, and acted as teacher at the theological seminary during
the school year 1896-7.

Westergreen enjoys the reputation of being a profound thinker and a good speaker. He is well versed, especially in the subjects of theology and church history. As a champion of Methodism among the

Rev. Albert Ericson

Swedish-Americans he has exerted a powerful influence. His ability as scholar and preacher has been recognized by a Methodist institution of learning, which some years ago gave him the degree of D. D.

Rev. Albert Ericson

The fourth of this group of eminent Swedish Methodist workers is Albert Ericson, a distinguished preached and educator, a biographical sketch of whom is found elsewhere in this work. He began preaching shortly after his coming to the United States in 1857. After having served as editor of "Sändebudet", the mouthpiece of the denomination, for two years, Ericson was called in 1866 as teacher of Swedish in the proposed theological seminary and went abroad to prepare himself for this work. Finding upon his return that the school was not yet opened, he again assumed the editorship of the official church paper. After laboring as a preacher in the eastern field for some ten years he was called to the presidency of the Swedish Theological Seminary in Evanston. In this responsible position, held by him for a quarter of a century, he continues to render efficient service to his church and to wield great influence in the training of its teachers.

The Swedish Theological Seminary

As early as 1865, a year before the Methodist Episcopal Church of America celebrated its one hundredth anniversary, steps were taken toward the establishment of a divinity school for the Scandinavian element of the denomination. The initiative was taken by Rev. Victor Witting. In October of that year a general convention of all Scandinavian Methodist preachers and a number of laymen was held to discuss the matter. The meeting resolved that a Scandinavian seminary be founded at the earliest possible time. Rev. Witting and other pastors were appointed as solicitors of funds, and teachers were designated. The project met with favor everywhere and a considerable amount was subscribed. When Witting, who was the soul of the movement, was sent to Sweden, the work lagged, and more than half of the amount promised was lost through negligence in making collections.

Ere long it proved impracticable to carry out the original plan of a common institution for all Scandinavian Methodists. A separation between the Swedish and Norwegian brethren followed, each group continuing to carry forward its plans, after an equal division of the existing funds had been made. The split delayed the establishment of a Swedish seminary until 1870, when it was finally founded at Galesburg. On Feb. 28th of that year it opened with two students and Rev. N. O. Westergreen as teacher. During the entire first year the attendance stopped at a total of four. The upper story of a private house, belonging to one Peter Hillgren, was at first used for studies and recitation rooms. From there the school moved into another private house and then occupied rooms on the second floor in the private

The Swedish Theological Seminary, Evanston

residence of Rev. Westergreen. Not more than a dozen persons availed themselves of the instruction given while the school was in Galesburg, but this number includes not a few of the leading members of the Swedish Methodist clergy. From that time the school has had a permanent existence, although the location has varied. In 1872 it was removed from Galesburg to Galva, and Westergreen was succeeded by Rev. C. A. Wirén. Three years afterward, in 1875, the institution was located in Evanston, in organic connection with the Northwestern University. At this time Dr. William Henschen was placed at its head, a position retained by him until the close of the school year in the spring of 1883. Part of this time the first class had been maintained and taught partly at Galva, partly in St. Paul and Minneapolis, Fredrick Ahlgren acting as teacher at the former place in 1877-9, and J. O. Nelson at the latter in 1879-82. After that the institution was consolidated at Evanston, with Prof. Albert Ericson at the head. He was the sole teacher up to 1889, when C. G. Wallenius was elected assistant professor. He resigned in 1896, and was succeeded by Westergreen, but returned to the position after an interval of three years, and remained with the institution until 1906.

Many of the students of the seminary have availed themselves of its connection with the university to take special courses in its various departments, a number graduating from the college. From 1886 a special teacher of English has been a member of the seminary faculty.

The control of the institution is vested in a board of nine directors, five clergymen and four laymen, representing the Central, the Western, the Northern and the Eastern Swedish Methodist Conferences.

The institution was started on a fund of $4,000, which has since grown to $45,000. This does not include the sum of about $8,000 expended on the building erected in 1883 on ground owned by the university. This building was a three story structure, containing recitation rooms, dining room, kitchen and 16 living-rooms for students. The money expended on the building was raised chiefly through the efforts of Rev. Charles G. Nelson.

Recently a more commodious building has been erected at a cost of $35,000, the dedication of which on Sept. 21, 1907, marked a great stride in the progress of the institution. The new building is located at Orrington avenue and Lincoln street; on a campus, 246 feet front by 211 deep, costing $12,000. The present valuation on the seminary property is $47,000, on which rests a debt of about $14,000.

The Bethany Home

The question of establishing a Swedish Methodist home for the aged in Chicago was first broached at the annual meeting of the ministerial association of the Chicago district, held at Donovan, Ill., in 1889.

A committee appointed to present plans for such an institution included Mr. John R. Lindgren, the banker. At a subsequent meeting, held New Year's Day, 1890, he gave a promise of $5,000 to the proposed home, conditioned on the raising of a like amount. Rev. Alfred Anderson set to work soliciting donations, and when through his efforts the condition had been fully met, Mr. Lindgren promised another substantial donation on the same terms.

With such a lift at the start, it was comparatively easy to acquire the funds needed for the early realization of the plan. In February, 1891, a house in south Evanston was rented and on the 3rd of March following the home was formally opened. In August of the same year ground was purchased in the Ravenswood district, Chicago, for the sum

The Bethany Home, Chicago

of $13,000. A building was erected thereon, at a cost of nearly $15,000. Upon its completion, the temporary quarters were abandoned and the wards transferred to the new building. This contained mainly living-rooms for the aged, but two rooms were set aside for the accommodation and care of the sick, and two physicians and a trained nurse were engaged. In this way charity was extended in the form of medical attendance free of cost, wholly or in part, until the entire building was needed for its original purpose, when the hospital department was discontinued.

In the year 1896 a six-flat building was erected on the grounds, the rental of which goes toward the maintenance of the home. This was ready for occupancy in April, 1897, and has since yielded the institution a handsome steady income, supplemented by gifts and contributions from churches, societies and individuals, and an annual offering in the churches on Thanksgivings Day. Applicants for admission have paid in various sums, varying from $50 to $500 a person, no specified fee being required.

The affairs of the Bethany Home are in the hands of a board of trustees, with Rev. Alfred Anderson as president and Rev. John Bendix as financial agent, the latter having filled that position for the past eleven years. The institution, now free of debt, owns property valued at $75,000.

At the close of the year 1907 the number of inmates of the home was thirty. The total number of persons cared for since the opening was 179, of whom 41 have passed away.

Growth of Swedish Methodism

In 1875 Swedish Methodism in the West had grown to such an extent that its ministers, with two or three exceptions, all deemed it not only desirable but absolutely necessary to hold a Swedish conference comprising all the Swedish Methodist congregations in the states of Illinois, Indiana, Iowa, Kansas, Nebraska, Minnesota, Wisconsin and Michigan, and to this end a petition was submitted at the General Conference which convened at Baltimore in May, 1876. The petition was granted, and Sept. 6th the following year Bishop Jesse T. Peck organized in Galesburg the Swedish Northwestern Conference. From its inception the conference embraced three districts, those of Galesburg, Iowa and Minnesota, with a total of 36 ministers, 39 pastorates, 4,105 members. 44 church edifices, valued at $121,750, and 22 parsonages, at $19,225.

In 1893, after 16 years of progress, there were five districts in all, viz., Chicago, Burlington, Kansas, Nebraska, St. Paul and Superior, with 85 ministers, 105 pastorates, 9,800 members, 131 church edifices and 61 parsonages, with a total property value of $564,880. After three years of preparation, the Northwestern Conference at a meeting in Galesburg was divided into three conferences, the Central, the Western and the Northern Swedish conferences. The Central Conference included Illinois, Indiana, Ohio, western New York, western Pennsylvania, and the city of Racine, Wis. It was divided into three

SVENSKA M. E. KYRKANS
FÖRSTA PREDIKANT MÖTE
SOM HÖLLS I CHICAGO 1866

1. N. O. Westergreen.
2. Ole Peter-en.
3. C. J. Anderson.
4. O. Gunderson.
5. O. C. Simjson.

6. S. B. Newman.
7. N. Peterson.
8. J. H. Ekstrand.
9. A. Vigdal.
10. J. H. Johnson.

11. A. Haugensen.
12. O. G. Hedström.
13. Karl Schon.
14. A. Westergren.
15. Albert Ericson.

16. O. P. Peterson.
17. L. Lindqvist.
18. N. Christofferson.
19. John Wigren.

20. J. Östlund.
21. P. Nyberg.
22. P. Jensen.
23. R. Peterson.

24. C. J. Hoflund.
25. Gustaf Wetterland.
26. A. J. Anderson.
27. V. Witting.

Participants in the First Conference of Swedish M. E. Clergymen, Chicago, 1866 districts, Chicago, Galesburg and Jamestown, numbering altogether 43 ministers, 43 pastorates, 5,321 members, 47 church buildings and 22 parsonages.

The Western Conference embraced Iowa, Missouri, Kansas and Nebraska and was divided into two districts, Iowa and Kansas-Nebraska, with a total of 27 pastors, 29 pastorates, 2,299 members, with 39 church edifices and 19 parsonages, worth altogether $100,500.

The Northern Conference comprised Minnesota and Wisconsin, with the exception of the city of Racine, and the northern peninsula of Michigan. The following year, this conference was organized into three districts, Lake Superior, Minneapolis and St. Paul, and had at that time 32 ministers, 39 pastorates, 2,634 members, 52 church build-

Swedish Methodist Tabernacle at Desplaines,
Dedicated 1907

ings and 23 parsonages. At the seventh annual meeting of the conference in Calumet, Mich., in 1900, it was reorganized into a regular annual conference called the Northern Swedish Conference. In 1903 it numbered 30 ministers, 43 pastorates, 2,906 members, 64 church buildings and 40 parsonages.

The Swedish Methodist work in the East is of a more recent date than that in the West. With a couple of exceptions, the eastern congregations have all been organized later than 1878. Originally these belonged to the various American annual conferences, but in 1900 they petitioned for permission to form a conference of their own. This being granted, the Eastern Swedish Conference was organized April 24, 1901, at a meeting held in the Immanuel Church of Brooklyn, N. Y. The conference was divided into the four districts of Brooklyn, New York, Worcester and Boston, these embracing a membership of 3,642, with 26 ministers, 28 pastorates, 28 churches and 10 parsonages, the property being valued at $343,200.

In Texas work was taken up among the Swedish people as early as 1873. At first this was carried on under the direction of the American Texas conference of the Southern M. E. Church, but in 1881 a Swedish district was formed, as a part of the Austin Conference of the Northern M. E. Church. In 1903 this district had 10 ministers, 10 pastorates, 572 members, 13 churches and 9 parsonages, the property being valued at $51,400.

The Swedish Methodist work in California dates from the early seventies, but not until 1892 was a Swedish district formed. This numbered in 1903 seven congregations, with 342 members, and had 7 churches and 2 parsonages. The value of its church property was $45,050.

In the summer of 1881 the Swedish Methodists extended their endeavors to the states of Oregon and Washington, and in 1890 a Swedish district was formed, embracing these two states and Idaho. Its statistics in 1903 were as follows: 12 congregations, 395 members, 11 church buildings and 8 parsonages. The total value of the church property was $39,935.

Eliminating the Jamestown, N. Y., district from the Central Conference, its statistics will practically cover only the state of Illinois. The strength of the Swedish Methodists in the state will then appear from the following figures, compiled in 1907, covering the Chicago and Galesburg districts: regularly ordained ministers, 47; churches, 49; members, on probation, 383, in full connection, 5,222; church buildings, 49, the estimated value of which was $372,200; parsonages, 27; estimated value, $102,000, making a total church property value of $474,000.

CHAPTER VII

The Swedish, Episcopal Church

The First Swedish Episcopal Clergyman in the United States

THE story of the founding of the Pine Lake settlement in Wisconsin, the first Swedish colony in the Northwest, by Gustaf Unonius, has been recounted in previous pages. In the history of the Swedish-Americans this man is remarkable also for being the first Swedish Episcopal clergyman in this country and the organizer of the first Swedish church of that denomination. This congregation was followed in later years by others, in various parts of the country. Although these do not, like those of the other Swedish denominations, have an organization of their own, but are merely part of the respective American bishoprics, yet they are not without influence on the religious development of the Swedish-Americans. That influence increases in direct ratio to the increasing number and size of the congregations, most of which up to the present time are few and comparatively small.

Already during his pioneer days, Unonius, then a mere layman, acted as pastor for the surrounding community. Every Sunday he would conduct services in his rude dwelling, the order of service consisting of the singing of hymns and reading of a sermon from some postil brought over from the old country. These services gradually attracted the neighbors throughout the settlement, even those living at considerable distance, and in all their simplicity these hours of worship grew to be spiritual feasts to the settlers. In the meantime the Episcopal Church had started a mission in the vicinity of the colony, where its ministers, at the invitation of the settlers, would administer the sacraments and perform other official acts. But since the English language was still incomprehensible to most of the settlers, who constantly required the services of Unonius as interpreter, they soon recognized the demand for a man who could officiate in their own language and requested Unonius, in whom they had implicit confidence, to enter the ministry. He hesitated at first, but finding himself gradually drawn to the ministry and discovering his unfitness for the farmer's vocation, he finally gave way to their gentle persuasion and resolved to study for the priesthood.

Of all the religious denominations with which the settlers had come in contact up to this time, they considered the Epicopalian the nearest approach to their own faith, both in the matter of creed and of polity. They therefore urged Unonius to seek ordination in that church, and he acceded to their wishes the more readily as he himself was convinced of the superiority of the Episcopalian over other churches. Entering the theological seminary just established by the Episcopalians at Nashota, Wis., he was after three years of study ordained in 1845 by Bishop Kemper and assigned as missionary to the Swedish and Norwegian immigrants in Pine Lake and vicinity. According to his own statement, Unonius was the first Episcopal clergyman ordained in Wisconsin. He soon discovered that the ministry also had its drawbacks. Things went fairly well so long as he was in the pay of the missionary board, but when he endeavored to form an organized congregation and asked its members to contribute regularly to the support of the minister, he was met with the reply that "in this country the gospel is free."

Under such circumstances the ministry became a hard and disagreeable task, but undismayed he continued the work under great privations until he became pastor of a newly organized American church in Manitowoc, Wis., when his cares were somewhat lightened.

The First Scandinavian Church in Chicago

In the meantime, religious needs had begun to be felt among the few Swedes of Chicago, but at least for a time, these needs were only imperfectly supplied. As early as the fall of 1847, there appeared among them a certain Gustaf Smith who claimed to be a Lutheran minister but who seems to have been an adventurer and a mere imposter. Nevertheless, he succeeded in gaining the confidence both of his own fellow countrymen and of the Norwegians of the city so as to be able to organize a congregation. A lot was purchased at Superior street, near La Salle avenue, on the spot where the Passavant Hospital is now located, and a small church building was begun, whereupon Smith, accompanied by one of the leading members of the church, went to St. Louis to solicit money for the building fund among the German Lutherans of that city. They succeeded well, bringing back no less than $600. The resultant joy soon turned to sorrow and regret when "Rev." Smith absconded with the greater part of the funds. About the same time another misfortune befell the congregation in that the still unfinished edifice was torn from its foundations by a storm and badly damaged. Worst of all, strife and dissension arose, which tore the congregation itself to pieces.

Among the Norwegians of Chicago there were at this time several intelligent Christian men who had not been duped by Smith and his followers. These organized in the winter of 1848 the first Norwegian Lutheran church in Chicago and called a student of their own nationality, named Paul Andersen, as their pastor. The same year this congregation purchased the half-ruined church belonging to Smith's congregation and restored it to its foundation. The same church was sold in 1854 to the Swedish Lutheran Immanuel Church organized the year before and was used by them until 1869.

The aforesaid Smith afterward joined the Swedish Methodists and operated for several years in Iowa. In 1852-53 he was in charge of their church in New Sweden and in 1854 organized the churches of Dayton and Stratford. Suspicious actions soon caused his expulsion. He then joined the American Free Methodists and in his efforts to win his former brethren of the Swedish church over to that sect, caused a good deal of disaffection and disorder among the young Swedish Methodist congregations of Iowa. He met with little success, however, and when he was no longer able to support himself among his countrymen in Iowa, he went still farther west where the tracks of the "evangelist" are lost.

Unonius and the Erik Janssonists

After these adversities, the Swedish members of the congregation founded by Smith decided, on the advice of P. von Schneidau, to call as their pastor his friend Unonius, whom they knew from his former visits to Chicago. In the summer of 1848 he had visited the city and conducted the first religious meeting in the Swedish language ever held in Chicago. That meeting took place in a hall in a medical institute on the north side and was attended by 30 to 40 persons.

On this occasion an episode took place which deserves to be recorded. A party of Erik Jassonists which had just arrived from Sweden was stopping in Chicago awaiting the arrival of one of the apostles to guide them on their way to Bishop Hill. In a few days the expected apostle arrived, accompanied by five or six other men, bringing horses and wagons. It was Anders Anderson from Thorstuna. Upon learning that Swedish religious meetings were held in the city, he went there with some of his men. After the sermon, Unonius, knowing that there were Erik Janssonists in the audience, attempted to direct a few words of admonition to these deluded persons. Had he been aware of the trouble the Erik Janssonists had made for the Swedish clergy for the past four years, he would wisely have desisted from addressing them, but as he had been in the United States since 1841, he had not been in a position to follow the career of the sect. He was quickly made aware of the utter uselessness of engaging in a discussion with these people, infallible as they were in their own eyes. Hardly had he closed his remarks when Anders Anderson arose and began to defend the doctrines of Erik Jansson. A long debate on the subject of dead and living Christianity ensued between the two men, and Unonius was ignominiously defeated in the tilt, his opponent Anderson being almost the equal of Erik Jansson himself in the art of fencing with passages of Scripture as weapons. With an inexhaustible supply of memorized scriptural concordances and parallels, literally interpreted, these fanatics were capable of proving with the words of the Bible any proposition whatsoever. As against this volubility and mass of evidence all the learning and theological armament of Unonius availed nothing. Although Anderson worsted his opponent in argument, yet it does not appear that he made a single proselyte among the Swedes of Chicago, who were pretty well acquainted with the Erik Jansson movement.

Founding of the First Swedish Episcopal Church

"Rev." Smith's congregation seems to have been altogether too loosely organized to hang together for any length of time without reorganization. Besides, it appears to have lacked all connection with the Lutheran Church in general. One thing and another tended toward disintegration, and the Swedish members, at the instance of Von Schneidau and with the advice of Unonius, undertook to organize an Episcopal congregation. The original purpose was to make it all Swedish, but the Swedes being few and the Norwegian members of the church preferring to make common cause with them in church matters, it was decided to make it Scandinavian. A committee, known as the church committee, was appointed to draw up a constitution. This committee, consisting of Von Schneidau, Anders Larsson, Pehr Ersson and J. Fr. Björkman, Swedes, and And. B. Jonsen, Battolf Markusen, and Knut Gundersen, Norwegians, met at the home of Von Schneidau March 5, 1849. The name proposed was the St. Eric and St. Olaf Church, to indicate its Scandinavian character and to do honor to the patron saints of the countries of Sweden and Norway.

The congregation at first held its services in the basement of the American Episcopal Church of St. James where the organization was completed in May, 1849. For reasons unknown the proposed name was not adopted, the church being named St. Ansgarius, from the first Christian missionary in Sweden. The constitution was now adopted and signed by 34 voting members. the Swedes and Norwegians being about equally divided. Rev. Unonius was present and his name and

that of his wife head the list as it appears in the earliest church records.
The first trustees were, Polycarpus von Schneidau, W. Knudsen, Battolf
Markusen, Anders Jonsen, Anders Larsson, John Björkman, A. S.
Sheldon and John Andersson.

Immediately on his removal to Chicago, Rev. Unonius undertook
the laborious task of gathering funds for a church building. Accompanied by his faithful friend Von Schneidau, he made a trip to
Delaware and Pennsylvania to visit the descendants of the Delaware
Swedes and among these people he succeeded in soliciting for his church
fund a sum amounting to between $4,000 and $5,000. Early in the

Rev. Gustaf Unonius

spring of 1850 two building lots, located at the corner of Franklin and
Indiana streets, were purchased for the sum of $400. The work of
building was at once begun and progressed nicely so long as the funds
lasted. These, however, soon were exhausted and again Unonius and
Von Schneidau were obliged to begin soliciting. At this juncture Jenny
Lind, the great Swedish singer, visited New York city, and Unonius
succeeded in persuading the prima donna to donate the sum of $1,500
to his church building fund. After her departure in 1851, she added to
her munificence by donating, through one Max Hjortsberg of Chicago,
an altar service consisting of a beautifully worked communion cup and
plate, valued at $1,000. For the funds now available a handsome and

commodious church and a comfortable parsonage were built. The church was a frame edifice, provided with a semi-circular gallery, and had a total seating capacity of 300. Its dimensions were 33x50 feet. The parsonage was a two story frame house.

Unonius as a Pastor

For nine years Rev. Unonius carried on an energetic and richly blessed pastoral work combined with tireless endeavor in behalf of the needy. At this time the Swedish people of Chicago lived under conditions entirely different from those of today. They were few in number and generally poor, unable to give any material aid to other poor immigrants who followed. The latter, therefore, in the first place turned to the Swedish minister for assistance, demanding not only that he act as their spiritual adviser and teacher but also as their commissioner, assistant and adviser in all worldly matters. Unonius, who warmly sympathized with the poor, and mostly sick, Swedish immigrants, never spared himself, but was at their service at all times, so far as his strength and ability would permit. The cholera, which broke out epidemically almost every year, caused him much work and anxiety. The hardest part of his task was how to procure homes and foster-parents for all the children of immigrants who lost one or both parents in the epidemic.

After only four years of labor for the temporal and spiritual welfare of his countrymen, this warm-hearted philanthropist was so broken down by over-exertion that he was compelled in 1853 to seek rest and recreation in a trip to Sweden. He returned just in time to resume with renewed strength the arduous and self-sacrificing duties imposed by the terrible cholera outbreak of 1854 among the Swedish newcomers.

The membership of his church continually changed. In 1850, his second year, the congregation numbered 163, the following year it grew to 195, in 1855 it dropped down to 117, but in 1857 it had again increased to 142. In 1856 the little church was so prosperous as to be able to purchase an organ costing $700.

Notwithstanding his many duties at home, Unonius found time to pay occasional visits to neighboring places to serve his fellow countrymen by preaching and officiating at various religious acts. During his very first year in Chicago, he made an official trip westward, visiting almost every point where Swedes had settled. The main reasons why he did not afterward attempt to organize Swedish Episcopal congregations at these various places are the following: In the first place there was not sufficient material at hand at these points to found churches, in the second, he was the only Swedish Episcopal pastor in the whole country and had his hands more than full of work right in his home

Communion Chalice and Paten of solid silver, presented by Jenny Lind to the St. Ansgarius Church, bearing the inscription. "Gifvet till den Skandinaviska Kyrkan St. Ansgarius i Chicago af en Landsmaninna A. D. 1851."

field, and in the third place, after a few years the religious needs of the immigrants began to be provided for by the Swedish Lutheran clergymen who organized congregations wherever an opportunity offered. Had the American Episcopal Church, from the very encouraging beginning made by Unonius, displayed a warmer interest in mission work among the Swedish settlers it might then have obtained that foothold among them which it has, with partial success, sought to gain in later years. It must be admitted, however, that Unonius did his part in serv-

St. Ansgarius Episcopal Church and Rectory

ing his fellow countrymen who at that time, if ever, were in need of spiritual advice and comfort as well as material help. The exceptional zeal and unselfish efforts of Unonius in behalf of the early settlers entitle him to an honored place in the history of the Swedes of America.

At the time of his visit to Sweden in 1853, Unonius harbored the desire to remain in the old country and enter the service of the state church, but his duties called him back to Chicago. For several years more he labored here with his customary energy. His work was still further increased by his appointment to the office of vice consul for Sweden and Norway to succeed Von Schneidau who, after a few years of service, was compelled to retire on account of an incurable disease. Finally, in the year 1858, Unonius was able to realize his desire to return to Sweden.

He there sought admission as minister to the state church, but encountering various obstacles, he was forced to choose another calling in order to earn a living for himself and family. He entered the customs service and in 1863 was promoted to the position of collector of the port of Grisslehamn, an office which he held until 1888. Both before and after his retirement from the customs service Unonius would engage in pastoral work whenever called upon, and he retained to his old age the ecclesiastical office in the Anglican Church.

In 1859, the year after his return to Sweden, the riksdag voted him a gift of three thousand crowns in recognition of his long and useful service in behalf of his fellow countrymen in the United States.

Rev. Jacob Bredberg

During his last years Unonius was living at Hacksta, in the province of Upland, a country seat placed at his disposal by his son-in-law, Hugo Tamm, a landed proprietor and member of the riksdag. There he died October 14, 1902, at the high age of 92 years.

Alongside of his official duties, Unonius devoted himself quite extensively to literary pursuits. His best known works, both in Swedish, are: "Mormonism, its Origin, Development and Creed," published in 1883, and "Reminiscences of Seventeen Years in the American Northwest," published in 1861-2. At the age of 86, he added a supplement to the latter volume.

The St. Ansgarius Church

After the return of Unonius to Sweden the St. Ansgarius Church for several years had to pass through many hard struggles. No Swedish pastor was to be had, and it was for a time served by American Episcopal clergymen. During this period it was known as the St. Barnabe's Mission, and its membership seems to have been very small.

This stagnation period lasted until 1862 when Rev. Jacob Bredberg, a former curate from Sweden, who for several years had been in the service of the Methodist Church, assumed the pastorate. Its membership was very materially reduced that same year by the withdrawal of the Norwegian members, but it rallied from the stroke and added quite

Rev. John Hedman

Rev. Herman Lindskog

a number of new members during the many years that Rev. Bredberg was in charge. In 1868 the church was extensively remodeled and enlarged at an outlay almost equal to the original cost of the edifice. The renovated temple had not been long in use when it was destroyed in the great fire of 1871. Three of the trustees, Schönbeck, Norström and Lind, succeeded in saving the altar-piece, painted in 1868 by the Norwegian artist Clason, and also the church records, which were taken to the cathedral of the Episcopal bishopric of Illinois, located on the west side, and there placed in safe keeping. The communion service donated by Jenny Lind was kept in the safe of one of the church members who saved it from destruction, and it is used at the communion services of the church to this day.

Before the end of the disastrous year of 1871 the congregation had begun to erect a new church which was ready for occupancy on Christmas morning, 1872. This was the same church that is still used by the St. Ansgarius congregation. It is situated on Sedgwick street and is built in the Gothic style, its cost being approximately $30,000. To that sum the Illinois bishopric of the American Episcopal Church contributed $20,000. Adjacent to the church a spacious parsonage was erected.

Old age and resultant illness in 1877 compelled Rev. Bredberg to resign. His successor was Nils Nordeen who was replaced by P. Arvidson the following year. Arvidson was succeeded by John Hedman in the fall of 1879. Rev. Hedman was a native of Krokstad parish, in Bohuslän, where he was born June 25, 1848. He studied in Sweden and Germany before coming to America in 1873, and in 1877 he entered the Episcopal institution of Seabury Hall, at Faribault, Minn., where he finished his theological course in June, 1879. The following September he was ordained in the St. Ansgarius Church to which he was assigned as assistant pastor. In May, 1880, Hedman was unanimously elected rector and served in this capacity until 1887.

From that year the rectorate of the St. Ansgarius Church has been entrusted to Rev. Herman Lindskog whose biography appears elsewhere in this volume.

There are three other Swedish Episcopal congregations in this state, but these are of quite recent date. The largest doubtless is that of Galesburg; next in point of size comes the Immanuel Church of Englewood. The third in order is the Woodhull church which during the last few years has shown but faint signs of life.

The Swedish Episcopal churches in the eastern states are not the fruits of the fundamental work accomplished in Illinois and Wisconsin and therefore cannot properly be mentioned under this head.